# Medical Law and Ethics

## Second Edition

Bonnie F. Fremgen, Ph.D.

PEARSON
Prentice
Hall

*Upper Saddle River, New Jersey 07458*

**Library of Congress Cataloging-in-Publication Data**

Fremgen, Bonnie F.
    Medical law and ethics / Bonnie F. Fremgen.— 2nd ed.
        p.   cm.
    Includes bibliographical references and index.
    ISBN 0-13-117708-7
    1. Medical laws and legislation—United States.   2. Medical care—
Law and legislation—United States.   3. Medical ethics.   I. Title.

KF3821.F74 2005
344.7304'1—dc22

2004023763

**Notice:** The material in this textbook contains the most current information about the topic at the time of publication. This text is not meant to be used in lieu of qualified legal advice for situations that arise in either one's professional practice or personal life. An attorney should always be consulted for legal advice. Since laws for health care professionals vary from state to state, it is always wise to consult specific laws within one's state of practice.

**Note Re Case Studies:** The names used in the case studies throughout the text are fictitious.

**Publisher:** Julie Levin Alexander
**Publisher's Assistant:** Regina Bruno
**Senior Acquisitions Editor:** Mark Cohen
**Associate Editor:** Melissa Kerian
**Editorial Assistant:** Jaquay Felix
**Director of Manufacturing and Production:** Bruce Johnson
**Managing Editor for Production:** Patrick Walsh
**Production Liaison:** Christina Zingone
**Production Editor:** Karen Berry/Pine Tree Composition, Inc.
**Manufacturing Manager:** Ilene Sanford
**Manufacturing Buyer:** Pat Brown
**Creative Director:** Cheryl Asherman

**Senior Design Coordinator:** Christopher Weigand
**Cover Designer:** Blair Brown
**Director of Marketing/Marketing Manager:** Karen Allman
**Channel Marketing Manager:** Rachele Strober
**Marketing Coordinator:** Michael Sirinides
**Marketing Assistant:** Patricia Linard
**Media Editor:** John Jordon
**Media Production Manager:** Amy Peltier
**Media Project Manager:** Stephen Hartner
**Composition:** Pine Tree Composition, Inc.
**Printer/Binder:** RR Donnelley & Sons, VA
**Cover Printer:** Coral Graphics

Credits and acknowledgments borrowed from other sources and reproduced, with permission, in this textbook appear on appropriate page within text.

Pearson Education, LTD.
Pearson Education Singapore, Pte. Ltd.
Pearson Education, Canada, Ltd.
Pearson Education–Japan
Pearson Education Australia PTY, Limited

Pearson Education North Asia Ltd.
Pearson Educación de Mexico, S.A. de C.V.
Pearson Education Malaysia, Pte. Ltd.
Pearson Education, Upper Saddle River, New Jersey

10  9  8  7  6  5  4
**ISBN 0-13-117708-7**

*To my children, who have always
been my inspiration for ethical behavior.*

# Contents

# Preface

The allied health professional has always been an important member of the medical team. This team awareness is even more critical in today's health care environment, since the physician no longer practices medicine alone.

*Medical Law and Ethics* is written in straightforward language that is aimed at the nonlawyer health professional who must be able to cope with multiple legal and ethical issues. This text is appropriate for those persons studying in a college or university who are working toward careers in the allied health field in a variety of settings, such as medical offices, hospitals, clinics, and skilled-nursing facilities. A wide range of pertinent topics is discussed, such as the legal system, the physician–patient relationship, professional liability and medical malpractice, public duties of the physician, the medical record, and ethical and bioethical issues. There is an in-depth discussion of the regulations affecting the health care professional, including up-to-date information about the Health Insurance Portability and Accountability Act of 1996 (HIPAA). The intent is to help health care professionals to better understand our ethical obligation to ourselves, our patients, and our employer.

Many legal cases are sprinkled throughout the text to demonstrate the history of the law as it pertains to subjects such as patient confidentiality, managed care, federal regulations affecting the employee, death and dying, and abortion. In some examples, the cases may seem old; but since our legal system is based on case law, they are still pertinent today. A legal icon (scales of justice) appears in the left margin to indicate legal case citations.

A special feature called Med Tips provides quick information about the law and ethics. These brief scenarios and hints help to maintain interest in this vital subject. Each chapter includes glossary terms highlighted in bold on first reference, extensive end-of-chapter exercises, and one actual practice case. The appendices include a thorough compilation of codes of ethics that form a basis for current practice, a listing of health care regulatory agencies and useful medical Web sites, case citations, and supplemental cases for discussion.

This text provides an overview of medical law and ethics. Practicing health care professionals should know the legal requirements in their own jurisdictions.

## CHAPTER STRUCTURE

**Learning Objectives** These include an overview of the basic knowledge discussed within the chapter and can be used as a chapter review.

**Key Terms** Important vocabulary terms are listed alphabetically at the beginning of each chapter and printed in bold the first time they are defined in the text.

**Introduction** Each chapter begins with an introductory statement that reflects the topic of the chapter.

**End-of-Chapter Exercises** A selection of matching and multiple-choice questions are included to test the student's knowledge of the chapter material.

**Case Study** The case studies are based on real-life occurrences and offer practical application of information discussed within the chapter. These are included to stimulate and draw upon the student's critical-thinking skills and problem-solving ability.

**References** These useful resources provide further information on the topics included within the chapter.

## SPECIAL FEATURES

**Med Tip** Med Tips are placed at strategic points within the narrative to provide helpful hints and useful information to stimulate the student's interest in the topic.

**Legal Case Citations** Discipline-specific cases are used throughout the text to illustrate the topic under discussion. The cases reflect the many medical disciplines, including that of the physician, that come together in the care of the patient. While this book is not meant to be a law book, nevertheless, the cases cited in the book are meant to emphasize the importance of the law for the students.

**Points to Ponder** Thought-provoking questions give students an opportunity to evaluate how they might answer some of the tough, medically related ethical dilemmas in today's society. These questions can also be used for critical debate among students during a class activity.

**Discussion Questions** These end-of-chapter questions encourage a review of the chapter contents.

**Put It into Practice** These thought-provoking activities appear at the end of each chapter. They provide a clinical correlation with the topics discussed in the chapter and stimulate the student's own contemplation of legal and ethical issues that are apparent in everyday life.

**Web Hunt** This end-of-chapter Internet activity encourages the student to access the multitude of medical resources available through this medium.

**Appendices** Codes of Ethics are included in Appendix A; a list of U.S. regulatory agencies appears in Appendix B; useful medical Web sites are listed in Appendix C; the case citations used throughout the book are listed in Appendix D; and supplemental cases for discussion are included in Appendix E.

**Additional Examination Review Questions** These are included in the Instructor's Manual.

# Letter to the Student

For a successful start to your study of medical law and ethics, consider following the ABCs of classroom success: **A**ctively participate, **B**enefit from the experience, and **C**ommit to learning. It is necessary for you to attend class to truly benefit from your ethics education. So much happens in the classroom—especially the interaction between you and your classmates. The discussion portion of an ethics class is one of the most important components. You must be present to contribute. The text serves as an information source and as the first step in your education—the dynamics of classroom interaction between you, your instructor, and the other students is critical for success in learning.

> **Actively** participate when you attend class. It is necessary to absorb what takes place during the class session. Listen carefully to what your instructor and fellow students say. If you don't share your ideas, experiences, and questions, then the rest of the class is losing what you have to offer. The dialogue about ethics that you have with your instructor and fellow classmates can be one of the most meaningful learning experiences.

> **Benefit** from the experience and ideas of your peers (classmates). Listen to the opinions of others during class discussions. Pay particular attention to the opinions that differ from your own. As a member of the health care team, you will frequently hear opinions that differ from your own—both from your coworkers and your patients. You do not have to change your opinions or beliefs, but try to keep an open mind.

> **Commit** to learning by carefully reading and analyzing the textbook material. Look for new information and also for discussion points that both agree and disagree with your own perspective. Keep an open mind to the opinion of others. Take this course seriously so that it is not a waste of your time. In fact, your ethics class can be one of the most important classes that you take! Communicate what you have learned. Your perspective is important for others to hear. Use your time wisely in class, share your ideas, and listen to the thoughts of others.

The law is dynamic and often is revised as changes take place in society. For example, one of the newest laws affecting health care, the Healthcare Insurance Portability and Accountability Act of 1996 (HIPAA), has recently had an added impact regarding the necessity for health care organizations, including physicians' offices, to provide notice to all patients concerning their privacy practices. This textbook is not meant to be a study of the law, but rather to introduce students to the impact that law and ethics have on their professional lives.

# How to Interpret Case Citations

Selected legal cases are used in this textbook to illustrate various legal principles. At the end of each case summary is a citation such as, *Moon Lake Convalescent Center v. Margolis,* 433 N.E.2d 956 (Ill. App. Ct. 1989). This citation, similar to a street address, tells you where you can find this case among the many sets of reported cases (called *reporters*) in the library. Most case citations end with information in parentheses, such as (Ill. App. Ct. 1989), which tells you what court (the Illinois Appellate Court) decided the case and the year (1989) of the decision; but you do not need that information when you are simply trying to locate a particular case in the library. The small *v.* between the litigants' names stands for "versus." A case citation consists of

- the italicized case name—usually the name of the plaintiff and the defendant. In our example, *Moon Lake Convalescent Center* (defendant) and *Margolis* (plaintiff).
- the name of the reporter(s) where the case is published (Northeast Reporter, 2d series)
- the volume number(s) of the reporter(s) where the case is published (433)
- the page number of the volume where the case begins (956)
- the year the case was decided (1989)
- for federal Court of Appeals cases, a designation of the circuit; for federal District Court cases, the state and judicial district where the court is located; for state cases, an indication of the state if it is not apparent from the name of the reporter (Illinois Appellate Court).

Therefore, our example case between Moon Lake Convalescent Center and Margolis is found in volume 433 of the Northeast Reporter, 2d series, on page 956.

Abbreviations for other reporters (books) are:

A (Atlantic Reporter)
P (Pacific Reporter)
U.S. (United States Reports)
F. Supp. (Federal Supplement)
F (Federal Reporter)
NE (Northeast Reporter)
NW (Northwest Reporter)

NYS (New York Supplement)
So (Southern Reporter)
SW (Southwestern Reporter)

Most reporters have been published in two or more series, such as 2d, meaning second series. The student should not be concerned with memorizing the names of the reporters. The abbreviations for them are found at the beginning of most of the legal research publications that we use. As you do research within your own state, you will become familiar with the abbreviations that are most commonly used. Legal research can be done through a law library or via the Internet from Lexis-Nexis, which is a subscription service used by law firms and libraries.

# Acknowledgments

This book would not have been possible without the assistance and guidance of many people. I am grateful to the editorial and production staffs at Prentice Hall for their skill and patience with this project. I thank Mark Cohen, acquisitions editor, for his leadership with this project; Melissa Kerian, whose courtesy and thoroughness are greatly appreciated; Pat Walsh, managing production editor, whose calm presence is always available; and especially Karen Berry, production editor at Pine Tree Composition, Inc., and Christina Zingone, production liaison, for their great attention to detail and all their hard work.

The following reviewers provided valuable feedback during the writing process. We thank all these professionals for their contributions and attention to detail.

Anne M. Arto
District Coordinator of Continuing Education
Pasco-Hernando Community College
Brooksville, FL

Deborah J. Bedford, CMA, AAS
Program Coordinator/Instructor
Medical Assisting Program
North Seattle Community College
Seattle, WA

Norma Bird, M.Ed, BS, CMA
Medical Assisting Program Director/Instructor
Idaho State University College of Technology
Pocatello, ID

Rafael Castilla, MD
Dean of Academics
Hohokus School of Business and Medical Sciences
Ridgefield, NJ

Michael W. Cook, MA, RRT
Professor of Respiratory Therapy
Mountain Empire Community College
Big Stone Gap, VA

Tonya Hallock
Medical Assisting Program Director
Concorde Career Institute
Garden Grove, CA

Janice C. Hess, MA
Office Skills and Technology Instructor
Metropolitan Community College
Elkhorn, NE

Jennifer Lame, BS, RHIT
Health Information Instructor
Idaho State University
Pocatello, ID

Valeria Truitt, BS, MA, Ed.
Lead Instructor and Curriculum Coordinator
Craven Community College
New Bern, NC

Lori Warren, MA, RN, CPC, CCP, CLNC
Medical Department Co-Director/Instructor
Spencerian College
Louisville, KY

# About the Author

Bonnie F. Fremgen, Ph.D., is a former associate dean of the Allied Health Program at Robert Morris College. She has taught medical law and ethics courses as well as clinical and administrative topics. In addition, she has served as an advisor for students' career planning. She has broad interests and experiences in the health care field, including hospitals, nursing homes, and physicians' offices.

Dr. Fremgen holds a nursing degree as well as a master's in health care administration. She received her Ph.D. from the College of Education at the University of Illinois. She has performed postdoctoral studies in medical law at Loyola University Law School in Chicago.

Dr. Fremgen has taught ethics at the University of Notre Dame, South Bend, Indiana; University of Detroit, Detroit, Michigan; and Saint Xavier University, Chicago, Illinois.

CHAPTER **1**

# Introduction to Medical Law, Ethics, and Bioethics

## LEARNING OBJECTIVES

1. Define the glossary terms.
2. Describe the similarities and differences between laws and ethics.
3. Discuss the difference between ethics and bioethics.
4. Describe how to apply the three decision-making models discussed in this chapter.
5. Explain why ethics is not just about the sincerity of one's beliefs, emotions, or religious viewpoints.

## KEY TERMS

| | | |
|---|---|---|
| **Applied ethics** | **Due process** | **Medical ethics** |
| **Beneficence** | **Empathy** | **Medical practice acts** |
| **Bioethicists** | **Ethics** | **Statutes** |
| **Bioethics** | **Fidelity** | **Sympathy** |
| **Comparable worth** | **Integrity** | **Tolerance** |
| **Cost/benefit analysis** | **Laws** | **Utilitarianism** |

## INTRODUCTION

Medical professionals encounter health care dilemmas that are not experienced by the general population. They are faced with individual choices that must, of necessity, always take into consideration the common good of all patients. Medical-ethical decisions have become increasingly complicated with the advancement of medical science and technology. The topics of medical law, ethics, and bioethics, while having very specific definitions, are interrelated. One cannot practice medicine in any setting without an understanding of the legal implications for both the practitioner and

1

the patient. Medical ethics is an **applied ethics,** meaning that it is the practical application of moral standards that concern benefiting the patient. Therefore, the medical practitioner must adhere to certain ethical standards and codes of conduct. Bioethics, while closely related to applied ethics, is a field resulting from modern medical advances and research. Many medical practitioners, patients, and religious organizations believe that advances in bioethics, such as cloning, require close examination, control, and even legal constraints.

## WHY STUDY LAW, ETHICS, AND BIOETHICS?

Without a moral structure for one's actions, people would be free to pursue their own self-interests. In many cases, people would behave in a moral fashion within the constraints and framework of their culture and religious beliefs. However, upon closer examination of living without the constraints and limitations imposed by moral standards and laws, a state of hostility may arise in which only the interests of the strong would prevail. The words *justice* and *injustice* would have little meaning. We all believe we know the difference between right and wrong. We may firmly believe that while some decisions are difficult to make, we would intuitively make the right decision. However, there is ample proof in medical malpractice cases that in times of stress and crisis, people do not always make the correct ethical decisions. Because what is illegal is almost always unethical, it is important to have a basic understanding of the law as it applies to the medical world.

 **MED TIP**   An understanding of the law will help to protect you and your employer from being sued.

Medicine is based on the professional skills of many persons, including physicians, nurses, radiology technicians, pharmacists, and a multitude of other allied health professionals. The health care team, composed of these professionals, with the addition of health care administrators, often must decide on critical issues relating to patient needs. In some cases, the decisions of these professionals are at odds with one another. For example, when an obstetrician withholds resuscitation attempts on a severely handicapped newborn, such as one born without a brain (anencephalic), he or she may be acting in opposition to the law in many states and the ethics of many people. Does a nurse have an ethical responsibility to override this order if he or she believes it to be wrong? Is there a better way to handle such an ethical dilemma without the patient suffering in the process? It is generally understood that nurses and other allied health care professionals carry out the orders of their employer/physician. However, as illustrated in the above case, in some situations, confusion arises about what is the right thing to do.

 **MED TIP**   A study of law, ethics, and bioethics can assist the medical professional in making a sound decision based on reason and logic rather than on emotion or a "gut feeling."

Ethics asks difficult questions, such as "How should we act?" and "How should we live?" The answers to such questions are often subjective and can change according to circumstances, so it is realistic to ask, "Why study ethics?" The short answer is that in spite of the many gray areas of ethics, we are expected to take the right action when confronted with an ethical dilemma. We must consider the consequences of wrong-doing. We must learn how to think about an action and then how to translate those thoughts into action. So, even if the "right thing" isn't always clear, we can prepare minds to think about action and to see how the experiences of others can influence our own actions. The important thing is to be able to think and then take action!

While studying ethics, ask yourself the following questions. Do you know what you would do in each of the following situations? Do you know whether you are exposing yourself to a lawsuit?

- A fellow student says, "Sure, I stole this book from the bookstore, but the tuition is so high that I figured the school owed me at least one book." What do you do? (Chapter 1, Introduction to Medical Law, Ethics, and Bioethics.)
- An orderly working in a skilled-nursing facility is left alone in the dining room in charge of a group of elderly residents who are finishing their dinner. One of the residents does not want to eat but wishes to go back to his own room, which he cannot find by himself. The orderly has been instructed never to leave patients alone. Since he cannot leave the dining room full of patients, nor can he allow the one elderly resident to find his own room, the orderly locks the dining room door. The elderly resident claims he has been falsely imprisoned. Is he correct? (Chapter 2, The Legal System.)
- You are drawing a specimen of blood on Emma Helm, who says that she doesn't like having blood drawn. In fact, she tells you that the sight of blood makes her "queasy." While you are taking her blood specimen, she faints and hits her head against the side of a cabinet. Are you liable for Emma's injury? If you are not liable, do you know who is? (Chapter 3, Importance of the Legal System for the Physician.)
- You are answering the phone calls in a physician's office while the receptionist is having lunch. A patient calls and says he must have a prescription refill for blood-pressure medication called in right away to his pharmacy, since he is leaving town in thirty minutes. He says that he has been on the medication for four years and that he is a personal friend of the physician. No one except you is in the office at this time. What do you do? (Chapter 4, Medical Practice and Allied Health Professionals.)
- Terry O'Rourke, a 25-year-old female patient of Dr. Williams, refuses to take her medication to control diabetes and is not following her dietary plan to control her disease. After repeated attempts to help this patient, Dr. Williams has decided that she can no longer provide care for Terry. The office staff has been advised not to schedule Terry for any more appointments. Is there an ethical or legal concern (or both) regarding this situation? Is there anything else that either Dr. Williams or her staff should do to sever the patient relationship with Terry? (Chapter 5, The Physician–Patient Relationship.)
- You drop a sterile packet of gauze on the floor. The inside of the packet is still considered sterile; however, the policy in your office is to resterilize anything that

drops on the floor. This is the last sterile packet on the shelf. The chances are very slight that any infection would result from using the gauze within the packet. What do you do? (Chapter 6, Professional Liability and Medical Malpractice.)

■ The pharmaceutical salesperson has just brought in a supply of nonprescription vitamin samples for the physicians in your practice to dispense to their patients. All the other staff members take samples home for their families' personal use. They tell you to do the same, since the samples will become outdated before the physician can use all of them. It would save you money. What do you do? Is it legal? Is it ethical? (Chapter 7, Public Duties of the Physician.)

■ You feel a slight prick on your sterile glove as you assist Dr. Brown on a minor surgical procedure. Dr. Brown has a quick temper, and he will become angry if you delay the surgical procedure while you change gloves. Will it hurt to wear the gloves during the procedure, since there was just a slight prick and the patient's wound is not infected? Who is at fault if the patient develops a wound infection? Is this a legal and/or ethical issue? (Chapter 8, Federal Regulations Affecting the Medical Professional.)

■ Demi Daniels calls to ask you to change her diagnosis in her medical record from R/O (rule out) bladder infection to "bladder infection" because her insurance will not pay for an R/O diagnosis. In fact, she tested negative for an infection, but she was placed on antibiotics by the physician anyway. What do you do? Is this legal? Is it ethical? (Chapter 9, The Medical Record.)

■ A physician from another office steps into your office and asks to see the chart of a neighbor whom he believes may have an infectious disease. He states that the neighbor is a good friend and that she will not mind if he reviews her medical chart. Is it legal for you to give the chart to this physician? (Chapter 10, Confidentiality in Medical Practice.)

■ A well-known baseball Hall of Fame fielder received a liver transplant in 1995. It took only two days for Baylor Medical Center's transplant team to locate an organ donor for this national hero when his own liver was failing due to cirrhosis and hepatitis. The patient was a recovering alcoholic who also had a small cancerous growth that was not believed to be life-threatening. Since there are relatively few liver donor organs available, there were mixed feelings about speeding up the process for a famous person. He subsequently died a few years later from cancer. What are the ethics of giving a scarce liver to a recovering alcoholic? What are your thoughts about the statement "People should not be punished just because they are celebrities"? (Chapter 11, Ethic and Bioethic Issues in Medicine.)

■ A physician used his own sperm to artificially inseminate his patients. He told the court that he didn't see anything wrong with this practice because these women came to him wanting to have a child. However, his patients were unaware that he was using his own sperm for the procedure. Some of his office staff became suspicious of the physician's methods but failed to report their suspicions immediately. Many children were conceived as a result of this physician's sperm being implanted into their mothers. Is this a legal, ethical, or bioethical issue? Was the office staff also at fault? (Chapter 12, Ethical Issues Relating to Life.)

■ A 55-year-old man, Glenn Ross, with pancreatic cancer has been told by his physician that he has only a few months to live. He has received several series of chemotherapy that were of little or no benefit. Mr. Ross, who is now bedridden in a nursing home for the terminally ill, has requested that he receive no further treatment. His son, who lives in another state, demands that his father be hospitalized and placed back on chemotherapy. When the physician explains that there is little hope for the father's recovery, the son threatens to sue the physician for withdrawal of care. What are the ethical issues in this case? (Chapter 13, Death and Dying.)

These situations, and others like them, are addressed throughout this book.

## MEDICAL LAW

**Laws** are rules or actions prescribed by an authority such as the federal government and the court system that have a binding legal force. Medical law addresses legal rights and obligations that affect patients and protect individual rights, including those of health care employees. For example, practicing medicine without a license, Medicaid fraud, and patient rape are violations of medical laws that are always illegal, and immoral or unethical.

It is easy to become confused when studying law and ethics, because, while the two are different, they often overlap. Some illegal actions may be quite ethical—for example, exceeding the speed limit when rushing an injured child to the hospital. Of course, many unethical actions may not be illegal, such as cheating on a test. Law and ethics exist in everyday life and thus are difficult to separate. An insurance company denying payment for a life-saving heart transplant on a 70-year-old male is not illegal, but it may well be unethical.

**MED TIP**   In general, an illegal act, or one that is against the law, is always unethical. However, an unethical act may not be illegal. For instance, when an employee looks at a neighbor's medical record out of curiosity, it is not necessarily against the law, but it is unethical.

The law provides a type of yardstick by which to measure our actions, and it punishes us when our actions break the laws. Many of the actions punishable by law are considered morally wrong, such as rape, murder, and theft. The problem with measuring our actions using only the law, and not considering the ethical aspects of an issue, is that the law allows many actions that are morally offensive, such as lying and manipulating people. Laws against actions such as adultery, which most people agree is immoral, exist, but they are rarely enforced. Some situations involving interpersonal relationships between coworkers, such as taking credit for someone else's work, are difficult to address with laws. Other work issues such as lying on job applications, padding expense accounts, and making unreasonable demands on coworkers are usually handled on the job and have not been regulated by laws.

A further caution about relying on the law for moral decision making is the concern that the requirements of the law often tend to be negative. The standards of morality, on the other hand, are often seen to be positive. The law forbids us to harm, rob, or defame others; but it does not require us to help people. Morality would tell us to give aid to the drowning victim even if the law does not mandate that we do so. Many people believe that something is wrong, or unethical, only if the law forbids it. Conversely, they reason that if the law says it's all right, then it is also ethical. Unfortunately, these people believe that until the law tells them otherwise, they have no ethical responsibility beyond the law. Finally, laws are often reactive and may lag behind the moral standards of society; slavery is the most obvious example. Sexual harassment and racial discrimination existed as moral problems long before laws were enacted to suppress this behavior.

There are a multitude of laws, including criminal and civil **statutes** (laws enacted by state and federal legislatures) as well as state medical practice acts that affect health care professionals. **Medical practice acts,** established in all 50 states by statute, apply specifically to the way medicine is practiced in a particular state. These acts define the meaning of the "practice of medicine" as well as requirements and methods for licensure. They also define what constitutes unprofessional conduct in that particular state. While the laws vary from state to state, the more common items of unprofessional conduct include

- impaired ability to practice medicine due to addiction or mental illness.
- conviction of a felony.
- insufficient record keeping.
- allowing an unlicensed person to practice medicine.
- physical abuse of patients.

## ETHICS

**Ethics** is the branch of philosophy related to morals, moral principles, and moral judgments. Morality is the quality of being virtuous. However the terms *ethics* and *morality* are used interchangeably by many people. Ethics, as part of philosophy, uses reason and logic to analyze problems and find solutions. Ethics, in general, is concerned with the actions and practices that are directed at improving the welfare of people in a moral way. Thus, the study of ethics forces us to use reason and logic to answer difficult questions concerning life, death, and everything in between. In modern terms, we use words such as *right, wrong, good,* and *bad* when making ethical judgments. In other cases, people refer to issues or actions that are *just* and *unjust* or *fair* and *unfair.* **Medical ethics** concerns questions specifically related to the practice of medicine. This branch of ethics is based on principles regulating the behavior of health care professionals including practitioners such as physicians, nurses, and allied health professionals. It also applies to patients, relatives, and the community-at-large.

 **MED TIP**   Medical ethics mandates that the welfare and confidentiality of the individual patient must be the chief concern.

Ethics is meant to take the past into account, but also to look to the future and ask, "What should I do now?" Unfortunately, using moral views based only on those of parents and peers can lead to radical subjectivism that can make ethical discussion of issues such as euthanasia, abortion, or cloning difficult if not impossible. Whenever you are involved in an ethical dilemma, you must analyze actions and their consequences to all concerned parties. Law also does this by directing actions into "legal" and "illegal" human actions. As we study ethics, we will also analyze various actions and their effects.

 **MED TIP**   Remember that ethics always involves formal consideration of the interests of others in deciding how to act or behave.

Basic questions relating to the study of ethics have been the subject of much debate and analysis, particularly among philosophers. Ethics has been defined by various philosophers under several categories, such as utilitarianism, natural rights or rights-based, duty-based, and virtue-based ethics.

## Utilitarianism

**Utilitarianism** is an ethical theory based on the principle of the greatest good for the greatest number. This ethical theory is concerned with the impact of actions, or final outcomes, on the welfare of society as a whole. Additionally, utilitarianism is a consequences-based ethical theory that follows the premise that the ends (consequences) justify the means (methods for achieving the ends). For example, in the case of limited financial resources, money would be spent in a way to benefit the greatest number of people. In this respect, utilitarianism is considered to be an efficient allocation of resources. In a professional context, a **cost/benefit analysis** justifies the means of achieving a goal. In other words, if the benefit (or well-being) of a decision outweighs the cost (financial or otherwise) of achieving a goal, then the means to obtain the goal would be justified. A problem arises when utilitarianism, or cost/benefit analysis, is used for making ethical decisions, since some people will inevitably "fall through the cracks."

The nation's Medicare system, in which all persons over the age of 65 receive health care benefits, is one example of utilitarianism. Congress has limited amounts to allocate for medical coverage and uses those funds to cover the elderly and others, such as the disabled, under the Medicare Act. However, not *all* people require the benefit. In the case of Medicare, for example, not all elderly persons need to have medical coverage provided for them, since some are wealthy and can afford their own coverage.

Another example of utilitarianism occurs when there is a limited supply of donor organs. Under a utilitarianism approach, patients with the most immediate need (and who would benefit the most) would receive the organ. Using this approach to organ distribution, terminally ill or elderly persons with a limited lifespan would not be the first to receive a scarce resource such as a new heart.

## Rights-Based Ethics

A natural rights or rights-based ethical theory places the primary emphasis on a person's individual rights. This theory, based on justice, states that rights belong to all people purely by virtue of their being human. Under our rights-based democracy, all Americans have the right to freedom of speech. Employees have the right to due process, which entitles them to a fair hearing in the case of dismissal from their jobs. In the above example of limited donor organs, using a rights-based ethical approach, every patient needing a donor organ would have the same right to receive the available organ.

## Duty-Based Ethics

Duty-based ethics focuses on performing one's duty to various people and institutions such as parents, employers, employees, and customers (patients). Americans have a duty to adhere to laws enforced by government authorities. One of the problems encountered with a duty-based approach is that we may hear conflicting opinions about what our "duty" or responsibility is. If our employer asks us to do something that we believe is wrong or unethical, we have a duty not to perform the action. However, this violates our duty to our employer. Most religions have statements that address one's duty as a member of that faith or religion. However, many people do not accept their faith's belief concerning issues such as birth control and working on the Sabbath, but do adhere to other doctrines of their religion.

## Virtue-Based Ethics

A moral virtue is a character trait that is morally valued. The emphasis of virtue-based ethics is on persons and not necessarily on the decisions or principles that are involved. Most people agree that virtues are just good habits, such as fairness and honesty. Other examples of virtues and good character traits are integrity, trust, respect, empathy, generosity, truthfulness, and the ability to disclose mistakes.

Virtue-based ethics, or seeking the "good life," is our legacy from the philosopher Aristotle. According to him, the end of life, for which we all aim, is happiness. He believed that happiness is founded not solely on what we gain in life, but also on who we are. For example, the joy of being a medical professional cannot be present without having the traits or virtues that make one a good nurse, medical assistant, technologist, or physician.

While each of these four ethical theories can have positive outcomes and are useful in certain circumstances, no one ethical theory or system is perfect. See Table 1-1 for a comparison of the advantages and disadvantages of the four ethical theories.

Ethical standards that relate to the medical profession are set and defined by professional organizations such as the American Medical Association. Most professional disciplines, such as nursing, have their own organizations and standards of guiding ethical codes of conduct. Codes of ethics are discussed more fully in Chapter 11.

In general, people believe an action is wrong or unethical if it

- causes emotional or physical harm to someone else.
- goes against one's deepest beliefs.
- makes a person feel guilty or uncomfortable about a particular action.

**TABLE 1–1**   Advantages and Disadvantages of Four Ethical Theories

**Utilitarianism:** The principle of the greatest good for the greatest number. Also called a cost/benefit analysis. A consequence-based theory—or a means to an end.

*Advantages:* Encourages efficiency and productivity by looking beyond the individual to access the impact of decisions on all who will be affected. It is consistent with profit maximization: getting the most value (benefit) for the least cost.

*Disadvantages:* Virtually impossible to quantify all important variables. It can result in a biased allocation of resources, especially when some people lack a representation of voice (i.e., the poor, elderly, and handicapped). The rights of some people may be ignored in order to achieve a utilitarian outcome.

**Rights-based ethics:** Based on the premise that there are moral entitlements by virtue of being human (i.e., the right to health care, the right to free speech).

*Advantages:* Protects the individual from injury; consistent with rights to freedom and privacy. It is consistent with an accepted standard of social behavior, independent of outcomes.

*Disadvantages:* Can imply individualistic selfish behavior that, if misinterpreted, may result in anarchy. Can foster personal liberties that may create obstacles to productivity and efficiency.

**Duty-based ethics:** Based on absolute moral rules. This theory is based on the premise that universal principles should guide all actions. These absolute rules or principles will help us to determine what constitutes our duty toward others.

*Advantages:* People are not treated as a means to an end with this theory. There is a mandate for respect and impartiality toward people.

*Disadvantages:* Difficult to identify who should determine what the rules and principles of moral behavior should be. Who determines what our duty to one another is?

**Virtue-based ethics:** Based on the premise that there is an acquired human quality which tends to enable us to achieve those goods (or rewards) which are the result of virtuous practices.

*Advantages:* Virtuous behavior includes such attributes as perseverance, courage, integrity, compassion, fidelity, humility, and justice.

*Disadvantages:* While there are few disadvantages with this ethical theory, there is a concern that persons can be taken advantage of if they become too complacent and trusting.

- breaks the law or traditions of their society.
- violates the rights of another person.

## Principles or Values That Drive Ethical Behavior

Most people have established throughout their lifetime their own set of principles or values that drive their ethical behavior. Benjamin Franklin included in his list of virtues such things as cleanliness, silence, and industry. In today's world, we don't think of these things as virtues; they are assumed by many people to be a part of everyday life.

However, in today's fast-paced health care environment, it is important to slow down enough to consider some of the most respected virtues. Some of these virtues include beneficence, fidelity, gentleness, humility, justice, perseverance, responsibility, sanctity of life, tolerance, and work.

- **Beneficence**—is the action of helping others and performing actions that would result in benefit to another person. It cautions all those working in the health care field to do no harm to anyone. In fact, when we prevent harmful actions from happening to our patients, we are using this virtue to its fullest extent.

- **Fidelity**—loyalty and faithfulness to others. Fidelity implies that we will perform our duty. We must use caution when practicing fidelity. A strict adherence to a sense of duty or loyalty to an employer does not mean that we must perform actions that are wrong or harmful to our patients.

- Gentleness—implies a mild, tenderhearted approach to other people. Gentleness goes beyond compassion since it can exist in the absence of a person's pain and suffering. A gentle approach to patient care is considered by patients to be one of the most welcome virtues. Both men and women have the ability to demonstrate gentleness.

- Humility—acquiring an unpretentious and humble manner. Humility is considered to be the opposite of vanity. It has been said that "honesty and humility are sisters." This means that to be truly humble, we must be entirely honest with ourselves. There is no greater virtue for health care workers than honesty. Vanity and a sense of self-importance have no place in medicine. When mistakes are made, they must be reported so that corrections can take place. It takes a humble—and honest—person to admit mistakes.

- Justice—implies fairness in all our actions with other people. It means that we must carefully analyze how to balance our behavior and be fair to all. Justice implies that the same rules will apply to everyone. This means that as health care workers we cannot demonstrate favoritism with our patients or our coworkers. The four cardinal virtues are justice, temperance, prudence, and courage. Of these four, only justice is considered to be an absolute good. To emphasize this point, the philosopher Immanuel Kant said, "If legal justice perishes, then it is no longer worthwhile for men to remain alive on this earth."

- Perseverance—to persist with a task or idea even against obstacles. This virtue implies a steady determination to get the job done. For example, it takes perseverance to complete one's education. This is an outstanding virtue for a health care worker to have. It implies that one will finish the job even if it is difficult.

- Responsibility—a sense of accountability for one's actions. Responsibility implies dependability. A sense of responsibility can become weakened when one is faced with peer pressure. Medical professionals must be able to "answer" or be accountable for their actions. Taking responsibility is a sign of maturity.

- Sanctity of life—refers to the sacredness of human life. All human beings must be protected. This means that we may have to become an advocate for people who cannot speak out for themselves, such as children and many elderly.

- **Tolerance**—a respect for those whose opinions, practices, race, religion, and nationality differ from our own. Tolerance requires a fair and objective attitude toward opinions and practices that differ from our own.

- Work—is an effort applied toward some end goal. Work, if performed well, is clearly a virtue that almost everyone enters into at one time or another. In its broadest sense, work is part of our everyday existence that includes activities such as studying, child-rearing, home maintenance, gardening, hobbies, and religious activities. The work we do to earn a living can be performed with pride or can be performed poorly and grudgingly. The most satisfying work involves achieving a goal that we believe is worthwhile and worthy of our talent.

## Interpersonal Ethics

The expectation of employees in the workplace is that they will be treated ethically with respect, integrity, honesty, fairness, empathy, sympathy, compassion, and loyalty. Professional health care employees are no different in their expectation of receiving such treatment.

 **MED TIP**   Remember to treat each person, whether patient or coworker, the way you wish to be treated.

- Respect implies the ability to consider and honor another person's beliefs and opinions. This is a critical quality for a health care worker, since patients come from a variety of racial, ethnic, and religious backgrounds. Coworkers' opinions must also be respected, even if contrary to one's own.
- **Integrity** is the unwavering adherence to one's principles. People with integrity are dedicated to maintaining high standards. For example, integrity means that health care professionals will wash their hands between each patient contact even when no one is looking. Dependability, such as being on time for work every day, is a key component of integrity.
- Honesty is the quality of truthfulness, no matter what the situation. Health care professionals must have the ability to admit an error and then take corrective steps. Anyone who carries out orders for a physician has a duty to notify the physician of any error or discrepancy in those orders.
- Fairness is treating everyone the same. It implies an unbiased impartiality and a sense of justice. This is a particularly important characteristic for supervisors.
- **Empathy** is the ability to understand the feelings of others without actually experiencing their pain or distress. Acting in this caring way expresses sensitivity to patients' or fellow employees' feelings. (See Figure 1-1.) **Sympathy,** on the other

**FIGURE 1–1**    Health care professional demonstrating empathy.

hand, is feeling sorry for or pitying someone else. Most people, including patients, react better to empathetic listeners than to sympathetic ones.

■ Compassion is the ability to have a gentle, caring attitude toward patients and fellow employees. Any illness, and in particular a terminal illness, can cause fear and loneliness in many patients. A compassionate health care professional can help to ease this fear. (See Figure 1-2.)

■ Loyalty is a sense of faithfulness or commitment to a person or persons. Employers expect loyalty from their employees. This loyalty should be granted unless the practice of one's employer is unethical or illegal. For example, it is never appropriate to recommend that a patient seek the services of another physician unless instructed to do so by the employer. By the same token, employees expect loyalty, or fair treatment, from their employer.

 **MED TIP**   Loyalty to one's employer does *not* mean hiding an error that has been committed by that employer or by a physician.

FIGURE 1–2   All patients are entitled to compassionate care.

Additionally, there are specific issues that affect the workplace such as privacy, due process, sexual harassment, and comparable worth:

- Privacy, or confidentiality, is the ability to safeguard another person's confidences or information. Violating patient confidentiality is both a legal and ethical issue that carries penalties. Employees have a right to expect the contents of their personnel records to be held in confidence by their employer. By the same token, it is inappropriate for employees to discuss the personal life of their physician/employer.
- **Due process** is the entitlement of all employees to have certain procedures followed when they believe their rights are in jeopardy. The Fourteenth Amendment of the Constitution acts to prevent the state's deprivation or impairment of "any person's life, liberty, or property without due process of the law." The Fifth Amendment also restricts the federal government from depriving individuals of these rights without due process of the law. In a work environment, this means that all employees accused of an offense are entitled to a fair hearing in their defense.
- Sexual harassment is defined in the Equal Employment Opportunity Commission guidelines, which are part of Title VII of the Amended Civil Rights Act of 1964:

Unwelcome sexual advances, requests for sexual favors, and other verbal or physical conduct of a sexual nature constitute sexual harassment when (1) submission to such conduct is made either explicitly or implicitly a term or condition of an individual's employment; (2) submission to or rejection of such conduct by an individual is used as the basis for employment decisions affecting such individual; or (3) such conduct has the purpose or effect of interfering with an individual's work performance or creating an intimidating, hostile, or offensive working environment.

Both males and females working in the health care field have reported sexual harassment.

 **MED TIP**  Any type of gender harassment is seen as one person exerting power over another.

- **Comparable worth,** also known as pay equity, is a theory that extends equal pay requirements to all persons who are doing equal work. The principle of fairness and justice dictates that work of equal value performed by men and women in the workplace should be rewarded with equal compensation. However, research demonstrates that there is a wage gap, with some estimates as high as 36 percent, due to the undervaluation of work performed by women. This results in injustice; equals are not treated equally. Since pay scales are the same for males and females in many of the health care professions, the situation is not as intense as it is in the business world. However, employers and supervisors who are involved in the hiring process must be committed to providing equal pay for equal work.

## MODELS FOR EXAMINING ETHICAL DILEMMAS

The decision maker must always be objective when making ethical decisions. It is critical to examine all the facts of a given situation by gathering as much information or data as possible. Alternative solutions to the problem must be assessed if they are available. Both sides of every issue should be studied before ethical decisions are made. The following are three decision-making models that can be helpful when resolving ethical issues: the three-step ethics model; the seven-step decision model; and Dr. Bernard Lo's clinical model.

### Three-Step Ethics Model

Kenneth Blanchard and Norman Vincent Peale advise the use of a three-step model when evaluating an ethical dilemma. The three steps are to ask yourself the following questions:

- Is it legal?
- Is it balanced?
- How does it make me feel?

When applying this model, if the situation is clearly illegal, such as inflicting bodily harm on another, then the matter is also clearly unethical and you do not even have to progress to the second question. However, if the action is not against the law, then you should ask yourself the second question, "Is it balanced?", to determine if another person or group of people is negatively affected by the action. In other words, is there now an imbalance so that one person or group suffers or benefits more than another as a result of your action? For example, in the case of a scarce resource such as donor organs, does one group of people have greater access? The final question, "How does it make me feel?", refers to how the action will affect you emotionally. Would you be hesitant to explain your actions to a loved one? How would you feel if you saw your name in the paper associated with the action? Can you face yourself in the mirror? If you can answer the first two questions with a strong "Yes" and the final question with a strong "Good," then the action is likely to be ethical.

For example, student cheating is clearly unethical. By using the three-step ethics model, we have an even clearer idea of why it is unethical to look at even one answer on another student's test. We ask the three questions:

1. Is it legal? Yes, as far as we know there is no law against cheating.
2. Is it balanced? No, it is not. This question is where the model really helps us. One group or person (in this case the cheater) does have an advantage over another group or person. In addition, the grades will be skewed for the entire class, since the person who cheated will receive a higher grade than what he or she earned.
3. How does it make me feel? Remember that we have to live with ourselves. The philosopher Thomas Aquinas said, "We become what we do," meaning that if we lie, we become a liar. Or in this case, if we cheat, we become a cheater.

**MED TIP** The three-step ethics model is a quick way to check yourself when you are uncomfortable about an ethical decision. Use it often!

## The Seven-Step Decision Model

I. Determine the facts by asking the following questions:
What do we need to know?
Who is involved in the situation?
Where does the ethical situation take place?
When does it occur?
II. Define the precise ethical issue.
III. Identify the major principles, rules, and values. For example, is this a matter of integrity, quality, respect for others, or profit?
IV. Specify the alternatives. List the major alternative courses of action, including those that represent some form of compromise. This may be a choice between simply doing or not doing something.
V. Compare values and alternatives. Determine if there is one principle or value, or a combination of principles and values, that is so compelling that the proper alternative is clear.
VI. Assess the consequences. Identify short-term, long-term, positive, and negative consequences for the major alternatives. The short-term gain or loss is often overridden when long-term consequences are considered. This step often reveals an unanticipated result of major importance.
VII. Make a decision. The consequences are balanced against one's primary principles or values.

The seven-step decision model forces us to closely examine the facts before we make an ethical decision. This model can be used to examine all of the end-of-chapter cases in this textbook.

## Dr. Bernard Lo's Clinical Model

Dr. Lo has developed a clinical model for decision making to ensure that no important considerations relating to patient care are overlooked. He believes this approach can be used to help resolve important patient-care issues, such as when to proceed with life-sustaining interventions (for example, cardiopulmonary resuscitation [CPR], or kidney dialysis).

I. Gather information.
If the patient is competent, what are his or her preferences for care?
If the patient lacks decision-making capacity, has he or she provided advance directives for care?
If the patient lacks decision-making capacity, who should act as surrogate?
What are the views of the health care team?
What other issues complicate the case?

   II.  Clarify the ethical issues.
        What are the pertinent ethical issues?
        Determine the ethical guidelines that people are using.
        What are the reasons for and against the alternative plans of care?
  III.  Resolving the dilemma.
        Meet with the health care team and with the patient or surrogate.
        List the alternatives of care.
        Negotiate a mutually acceptable decision.

Dr. Lo emphasizes that patients should play an active role in decisions. Everything should be done to ensure that the patient has been well informed by providing information in an easy-to-understand way. He requires that the entire health care team—including medical students, nurses, social workers, and all others who provide direct care for the patient—be involved in the decisions. These caregivers should voice any moral objections they have to the proposed care. Finally, the patient's best interests must always be protected. This model is more commonly used in a hospital or clinic setting.

## WHAT ETHICS IS NOT

Ethics is not just about how you feel, the sincerity of your beliefs, or your emotions; nor is it only about religious viewpoints.

Feelings, such as in the statement "I feel that capital punishment is wrong," are not sufficient when making an ethical decision. Others may feel that capital punishment is right in that it helps to deter crime. All people have feelings and beliefs. However, ethics must be grounded in reason and fact. For example, a statement such as "I feel that cheating is wrong" doesn't tell us why you believe it is wrong to cheat. A better statement reflecting ethics would be, "I think cheating is wrong because it gives one student an unfair advantage over another student."

The sincerity with which people hold their beliefs is also not an adequate reason when making an ethical decision. For example, Hitler sincerely believed that he was right in exterminating more than 6 million Jews. His sincerity did not make him right.

Emotional responses to ethical dilemmas are not sufficient either. Emotions may affect why people do certain things, such as the woman who kills her husband in a rage after discovering he had an affair. However, we should not let our emotions dictate how we make ethical decisions. We may have helplessly watched a loved one die a slow death from cancer, but our emotions should not cloud the issue of euthanasia and cause us to kill our ill patients.

Ethics is not just about religious beliefs. Many people associate ideas of right and wrong with their religious beliefs. While there is often an overlap between ethics and what a religion teaches as right and wrong, people can hold very strong ethical and moral beliefs without following any formal religion.

 **MED TIP**  Our determination of what is ethical or moral can have serious consequences in human action.

# BIOETHICS

**Bioethics,** also known as biomedical ethics, is one branch of applied, or practical, ethics. It refers to moral dilemmas and issues prevalent in today's society as a result of advances in medicine and medical research. The term *bio,* meaning life, combined with *ethics* relates to the moral conduct of right and wrong in life and death issues. Many of these dilemmas are the result of advances in medical research. Ethical problems of the biological sciences, including research on animals, all fall under the domain of bioethics. Some of the bioethical issues discussed in this text include the allocation of scarce resources, beginning-of-life issues, cloning, harvesting embryos, concerns surrounding death and dying, experimentation and the use of human subjects, and dilemmas in the treatment of catastrophic disease.

**Bioethicists,** specialists in the field of bioethics, give thought to ethical concerns that often examine the more abstract dimensions of ethical issues and dilemmas. For example, they might ask, "What are the social implications of surrogate motherhood?" Bioethicists are often authors, teachers, and researchers.

This branch of ethics poses difficult, if not impossible, questions for the medical practitioner. Examples of some of the difficult ethical and bioethical questions and situations that face the health care professional are listed under Points to Ponder.

## POINTS TO PONDER

1. Should an alcoholic patient, who may die of liver disease, be eligible for an organ transplant?
2. Should a suicidal patient be allowed to refuse a feeding tube?
3. Should prisoners be eligible to receive expensive medical therapies for illnesses?
4. Is assisting with suicide ever ethically justified?
5. Should medical personnel suggest other treatment modes or suggest the patient request a consultation with another physician?
6. Under what circumstances should you report a colleague or physician who is physically, psychologically, or pharmacologically impaired?
7. Is experimentation on human subjects ever justified?
8. When, if ever, should you disclose a patient's medical condition to the family?
9. Should parents be allowed to refuse medical treatment, such as chemotherapy, for their infant?
10. Should genetic counseling include recommendations by the medical personnel?
11. Should you protect your friend by telling him that his lover has tested positive for AIDS?

These questions, and others like them, are addressed throughout this book.

## DISCUSSION QUESTIONS

1. Discuss the difference between the terms *legal* and *moral.*
2. Give an example for each of the following: a medical ethics dilemma, a bioethics situation, and a medical-legal problem.

3. Determine if the eleven questions under Points to Ponder are ethical or legal issues or both.
4. Describe five ethical situations that you may face in the profession you intend to follow.

## PRACTICE EXERCISES

### Matching

Match the responses in column B with the correct term in column A.

**Column A**

_____ 1. bioethics
_____ 2. ethics
_____ 3. applied ethics
_____ 4. laws
_____ 5. medical ethics
_____ 6. utilitarianism
_____ 7. rights-based ethics
_____ 8. three-step ethics model
_____ 9. R/O
_____ 10. gut feeling

**Column B**

a. justice-based
b. decision based on emotion
c. binding rules determined by an authority
d. greatest good for the greatest number
e. moral dilemmas due to recent advances in medicine
f. practical application of moral standards
g. rule out a diagnosis
h. moral conduct to regulate behavior of medical professionals
i. branch of philosophy
j. Kenneth Blanchard and Norman Vincent Peale's approach to ethics

## MULTIPLE CHOICE

Select the one best answer to the following statements.

1. A problem that occurs when using a duty-based approach to ethics is
   a. the primary emphasis on a person's individual rights
   b. determining the greatest good for the greatest number of people
   c. the conflicting opinions regarding what our responsibility is
   d. remembering the three-step model approach to solving ethical dilemmas
   e. understanding the difference between what is fair and unfair

2. Moral issues that occur as a result of modern medical technology are covered under what specific discipline?
   a. law
   b. medicine
   c. philosophy
   d. bioethics
   e. none of the above

3. When trying to solve an ethical dilemma, it is necessary to
   a. do what everyone else is doing
   b. use logic to determine the solution
   c. do what we are told to do by others
   d. base the decision on religious beliefs only
   e. allow our emotions and feelings to guide us

4. The three-step approach to solving ethical dilemmas is based on
   a. asking ourselves how our decision would make us feel if we had to explain our actions to a loved one
   b. asking ourselves if the intended action is legal
   c. asking ourselves if the intended action results in a balanced decision
   d. a and b only
   e. a, b, and c

5. A utilitarian approach to solving ethical dilemmas might be used when
   a. allocating a limited supply of donor organs
   b. trying to find a just decision in which everyone will benefit
   c. finding a decision based on a sense of duty toward another person
   d. making sure that no one will "fall through the cracks" and not receive access to care
   e. none of the above

6. An illegal act is always
   a. hidden
   b. unethical
   c. performed with the full knowledge of the health care worker
   d. obvious
   e. all of the above

7. A practical application of ethics is
   a. philosophy
   b. the law
   c. illegal
   d. applied ethics
   e. b and d

8. An employee who is entitled to a fair hearing in the case of a dismissal from a job is an example of
   a. duty-based ethics
   b. utilitarianism
   c. rights-based ethics
   d. justice-based ethics
   e. c and d

9. Laws that affect the medical profession
   a. often overlap with ethics
   b. have a binding force
   c. are always fair to all persons

    d. are determined by a governmental authority

    e. a, b, and d

10. Modern laws
    a. may allow some unethical acts such as lying on job applications
    b. are interpreted by some people to require no ethical responsibility beyond what the law requires
    c. are not used as a type of yardstick for group behavior
    d. a and b only
    e. a, b, and c

## PUT IT INTO PRACTICE

Talk to someone who is currently working in the medical field that you are working in or plan to enter. Ask him or her for a definition of medical ethics. Then compare it with the textbook definition. Does it match? Discuss with that person an ethical dilemma that he or she has faced and handled.

## WEB HUNT

Search the Web site of the Joint Commission on Accreditation of Health Care Organizations (*www.jcaho.org*). Using either the heading "For the General Public" or "Quality Check," enter the name of a health care institution in your area and determine its quality rating, according to the JCAHO.

## REFERENCES

Bennett, W. 1993. *The book of virtues.* New York: Simon & Schuster.

Blanchard, K., and N. Peale. 1988. *The power of ethical management.* New York: William Morrow.

Boatright, J. 2000. *Ethics and the conduct of business.* Upper Saddle River, N.J.: Prentice Hall.

Brincat, C., and V. Wike. 2000. *Morality and the professional life.* Upper Saddle River, N.J.: Prentice Hall.

Buchholz, R., and S. Rosenthal. 1988. *Business ethics.* Upper Saddle River, N.J.: Prentice Hall.

Comte-Sponville, A. 2001. *A small treatise on the great virtues.* New York: Henry Holt.

Fredrick, C., and C. Atkinson. 1997. *Women, ethics and the workplace.* Westport, Conn.: Praeger.

Garrett, T., H. Baillie, and R. Garrett. 1993. *Health care ethics: Principles and problems.* Upper Saddle River, N.J.: Prentice Hall.

Klayman, E., J. Bagby, and N. Ellis. 1995. *Irwin's business law.* Burr Ridge, Ill.: Irwin.

Larmer, R. *Ethics in the workplace.* 1996. New York: West Publishing.

Lo, B. 1995. *Resolving ethical dilemmas: A guide for clinicians.* New York: Lippincott Williams & Wilkins.

Newton, L., and D. Schmidt. 1996. *Wake up calls.* New York: Wadsworth.

Sterba, J. 1998. *Ethics: The big questions.* Malden, Mass.: Blackwell.

Veatch, R., and H. Flack. 1997. *Case studies in allied health ethics.* Upper Saddle River, N.J.: Prentice Hall.

Weber, C. 1995. *Stories of virtue in business.* New York: University Press of America.

## CASE STUDY

Your friend shows you some books he took from the bookstore without paying for them. When you question him about it, he says, "Sure I took them. But I'm no different than anybody else around here. That's how we all manage to get through school on limited funds. I'll be a better medical professional because of all the knowledge I gain from these books."

1. Do you agree or disagree with his rationalization? Why or why not?

_____

_____

_____

_____

_____

2. What do you say to him?

_____

_____

_____

_____

_____

3. What ethical principles discussed in this chapter helped you with your answer?

_____

_____

_____

_____

_____

# PART I

# THE LEGAL
# ENVIRONMENT

## CHAPTER 2

# The Legal System

## LEARNING OBJECTIVES

1. Define the glossary terms.
2. Discuss why an understanding of the legal profession is necessary for the health care professional.
3. Describe the sources of law.
4. Describe the steps for a bill to become a law.
5. Discuss the difference between civil law and criminal law, explaining the areas covered by each.
6. List six intentional torts and give examples of each.
7. List examples of criminal actions that relate to the health care worker.
8. Discuss the difference between a felony and a misdemeanor.
9. Describe the types of courts in the legal system.
10. Explain the trial process.
11. Discuss why an expert witness might be used during a lawsuit.

## KEY TERMS

| | | |
|---|---|---|
| Administrative law | Defamation of character | Plaintiff |
| Breach | Defendant | Precedent |
| Breach of contract | Deposition | Prosecutor |
| Case law | Discovery | Regulations |
| Checks and balances | Embezzlement | Slander |
| Civil law | Expert witness | *Stare decisis* |
| Closing argument | Expressed contract | Statutes |
| Common law | Felony | Subpoena |
| Competent | Fraudulent | *Subpoena duces tecum* |
| Consideration | Implied contract | Tort |
| Constitutional law | Indictment | Tort law |
| Contract law | Libel | Unintentional torts |
| Criminal case | Litigation | Waive |
| Criminal laws | Misdemeanors | |

## INTRODUCTION

Health care professionals must have a good understanding of the legal system for a variety of reasons. The advanced state of medical technology creates new legal, ethical, moral, and financial problems for the consumer and the health care practitioner. Today's health care consumer demands more of a partnership with the physician and the rest of the health care team. Patients have become more aware of their legal rights. Court cases and decisions have had a greater impact than ever on the way health care professionals practice business in the medical field.

 **MED TIP**   Every effort should be made to provide a quality of care for patients that will not only help them to recover their health but will also avoid lawsuits.

## THE LEGAL SYSTEM

To understand the American legal system, it is important to first understand the two fundamental principles on which the United States system of government was founded—federalism and checks and balances. A federal form of government is one in which power is divided between a central government and smaller regional governments. The Constitution of the United States, which was drafted in Philadelphia in 1787, established a federal form of government, giving a limited and enumerated power to the central government (i.e., the federal government). All powers that have not been specifically delegated to the federal government by the Constitution are retained by the states.

The American legal system has one federal legal system and fifty separate and unique state systems. For example, the federal government administers the U.S. Tax Court and the U.S. Bankruptcy Court. The state governments administer such courts as traffic and small claims courts. The state governments also administer medical licensing acts.

The court system is only one part of the government, however. In establishing a federal government, the U.S. Constitution separated the government's power into three branches: legislative, executive, and judicial. The branches complement each other but do not take on the power of the other branches. The separation between the three branches created a system of **checks and balances** and was designed by the framers of the Constitution so that no one branch could have more power than another branch. See Figure 2-1 for an illustration of the branches of the U.S. government.

The legislative branch, referred to as Congress, is considered the lawmaking body. It is composed of members of the Senate and House of Representatives and is

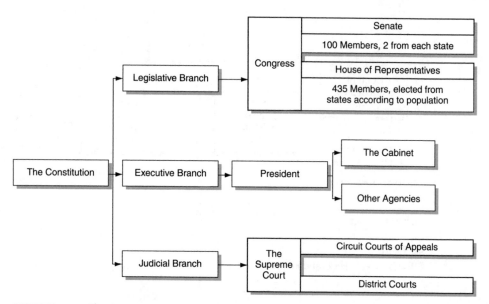

**FIGURE 2–1**   The branches of the U.S. government.

responsible for originating legislation. The executive branch (consisting of the President of the United States, his or her cabinet, and various advisers) administers and enforces the law. The judicial branch (consisting of judges and the federal courts, including the Supreme Court) interprets the laws. Congress has the power to make the law, but the President has the power to veto these laws, although Congress can then override the veto with a two-thirds majority vote. The President can appoint all federal and Supreme Court judges, but Congress must confirm appointments. The judicial branch can review legislation and interpret the laws passed by Congress and the President, but the President must enforce the law. Congress can, in many instances, pass new laws to override a judicial decision. See Figure 2-2 for an illustration of the federal court structure.

The states all have their own constitutions, which in many respects mirror the U.S. Constitution. The state constitutions likewise establish legislative, executive, and judicial branches within each state. See Figure 2-3 for an illustration of the separation of powers.

**MED TIP**   Federal law is administered the same in all states. However, individual states may vary on how they interpret and implement laws relegated to the states. Therefore, interpretation of legal acts for allied health professionals varies greatly from state to state.

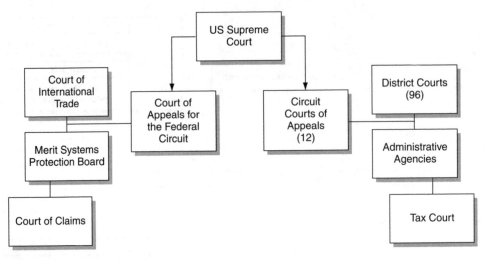

**FIGURE 2–2**   Federal court structure.

**FIGURE 2–3**   Separation of powers in the federal legal system.

# SOURCES OF LAW

All laws—those enforceable rules prescribed by a government authority—must come from somewhere. Let's say that you are pulled over and given a ticket for driving 70 miles an hour, when the speed limit is only 55. You obviously broke a law. But where did that law come from? Did someone just walk down the highway and put up signs saying how fast he or she thought you should drive? Of course not. The speed limit, like all other laws, originated from a government body authorized to establish rules. These rules fall into four different categories: constitutional; statutory; regulatory; and common, or case, law.

## Constitutional Law

**Constitutional law** consists of both the U.S. Constitution and the constitutions of the individual states. A constitution sets up a government, defines the government's power to act, and sets limits on the government's power (i.e., individual rights such as the right to free speech).

It is important to realize that the Constitution only addresses the relationship between individuals and their government; it does not apply to the relationship between private entities, whether they be individuals or businesses. For instance, a state-run hospital cannot violate your constitutional rights, but a private hospital can. That does not mean that private hospitals have free reign to do as they please. Rather, it means that the rules governing their conduct come from another source of law. For example, while it is not unconstitutional for a private hospital to discriminate, it is illegal because there is a federal statute that makes it illegal for private employers to discriminate.

## Statutory and Regulatory Law

**Statutes** are laws passed by legislative bodies, either Congress or the state legislature. This is called statutory or legislative law. Congress and the state legislatures have the authority to pass laws because in setting up our form of government, the Constitution authorized the legislature to make laws. Statutory law consists of ever-changing rules and regulations created by the U.S. Congress, state legislators, local governments, or constitutional lawmakers. These statutes are the inviolable rights, privileges, or immunities secured and protected for each citizen by the U.S. Constitution.

Legislatures sometimes authorize agencies to make laws. The legislature does this by passing a statute, called enabling legislature. This statute creates an agency and authorizes it to pass laws regarding specific issues. For instance, the Food and Drug Administration is a federal agency that can pass rules governing the sale of food and drugs. The rules or laws made by agencies are called **regulations.**

Statutes begin as bills submitted by legislators at the state or federal level. The first step is taken when the bill is introduced in either of the two legislative houses: Senate or House of Representatives. If the bill does not "die" (if it fails to be acted upon) in one of the houses, it then goes to a committee for discussion and consideration. (Note that 85 percent of all bills die before they reach a committee.) The committee studies the bill and may hold a hearing to gain more facts about the bill. This first committee issues a report, including a recommendation to either pass or fail the bill. The bill then goes back to the house (Senate or House of Representatives) in which it originated, where a discussion and vote takes place. After the bill passes in one house, it becomes an act. The act is then sent back to the other house, where it goes through the same steps as it did as a bill. The act can always be amended by the second house, which results in its being returned to the originating house for a discussion and vote on the amendment.

If the second house passes the act, then the heads of each house—Speaker of the House of Representatives and the President Pro Tem of the Senate (the Vice President of the United States)—sign it. The act is then sent to the chief executive, who is, in the case of a federal act, the President and, for a state act, the governor. The act becomes a law if it is signed by the chief executive and not vetoed within ten days.

After this complicated process, the act is referred to as a public law or statute.

 **MED TIP**    A new law is issued with a public law number, such as PL 94-104, which indicates that it was the 94th Congress that passed the law (the first two digits) and the 104th piece of legislation in that Congress.

Laws that are passed by city governments are called municipal ordinances. Federal laws have precedence over state laws; state laws have precedence over city or municipal laws. In other words, a state or city may make laws and regulations more stringent than the federal law, but cannot make laws less stringent.

## Common Law

The final source of law is common law. Unlike the laws established by legislative bodies (statutory laws), common law is made by judges when they apply previous court decisions to current cases. Thus, **common law,** as established from a court decision, may explain or interpret the other sources of law. Since common law evolves on a case-by-case basis, it is also called **case law.** For instance, a case may explain what the constitution, a statute, or a regulation means. In addition to interpreting the other sources of law, common law defines other legal rights and obligations. For example, a doctor's obligation to use reasonable care in treating a patient (i.e., not to commit medical malpractice) is a legal obligation created from actual court decisions.

Common law, or case law based on decisions made by judges, was originally established by English courts in the 12th century and brought to America by the early colonists. The only state that doesn't follow common law is the state of Louisiana, which bases its law on early French law. Common law is based on **precedent,** the ruling in an early case that is then applied to subsequent cases when the facts are the same. Each time common law is applied, it must be reviewed by the court to determine if it is still justified and relevant. As a result of this constant review of common law, many laws have been changed (or updated) over the years. The ultimate arbiter, or interpreter, of common law is the state supreme court or, if the law involves a federal question, the U.S. Supreme Court. The legal principle of *stare decisis,* or "let the decision stand," comes to us from the precedence of basing decisions on similar past case decisions.

Example of Case Law:

In the 1616 case of *Weaver v. Ward,* Weaver sued Ward after Ward's musket accidentally fired during a military exercise, wounding Weaver. Weaver won, and Ward had to pay damages for Weaver's injury. The court concluded that Weaver did not have to show that Ward intended to injure him. Even though the injury was an accident, Ward was still liable (*Weaver v. Ward,* 80 Eng. Rep. 284, 1616). In *Lambert v. Bessey,* decided in 1681, the court stated, "In all civil acts the law doth not so much regard the intent of the actor, as the loss and damage of the party suffering." (*Lambert v. Bessey,* 83 Eng. Rep. 220, 1681.) Cases such as these established the precedent that the person who hurt another person by unavoidable accident or self-defense was required to make good the damage inflicted.

> **MED TIP** Taken literally, *stare decisis* means to abide by, or adhere to, decided cases.

Many old case decisions, such as the ones described in the case law example, still influence today's medical practitioner.

Even though the facts of these cases are antiquated, we can still see their relevance when a patient suffers an injury while undergoing medical treatment. In the late 19th century, the courts recognized that there should be liability for a pure accident. Therefore, a person (defendant) may be liable for an injury to another person (plaintiff), even if the defendant did not intend to hurt the plaintiff.

## CLASSIFICATION OF LAWS

Laws are classified as private and public. Private (or civil) laws can be divided into six categories: tort, contract, property, inheritance, family, and corporate law. Only tort and contract law are discussed here, since they most often affect the medical professional. Public law can be divided into four categories: criminal, administrative, constitutional, and international law. This chapter discusses only criminal law.

### Civil (Private) Law

**Civil law** concerns relationships between individuals or between individuals and the government. It involves all the law that is not criminal law, although the same conduct may violate criminal and civil law. For instance, murder is a crime that the government prosecutes in order to punish the defendant by inflicting a prison term or even death, while the surviving family members can sue the person in a civil suit for wrongful death and receive compensation for their loss. Civil law cases generally carry a monetary damage or award. An individual can sue another person, a business, or the government. Some civil law cases include divorce, child custody, auto accidents, slander, libel, and trespassing.

Civil law includes tort law and contract law. **Tort law** covers acts that result in harm to another. **Contract law** includes enforceable promises and agreements between two or more persons to do, or not do, a particular action. Health care employees are most frequently involved in cases of civil law, in particular, tort and contract law. Most medical malpractice lawsuits fall within the category of the civil law of torts.

 **MED TIP**   In many cases, civil law matters are handled and settled outside of the courtroom.

### Tort Law

A **tort** is a civil injury, or wrongful act, that is committed against another person or property that results in harm and is compensated by money damages. To sue for a tort, a patient must have suffered a mental or physical injury that was caused by the physician or the physician's employee. A tort case is tried before either a judge or a jury. Torts can be either intentional or unintentional (accidental), and the patient may recover monetary damages.

 **MED TIP**   Under tort law, if a wrongful act has been committed against another person and there is no harm done, then there is no tort. However, in medical practice, every wrongful act or error must be reported, since patients may experience harm sometime later than when the tort occurs. For instance, if a woman in the first trimester (first three months) of her pregnancy has an x-ray procedure, the fetus may not demonstrate any harmful effects until several months later at birth.

*Intentional Torts*   Intentional torts include assault, battery, false imprisonment, defamation of character, fraud, and invasion of privacy. Table 2-1 provides a description and example of each.

*Assault*   No health care professional would knowingly perform torts against a patient or any other person. However, even a trained professional can make a mistake if he or she is not aware of what constitutes a "wrongful act" under these torts. For example, for a tort of assault, it is sufficient for the patient to just fear that he or she will be hurt or has an "imminent apprehension of bodily harm." So, if a health care professional threatens a patient by saying, "If you don't lie still, we will have to hold you down," and the patient believes this will cause him or her injury or harm, this is considered a tort of assault.

*Battery*   The tort of battery requires bodily harm or unlawful touching (touching without the consent of the patient). No procedure, including drawing blood for a laboratory test, can be performed without the patient's knowledge and consent. When a patient offers an arm or rolls up a sleeve for the phlebotomist, this constitutes a form of consent (implied) for the procedure.

**TABLE 2–1** Intentional Torts

| Tort | Description | Example |
|------|-------------|---------|
| Assault | The threat of bodily harm to another. There does not have to be actual touching (battery) for an assault to take place. | Threatening to harm a patient or to perform a procedure without the informed consent (permission) of the patient. |
| Battery | Actual bodily harm to another person without permission. This is also referred to as unlawful touching or touching without consent. | Performing surgery or a procedure without the informed consent (permission) of the patient. |
| False imprisonment | A violation of the personal liberty of another person through unlawful restraint. | Refusing to allow a patient to leave an office, hospital, or medical facility when he or she requests to leave. |
| Defamation of character | Damage caused to a person's reputation through spoken or written word. | Making a negative statement about another physician's ability. |
| Fraud | Deceitful practice that deprives another person of his or her rights. | Promising a miracle cure. |
| Invasion of privacy | The unauthorized publicity of information about a patient. | Allowing personal information, such as test results for HIV, to become public without the patient's permission. |

*Source:* Fremgen: *Essentials of Medical Assisting,* Prentice Hall, 1998.

*False Imprisonment* False imprisonment in health care occurs when a medical professional, or a person hired by that professional, takes an action to confine a patient. There have been cases in which patients were not allowed to leave a room or building when they wished, resulting in a tort of false imprisonment in which the patient (plaintiff) won the case. This occurred in a Texas case in which the patient, who was assessed as being competent, was detained against his will from leaving a nursing home. (*Big Town Nursing Home. v. Newman,* 461 S.W.2d 195, Tex. Civ. App. 1970.)

A more common situation occurs when a patient wishes to leave a hospital against medical orders. In this case, the patient must sign a statement that says he or she is leaving against the advice of the physician. There have also been a few cases of false imprisonment, resulting from hospitals trying to hold patients until their bills were paid. (*Williams v. Summit Psychiatric Ctrs.,* 363 S.E.2d 794, Ga. App. 1987.) However, no such cases have been reported in the last few years because hospitals now understand that this practice is unacceptable.

*Defamation of Character* Making false and/or malicious statements about another person constitutes **defamation of character.** Defamation can be in two forms: slander or libel. According to *Black's Law Dictionary,* **slander** is speaking false and malicious words concerning another person which brings injury to his or her reputation. There are four recognized exceptions that require no proof of actual harm to a person's reputation in order to recover damages for slander: accusing a person of a crime; accusing someone of a "loathsome" disease, such as a venereal disease; using words against a person's business or profession; and calling a woman unchaste. **Libel** is, in general, any publication in print, writing, pictures, or signs that injures the reputation of another person. Physicians and nurses are protected against an accusation of libel when complying with a law to report venereal disease or cases of abuse.

*Fraud*    **Fraudulent** practices consist of an attempt to deceive another person. For example, making a statement to a cancer patient that "Dr. Williams is a miracle worker; she'll have you feeling better in no time" is a false promise, since there are too many variables when dealing with cancer. However, a more common type of medical fraud consists of false billing practices, especially relating to Medicare and Medicaid.

Physicians are prohibited from accepting kickbacks, or payments of any kind, for the referral of Medicare and Medicaid patients under the Medicare-Medicaid Antifraud and Abuse Amendments. In some cases, physicians have received kickbacks from medical technology companies for using their products on patients. This is considered a criminal offense under the Antifraud law and could result in a large penalty and even imprisonment.

**Embezzlement,** the illegal appropriation of property, usually money, by a person entrusted with its possession, can occur in a physician's or dentist's office when a trusted office manager has total control over the office finances. To embezzle means to willfully take another person's money. For control purposes, more than one person should receive payments, issue receipts for payments, audit the accounts, and deposit the money.

*Invasion of Privacy*    An invasion of privacy can occur at any time during a patient's treatment, even after the patient has granted permission to allow publicity. For example, in the case of allowing photographs or videotapes to be taken, the patient may cancel the permission at any time. In *Estate of Berthiaume v. Pratt,* an invasion of privacy case was tried after a patient with cancer of the larynx died. The deceased patient had allowed his physician to take several photographs that were to be used for the medical record but not for publication. A few hours before the hospitalized patient died, the surgeon and a nurse attempted to take more photographs in spite of the patient's indication he did not want this done and his wife's protests. The wife sued the surgeon for assault, since he had moved the patient's head during the photo taking, as well as invasion of privacy. An appeals court found in favor of the plaintiff and stated that taking photographs, in spite of the patient's protests, was an invasion of his legal rights to privacy. (*Estate of Berthiaume v. Pratt,* 365 QA.2d 792, Me. 1976.)

The famous Supreme Court case in 1973, *Roe v. Wade,* gave strength to the argument that a woman had a right to privacy over matters that related to her body, which included pregnancy. (*Roe v. Wade,* 410 U.S. 113, 1973.)

*Unintentional Torts*    **Unintentional torts,** such as negligence, occur when the patient is injured as a result of the health care professional not exercising the ordinary standard of care. The term *standard of care* means that the professional must exercise the type of care that a "reasonable" person would use in a similar circumstance.

**MED TIP**  The term *reasonable* is a broad, flexible word used to make sure the decision is based on the facts of a particular situation rather than on abstract legal principles. It can mean fair, rational, or moderate. Reasonable care has been defined as "that degree of care a person of ordinary prudence (the so-called reasonable person or reasonable health care professional) would exercise in similar circumstances."

*Morrison v. MacNamara* illustrates the standard of care issue. In this case, MacNamara, a technician, took a urethral smear from the patient, Morrison, while the patient was standing. Morrison fainted, hit his head, and permanently lost his sense of smell and taste. An expert witness from Michigan testified that the national standard of care for taking a urethral smear requires the patient to sit or lie down. Thus, the court found in favor of the patient. (*Morrison v. MacNamara*, 407 A.2d 555, D.C. 1979.)

Negligence is the failure or omission to perform professional duties to an accepted standard of care, such as a "reasonable person" would do. Negligence can involve doing something carelessly or failing to do something that should have been done. Physicians and other health care professionals usually do not knowingly indulge in acts that are negligent. Malpractice, which is misconduct or demonstration of an unreasonable lack of skill, relates to a professional skill such as medicine or the law. Negligence and malpractice are similar in that both relate to wrongdoing. In medical malpractice, negligence is considered the predominant theory of liability. The topics of negligence and malpractice are discussed further in Chapter 3.

**MED TIP**  Remember that it is easier to prevent negligence than it is to defend it.

## Contract Law

Contract law addresses a **breach** or neglect of a legally binding agreement between two parties. The agreement or contract may relate to insurance, sales, business, real estate, or services such as health care.

**MED TIP**  Breach of contract refers to the failure, without legal excuse, to perform any promise or to carry out any of the terms of a contract.

A contract consists of a voluntary agreement that two parties enter into with the intent of benefiting each other. Something of value, which is termed **consideration,** is part of the agreement. In the medical profession, the consideration might be the performance of an appendectomy for a specific fee. An agreement would take place between the two parties that would include the offer ("I will perform the appendectomy") and the acceptance of the offer ("I will allow you to perform the appendectomy"). Therefore, a surgeon who has consent to perform a hysterectomy on a patient may not perform an appendectomy at the same time unless there is consent from the patient for both procedures.

In order for the contract to be valid (legal), both parties must be **competent.** The concerned party (patient) must be mentally competent and not under the influence of drugs or alcohol at the time the contract is entered into.

*Types of Contracts*   A contract can be either expressed or implied. An **expressed contract** is an agreement entered into orally or in writing. All the components of the contract must be clearly stated or in writing.

> **MED TIP**   Most contracts are enforceable, even if oral.

Each state identifies certain types of contracts that must be in writing. The sale of property, mortgages, and deeds is required to be in writing by most state statutes.

There are state statutes and federal laws that relate to the medical profession. For example, if a third party agrees to pay a patient's bill, a contract must be placed in writing and signed by the third party. A copy of this document should be kept in the patient's chart or file. If physicians agree to allow their patients to pay bills in four or more installments, the interest (if any) must be stated in writing (Truth in Lending Act of 1969, discussed in Chapter 8).

An **implied contract** is one in which the agreement is shown through inference by signs, inaction, or silence. For example, when a patient explains his or her symptoms to the physician, and the physician then examines the patient and prescribes treatment, a contract exists, even though it was not clearly stated; and both parties must follow through on the implied agreement. This can cause problems for both parties if there is not a clear understanding of the implied contract. For example, a New York court found an implied contract to pay for medical services existed when a physician listened to a patient describe his symptoms over the telephone. (*O'Neill v. Montefiore Hosp.*, 202 N.Y.S.2d, 436, App. Div. 1960.)

*Termination of the Contract*   A **breach of contract** occurs when either party fails to comply with the terms of the agreement. For example, if a physician refuses to perform a medical procedure he or she had agreed to perform, the physician has breached the contract. If a patient does not pay an agreed-upon fee, then the patient breached the contract with the physician.

The termination of a contract between patient and physician generally occurs when the treatment has ended and the fee has been paid. However, issues may arise that cause premature termination of a contract. It should be noted that both physicians and patients have the right to terminate the contractual agreement. A breach of contract occurs when one of the parties that entered into the contract does not keep his or her promise as, for example, when a patient refuses to pay a bill. A physician may be liable for breach of contract if he or she has promised to cure a patient and then failed to do so. The breach of contract can occur even if there were no negligence on the part of the physician.

When terminating a contract, physicians should be careful that they are not charged with abandonment of the patient. To protect against an abandonment charge, any letter from the physician to the patient should indicate the date his or her services will be terminated. A copy of this letter to the patient should be placed in the patient's record. In addition, there should be a notation in the patient's chart that a notification of termination letter was sent. See Chapter 5 for a complete discussion of abandonment. Some of the reasons for premature termination of a medical contract are

- failure to follow instructions.
- missed appointments.
- failure to pay for service.
- the patient states (orally or in writing) that he or she is seeking the care of another physician (for example, the patient's insurance may have changed and the physician may not be covered by the new insurance, or the patient may move).

## Public Law: Criminal Law

**Criminal laws** are made to protect the public as a whole from the harmful acts of others. The purpose of criminal law is to define socially intolerable conduct that is punishable by law. A criminal act is one in which a person or institution commits an illegal act or a failure to act.

In a **criminal case,** the government (the state in most cases) brings the suit against a person or group of people accused of committing a crime, resulting in a fine, imprisonment, or both if the defendant is found guilty. Federal criminal offenses include illegal actions that cross state lines—kidnapping, treason, or other actions that affect national security. Crimes involving the borders of the United States (for example, illegal transport of drugs, and any illegal act against a federally regulated business, such as a bank) are also federal criminal offenses. Historically, state criminal offenses included murder, robbery, burglary, larceny, rape, sodomy, and arson, but today they also include such things as practicing medicine without a license.

In the health care field, federal and state agencies, under authorization from Congress or state legislatures, have created a multitude of rules and regulations. **Administrative law,** a branch of public law, covers regulations that are set by government agencies. Violations of these regulations constitute criminal or civil actions. In most cases, they are civil law violations. Wide-ranging health care related regulations include

- licensing and supervision of prescribing, storing, and dispensing controlled substances.
- health department regulations, including reporting requirements of certain communicable diseases.
- Internal Revenue Service regulations.
- regulations against homicide, infanticide, euthanasia, assault, and battery.
- regulations against fraud.

Criminal acts fall into two categories: felony and misdemeanor. A **felony** carries a punishment of death or imprisonment in a state or federal prison for more than one year. These serious crimes include murder, rape, robbery, tax evasion, and practicing medicine without a license. **Misdemeanors** are less serious offenses. They include traffic violations, disturbing the peace, and theft. A misdemeanor carries a punishment of fines or imprisonment in jail for up to a year. See Figure 2-4 for an illustration of the felony case process and Figure 2-5 for an illustration of the misdemeanor case process.

A physician's license may be revoked by the state licensing board if he or she is convicted of a crime. Criminal cases in the health care field have included revocation of a license for sexual misconduct, income tax evasion, counterfeiting, murder, and violating narcotics laws.

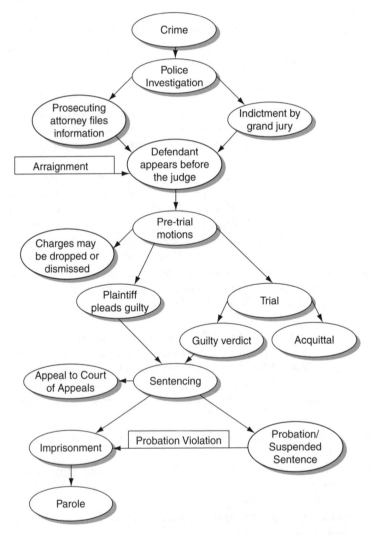

**FIGURE 2–4**   Felony case process. *(Adapted from "A Citizen's Guide to Washington Courts," Washington State Office of Administrator for the Courts, 1997.)*

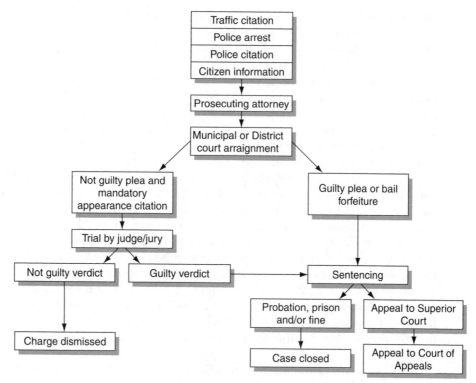

**FIGURE 2–5** Misdemeanor case process. *(Adapted from "A Citizen's Guide to Washington Courts," Washington State Office of Administrator for the Courts, 1997.)*

## THE COURT SYSTEM

There are two court systems in the United States: state and federal. Each system has specific responsibilities that may be either exclusive, meaning that only that particular court can hear a case, or concurrent, meaning both courts have the power to hear the case. Which court hears the case depends on what type of offense has been committed. For a criminal case, this depends on the type of crime and where the criminal action occurred. For example, a bank robbery that took place in Alabama will usually be tried by a federal court in that state. In a civil case, the type of court used depends on where the incident occurred and the type of lawsuit.

### Types of Courts

The federal court system has jurisdiction, or power to hear a case, when one of the following conditions is present:

- the dispute relates to a federal law or the U.S. Constitution
- the U.S. government is one of the parties involved in the dispute
- different states' citizens are involved in the dispute and the case involves over $75,000

- citizens of another country are involved in a dispute with a U.S. citizen and the case involves over $75,000
- the actual dispute occurred on or in international waters

If the case does not involve one of these situations, it must be tried in state court. However, even if one of these situations exists, the case may still be heard in state court unless Congress has prohibited state courts from hearing the case, such as with a kidnapping that takes place across state lines. Cases involving a federal crime, bankruptcy law, and patent law must be heard in federal court. Cases involving divorce, child custody, and probate must be heard in state court.

The court system is divided into three levels. The levels for the federal court system are district (or municipal), court of appeals (or circuit courts), and the U.S. Supreme Court. A case is tried at the lowest level court first. If that court's decision is appealed, or challenged, then the next higher court examines the decision.

The state courts, from lower to higher, are divided into district or municipal trial courts, state court of appeals, and the state's highest court for final appeals. The lower state courts hear cases such as small claims and traffic violations.

Physicians may have to take a patient who has a delinquent account to small claims court. Physicians may authorize their office manager, bookkeeper, or other office assistant to appear in court for the hearing. The clerk of small claims court can provide information on the requirements and procedures relating to this type of lawsuit.

Probate court, or estate court, handles cases involving estates of the deceased. A physician may have to contact the county court recorder for information about filing a claim for payment from the estate of a deceased patient.

 **MED TIP**   It is always advisable to seek payment for all medical services that have been provided to dying or deceased patients. Failure to seek payment may be thought of as an indication of guilt or negligence over a patient's treatment or death.

## THE TRIAL PROCESS

### The Grand Jury

The federal government and many states use the grand jury process. A grand jury, usually consisting of 23 private citizens, hears evidence about a criminal case in order to determine if the case has enough merit to be heard in court. Thus, a grand jury can serve as a filter to prevent cases from being heard when there is insufficient evidence. The grand jury hearings are held in private, and the **defendant,** the person being sued in a court of law, does not generally appear to speak before the grand jury. The grand jury can ask to see documents relating to the investigation and to speak with witnesses. After hearing all the evidence and deliberating among themselves, the grand jury votes on whether they should move the **indictment,** a written legal charge against the defendant, to a trial court.

## The Procedure

When two parties are unable to solve a dispute by themselves, it may result in **litigation,** a dispute or lawsuit that is tried in court. A physician may be the **plaintiff,** the person bringing an action into litigation, or the defendant. A **prosecutor** brings a criminal lawsuit on behalf of the government. Not all lawsuits end up in court. In many situations, attorneys for both sides work out a settlement, or agreement, between the parties, so there is no need for a trial. This is called settling out of court.

If the parties are unable to settle the dispute, a trial is held. A court case can be tried before a judge only, or before a judge and jury of the defendant's peers. Both parties (defendant and plaintiff) in the case may **waive,** or give up their right to, a jury trial or request a jury trial.

If a jury is requested, then six to twelve people are selected from a large pool of potential jurors. The jurors are summoned from a list of residents of a particular region, registered voters, or drivers license holders. The judge and attorneys for both sides of the case (plaintiff and defendant) question the potential jurors to find an impartial jury. Once the final selection of jurors is made, the case is ready to begin.

A trial begins with opening statements made by the attorneys for each side of the case that describe the facts they will attempt to prove during the case. The plaintiff's attorney then questions the first witness. A witness is generally someone who has knowledge of the circumstances of the case and can testify, under oath, as to what happened. This witness can then be cross-examined (asked questions) by the defendant's attorney. After all of the plaintiff's witnesses have been examined and cross-examined, the defendant's attorney (defense counsel) presents witnesses for their side of the case. The plaintiff's attorney then has an opportunity to cross-examine the defense witnesses. When this portion of the case has been completed, both sides "rest their case," which means that all the evidence and witnesses have been examined.

 **MED TIP** The American legal system is based on the premise that all persons are innocent until proven guilty. Because the plaintiff is claiming that the defendant violated a law, the *burden of proof* is placed upon the plaintiff to prove that the defendant is liable.

Attorneys for both the plaintiff and the defendant then make closing speeches or summaries of their case, called **closing arguments.** In a jury trial, the judge instructs the jury on the areas of law that affect the case. The jury is then excused and taken to another room so they can deliberate, examine the evidence presented, and come to a conclusion, or verdict. If the trial has been conducted in front of a judge without a jury, then the judge makes a decision based on the evidence presented and the law. In a civil case, if the judge or jury finds in favor of the plaintiff, then the defendant is ordered to pay the plaintiff a monetary award. In a criminal case, if the defendant is found guilty, the judge sentences the defendant with either a fine and/or a prison

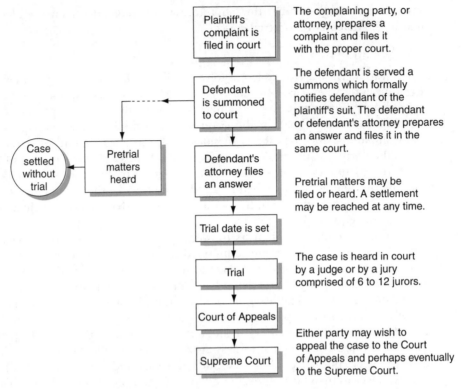

The complaining party, or attorney, prepares a complaint and files it with the proper court.

The defendant is served a summons which formally notifies defendant of the plaintiff's suit. The defendant or defendant's attorney prepares an answer and files it in the same court.

Pretrial matters may be filed or heard. A settlement may be reached at any time.

The case is heard in court by a judge or by a jury comprised of 6 to 12 jurors.

Either party may wish to appeal the case to the Court of Appeals and perhaps eventually to the Supreme Court.

**FIGURE 2–6** The procedure for a civil trial. *(Adapted from "A Citizen's Guide to Washington Courts," Washington State Office of Administrator for the Courts, 1997.)*

sentence or even the death penalty. If the defendant wins in either a civil or criminal case, the case is over unless an appeal to the verdict is taken. See Figure 2-6 an illustration of a civil trial procedure.

A plaintiff or defendant may appeal the decision to a higher court. Ultimately a case can be appealed to the highest court, either the state supreme court or, in a federal case, the U.S. Supreme Court.

 **MED TIP** A judgment of not guilty, or not liable as in a malpractice case, does not mean that the defendant did not commit the crime or perform the misconduct. It only means that, based on the evidence presented, the plaintiff failed to prove it to a jury.

## Subpoena

**Discovery** is the legal process by which facts are discovered before a trial begins. A court of law may need to subpoena a person or records. A **subpoena** is a court order for a person or documents to appear in court. In some cases, a **deposition** can be taken, meaning that the person's statement is recorded with witnesses present, and the person is then not required to appear in court. The deposition is submitted by an attorney during the court case. A *subpoena duces tecum,* a Latin phrase meaning "under penalty, take with you," is a court order requiring a witness to appear in court and to bring certain records or other material to a trial or deposition. There is a penalty for failure to appear, or present documents, if subpoenaed by the court. A person or document may also be produced in court on a voluntary basis, thus not requiring a subpoena.

A subpoena must be hand-delivered, or served, to the person who is being requested to appear in court, that is, the person who is named on the subpoena. An assistant cannot accept a subpoena on behalf of a physician without his or her knowledge; otherwise the subpoena is considered "not served." The physician may delegate the responsibility to an assistant to accept a subpoena on his or her behalf, but this practice is not encouraged. It is always a good idea to consult with an attorney if you are served a subpoena.

 **MED TIP**   Ordinarily, medical records cannot be sent to anyone without consent in writing from the patient and the physician's approval. One exception to this is when a record is subpoenaed.

When a record such as a medical file or chart is subpoenaed, only the parts of the record requested should be copied and mailed to the requesting attorney. Unless the original document is subpoenaed, a certified photocopy may be sent. If the original record is subpoenaed, then a photocopy is made, and this is returned to the file. A receipt for the subpoenaed record should be placed in the file, and the patient should be notified that the record has been subpoenaed. Any notice relating to subpoenaed records should be sent to the patient by certified mail.

 **MED TIP**   Particular care should be taken when using a fax transmission of a medical record. The sender should be assured by the person receiving the fax that the machine is located in a restricted area. Confidential material should generally not be transmitted by fax, and a fax transmission is usually not acceptable when an original document is requested.

## Expert Witness

An **expert witness** is a person called as a witness in a case where the subject matter is beyond the general knowledge of most people in the court or on the jury. This person, usually a medical professional, has special knowledge or experience not only about the facts of a case but also about the professional conclusions that are drawn from the facts. The testimony of the expert witness should assist the jury or judge in determining the accuracy of the facts in a particular case. In a medical malpractice suit, an expert witness often is called to testify as to what the standard of care for a patient is in a similar circumstance and locality. An expert witness in a medical malpractice suit is generally a physician.

Expert witnesses, who are generally paid a fee, may use visual aids such as charts, photos, x-rays, models, and diagrams. They do not testify about the actual facts of the case, but clarify points of knowledge that may not be readily understood by all present. For example, an expert witness on the topic of DNA may be called to testify in a paternity case.

## Testifying in Court

If called to testify in court, remember:

- Always tell the truth.
- Be professional. People are judged by their appearance as well as by their behavior in court. An attorney can offer further advice on this.
- Remain calm, dignified, and serious at all times. The opposing attorney may try to make the witness nervous by asking difficult questions.
- Do not answer a question you do not understand. Simply ask the attorney to repeat the question or state, "I don't understand the question."
- Just present the facts surrounding the case. Do not give any information that is not asked for. Do not insert your opinion. "The patient was shouting" is stating a fact; "He was angry" is your opinion.
- Do not memorize your testimony ahead of time. You will generally be allowed to take some notes with you to refresh your memory concerning such things as dates.

### POINTS TO PONDER

1. Why do I have to know how a bill becomes a law?
2. Why is common law important?
3. How can I avoid a lawsuit?
4. Can I restrain a person against his or her will if I know it is for his or her own good?
5. Can I be sued if I make a statement to a patient about a mistake a physician has made?
6. What should I do if I see a physician or another health care employee make an error?
7. Can I be sued if I unintentionally leave a patient record with a diagnosis of AIDS within sight of another patient?
8. What do I do if I am subpoenaed?

### DISCUSSION QUESTIONS

1. Discuss the significance of common laws for the health care professional.
2. Explain what is meant by the statement, "It is easier to prevent negligence than it is to defend it."
3. Differentiate between common law and statutory law.
4. Explain what the numbering system in public law means.

5. Discuss what is meant by the term *abandonment* and describe ways that this claim can be avoided.
6. What is meant by *burden of proof*?

## PRACTICE EXERCISES

### Matching

Match the responses in column B with the correct term in column A.

**Column A**

_____ 1. breach
_____ 2. deposition
_____ 3. plaintiff
_____ 4. defendant
_____ 5. felony
_____ 6. misdemeanor
_____ 7. waive
_____ 8. tort
_____ 9. subpoena
_____ 10. precedent

**Column B**

a. order for a person or documents to appear in court
b. person who is being sued
c. give up the right to something
d. law that covers harm to another person
e. earlier ruling applied to present case
f. failure
g. person who sues another party
h. less serious crime such as a traffic violation
i. oral testimony to be used in court
j. serious crime such as practicing medicine without a license

## MULTIPLE CHOICE

Select the one best answer to the following statements.

1. Sources of law include all of the following except
   a. regulatory law
   b. executive law
   c. statutory law
   d. common law
   e. constitutional law

2. *Subpoena duces tecum* means
   a. "let the master answer"
   b. "under penalty, take with you"
   c. "let the decision stand"
   d. "the thing speaks for itself"
   e. "the thing has been decided"

3. *Stare decisis* means
   a. "let the master answer"
   b. "under penalty, take with you"

   c. statutory law has been invoked

   d. constitutional law has been invoked

   e. "let the decision stand"

4. Administrative law covers all of the following except
   a. health department regulations
   b. licensing of prescription drugs
   c. Internal Revenue Service regulations
   d. fraud
   e. all of the above are correct

5. The person who brings the action into litigation is called a(n)
   a. attorney
   b. plaintiff
   c. defendant
   d. judge
   e. jury

6. A court order that requires a witness to appear in court with certain records is called a
   a. deposition
   b. discovery
   c. *subpoena duces tecum*
   d. *res judicata*
   e. waiver

7. The common law of the past that is based on a decision made by judges is called
   a. civil law
   b. constitutional law
   c. case law
   d. criminal law
   e. statutory law

8. The threat of doing bodily harm to another person—stating, for example, "If you won't allow us to continue this procedure, we will have to tie your hands"—is
   a. assault
   b. battery
   c. fraud
   d. invasion of privacy
   e. all of the above

9. Standard of care refers to that care which
   a. a reasonable person would use
   b. is ordinary care
   c. a prudent person would use
   d. health care professionals in all specialties must practice
   e. all of the above

10. Removing one's clothing in order to allow the physician to perform a physical examination is a(n)
    a. invasion of privacy
    b. defamation of character
    c. implied contract
    d. abandonment
    e. none of the above is correct

## PUT IT INTO PRACTICE

Give an example of a violation of each of the six torts mentioned in this chapter (assault, battery, false imprisonment, defamation of character, fraud, and invasion of privacy) as it might affect your particular area of medical specialization.

## WEB HUNT

Search the Web site of the National Institutes of Health (*www.nih.gov*). What types of information and services does this site offer?

Search the Web site *www.findlaw.com* and click on "Medical Malpractice." Read the article "Lessons Learned the Hard Way: Medical Malpractice." Summarize the six examples of successful medical malpractice claims discussed in that article.

## REFERENCES

Black, H. 2004. *Black's law dictionary*. 8th ed. St. Paul, Minn.: West Publishing.

Hall, M., and M. Bobinski. 2003. *Health care law and ethics in a nutshell*. St. Paul, Minn.: West Publishing.

Havinghurst, C. 1998. *Health care law and policy: Readings, notes and questions*. Westbury, N.Y.: Foundation Press.

Miller, R. 1990. *Problems in hospital law*. Rockville, Md.: Aspen.

Oran, D. 1985. *Law dictionary for nonlawyers*. New York: West Publishing.

Sanbar, S., A. Gibofsky, M. Firestone, and T. LeBlang. 1998. *Legal medicine*. Chicago: Mosby.

Wade, J., V. Schwartz, K. Kelly, and D. Partlett. 1994. *Prosser, Wade, and Schwartz's cases and material on TORTS*. Westbury, N.Y.: Foundation Press.

## CASE STUDY

Adam Green is an orderly in the Midwest Nursing Home. His supervisor, Nora Malone, has asked him to supervise the dining room while 20 residents eat their evening meal. Bill Heckler is an 80-year-old resident who is very alert and ambulatory. He tells Adam that he doesn't like the meal that's being served, and he wants to leave the dining room and go back to his own room. Adam is quite busy, since he has to watch the behavior of several patients who are confused. He's concerned that patients might choke on their food or otherwise harm themselves. Adam becomes impatient with Bill and tells him that he cannot leave the room until everyone is finished eating. Adam then locks the dining room door. Bill complains to the nursing home administrator that he was unlawfully detained. He then hires an attorney, who brings forth a charge of false imprisonment.

1. Was Adam's action justified?

_____

_____

2. In your opinion, was this a case of false imprisonment?

_____

_____

3. What could Adam have done to defuse the situation?

_____

_____

4. Do the nursing home administrator and Nora Malone have any legal responsibility for Adam's action?

_____

_____

5. What would a "reasonable and prudent" person do in the same circumstances?

_____

_____

CHAPTER **3**

# Importance of the Legal System for the Physician

## LEARNING OBJECTIVES

1. Define all glossary terms.
2. List the four basic characteristics of state medical practice acts.
3. Describe the three methods by which a state grants a license to practice medicine.
4. Discuss conduct that may result in a physician's loss of license to practice medicine.
5. Identify the difference between licensure and certification.
6. Discuss what the term *standard of care* means for the physician and what it means for someone in your profession.
7. Describe the importance of the discovery rule as it relates to the statute of limitations.
8. Discuss the importance of the phrase *respondeat superior* as it relates to the physician.

## KEY TERMS

| | | |
|---|---|---|
| Discovery rule | Medical practice acts | Revoke |
| Endorsement | Prudent person rule | Risk management |
| Good Samaritan laws | Reciprocity | Standard of care |
| *Guardian ad litem* | *Respondeat superior* | Statute of limitations |

## INTRODUCTION

Even though only a small portion of malpractice suits actually end up in court, it is still important that all health care professionals realize how the law impacts the physician's practice. The physician has a responsibility to respect the conditions of licensure. Health care employees must understand their obligations to their physician/employer and to the patients they serve.

## MEDICAL PRACTICE ACTS

Each state has statutes that govern the practice of medicine in that state. These are called **medical practice acts** and are meant to protect the health and safety of the general public. The acts were originally established in a limited number of states to protect the general public from quackery, or persons practicing medicine without a legitimate education and training. Each state legislature establishes a state medical board that has the authority to control the licensing of physicians. While some slight differences exist from state to state, in general these practice acts define who must be licensed to perform certain procedures. These acts also specify the requirements for licensure; the duties of the licensed physician; grounds on which the license may be revoked, or taken away; and reports that must be made to the government or other appropriate agencies. Medical practice acts also define the penalties for practicing without a license. These state acts seek to protect patients from harm caused by persons who are not qualified to practice medicine. Therefore, each state licensing board has the authority to grant a medical license to qualified individuals as well as to revoke or take away that license for cause, and to fine, reprimand, and censure the physician.

 **MED TIP**   Every state has a state board set up to handle issues relating to physician registration. The title for these boards varies from state to state (for example, State Board of Registration or State Board of Medical Examiners). However, the functions are similar for all state boards.

State licensing boards receive complaints about physicians from a variety of sources: patients, other physicians, employees including hospital employees, the media, and insurance companies. The board has the authority to investigate each complaint, but cannot prosecute the physician. However, the board may access records that relate to each incident, including patient hospital records, individual physician medical records, and insurance reimbursement records. The board may declare the name of the physician but is obligated to keep a patient's name confidential.

A physician who moves to another state must obtain a license to practice in that state also. The physician may be required to pass another state's medical examination, or the physician may receive reciprocity or endorsement from the state.

Generally, physicians in different states may consult with each other without being licensed in each other's state. Additionally, physicians who practice only in governmental institutions such as Veterans Administration hospitals, for the Public Health Service, or on military bases may practice without the local licensure from the state in which they are practicing.

Thus, while medical practice acts vary from state to state, they generally

- provide for the establishment of a medical examining board, also called a State Board of Registration or State Board of Examiners, that has authority to license physicians.
- establish the baseline for the practice of medicine in that state.
- determine the prerequisites for licensure.
- forbid the practice of medicine without a license.
- specify the conditions for license renewal, suspension, and revocation.

## LICENSURE OF THE PHYSICIAN

The board of examiners in each state may grant licensure through examination, endorsement, or reciprocity.

### Examination

Each state offers its own examination for licensure. Some states also accept or endorse the National Board of Medical Examiners (NBME) licensing examination, usually taken before the end of medical school, for licensure. Within the United States, the official medical licensing exam is the Federal Licensing Examination (FLEX). The license is issued to those who pass the examination, graduate from an accredited school, and complete an internship. Successful completion of these criteria entitles one to set up private practice as a general practitioner.

In addition, the U.S. Medical Licensing Examination (USMLE), which was introduced in 1992, is a single licensing examination for graduates from accredited medical schools that allow them to practice medicine. In addition to successfully passing the examination (written and oral), applicants are required by most states to

- provide proof that he or she has completed the professional education as required by his or her state.
- provide proof of the successful completion of an approved internship/residency program.
- provide information about any past convictions, history of drug or alcohol abuse.
- have obtained an age of majority, generally 21 years old.
- be of good moral character.
- be a resident of that state.

### Endorsement

**Endorsement** means an approval or sanction. A state will grant a license by endorsement to applicants who have successfully passed the NBME exam. In fact, most physicians in the United States are licensed by endorsement. Any medical school graduate who is not licensed by endorsement is required to pass the state board examination. Graduates of foreign medical schools must fulfill the same requirements as American graduates. Licensure by endorsement is considered for acceptance or denial on a case-by-case basis. In some cases, a physician trained in a particular country or foreign school may not be able to obtain a license to practice in the United States without attending a U.S. medical school.

## Reciprocity

Physicians must satisfy the licensure requirements of any and all states in which they practice. In some cases, the state to which the physician applies for a license will accept the state licensing requirements of the state from which the physician already holds a license. In that case, the physician will not have to take another examination. This practice of cooperation by which a state grants a license to practice medicine to a physician already licensed in another state is known as **reciprocity.** Reciprocity is automatic if a reciprocity agreement exists between the two states where licensure is being sought and if the requirements of the agreement are satisfied. For instance, some states require a physician to be licensed for a certain number of years before qualifying for reciprocity.

## Registration

It is necessary for physicians to maintain their license by periodic re-registration or renewal either annually or biannually. In addition to paying a fee to renew their license, physicians are required to complete 75 hours of continuing medical education (CME) units in a three-year period to assure that they remain current in their field of practice. While state requirements differ for renewal of a medical license, they generally include (1) attending approved workshops, courses, and seminars; (2) completing self-instruction modules; (3) teaching other health professionals; and (4) reading a variety of approved medical literature.

There are a few exceptions to the requirement of having a valid state license to practice medicine within that state: These include

- a physician employed by a federal medical facility, such as a Public Health Service wellness center or a VA hospital.
- an out-of-state physician who is providing emergency medical care.
- a physician who is waiting to become a qualified resident in a state in order to obtain a license.
- a research physician who does not practice patient-based medicine.

## Revocation and Suspension of Licensure

A state may **revoke** a physician's license for cases of severe misconduct, including unprofessional conduct, commission of a crime, or personal incapacity to perform one's duties. Unprofessional conduct involves behavior that fails to meet the ethical standards of the profession, such as inappropriate use of drugs or alcohol, gross immorality, or falsifying records. Crimes may include Medicare/Medicaid fraud, rape, murder, larceny, and narcotics convictions. Personal incapacity often relates to a physical or mental incapacity that prevents the physician from performing professional duties. Professional incompetence, such as malpractice or negligence, can also result in revocation of a medical license.

The physician's state licensing board generally oversees the suspension or revocation of a license. The board will provide the physician with sufficient notice of any charges and then perform a thorough investigation of the charges. In some states, the licensing board can temporarily suspend a physician's license to practice if a potentially dangerous situation exists, such as drug impairment or criminal charges. The physician is always accorded due process of the law, which includes a written description of the claim and a hearing before the state medical examiners. The physician can then appeal the board's decision.

**MED TIP**   An allied health care professional must use caution when submitting patient claims for medical reimbursement. Filing a false claim for programs such as Medicare or Medicaid is a federal crime. The employee's physician/employer could be severely fined and even lose his or her license for this type of fraudulent act.

## LICENSURE AND CERTIFICATION OF ALLIED HEALTH PROFESSIONALS

In addition to being licensed to practice medicine, physicians may be certified in a particular specialty area, such as orthopedics, on a voluntary basis. They earn the title "board certified" by completing the requirements of the national board in that specialty area. Physicians who are both licensed and board certified have thus fulfilled the licensing requirements in their state and also achieved a special competence, or certification, in a medical specialty.

Other health professionals may also be licensed and/or have certification depending on the particular professional specialty. Nurses and pharmacists are licensed by the state in which they practice. They must graduate from an accredited educational program and pass a national examination that shows competency in their chosen medical field. Certification indicates that the allied health professional has met the standards set by an accreditation body but is not licensed. For example, a certified medical assistant has met the standards of the American Association of Medical Assistants (AAMA). A registered medical assistant (RMT) has met the standards set by the American Medical Technologists (AMT) Association. The national professional associations maintain a registry of the licensed and certified individuals within their profession.

Licensed medical professionals, other than physicians, can place their license in jeopardy or even lose their license to practice their profession if they abuse drugs or alcohol, steal from their employer or patients, lie about their education and training, or commit a criminal action.

**MED TIP**   Physicians, and their staff who assist with hiring personnel, have a responsibility to check the licensure and certification of all the employees. For example, patients expect that when they see the initials R.N. after an employee's name, that person will be able to function as a registered nurse.

## Practicing Medicine Without a License

No physician wishes to have a license expire for failure to renew or be revoked for inappropriate behavior. A physician cannot practice medicine without this license.

 **MED TIP** Remember that if a physician continues to practice medicine without renewal of his or her license, it is considered practicing medicine without a license, under the law.

Non-physician health professionals also cannot practice medicine outside of their own licensure and expertise. If one acts outside the area of his or her competency and the patient is injured as a result, that health care practitioner is liable for malpractice or, in other terms, medical negligence. In this situation, the health care practitioner could be fined and/or lose his or her license. For example, it is against the law for a nurse or medical assistant to prescribe medications; this function lies only within the domain of the physician. A phlebotomist is not licensed to discuss the results of a patient's laboratory tests with the patient; only the physician is licensed to interpret and discuss this information with the patient.

## Accreditation

Accreditation is a voluntary process in which an agency is requested to officially review and authorize health care institutions such as hospitals, nursing homes, and educational programs. This is accomplished by sending in an objective third party, such as the Joint Commission on Accreditation of Healthcare Organizations (JCAHO), to examine the policies and procedures of the organization being accredited. The accreditation process can be rigorous and generally requires an onsite examination of the program under review. The institution or program must demonstrate that it maintains high standards of care for patients or education of its participants.

The JCAHO accredits such organizations as all types of hospitals, including psychiatric, long-term care facilities, managed care organizations such as HMOs, and clinical laboratories. A JCAHO survey team visits the organization for an onsite inspection every three years. Upon successful completion of the accreditation process, an institution may display signage that it is accredited by the JCAHO.

Another organization that provides accreditation for the health care profession is the Commission on Accreditation of Allied Health Education Programs (CAAHEP). CAAHEP provides accreditation for programs such as medical assisting, emergency medical technicians (EMTs), physician's assistants, and respiratory therapists.

## STANDARD OF CARE

**Standard of care** refers to the ordinary skill and care that medical practitioners such as physicians, nurses, physician's assistants, medical assistants, and phlebotomists must use. This level of expertise is that which is commonly used by other medical practitioners in the same locality and medical specialty when caring for patients.

The standard of care for particular professions has changed somewhat over the years. For instance, in a Louisiana case, the court concluded that because doctors and nurses are both members of the medical profession, they should be held to the same high standard of professional competence. (*Norton v. Argonaut Ins. Co.,* 144 So.2d 249, La.App.1962.) However, in a later case, the court recognized that "situations could arise in which a doctor would be considered negligent in his performance of some task where he failed to act to the best of his ability as a physician, while a nurse, performing the same task in the same manner, could be acting to the best of her ability as a nurse." (*Thompson v. Brent,* 245 So.2d 751, La.App.1971.)

While physicians are not obligated to treat everyone (except in the case of an emergency), once a physician accepts a patient for treatment, he or she has entered into the physician–patient relationship (contract) and must provide a certain standard of care. This means that the physician must provide the same knowledge, care, and skill that a similarly trained physician would provide under the same circumstances in the same locality. The law does not require the physician to use extraordinary skill. The law requires only reasonable, ordinary care and skill. The physician is expected to perform the same acts that a "reasonable and prudent" physician would perform. This standard also requires that a physician not perform any acts that a "reasonable and prudent" physician would not.

Physicians are expected to exhaust all the resources available to them when treating patients and not expose patients to undue risk. If they violate this standard of care, they are liable for negligence.

## The Prudent Person Rule

The **prudent person rule,** also called the reasonable person standard, means that a health care professional, usually a physician, must provide information to a patient that a reasonable, prudent person would want before he or she makes a decision about treatment or refusal of treatment. In general, a reasonable, prudent person would want to know the following:

- the diagnosis
- the risks and potential consequences of the treatment, excluding any remote or improbable outcomes; this information should include the success and failure rates of the physician and/or institution
- the expected benefits of the treatment or procedure
- potential alternative treatments
- the prognosis if no treatment is received
- the costs, including the amount of expected pain

In general, the physician discusses these issues with the patient; however, ancillary health care professionals may be present during these conversations. The patient should always be considered in terms of a "reasonable, prudent person." Unfortunately, not all patients are provided the same courtesy.

# CONFIDENTIALITY

Confidentiality refers to keeping private all information about a person (patient) and not disclosing it to a third party without the patient's written consent. The duty of medical confidentiality is an ancient one. The Hippocratic Oath states, "What I may see or hear in or outside the course of the treatment . . . which on no account may be spread abroad, I will keep to myself, holding such things shameful to speak about." This duty seeks to respect the patient's privacy, and it also recognizes that if the physician does not keep information confidential, patients may be discouraged from revealing useful diagnostic information to their physician.

According to the Medical Patients Rights Act, a law passed by Congress, all patients have the right to have their personal privacy respected and their medical records handled with confidentiality. Information such as test results, patient histories, and even the fact that the person is a patient, cannot be told to another person. No information can be given over the telephone without the patient's permission. No patient records can be given to another person or physician without the patient's written permission or unless the court has subpoenaed it.

In short, any information that is given to a physician by a patient is considered confidential, and it may not be given to an unauthorized person. Information should be communicated only on a need-to-know basis. (See Chapter 10 for a more detailed discussion of confidentiality and the Health Insurance Portability and Accounting Act of 1996, or HIPAA.)

**MED TIP**   Be especially careful about discussing anything relating to a patient within earshot of others. A comment such as, "Did Ms. Jones come in for her pregnancy test?" can result in a breach-of-confidentiality lawsuit against the physician. Remember: "Walls have ears."

## STATUTE OF LIMITATIONS

The **statute of limitations** refers to the period of time that a patient has to file a lawsuit. The court will not hear a case that is filed after the time limit has run out. This time limit varies from state to state, but typically is one to three years. The only exception is that there is no statute of limitations for murder. One of the purposes of the statutes is to prevent potential plaintiffs from "sitting on their rights" while the memories surrounding the controversy grow dim or witnesses die or move away. In addition, the statutes allow potential defendants to go on with their lives without worry about a lawsuit that could be filed relating to some long-ago occurrence.

The statute of limitations, or the time period, however, does not always start "running" at the time of treatment. It begins when the problem is discovered or should have been discovered, which may be some time after the actual treatment. This is known as the **discovery rule.** In *Teeters v. Currey,* the plaintiff sued her doctor, alleging that as a result of Dr. Currey's negligence in performing surgery to sterilize Teeters, she gave birth to a premature child with severe complications several years later. Teeters brought an action for malpractice, and Currey pleaded the statute of limitations. The court found in favor of the defendant, Currey; however, Teeters appealed and won the case. The court adopted the "discovery doctrine" under which the statute does not begin to run until the injury is, or should have been, discovered.  (*Teeters v. Currey,* 518 S.W.2d 512, Tenn. 1974.)

In some cases, the statute of limitations is *tolled,* or stops running. For instance, most states say that the statute of limitations does not begin to run until the injured person reaches age 18. So, when a minor is injured, the minor may sue years after learning of the injury. While generally the court will appoint a ***guardian ad litem,*** an adult to act in the court on behalf of a child in litigation, the child does not have to sue through the *guardian ad litem* but may wait until he or she reaches adulthood. An example of this would be suing an obstetrician and his or her health care assistants 18 years (plus the statute of limitations period, which varies slightly in each state) after a birth injury has occurred.

 **MED TIP**   The statute of limitations is a state law that varies by state.

## GOOD SAMARITAN LAWS

**Good Samaritan laws** are state laws that help to protect from liability health care professionals who provide emergency care to an accident victim. These laws exist in most states to encourage such aid. Those professionals who do offer aid outside their work environment in good faith, without gross negligence, are protected by this law.

No one is required to provide aid in the event of an emergency, except in the state of Vermont. Someone responding in an emergency situation is only required to act within the limits of acquired skill and training. For example, a nursing assistant would not be expected, or advised, to perform advanced emergency treatment that is considered within the scope and practice of a physician or nurse.

Even though trained health professionals are not under a legal obligation to offer aid to an emergency victim, they do have an ethical obligation. Their personal ethics set the guidelines for care provided in emergency situations. (See Figure 3-1.)

**FIGURE 3–1**   A hospital employee providing emergency aid.

**MED TIP** The Good Samaritan laws do not protect physicians or their employees from liability while practicing their profession in their work environment. The laws are meant to encourage medical professionals to assist with emergencies outside of the work setting.

## RESPONDEAT SUPERIOR

***Respondeat superior*** is a Latin phrase meaning, "Let the master answer." Under the principle of *respondeat superior,* an employer is liable for acts of the employee within the scope of employment. What this means for physicians is that they are liable for negligent actions of the employees working for them. (See Figure 3-2.)

**MED TIP** Even though the doctrine of *respondeat superior* mainly refers to the employer, in all states both the physician and the employee may be liable.

In effect, when a physician delegates certain duties to staff employees—nurses, physician's assistants, and medical assistants—the ultimate liability for the correct performance of those duties rests with the physician. For example, in the case of *Thompson v. Brent,* a medical assistant removed a cast from Thompson's arm with an electrically powered saw, known as a Stryker saw. While sawing through the cast, the medical assistant cut the plaintiff's arm, causing a scar almost the length of the cast

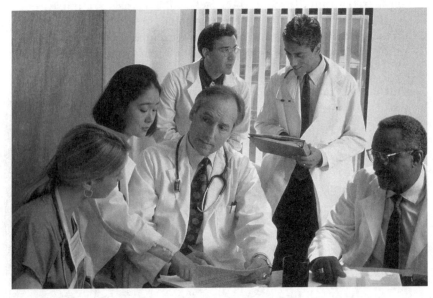

**FIGURE 3-2** Physician working with the rest of the health care team.

and the width of the saw blade. The court held that even though the medical assistant was negligent in the use of the saw, the physician was liable for the assistant's actions under the doctrine of *respondeat superior.* (*Thompson v. Brent,* 245 So.2d 751, La. Ct. App. 1971.)

In similar cases, the courts have consistently found both the employer *and* the health care employee negligent. In the case of *Goff v. Doctors General Hospital,* the court held that the nurses who attended a mother, and who knew that she was bleeding excessively, were negligent in failing to report the circumstances so that prompt measures could be taken to safeguard her life. (*Goff v. Doctors General Hospital,* 333 P.2d 29, Cal. Ct. App. 1958.)

The most well-known case in which a nurse failed to bring the condition of the patient to the doctor's attention was *Darling v. Charleston Community Memorial Hospital.* This case involved a minor patient who sued a hospital and a physician for allegedly negligent medical and hospital treatment, which resulted in the amputation of the patient's right leg below his knee. On November 5, 1960, the 18-year-old plaintiff broke his leg while playing football. At the hospital emergency room, his leg was set and placed in a cast, and he was hospitalized. He complained of great pain in his toes, which became swollen, dark, and eventually cold and insensitive. Over the next few days, the physician relieved the pressure in the cast by "notching" the cast and cutting it three inches above the foot. On November 8, the physician split both sides of the cast, cutting the patient's leg as the cast was removed. Blood and seepage were observed coming from the leg as the cast was removed. The plaintiff was eventually transferred to another hospital on November 19 under the care of a specialist. After several attempts to save the plaintiff's leg, it was finally amputated eight inches below the knee. The plaintiff's attorney argued that it was the duty of the nurses to check the circulation of the leg frequently and the duty of the hospital to have, at the bedside, a staff of trained nurses who could recognize gangrene of the leg and bring it to the attention of the medical staff. If the physician failed to act, it was the duty of the nurse to then advise hospital authorities so that medical action could be taken. In this famous case, the court found liability existed on the part of all three: the physician, the hospital, and the nurse. (*Darling v. Charleston Community Mem. Hosp.,* 211 N.E. 2d 253, 1965.)

## Employee's Duty to Carry Out Orders

Health care employees have a duty to interpret and carry out the orders of their employer/physician. They are expected to know basic information concerning procedures and drugs that may be used. The nurse or other health care professional has a duty to clarify the physician's orders when they are ambiguous or erroneous. If the procedure or drug appears to be dangerous for the patient, the health care professional has a duty to decline to carry out the orders and should immediately notify the physician. In the case of *Cline v. Lund,* a hospital was held liable for the death of a patient because a nurse failed to check the patient's vital signs every 30 minutes as ordered by the physician. The nurse also failed to notify the physician when the patient's condition became life threatening. (*Cline v. Lund,* 31 Cal.App.3d 755, 1973.)

**MED TIP**   Health care workers have a duty to be assertive and question those orders that they believe are erroneous or appear to be harmful to the patient.

## Scope of Practice

Every employee in a medical setting must clearly understand and work within the scope of practice for his or her discipline. This means that a nurse can legally, through licensure, provide care and treatment to patients that a medical assistant is not licensed or certified to perform. For example, a nurse can renew medical prescriptions, with the physician's knowledge and authority, to a pharmacy over the telephone. A medical assistant is not licensed to do this. However, some states allow this function to be delegated to a certified medical assistant by a physician. A trained and certified medical assistant can draw a sample of blood from a patient and perform certain tests on the sample, such as a blood count. However, a nurse's aid is not qualified or certified to perform these procedures.

It is imperative that employees understand and practice within the guidelines of their profession. However, the physician/employer also has a responsibility. The physician must not require members of the health care team to perform activities that are outside their scope of practice.

In addition, a physician/employer must clearly designate a chain of command for the health care team, assigning a person to oversee the functions of the health care team. In some cases, the physician assumes this duty. However, a nurse manager may also be designated for this role. In some medical offices, medical assistants can assume this function due to the intensive administrative portion of their training. Each employee must understand the chain of command so that when a question occurs regarding patient treatment or procedure, there is a clear route for obtaining the correct answer. A clear chain of command provides a "failsafe" mechanism so that no employees are left to make decisions that they are unqualified to make.

 **MED TIP**   All employees must understand that there are limits to their authority when it comes to health care decisions. The ultimate decision always rests with the physician.

## Employer's Duty to Employees

Physicians/employers have a responsibility to provide a safe environment for their employees and staff. However, accidents and unforeseen incidents do happen, such as theft, fires, auto accidents while performing work-related tasks, and injuries from falls. Most physicians have liability insurance to cover any injuries or thefts occurring on the owner's grounds and within the buildings. They may also bond employees who handle money. Bonding is a special type of insurance made with a bonding company that covers employees who handle financial statements, records, and cash. If the employee embezzles (steals) money from the physician/employer, the physician can then recover the loss up to the amount of the bond.

Some physicians also carry liability insurance to cover the employee who has an automobile accident while conducting work-related business, such as making a bank deposit, for the employer.

## RISK MANAGEMENT

**Risk management** is a practice used to control or minimize the incidence of problem behavior that might result in injury to patients and employees, and ultimately to liability for the physician/employer. A key factor in risk management is to identify problem behaviors and practices in an organization such as a hospital or medical office. A plan of action is then put into practice to eliminate these problem behaviors. Risk management factors include environmental issues such as wet floors, improper grounding of electrical equipment, and poor security. Risk factors that affect employees include poor record keeping, improper storage of drugs and needles, improper follow-up for patient care, and abandonment of patients. Corrective actions for these factors are often addressed in updated policies and procedures books and employee handbooks. Many offices and hospitals employ risk managers whose sole job is to oversee the practices and behaviors that might harm patients and even result in malpractice suits.

 **MED TIP**　Everyone in a health care institution—not just the risk manager—is responsible for risk management.

### POINTS TO PONDER

1. If a patient who suffers from cirrhosis tells me in confidence that she has started drinking again, what should I do?
2. Does *respondeat superior* mean that I am fully protected from a lawsuit? Why or why not?
3. Does the Medical Practice Act in my state allow a registered nurse to prescribe birth control pills for patients? Why or why not?
4. Is it really beneficial for me to become a licensed or certified member of my profession? Why or why not?
5. Am I expected to maintain the same standard of care for patients that my physician/employer is held to?
6. Am I protected by Good Samaritan laws if I perform CPR on a patient in a hospital emergency room waiting area and the patient dies?
7. Am I protected from a lawsuit if I have reported a medical emergency to my supervisor that I did not believe I was capable of handling?
8. If an injury occurred four years ago, am I protected from a lawsuit if the statute of limitations is two years in my state?

## DISCUSSION QUESTIONS

1. You have been asked to discuss the importance of the legal system for the physician at your next staff meeting. Draft an outline of what your talk would include.
2. You have a patient collapse on the floor in your department (office) and you must administer CPR. If the patient is injured when you administer CPR, are you protected from a malpractice suit under the Good Samaritan laws?
3. Describe the process Dr. Williams might use to become licensed to practice medicine when she moves from Chicago to New York.
4. Describe what *reasonable and prudent* means as it relates to standard of care.

## PRACTICE EXERCISES

### Matching

Match the responses in column B with the correct term in column A.

**Column A**

_____ 1. endorsement
_____ 2. *guardian ad litem*
_____ 3. revoked
_____ 4. *respondeat superior*
_____ 5. statute of limitations
_____ 6. discovery rule
_____ 7. reciprocity
_____ 8. standard of care
_____ 9. Good Samaritan law
_____ 10. nonrenewal of license

**Column B**

a. begins at the time the injury is noticed or should have been noticed
b. ordinary skill that medical practitioners use
c. "let the master answer"
d. court-appointed representative
e. law to protect the health care professional
f. period of time that a patient has to file a lawsuit
g. sanction
h. medical license taken away
i. practicing medicine without a license
j. one state granting a license to a physician in another state

## MULTIPLE CHOICE

Select the one best answer to the following statements.

1. According to the Medical Patients Rights Act, patient information
   a. may be given over the telephone without the patient's consent
   b. must be communicated on a need-to-know basis
   c. can always be given out to another physician
   d. other than test results, cannot be given out to a relative
   e. can never be given out to a third party

2. The term for a court-appointed person to represent a minor or unborn child in litigation is
   a. *respondeat superior*
   b. advanced directive
   c. *guardian ad litem*
   d. durable power of attorney
   e. living will

3. Standard of care refers to
   a. ordinary skill
   b. type of care given to patients by other practitioners in the same locality
   c. only the care given by the physician
   d. a, b, and c
   e. a and b only

4. The statute of limitations varies somewhat from state to state but is typically
   a. ten years
   b. five years
   c. one to three years
   d. there is no limitation
   e. none of the above

5. *Respondeat superior* means that
   a. a health care employee can act independently of the employer
   b. the health care employee is never found negligent by the courts
   c. the employer is liable for the actions of the employee
   d. health care employees have a duty to carry out the orders of their employers without question
   e. all of the above

6. A process by which a physician in one state is granted a license to practice medicine in another state is
   a. endorsement
   b. reciprocity
   c. statute of limitations
   d. revocation
   e. suspension

7. Patients' rights to have their personal privacy respected and their medical records handled with confidentiality is covered in the
   a. statute of limitations
   b. rule of discovery
   c. FLEX act
   d. Medical Patients Rights Act
   e. Good Samaritan laws

8. A well-known malpractice case in which a nurse failed to bring the patient's condition to the doctor's attention is
   a. *Teeters v. Currey*
   b. *Darling v. Charleston Memorial Hospital*

    c. *Thompson v. Brent*

    d. *Norton v. Argonaut Insurance Company*

    e. none of the above

9. When a physician places an ambiguous order, the health care professional
   a. has a duty to carry out the order
   b. can decline to carry out the order
   c. should immediately notify the physician
   d. b and c only
   e. none of the above is correct

10. Both physicians and employees are
    a. liable in a lawsuit
    b. have the same responsibility to protect patient's confidentiality
    c. operate under a standard of care
    d. must be trained to perform a procedure before attempting it
    e. all of the above

## PUT IT INTO PRACTICE

Ask a physician who practices in a medical specialty area what is considered to be the standard of care in that field. Does this coincide with what you thought would be that physician's standard of care?

## WEB HUNT

Search the Web site of the American Health Lawyers Association (*www.health lawyers.org*). Discuss what type of information this site offers to physicians.

Using a search engine, search the law relating to Good Samaritan laws in your state.

## REFERENCES

American Medical Association. 1998. *Current opinions of the judicial council of the American Medical Association.* Chicago: American Medical Association.

Badasch, S., and D. Chesebro. 2004. *Introduction to health occupations.* Upper Saddle River, N.J.: Prentice Hall.

Black, H. 2004. *Black's law dictionary.* 8th ed. St. Paul, Minn.: West Publishing.

Fremgen, B. 1998. *Essentials of medical assisting: Administrative and clinical competencies.* Upper Saddle River, N.J.: Prentice Hall.

Garrett, T., H. Baillie, and R. Garrett. 1993. *Health care ethics: Principles and problems.* Englewood Cliffs, N.J.: Prentice Hall.

Jensen, A., M. Siegler, and W. Winsdale. 1992. *Clinical ethics: A practical approach to ethical decisions in clinical medicine.* New York: McGraw-Hill.

Lipman, M. 1994. *Medical law & ethics.* Upper Saddle River, N.J.: Prentice Hall.

Miller, R. 1990. *Problems in hospital law.* Rockville, Md.: Aspen.

Sanbar, S., A. Gibofsky, M. Firestone, and T. LeBlang. 1998. *Legal medicine.* Chicago: Mosby.

Stanfield, P. 2002. *Introduction to the health professions.* Boston: Jones & Bartlett.

*Taber's cyclopedic medical dictionary.* 2001. 19th ed. Philadelphia: F. A. Davis.

## CASE STUDY

You are drawing a specimen of blood on Emma Helm, who says she doesn't like having blood drawn. In fact, she tells you that the sight of blood makes her "queasy." You attempt to make her feel relaxed by quietly talking to her as you help her onto a chair. While you are taking her blood specimen, she faints and hits her head against the side of a cabinet.

1. Are you liable for Emma's injury? Why or why not?

_____

_____

_____

_____

2. If you are not liable, do you know who is?

_____

_____

_____

_____

3. Is Emma Helm at fault for her accident? Why or why not?

_____

_____

_____

_____

4. What might you do to prevent this type of injury from happening?

_____

_____

_____

_____

CHAPTER **4**

# Medical Practice and Allied Health Professionals

## LEARNING OBJECTIVES

1. Define all glossary terms.
2. Describe today's health care environment.
3. Discuss the similarities and differences among HMOs, PPOs, and EPOs.
4. Describe five types of medical practice.
5. Discuss the term *diplomat* as it relates to medical specialty boards.
6. Identify three categories of licensed nurses and describe their educational requirements.
7. Describe five categories of certified health care professionals.
8. Describe the diagnostic related group (DRG) system of classification.
9. State the differences between Medicare and Medicaid.

## KEY TERMS

Associate practice
Capitation rate
Copayment
Corporation
Diagnostic Related
   Groups (DRGs)
Exclusive Provider
   Organization (EPO)
Fee splitting
Fixed-payment plan

Franchise
Franchisees
Gatekeeper
Group practice
Health Maintenance
   Organization (HMO)
Indigent
Managed Care
   Organization (MCO)
Medicaid

Medicare
Partnership
Preferred Provider
   Organization (PPO)
Sole proprietorship
Solo practice
Third-party payers

# INTRODUCTION

Today's health care professionals are immersed in an ever-changing environment. The advent of managed care, a variety of medical practice arrangements, and a multitude of health care specialty areas have resulted in the continual need to understand health care law. Unfortunately, due to the rise of malpractice suits, many physicians are protecting themselves by ordering multiple testing procedures, some of which might not be needed, on patients. In addition, patients no longer want older, more conservative approaches to testing and diagnosis—and these newer tests are more expensive.

# TODAY'S HEALTH CARE ENVIRONMENT

Health care has undergone major changes during the past fifteen years. The growth rate of the older adult population and the remarkable technological discoveries and applications, such as heart and kidney transplants and mobile mammogram units, are just a few of the developments that have caused a rapid expansion of the health care system. In addition, insurance companies, managed care plans—such as health maintenance organizations (HMOs), which stress preventive care and patient education—and government legislation have significantly impacted the way health care is delivered.

Currently, about $3 billion a day is spent on health care in the United States. However, this does not mean that all Americans are receiving good care, or even any care. We, as a nation, are far from the top in life expectancy at birth. Traditionally, the emphasis in health care has been on quality. However, with rising health care costs, many U.S. citizens are concerned about the cost of services and access to medical care. Another critical dilemma is the crisis in health insurance coverage: many Americans do not have adequate medical insurance.

Health insurance includes all forms of insurance against financial loss resulting from illness or injury. Private health insurance is more than a $200 billion business annually. The most common type of health insurance covers hospital care. Relatively new types of insurance are the fixed-payment plans. These are offered by organizations that operate their own health care facilities or that have made arrangements with a hospital or health care provider within a city or region. The **fixed-payment plan** offers subscribers (members) complete medical care in return for a fixed monthly fee. HMOs, for example, base their operations on fixed prepayment plans.

Insurance companies and other **third-party payers,** such as HMOs, recognize that persons who are well covered by medical insurance have no incentive to economize. Insurers, however, want to keep their costs for reimbursement as low as possible. Physicians want to order more tests to avoid malpractice suits. Patients want adequate tests and complete care. Keeping these differing viewpoints in mind, who then decides on the allocation of the health resources?

## Managed Care

Managed care provides a mechanism for a **gatekeeper,** such as the insurance company, to approve all nonemergency services, hospitalizations, or tests before they can be provided. A primary care physician also acts in a gatekeeper capacity, since he or she is responsible for the patient's medical care and any referrals to other physicians or services. Physicians used to receive a fee for each service, procedure, test, or surgery they provided, called the fee-for-service (FFS) method of payment. In addition, patients could select any physician or specialist to treat them.

 **MED TIP**   One of the fundamental principles of managed care is "managed choice." Patients have a choice about their medical care but only within certain parameters that are determined by the managed care organizations (MCOs).

**Managed care organizations (MCOs)** pay for and manage the medical care a patient receives. One of the means an MCO uses to manage costs is to shift some of the financial risks back onto the physician and hospitals—when the costs go up, their income from the MCO goes down. This mechanism poses many ethical dilemmas. MCOs offer a variety of financial incentives including bonuses to physicians for reducing the number of tests, treatments, and referrals to hospitals and specialists. These incentives can create a conflict of interest for physicians. In addition, some MCOs implement gag clauses in contracts with physicians, which prohibit the physician from discussing these financial incentives. The federal government has banned gag clauses from contracts involving Medicare and Medicaid.

The offer of financial inducements to physicians who order fewer tests and hospitalizations for their patients is a widely discussed concern. Many fear that physicians may withhold services from patients in order to increase their own profits. Some of the reasons for these concerns are that MCOs attempt to limit the

- choice of physician
- treatments a physician can order
- number and type of diagnostic tests that can be ordered
- number of days a patient can stay in the hospital for a particular diagnosis
- choice of hospitals
- drugs a physician can prescribe
- referrals to specialists
- choice of specialists
- ordering of a second opinion for diagnosis and treatment

The managed care movement—with the implementation of health maintenance organizations (HMOs), preferred provider organizations (PPOs), and exclusive provider organizations (EPOs)—sought to bring health care costs under control by monitoring health care and hospital usage.

1. **Health Maintenance Organization (HMO)**—a type of managed care plan in which a range of health care services are made available to plan members for a predetermined fee (the **capitation rate**) per member, by a limited group of providers (such as physicians and hospitals).
2. **Preferred Provider Organization (PPO)**—a plan in which the patient uses a medical provider (physician or hospital) who is under contract with the insurer for an agreed fee in order to receive **copayment** (usually $10 to $20) from the insured. PPOs differ

from HMOs in two main areas: (a) a PPO is a fee-for-service (FFS) program not based on a prepayment or a fixed monthly fee paid to the health care provider for providing patient services **(capitation rate)** as with an HMO—physicians and hospitals designated as PPOs are reimbursed for each medical service they provide; and (b) PPO members are not restricted to certain designated physicians or hospitals.

3. **Exclusive Provider Organization (EPO)**—a new managed care concept that is a combination of HMO and PPO concepts. In an EPO, the selection of providers (such as physicians and hospitals) is limited to a defined group, but the providers are paid on a modified fee-for-service (FFS) basis. Unlike a PPO, there is no insurance reimbursement if nonemergency service is provided by a non–EPO provider.

## Federal Assistance Programs

### Medicare

**Medicare** is the federal program that provides health care coverage for the elderly and for disabled persons or those who suffer from kidney disease or other debilitating ailments, regardless of wealth or income. When Medicare was enacted in the 1960s, it was designed as a traditional third-party private insurance that emphasized free choice of health care. The accounting details were handled by private insurance companies, usually Blue Cross and Blue Shield. Medicare expenditures quickly rose beyond the initial projections. In addition, traditional Medicare reimbursement became very complex in both the administration and review process. This led to several problems, including a long delay for physicians and hospitals to receive reimbursement for providing services.

As a result of the rising costs of the Medicare program, a rationing of health care under Medicare has occurred. For example, the first $500 of the hospital care costs may have to be paid by the recipients once during each benefit period as a deductible; there is a cutoff of reimbursement of care beyond sixty days; and long-term care is not fully reimbursed. These cost-saving devices result in a fixed allocation of health care services for many elderly who will not use a hospital or nursing home facility because they cannot afford the deductible payment. In addition, most Medicare recipients who can afford to also pay for supplemental insurance to cover those costs not covered under Medicare.

Medicare patients have a right to care that may be denied under existing Medicare rules and regulations. As a result of a court case, new rules by the Department of Health and Human Services for HMOs went into effect in August 1997. In the case of *Grijalva v. Shalala* (Donna Shalala was secretary of the department when the suit was filed), an Arizona court found that a 71-year-old Medicare patient, whose health care coverage was refused by her HMO, was denied the right to appeal when her request for home health care was refused by her HMO. The judge ruled that the Department of Health and Human Services, which oversees Medicare, was at fault for failing to force HMOs to follow federal law that mandates allowing appeals when there are denials for treatment. Under the current rules, a Medicare patient in an HMO may appeal when there are denials for treatment. (*Grijalva v. Shalala*, 946 F. Supp. 747, Ariz. 1996.)

## Medicaid

**Medicaid** is a federal program implemented by the individual states, with the federal government paying 57.3 percent of Medicaid expenditures. Enacted at the same time as Medicare, it provides financial assistance to states for insuring certain categories of the poor and **indigent** (a person without funds). There is a growing concern that these two programs operate at cross purposes, since they serve some of the same beneficiaries, and that better coordination of the two programs is needed. Cases of abuse and fraud are reported within both programs. For example, there are cases of physicians and others employed in the health care field submitting bills for reimbursement under these two programs for patients they have never treated.

Rationing also takes place in the Medicaid program. For instance, several state Medicaid programs have resisted funding procedures such as liver transplants. The state of Oregon voted to abolish Medicaid funding for liver transplants and instead fund intensive prenatal screening programs. Voters apparently believed that the millions spent to save a few lives with liver transplants is better spent on effective prenatal screening that would help to prevent premature births and thus save more lives.

Individual states enact their own legislation to direct the way funds such as Medicaid are spent. Ethical dilemmas surface as patients on Medicaid find they have little or no access to funds within their own state.

## Diagnostic Related Groups (DRGs)

Another method of rationing health care was implemented in 1983, when Medicare instituted a hospital payment system—**diagnostic related groups (DRGs)**—that classifies each Medicare patient by illness. DRGs are designations used to identify reimbursement per condition of the patient. There are 467 illness categories of medical conditions under the DRG system.

Hospitals receive a preset sum for treatment of an illness category, regardless of the actual number of "bed days" of care used by the patient. This method of payment provides a further incentive to keep costs down. However, it has also discouraged the treatment of severely ill patients due to the high costs associated with their care. In addition, patients are often discharged before they are ready to take care of themselves. This has resulted in hospital readmissions and, in some cases, death from embolisms (blood clots) which could have been prevented if the patient had remained under hospital supervision a few days longer.

## Ethical Considerations of Managed Care

Managed care, including Medicare and Medicaid, has many flaws. Since the basis for a managed care approach is an economic one of cost containment, those who know how to use the system will fare better than the poor and ignorant. The wealthy patient may receive better care than the poor patient. For example, the wealthy Medicare patient may be able to carry a supplemental health insurance policy to cover the items, such as prescription drugs and long-term care, that are not fully covered under Medicare. Other ethical considerations and questions concerning managed care include the following:

■ Many believe it is difficult, if not impossible, to provide a decent minimum standard of care or treatment to everyone under the managed care concept.

- Are all the families and patients who agree to a managed care contract at the closest clinic fully informed of the consequences of trying to obtain health care elsewhere?
- Is a bait-and-switch approach being used by the MCO in which the patient is lured into joining a managed care plan only to realize that only minimal services are provided in such areas as rehabilitation or long-term care?
- Are the patient's interests being sacrificed to the bottom line? In other words, does a profit for the MCO become more important than the patient?

Medicare and Medicaid laws prohibit physicians referring their patients to any service, such as physical therapy or dialysis centers, in which they may have a financial ownership or interest. In addition, physicians must be cautious that their patient charges do not violate Medicare's fee-for-service reimbursement rule.

In spite of the potential problems with managed care, it is not an inherently unethical system of health care. Under this system, monitoring and control of the excessive use of testing and surgical procedures have improved. In addition, a reputable MCO can provide better preventive programs and health care screening for early detection of disease. It can also reduce the unnecessary testing, treatments, and hospitalizations that were present under the old fee-for-service (FFS) system.

## TYPES OF MEDICAL PRACTICE

In the early part of the twentieth century, the main form of medical practice was the solo practice set up by a family practitioner within a designated town or geographic area. Over the years, the practice of medicine and the legal environment have changed. Few physicians make house calls any longer. However, patients now expect to be able to reach their physicians on a 24-hour basis.

 **MED TIP**   The increase in patients who have initiated malpractice lawsuits has necessitated not only increased insurance coverage costs for physicians and patients, but different methods of practice.

Other forms of medical practice have become popular, including some that meet patient needs for around-the-clock coverage and some that provide the opportunity for a group of physicians to share insurance premium costs, staff, and facilities investments.

### Solo Practice

In **solo practice,** a physician practices alone. This is a common type of practice for dentists. However, physicians generally enter into agreements with other physicians to provide coverage for each other's patients and to share office expenses. Physicians are becoming increasingly reluctant to enter into solo practice because of the large burden of debt they incurred during their medical training and the high cost of operating an independent office.

A type of solo practice called **sole proprietorship** is one in which a physician may employ other physicians and pay them a salary. However, the sole proprietor of the medical practice is still responsible for making all the administrative decisions. The physician-owner pays all expenses and retains all assets.

The advantages of this type of practice include being able to retain all of the profits and to make the major decisions concerning policies and staffing. However, in a sole proprietorship, the owner is responsible and liable for the actions of all the employees. In addition, the physician may have to work long hours to provide his or her patients with the care they need. It is often difficult to find the correct balance of qualified physicians to help out during vacations and illnesses of the solo practitioner. This form of practice is diminishing rapidly due to increasing expenses and the lack of another physician to share the patient load.

## Partnership

A **partnership** is a legal agreement to share in the business operation of a medical practice. A partnership may exist between two or more physicians. In this legal arrangement, each partner becomes responsible for the actions of all the other partners. This responsibility includes debts and legal actions unless otherwise stipulated in the partnership agreement. It is always advisable to have partnership agreements in writing. A document or "certificate of doing business as partners" is registered in the local county clerk's office.

The advantages of a partnership include greater earning power than a physician just working alone can realize. There are also other physicians in a partnership to carry any burden of patient care, liability, overhead expenses, or capital requirements to improve the office facility. The disadvantages often relate to personality conflicts. In addition, all the partners in the group must share in the liabilities even if only a few of the members are responsible for incurring them.

## Associate Practice

The **associate practice** is a legal agreement in which physicians agree to share a facility and staff but not the profits and losses. They do not generally share responsibility for the legal actions of each other, as in a partnership. The legal contract of agreement stipulates the responsibilities of each party. The physicians act as if their practice is a sole proprietorship.

The legal arrangement of an associate practice must be carefully described and discussed with patients. Patients may mistakenly believe that there is a shared responsibility by all the physicians in the practice. This can lead to legal difficulties if one physician is accused of committing malpractice.

 **MED TIP**   To avoid the appearance that a partnership exists when one does not, physicians must be sure the signage on their offices, their letterhead and other stationery, and the manner in which the staff answers the telephone is not misleading.

## Group Practice

A **group practice** consists of three or more physicians who share the same facility (office or clinic) and practice medicine together. This is a legal form of practice in which the physicians share all expenses and income, personnel, equipment, and records. A physician may be a member of a group practice as a partner or as an employee. Some areas of medicine frequently found in group practice are anesthesiology, rehabilitation, obstetrics, radiology, and pathology. In some cases, physicians who practice in a single specialty area such as radiology join together in group practice. The membership of a group practice can be quite large, and thus it may be a difficult setting to work in for those who prefer to work alone. In some cases, the income level may not be as high as in a more limited type of partnership due to the large number of physicians creating the expenses. (See Figure 4-1.)

A group practice can be designated as a health maintenance organization (HMO) or as an independent practice association (IPA). Group practices have grown rapidly during the last decade, and large groups of more than one hundred doctors are not uncommon. A large group practice often forms a legal professional corporation.

## Professional Corporations

During the 1960s, state legislatures passed laws (statutes) allowing professionals—for example, physicians and lawyers—to incorporate. A **corporation** is managed by a board of directors. There are legal and financial benefits to incorporating the practice.

**FIGURE 4–1** Group practice.

Professional corporation members are known as shareholders. Some of the benefits that can be offered to employees of a corporation include medical expense reimbursement, profit-sharing, pension plans, and disability insurance. These fringe benefits may not always be taxable to the employee and are generally tax deductible to the employer. While a corporation can be sued, the individual assets of the members cannot be touched (as they can in a solo practice). In some cases, a physician in solo practice will take legal steps to incorporate in order to provide some protection of assets. A corporation will remain until it is dissolved. Other forms of practice, such as the sole proprietorship, stop with the death of the owner. Today, most medical practices are corporations.

Table 4-1 describes the types of medical practice along with the advantages and disadvantages of each.

 **MED TIP**    Physicians are moving away from solo practice and forming partnerships or corporations to better serve patient needs, share the costs of insurance, and in the case of corporations, provide legal protection.

**TABLE 4–1**    Types of Medical Practices

| Type of Practice | Advantages | Disadvantages |
|---|---|---|
| Solo practice (only one physician) | Physician retains independence; simplicity of organization; physician retains all assets | Difficulty raising capital, sole responsibility for liability and management functions; inadequate coverage of patients' needs; practice may die with the owner |
| Sole proprietorship | Physician retains all assets; autonomy; hires other physicians to provide assistance | Pays all expenses; responsible for all liability |
| Partnership | Legal responsibility is shared among partners; work, assets, and income are shared | Partners may have personality differences; all partners are liable for actions of the other partners |
| Associate practice | Work is shared | Legal responsibility is not shared by all members |
| Group practice | All expenses and income are shared; all equipment and facilities are shared | Income may not be as great as when a physician practices alone; possible personality clashes among members |
| Single specialty | Expenses and staff are shared | Possible competition among specialists within the group |
| Corporation | Protection from loss of individual assets; many fringe benefits offered; corporation will remain | Income may not be as great as in other forms of practice |

## THE ETHICS OF FEE SPLITTING

**Fee splitting** occurs when one physician offers to pay another physician for the referral of patients. Fee splitting has long been considered unethical and is a basis for professional discipline. The payment of a referral fee is also considered a felony in states such as Alaska, New Mexico, Vermont, and California. However, the most prohibitive statements against accepting a fee for referrals are at the federal level. The Medicare and Medicaid programs both contain antifraud and abuse provisions. These provisions declare that anyone who receives or pays any money directly or indirectly for the referral of a patient for service under Medicare or Medicaid is guilty of a felony punishable by five years' imprisonment or a $25,000 fine, or both.

Fee splitting is not the same as referrals to a hospital **franchise,** such as a pharmacy or radiology department. In this case, the holder of the franchise, or the **franchisee,** may legally pay the hospital in proportion to the amount of business received from hospital patients.

It is not necessarily considered fee splitting if the franchisee is paying an amount equal to expenses incurred. For instance, in a California case, a court held that a radiologist's payment of two-thirds of his receipts to a hospital did not constitute fee splitting because the evidence showed that fees paid to the hospital were equal to expenses incurred by the hospital to furnish the diagnostic center. (*Blank v. Palo Alto-Stanford Ctr.,* 44 Cal. Rptr. 572, Cal. Ct. App. 1965.)

## MEDICAL SPECIALTY BOARDS

Of the 9 million people employed in the health care system, there are approximately 600,000 physicians, 35,000 doctors of osteopathy, and 150,000 dentists. Of the 600,000 physicians, only 150,000 practice primary patient care: family medicine, internal medicine, obstetrics, and pediatrics. The majority of physicians work in specialty fields such as anesthesiology, psychiatry, or a surgical specialty. Many physicians now work at salaried staff positions in hospitals, as members of group practices, for a corporate-sponsored medical care firm, or for community clinics.

Currently, 23 specialty boards are covered by the American Board of Medical Specialists. Included among these specialties are the American Board of Allergy and Immunology, American Board of Anesthesiology, American Board of Emergency Medicine, American Board of Internal Medicine, American Board of Surgery, and American Board of Urology. The specialty boards seek to improve the quality of medical care and treatment by encouraging physicians to further their education and training. The board evaluates the qualifications of candidates who apply and pass an examination. The physicians who pass the board review become certified as diplomats. As board certified physicians, they may be addressed as either diplomats or fellows, a designation they can use after their name—for instance, Paul Smith, M.D., Diplomat of the American Board of Pediatrics.

Due to the dramatic advances in medicine over the past two decades, there continues to be an interest in specialization among physicians. Transplant surgery, including liver, kidney, lungs, and pancreas, has expanded the need for medical and surgical specialties. A description of some of the more common medical and surgical specialties is found in Table 4-2.

## American College of Surgeons

The American College of Surgeons also confers a fellowship degree upon applicants who have completed additional training and submitted documentation of 50 surgical cases during the previous three years. A successful candidate becomes a Fellow of the American College of Surgeons (FACS).

**TABLE 4–2**    Medical and Surgical Specialties

| Medical Specialty | Description |
| --- | --- |
| Adolescent medicine | Treats patients from puberty to maturity (ages 11 to 21) |
| Allergy and immunology | Treats abnormal responses or acquired hypersensitivity to substances with medical methods such as testing and desensitization |
| Anesthesiology | Administration of both local and general drugs to induce a complete or partial loss of feeling (anesthesia) during a surgical procedure |
| Cardiology | Treats cardiovascular disease (of the heart and blood vessels) |
| Dermatology | Treats injuries, growths, and infections to the skin, hair, and nails |
| Emergency medicine | Trained as an emergency medicine resident with the ability and skills to quickly recognize and prioritize (triage) acute injuries, trauma, and illnesses |
| Family practice | Treats the entire family regardless of age and gender |
| Geriatric medicine | Focuses on the care of diseases and disorders of the elderly |
| Hematology | Study of blood and blood-forming tissues |
| Infection control | Focuses on the prevention of infectious disease by maintaining medical asepsis, practicing good hygiene, and promoting immunizations |
| Internal medicine | Treats adults who have medical problems |
| Neurology | Treats the nonsurgical patient who has a disorder or disease of the nervous system |
| Nephrology | Specializes in pathology of the kidney, including diseases and disorders |
| Nuclear medicine | Specializes in the use of radioactive substances for the diagnosis and treatment of diseases such as cancer |
| Obstetrics and gynecology | Treats the female through prenatal care, labor, delivery, and the postpartum period; gynecology provides medical and surgical treatment of diseases and disorders of the female reproductive system |
| Oncology | The study of benign tumors and cancer-related tumors |

*(continued)*

**TABLE 4–2** Medical and Surgical Specialties (*continued*)

| Medical Specialty | Description |
|---|---|
| Ophthalmology | Treats disorders of the eye |
| Orthopedics | Specializes in the prevention and correction of disorders of the musculoskeletal system |
| Otorhinolaryngology (ENT) | Specializes in medical and surgical treatment of the ear (otology), nose (rhinology), and throat (laryngology) |
| Pathology | Specializes in diagnosing abnormal changes in tissues that are removed during surgery or an autopsy |
| Pediatrics | Specializes in the care and development of children |
| Physical medicine/ rehabilitative medicine | Treats patients after they have suffered an injury or disability |
| Preventive medicine | Focuses treatment on the prevention of both physical and mental illness or disability |
| Psychiatry | Specializes in the diagnosis and treatment of patients with mental, behavioral, or emotional disorders |
| Radiology | Specializes in the study of tissue and organs based on x-ray visualization |
| Rheumatology | Treats disorders and diseases characterized by inflammation of the joints, such as arthritis |
| Surgery | Corrects illness, trauma, and deformities using an operative procedure |

| Surgical Specialty | Description |
|---|---|
| Cardiovascular | Surgically treats the heart and blood vessels |
| Colorectal | Surgically treats the lower intestinal tract (colon and rectum) |
| Cosmetic/plastic surgery | Surgically reconstructs underlying tissues |
| Hand | Surgically treats defects, traumas, and disorders of the hand |
| Neurosurgery (CNS) | Surgically intervenes for diseases and disorders of the central nervous system |
| Orthopedic | Surgically treats musculoskeletal injuries and disorders, congenital deformities, and spinal curvatures |
| Oral (periodontics/ orthodontics) | Treats disorders of the jaws and teeth by means of incision and surgery as well as tooth extraction; treats malocclusion (misalignment) of teeth |
| Thoracic | Surgically treats disorders and diseases of the chest |

## American College of Physicians

The American College of Physicians offers a similar fellowship and entitles the applicant to become a Fellow of the American College of Physicians (FACP) in a nonsurgical area.

The designation doctor (Dr.) is the proper way of addressing—verbally or in writing—someone who holds a doctoral degree of any kind. In the medical field, the title of doctor indicates that a person is qualified to practice medicine within the limits of

**TABLE 4–3**    Designations and Abbreviations for Doctors

| Designations | Abbreviations |
|---|---|
| Doctor of Chiropractic | D.C. |
| Doctor of Dental Medicine | D.M.D. |
| Doctor of Dental Surgery | D.D.S. |
| Doctor of Medicine | M.D. |
| Doctor of Optometry | O.D. |
| Doctor of Osteopathy | D.O. |
| Doctor of Philosophy | Ph.D. |
| Doctor of Podiatric Medicine | D.P.M. |

the degree received; in other fields, the title means that a person has attained the highest educational degree in that field. Several designations for doctor are listed in Table 4-3.

**MED TIP**    The term doctor comes from the Latin word *docere,* meaning "to teach."

## ALLIED HEALTH PROFESSIONALS

A physician works with a variety of trained personnel, depending on the area of specialization. Health care team professionals are also called allied health care practitioners. Licensed personnel include registered nurses, nurse practitioners, licensed practical nurses, and pharmacists. Certified, but not licensed, personnel include the physician's assistant, the certified medical assistant, the certified medical transcriptionist, the laboratory technician, and the laboratory technologist. See Table 4-4 for descriptions of allied health professionals.

**MED TIP**    Patients often refer to anyone wearing a white laboratory coat as "doctor" or a white uniform as "nurse." Always correct patients and tell them exactly what your position is. If you are a student, be sure to wear an identifying badge so that you will not be asked to perform an action outside of your scope of practice.

**TABLE 4–4**  Health Care Occupations

| Occupation | Description |
| --- | --- |
| Certified medical assistant (CMA) | Duties are grouped into two categories: administrative and clinical. Work in a variety of health care settings including physicians' offices and clinics. Must graduate from an accredited program and pass a national certification exam. |
| Certified medical transcriptionist (CMT) | Types dictation recorded by a physician or surgeon. Must pass a certification exam. |
| Dental assistant | Works under the supervision of a dentist to prepare the patient for treatment, take dental x-rays, and hand instruments to the dentist. |
| Dental hygienist | Works directly with the dental patient to clean teeth, take x-rays, and discuss results of the patient's dental exam with the dentist. |
| Electrocardiograph technologist | Operates electrocardiograph (EKG/ECG) machines to record and study the electrical activity of the heart. |
| Emergency medical technician (EMT)/paramedic | Provides emergency care and transports injured patients to a medical facility. |
| Laboratory or medical technologist (MT) | Performs laboratory analysis, directs the work of laboratory personnel, and maintains quality assurance standards for all equipment. |
| Licensed practical nurse (LPN) | Performs some of the same, but not all, tasks as the registered nurse. Must graduate from a recognized one-year program and become licensed by the National Federation of Licensed Practical Nurses. |
| Medical records technician (ART) | Skilled in health information technology; maintains medical records in health care institutions and medical practices. Successful completion of the Accredited Record Technician examination allows the initials ART to be used after the technician's name. |
| Nurse practitioner | A registered nurse who has additional training in a specialty area such as obstetrics, gerontology, or community health. This nurse usually holds a master's degree. |
| Occupational therapist (OT) | Provides treatment to people who are physically, mentally, developmentally, or emotionally disabled in the area of personal care skills; goal of OT is to restore the patient's ability to manage activities of daily living. |
| Pharmacist | A licensed professional who orders, maintains, prepares, and distributes prescription medications. |
| Pharmacy technician | Prepares and dispenses patient medications. |
| Phlebotomist | Draws blood from patients; certification is required in some states. |

*(continued)*

**TABLE 4–4    Health Care Occupations *(continued)***

| Occupation | Description |
| --- | --- |
| Physical therapist (PT) | Provides exercise and treatment of diseases and disabilities of the bones, joints, and nerves through massage, therapeutic exercises, heat and cold treatments, and other means. |
| Physician's assistant (PA) | Assists the physician in the primary care of the patient. Requires additional education similar to a master's level program, must work or have an internship experience and pass an accreditation exam. |
| Registered nurse (RN) | A professional care giver who has successfully completed a national licensure exam known as the National Council Licensure Examination (NCLEX). |
| Respiratory therapist (RT) | Evaluates, treats, and cares for patients who have breathing abnormalities. |
| Social worker | Provides services and programs to meet the special needs of the ill, physically and mentally challenged, and older adults. |
| Surgical technician | Trained in operating room procedures and assists the surgeon during invasive surgical procedures. |
| Ultrasound technologist (AART) | Uses inaudible sound waves to outline shapes of tissues and organs. |
| X-ray technologist (radiologic technologist) | Uses radiologic technology such as nuclear medicine and radiation. |

## POINTS TO PONDER

1. What impact will managed care have upon your career as an allied health professional?
2. What type of practice does your physician/employer have? If it is not a solo practice, what are the other specialties involved in the practice?
3. What are the advantages of forming a corporation?
4. Why is it important to include the medical specialty and initials indicating a particular degree or license after one's name?
5. What should you say if a patient refers to you as "doctor" or "nurse" even though your degree is in another discipline?
6. How should health care plans balance the interests of all the enrolled patients with the interests of a patient who has special medical needs and extraordinary expenses?
7. In the interests of maintaining a successful practice, should a physician refuse to provide care for patients who are uninsured or minimally insured?
8. Consider the question of ethics that arises when we ask ourselves if we are reducing unnecessary tests, as the HMOs and others believe we should, or if we are limiting tests for patients who really need them.

## DISCUSSION QUESTIONS

1. Discuss your role as a medical professional in relation to the physician and other health care providers.
2. Discuss the impact that managed care is likely to have on your career in health care.
3. What can be done to ensure that MCOs provide ethical care for all patients?

## PRACTICE EXERCISES

### Matching

Match the responses in column B with the correct term in column A.

**Column A**

\_\_\_\_\_ 1. HMO
\_\_\_\_\_ 2. EPO
\_\_\_\_\_ 3. PPO
\_\_\_\_\_ 4. solo practice
\_\_\_\_\_ 5. associate practice
\_\_\_\_\_ 6. sole proprietorship
\_\_\_\_\_ 7. corporation
\_\_\_\_\_ 8. third-party payer
\_\_\_\_\_ 9. Medicaid
\_\_\_\_\_ 10. Medicare

**Column B**

a. preferred provider organization
b. physicians agree to share expenses of a facility
c. health maintenance organization
d. managed by a board of directors
e. financial assistance for the elderly
f. exclusive provider organization
g. one physician may employ others
h. financial assistance for the indigent
i. physician practices alone
j. insurance company

## MULTIPLE CHOICE

Select the one best answer to the following statements.

1. Under this plan, a health care provider is paid a set amount based on the category of care provided to the patient.
   a. AMA
   b. DRG
   c. ANA
   d. HHS
   e. UNOS

2. Medicare patients who are members of HMOs may now, by law,
   a. not make any deductible payment
   b. select any physician they wish
   c. appeal a denial of treatment
   d. have all their nursing home expenses paid
   e. none of the above

3. A type of managed care in which the selection of providers is limited to a defined group who are all paid on a modified fee-for-service basis is
   a. exclusive provider organization
   b. group practice
   c. preferred provider organization
   d. health maintenance organization
   e. sole proprietorship

4. A legal agreement in which physicians agree to share a facility and staff but not the profits and losses is
   a. solo practice
   b. sole proprietorship
   c. partnership
   d. associate practice
   e. none of the above

5. The advantage of a corporation is that it
   a. offers protection from loss of individual assets
   b. may offer fringe benefits
   c. will remain in effect after the death of a member
   d. offers the opportunity for a large increase in income
   e. a, b, and c only

6. A physician who is board certified may be addressed as
   a. diplomat
   b. fellow
   c. partner
   d. associate
   e. a and b only

7. MCOs are able to manage costs by
   a. shifting some financial risk back to the physicians
   b. shifting some financial risk back to the hospitals
   c. using a fee-for-service payment method
   d. a and b only
   e. a, b, and c

8. This federal legislation provides health care for indigent persons and is administered by individual states.
   a. Medicare
   b. Medicaid
   c. HMO
   d. PPO
   e. COBRA

9. The managed care system
   a. has a gatekeeper to determine who will receive medical treatments
   b. provides a mechanism for approval for all nonemergency services
   c. provides care for a fixed monthly fee

    d. includes HMOs, PPOs, and EPOs

    e. all of the above

10. The American College of Surgeons confers a fellowship degree upon its applicants

    a. whenever a surgeon places a request

    b. when they complete additional training

    c. when they have documentation of 50 surgical cases during the previous three years

    d. a, b, and c

    e. b and c only

## PUT IT INTO PRACTICE

Interview a medical professional who works in a specialization with which you are unfamiliar. Ask the professional to talk about education, what type of certification or licensing, if any, is necessary, and what legal issues affect the profession.

Interview a senior citizen and ask about his or her health insurance needs. Does he or she have difficulty with the paperwork required by the insurance company? Ask what could be done to make this a less difficult task.

Call a managed care group in your area. Request information concerning the group's policies and discuss the main points of coverage with them.

## WEB HUNT

Discuss the type of information that is available on the Web site for the American Medical Association (*www.ama-assn.org*).

Review the Web site for an organization such as the American Nurses Association (*www.nursinworld.org/readroom*), the American Association of Medical Assistants (*www.aama-ntl.org*), or your own professional organization. What are the categories listed on this Web site?

## REFERENCES

Anderson, O. 1990. *Health services in the U.S.* 2nd ed. Chicago: Health Administration Press.

Badasch, S., and D. Chesebro. 1997. *Introduction to health occupations.* Upper Saddle River, N.J.: Prentice Hall.

Fremgen, B. 1998. *Essentials of medical assisting: Administrative and clinical competencies.* Upper Saddle River, N.J.: Prentice Hall.

Garrett, T., H. Baillie, and R. Garrett. 1993. *Health care ethics: Principles and problems.* Upper Saddle River, N.J.: Prentice Hall.

Gervais, K., R. Priester, D. Vewter, K. Otte, and M. Solberg. 1999. *Ethical challenges of managed care.* Washington, D.C.: Georgetown University Press.

Hall, M., and M. Bobinski. 2003. *Health care law and ethics: In a nutshell.* St. Paul, Minn.: West Publishing.

McConnell, T. 1997. *Moral issues in health care: An introduction to medical ethics.* Albany, N.Y.: Wadsworth.

Mechanic, D. 2000. Managed care and the imperative for a new professional ethic. *Health Affairs* 19, no. 5 (September/October): 100–111.

Stanfield, P. 2002. *Introduction to the health professions.* Boston: Jones & Bartlett.

Tindall, W., W. Williams, J. Boltri, T. Morrow, S. van der Vaart, and B. Weiss. 2000. *A guide to managed care medicine.* Gaithersburg, Md.: Aspen.

U.S. Department of Labor, Bureau of Labor Statistics. 1993. *Occupational outlook handbook.* Washington, D.C.: U.S. Government Printing Office.

Wirth, A. 1992. *Education and work in the year 2000.* San Francisco: Jossey-Bass.

Wong, K. 1998. *Medicine and the marketplace: The moral dimensions of managed care.* Notre Dame, Ind.: University of Notre Dame Press.

## CASE STUDY

Jerry McCall is Dr. Williams's office assistant. He has received professional training as both a medical assistant and an LPN. He is handling all the phone calls while the receptionist is at lunch. A patient calls and says he must have a prescription refill for Valium, an antidepressant medication, called in right away to his pharmacy, since he is leaving for the airport in 30 minutes. He says that Dr. Williams is a personal friend and always gives him a small supply of Valium when he has to fly. No one except Jerry is in the office at this time. What should he do?

1. Does Jerry's medical training qualify him to issue this refill order? Why or why not?

   _____

   _____

   _____

2. Would it make a difference if the medication requested were for control of high blood pressure that the patient critically needs on a daily basis? Why or why not?

   _____

   _____

   _____

3. If Jerry does call in the refill and the patient has an adverse reaction to it while flying, is Jerry protected from a lawsuit under the doctrine of *respondeat superior*?

   _____

   _____

   _____

4. What is your advice to Jerry?

   _____

   _____

   _____

PART **II**

# THE HEALTH CARE ENVIRONMENT

CHAPTER 5

# The Physician–Patient Relationship

## LEARNING OBJECTIVES

1. Define the glossary terms.
2. Describe the rights a physician has when practicing medicine and when accepting a patient.
3. Discuss the seven principles of medical ethics as designated by the American Medical Association (AMA).
4. Summarize "A Patient's Bill of Rights."
5. Understand standard of care and how it is applied to the practice of medicine.
6. Discuss three patient self-determination acts.
7. Describe the difference between implied consent and informed consent.

## KEY TERMS

Abandonment
Acquired immune deficiency (AIDS) syndrome
Advance directive
Agent
Consent

Durable power of attorney
Human immunodeficiency virus (HIV)
Implied consent
Informed (or expressed) consent
*In loco parentis*

Living will
Minor
Privileged communication
Proxy
Uniform Anatomical Gift Act

## INTRODUCTION

Few topics are as important as the physician–patient relationship. This relationship impacts the entire health care team. All persons who interact with the patient must understand their responsibilities to both the patient and the physician. The patient's right to confidentiality must always be paramount.

## THE PHYSICIAN–PATIENT RELATIONSHIP

Both physician and patient must agree to form a relationship for there to be a contract for services. Once a doctor has agreed to treat a patient, the patient can expect that the doctor will provide medical services for as long as necessary. See Figure 5-1. In order to receive proper treatment, the patient must confide truthfully in the physician. Failure to do so may result in serious consequences for the patient, and the physician is not liable if the patient has withheld critical information.

## PHYSICIAN'S RIGHTS

Physicians have the right to select the patients they wish to treat. They also have the right to refuse service to patients. From an ethical standpoint, most physicians treat patients who need their skills. This is particularly true in cases of emergency.

Physicians may also state the type of services they will provide, the hours their offices will be open, and where they will be located. The physician has the right to expect payment for all treatment provided, and a physician can withdraw from a relationship if the patient is noncooperative or refuses to pay bills when able to do so.

Physicians have the right to take vacations and time off from their practice, and to be unavailable to care for their patients during those times. It is legally prudent for physicians to arrange for coverage during an absence. In most cases, other physicians will cover for them and take care of their patients. Physicians should notify their patients when they will be unavailable.

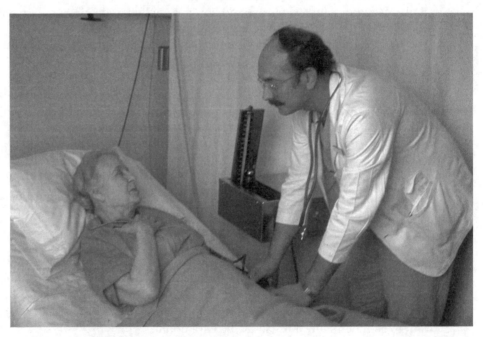

**FIGURE 5–1**   The physician–patient relationship.

Some physicians now charge for services such as answering after-hours phone calls and filling out insurance forms. Many physicians feel that the large increases in their malpractice insurance premiums and the tighter regulations by HMOs have forced them to charge for services that they previously performed without charge.

## PHYSICIAN'S RESPONSIBILITIES

While a physician has the right to accept or decline to establish a professional relationship with any person, once that relationship is established, the physician has certain responsibilities. For example, federal law and many state laws prohibit hospitals from giving physicians kickbacks of money or other benefits in return for referring patients. In 1994, NME Psychiatric Hospitals pleaded guilty to making unlawful payments to physicians in order to induce them to refer patients to their institutions. NME agreed to pay the federal government $379 million to settle the case. (*United States v. NME Psychiatric Hosps.*, Inc., No. 94-0268.)

The physician has many other responsibilities, including ethical ones. The American Medical Association (AMA) has taken a leadership role in setting ethical standards for the behavior of physicians. The AMA, organized in 1846, formed its first code of ethics in 1847. Table 5-1 presents the AMA's current statement of principles in its entirety.

## PROFESSIONAL PRACTICE RESPONSIBILITIES

Medical practice responsibilities include such commonplace routines as effective handwashing techniques before touching any patient. A recent survey cited in the *Chicago Tribune* of over 900 hospitals reports that medical mistakes kill anywhere from 44,000 to 98,000 Americans every year. According to the report, many often-preventable complications, such as postoperative infections, lead to more than 32,000 hospital deaths and more than $9 billion in extra costs annually. One of the most serious complications is postsurgery sepsis (bloodstream infections). Researchers believe that improved handwashing might reduce these high rates of death.

Physicians have many duties upon entering the practice of medicine. Examples of professional duties are described in Table 5-2.

### Duties During a Medical Emergency

A physician cannot ethically or legally turn away a patient who is in an emergency situation. If the physician is unable to adequately treat the patient, then he or she must call for emergency assistance from paramedics (a 911 call). For instance, allergy specialists may be unable to give life-saving medications to a stroke victim, since the drugs won't be available in their offices. However, allergy specialists can handle victims who are in respiratory distress as well as, or better than, some other medical specialists. It is especially important to remember that patients cannot be turned away from a hospital or physician's office if they are indigent or uninsured.

## TABLE 5-1    AMA Principles of Medical Ethics

### Preamble

The medical profession has long subscribed to a body of ethical statements developed primarily for the benefit of the patient. As a member of this profession, a physician must recognize responsibility not only to patients, but also to society, to other health professionals, and to self. The following principles adopted by the American Medical Association are not law, but standards of conduct which define the essentials of honorable behavior for the physician.

### Human Dignity

I. A physician shall be dedicated to providing competent medical service with compassion and respect for human dignity.

### Honesty

II. A physician shall deal honestly with patients and colleagues, and strive to expose those physicians deficient in character or competence, or who engage in fraud or deception.

### Responsibility to Society

III. A physician shall respect the law and recognize a responsibility to seek changes in those requirements that are contrary to the best interests of the patient.

### Confidentiality

IV. A physician shall respect the rights of patients, of colleagues, and of other health professionals, and shall safeguard patient confidence within the constraints of the law.

### Continued Study

V. A physician shall continue to study, apply, and advance scientific knowledge, make relevant information available to patients, colleagues, and the public, obtain consultation, and use the talents of other health professionals as needed.

### Freedom of Choice

VI. A physician shall, in the provision of appropriate health care, except in emergencies, be free to choose whom to serve, with whom to associate, and the environment in which to provide service.

### Responsibility to Improved Community

VII. A physician shall recognize a responsibility to participate in activities contributing to an improved community.

*Source:* American Medical Association, Code of Medical Ethics © 1998.

**MED TIP**   Remember that all physicians receive the same basic medical training regardless of their medical specialty. They and their staff should be able to assist with basic CPR.

## Duty to Treat Indigent Patients

There is currently a "dumping crisis" of indigent patients who lack medical insurance in American hospitals. There are many stories of deaths occurring after a patient has been shuffled from a private hospital emergency room to a public hospital that ac-

TABLE 5–2    Examples of Physicians' Duties

| | |
|---|---|
| Accepting gifts | Gifts to physicians from medical companies can be accepted only if they relate to the physician's medical practice. However, drug samples from pharmaceutical companies can be accepted for patient use. |
| Conflict of interest | Physicians should not place their own financial interests above the patient's welfare. |
| Professional courtesy | Historically, there is an unwritten practice among many physicians that they would not charge each other for professional services. However, this practice has lost favor because many physicians are concerned about the lack of documentation when seeing a fellow physician free of charge. |
| Reporting unethical conduct of other physicians | A physician should report any unethical conduct by other physicians. |
| Second opinions | Physicians should recommend that patients seek a second opinion whenever necessary. |
| Sexual conduct | It is unethical for the physician to engage in sexual conduct with a patient during the physician–patient relationship. |
| Treating family members | Physicians should not treat members of their families except in an emergency. |

cepts indigent patients. While the hospital treatment may not be to blame for the death, the long delay in treatment while the patient is being transferred might. The Comprehensive Omnibus Budget Reconciliation Act (COBRA) contains an amendment that prohibits "dumping" patients from one facility to another. It is now a federal offense to do this. This amendment does not mandate treatment, but it does require a hospital to stabilize a patient during an emergency situation.

Does a physician have a duty to treat a patient who is unable to pay? According to the Summary of Opinions of the Council on Ethical and Judicial Affairs of the AMA, a physician has the right to select which patients to treat. However, physicians do not have the same freedom to drop patients once they have agreed to treat them. The health care professional has the right to earn a living and charge for services, but from an ethical standpoint, a physician cannot abandon any patient, even in a non-emergency situation. Abandonment might expose the patient to dangers due to lack of oversight of medications and treatment.

## Duty Not to Abandon a Patient

Once a physician has agreed to take care of a patient, that contract may not be terminated improperly. Physicians may be charged with **abandonment** of the patient if they do not give formal notice of withdrawal from the case. In addition, the physician must allow the patient sufficient time to seek the service of another physician. This does not mean the physician may never withdraw from a case. Physicians may decide they can no longer accept responsibility for the medical treatment of a patient because the patient refuses to come in for periodic checkups or take prescribed medications and treatments. Abandonment could occur if the physician does not give enough notice to the patient so that other arrangements for medical care can be made.

**MED TIP**   Sending a letter by certified mail is the best method physicians can use to protect themselves from a charge of abandonment when they have to sever a relationship with a patient.

## Duty to Treat Patients with AIDS

**Acquired immune deficiency syndrome (AIDS)** is a disease resulting in infections that occur as a result of exposure to the **human immunodeficiency virus (HIV),** which causes the immune system to break down. AIDS was first documented in the United States in 1980. According to the Centers for Disease Control (CDC) in Atlanta, Georgia, this disease has become a major health concern in the world. About 1.5 million Americans are infected with HIV, which causes AIDS, and more than a quarter million people have AIDS. Globally, the World Health Organization (WHO) suspects there are as many as 15 million cases of HIV and 5 million full-blown cases of AIDS.

The infectious HIV virus causes the immune system, which is the body's shield against infection, to break down and eventually become ineffective by invading the body's macrophages (cells that engulf bacteria and other pathogens) and T-cells, which fight disease. There is presently no cure for HIV or AIDS, and people with the disease will have it for the rest of their lives.

The various means by which the AIDS virus can enter the body include

- vaginal, anal, or oral intercourse with a person who has the virus.
- sharing needles or syringes with a person who has the virus.
- receiving transfusions of blood or blood products donated by someone who has the virus.
- receiving organ transplants from a donor who has the virus.
- contaminating open wounds or sores with blood, semen, or vaginal secretions infected with the virus.
- having artificial insemination with the sperm of a man who has the virus.

Not all HIV patients develop AIDS or any other HIV-related condition. The CDC estimates from 50 to 90 percent of patients develop full-blown AIDS. It may take eight to ten years for symptoms of HIV infection to develop and twelve years or more for symptoms of AIDS to develop. The final stage of AIDS includes a variety of viral, fungal, bacterial, and parasitic infections; nervous disorders; and cancers. These infections, which are often present in the healthy body, can normally be overcome by the immune system; in the AIDS patient, the immune system is no longer effective and the infections become life-threatening. These infections, called opportunistic infections, include

- *Pneumocystis carinii pneumonia (PCP)*—a pulmonary disease characterized by cough, fever, and dyspnea (labored breathing) that can be fatal
- *Kaposi's sarcoma*—a type of skin cancer
- *Toxoplasmosis*—infestation of parasites that infect the brain and central nervous system

Testing for HIV is useful, since medications are available that can slow or even stop the advancement of the disease. Since there is a strong stigma attached to this disease, it is important to respect the confidentiality of anyone having an HIV or AIDS test. Patients must give their informed consent for the test.

> **MED TIP**    Note that testing positive for HIV does not necessarily mean that a person has, or will develop, AIDS. Positive test results, if leaked to an employer, can lead to loss of job, on-the-job harassment, or other serious consequences, even though such actions may be illegal.

### Ethical Considerations When Treating AIDS Patients

A physician who knows that the patient may endanger the health of others has certain ethical obligations, which include

1. persuading the patient to inform his or her partner(s)
2. notifying authorities if there is a suspicion that the patient will not inform others
3. as a last resort, notifying the patient's partner(s)

It is unethical to refuse to treat, work with, or provide housing for a person who is HIV- or AIDS-infected. In addition, the Americans with Disabilities Act (ADA), a federal law, protects HIV and AIDS patients from discrimination.

Physicians have been faced with the dilemma of honoring the confidentiality of their patients and then risk being sued for failure to warn or protect third parties who may have been exposed to HIV/AIDS through the activity of the patient. This is of particular concern when the patient is a child. AIDS has become the ninth leading cause of death among children ages one to four and is the sixth leading cause of death among the population aged 15 to 24. Many of these infected cases in children are due to childhood sexual abuse. The patients may be shunned by friends or others who are afraid of being exposed to the virus. In *Doe v. Borough of Barrington,* the court cited the plaintiffs' brief for numerous examples of hysteria caused as a result of AIDS. These included a Florida family, with hemophiliac children who tested positive for AIDS, driven out of town after their house was firebombed; a teacher with AIDS who was removed from teaching duties; and children with AIDS who were denied schooling in Colorado. (*Doe v. Borough of Barrington,* 729 F. Supp. 376, N.J. 1990.) The physician, by law, must make a full report to the state about any patient who is HIV- or AIDS-positive, despite the potentially serious consequences to the patient by reporting the case.

> **MED TIP**    Patients with AIDS or who are HIV-positive need to be treated with the same compassion and care that would be given to any patient with a life-threatening illness.

### Exposure of Health Care Workers to a Patient's Blood

Unfortunately, needlestick injuries in health care settings are common even when physician and health care workers take special precautions, such as using gloves. After exposure to an HIV-positive patient's blood, a physician or health care worker has a 0.3 percent risk of contracting HIV, according to the CDC estimates. In one study of medical school residents, it was found that 69 percent reported they had received a needlestick during their medical training. Understandably, health care workers who have received needlestick injuries wish to know if the patient's blood contained the HIV or AIDS virus.

If the patient refuses to be tested for HIV or AIDS, can the physician order blood work to test for the virus without the patient's consent? This presents both legal and ethical concerns. HIV testing without the patient's consent is illegal. However, some states have allowed HIV testing without the patient's consent when a serious situation warrants the testing. From an ethical standpoint, HIV testing in spite of the patient's objection violates the patient's autonomy and privacy.

### Restriction on HIV-Infected Health Care Workers

Public health concerns about HIV-infected health care employees has always been an issue. Several questions have been presented:

- Should health care workers, especially those who perform invasive procedures such as drawing blood specimens, be tested for HIV?
- Should HIV-infected health care workers inform their patients that they are positive for the virus?
- Should the practice of HIV-infected workers be restricted?

As patient/consumers, it is relatively easy for us to answer yes to these three questions. For example, physicians have an ethical obligation that requires that they do no harm to their patients. However, physicians must disclose information to their patients that a reasonable person would require in order to make an informed decision about their own testing for the virus. Most patients would certainly want to know if their physician or health care worker is infected with HIV. A *Newsweek* poll found that 94 percent of their readers responding to the poll agreed that all physician and dentists should be required to tell their patients if they are HIV-infected.

The American Medical Association (AMA) recommends that HIV-positive health care workers should not perform invasive procedures that pose a risk to their patients and that physicians should always "err on the side of protecting patients." The American Academy of Orthopedic Surgeons recommends that HIV-positive surgeons not perform procedures that involve the placement of internal devices, such as hip replacements, wires, or even blind probing of tissue. Probably the strongest statements come from the Federation of State Medical Boards, which states that it would be professional misconduct for health care workers to perform invasive procedures if they *do not* know their HIV-status. Furthermore, the Federation recommends that all state boards require that the names of HIV-infected health care workers be reported to them.

There are strong arguments for ignoring confidentiality issues and reporting HIV-positive workers if their actions put patients' health at risk. For example, surgeons, gynecologists, dentists, phlebotomists, surgical nurses, and emergency medical technicians all take part in invasive procedures in which HIV could be transmitted. In addition, removing the HIV-positive health care worker from close patient contact could ultimately provide protection from patients' infections and diseases such as tuberculosis.

There are valid arguments against requiring mandatory testing and restricting the activities of HIV-positive health care workers. For example, health care workers have a right to freedom from discrimination and to privacy. There are statistics that show that the risk of transmitting the HIV to another person is very low. In addition, the cost of testing all health care workers for HIV is prohibitive. The CDC has estimated that it would cost more than $250 million for testing alone. This money would have to be diverted from research and other programs. The CDC guidelines also declare that health care workers have no ethical duty to disclose their HIV status if they present no significant risk to their patients.

## On-the-Job Protection for the Health Care Worker

There is a relatively low risk of infection for persons working in the fields of medical transcription, secretarial, or office management in which there is little patient contact. There is a greater risk of infection for health care professionals, such as a physician, nurse, or medical assistant, since they have direct patient contact. The bottom line for all health care organizations is that there should be a clearly stated policy on how to handle all needlestick situations (see Figure 5-2) and patients' bodily fluids. Medical offices, clinics, and hospitals should use special absorbent cleaning material available in case of a blood spill. Directions on what to do when a blood spill or other accident occurs should be placed where they are visible for the entire staff.

**FIGURE 5–2**    Needlestick protection.

Some general safety precautions concerning HIV and AIDS exposure when working in a health care setting include

1. Since it is not possible to tell if a person is ill with HIV or AIDS just by looking at him or her, use standard safety precautions as if everyone you come into contact with has HIV or AIDS.
2. Use excellent hand-washing techniques before and after touching patients.
3. Wear latex or rubber gloves if you have any contact with blood, blood-tinged body fluids, urine, feces, or vomit.
4. Handle all needles with care. Never replace caps on needles or remove needles from syringes.
5. Dispose of all needles in puncture-proof, preferably locked, containers out of the reach of children.
6. Any open sores on either the patient or health care worker should be covered with a bandage.
7. Anyone with boils, fever blisters (herpes simplex), or shingles should avoid close contact with an HIV-infected person.
8. Wear protective gloves, clothing, and apparel, such as eye goggles, when testing blood products.

## Duty to Properly Identify Patients

Many medical errors occur because the patient was not properly identified. It is necessary to identify the patient both by stating his or her name and examining any other identification such as a medical wrist band. If in doubt about the identity of a patient, always ask to see some personal identification such as a driver's license.

Medical personnel should use a low voice when speaking to patients over the telephone or speaking about patients to other staff members within hearing distance of any patients in the waiting room. Ideally, a glass enclosure should be present at the front desk in all waiting rooms to separate the receptionist from the patients and provide an additional aid for patient confidentiality. The sign-in sheet or patient register should be designed so those patients who are signing in or registering cannot view other patients' names.

 **MED TIP**    Remember, if an error is made, such as not properly identifying the correct patient, admit it immediately. Then seek to correct the situation. You may save a life.

## Duty to Tell the Truth

There has been a major change in physicians' attitudes concerning truth-telling during the past several decades. Originally, many physicians believed in a paternalistic, or protective, approach in which they avoided upsetting their terminally ill patients by telling them the truth about their condition. In a research study conducted in 1961, Donald Oken reported that 88 percent of U.S. physicians surveyed said it was their policy not to tell their patients if they had a terminal malignancy. The physicians believed it would be too upsetting to the patient. In a follow-up study 20 years later, these findings were completely reversed, with 98 percent of the physicians surveyed following a position of telling the truth to patients. This position of truth-telling has continued to the present day. The openness for cancer patients came about, in part, due to the necessity to seek consent for chemotherapy and radiation therapy.

Is this change in honesty for the benefit of the patient? Should physicians inform their Alzheimer's patients if their families want the information withheld? Should elderly patients be lied to when they have to move into a nursing home? Should family members be misled over the phone when called to come into a hospital after a family member has expired? These difficult questions have caused many health care professionals to reexamine the truth-telling issue.

For example, a medical ethicist, Joseph Fletcher, states that maintaining the lie of a diagnosis becomes very difficult for everybody on the health care team. He believes in focusing on the consequences of an action while protecting the patient. Furthermore, according to Fletcher, medicine has now become too complex to keep secrets from patients. He states that in the long run it is better for the patient if the truth is told.

**MED TIP**   There are various interpretations of what constitutes lying. However, most people believe that a lie is a falsehood told in those circumstances in which the other person has a reasonable expectation of the truth.

False results of research studies also have had a negative impact upon patients. For example, a Canadian physician working with researchers at a major U.S. medical school reported fictitious results about a mastectomy study. The researchers falsely claimed, and advised the medical community, that the "less radical" surgical procedure, other than mastectomy, was an effective treatment for cancer of the breast. This deception took place over a fifteen-year period until finally they retracted their false claims.

Many believe that when dealing with the issue of truth-telling, one should apply principles of justice. In other words, try to determine what a "just" action would be for the patient. Thomas Hackett, in writing about psychological assistance for the dying patient, cites an example of a typical victim in which there was a failure to inform:

> A woman with terminal breast cancer asked her doctor why her headaches persisted. When the doctor said it was probably nerves, she asked why she was nervous. He returned the question. She replied, "I am nervous because all the tests have stopped, nobody wants my blood, and I get all the pills I want. The priest comes to see me twice a week, which he never did before, and my mother-in-law is nicer to me even though I am meaner to her. Wouldn't this make you nervous?" There was a pause. Then the doctor said, "You mean you think you are dying?" She said, "I do." He replied, "You are." Then she smiled and said, "Well, I broke the sound barrier; someone finally told me the truth."

In some circumstances, truth-telling is at variance with the medical profession's obligation of confidentiality. For example, in the famous Tarasoff case, the court held that a psychiatrist should have warned Tatiana Tarasoff that one of his patients was threatening to kill her. The court stated that the therapist was under an obligation to take reasonable steps to protect all third parties from the ill patient. (*Tarasoff v.*

*Regents of the University of California,* 17 Cal. 3d 342, 1976.) However, in a later case, the same California court that tried the Tarasoff case stated that the therapist did not have a duty to warn a third party of a threat, since the patient had not made threats against a particular person. While these two cases seem to be at odds with each other, the current thinking is that this later verdict is more reasonable. It is difficult, if not impossible, for a psychiatrist to determine which threats a patient makes will result in murder. In reality, however, many mental health physicians are maintaining a conservative approach by hospitalizing patients who show violent tendencies.

The American Hospital Association's Committee on Biomedical Ethics states:

> Also subject to state law, confidentiality may be overridden when the life or safety of the patient is endangered such as when knowledgeable intervention can prevent threatened suicide or self-injury. In addition, the moral obligation to prevent substantial and foreseeable harm to an innocent third party usually is greater than the moral obligation to confidentiality.

## PATIENTS' RIGHTS

The patient has the right to approve or give consent—permission—for all treatment. In giving consent for treatment, patients reasonably expect that their physician will use the appropriate standard of care in providing care and treatment—that is, that the physician will use the same skill that other physicians use in treating patients with the same ailments in the same geographic locality. (Standard of care is discussed in more detail in Chapter 3.)

The patient's right to privacy prohibits the presence of unauthorized persons during physical examinations or treatments. This right has long been established. In an 1881 case, the plaintiff, a poor woman named Mrs. Roberts, sued Dr. DeMay for bringing in a third party, by the name of Scattergood, to assist him while she was in labor. Mrs. Roberts claimed that Scattergood "indecently, wrongfully, and unlawfully" laid hands on her and assaulted her. Even though Mrs. Roberts thought Scattergood was a physician, which he was not, he was present without her permission. The court found in the plaintiff's favor and awarded her damages for the "shame and mortification" she suffered. (*DeMay v. Roberts,* 9 N.W. 146, Mich. 1881.)

Additionally, patients have the right to be informed of the advantage and potential risks of treatment—including the risk of not having the treatment. They also have the right to refuse treatment. Some members of religious groups, such as Jehovah's Witnesses and Christian Scientists, do not wish to receive blood transfusions or other types of medical treatment. Physicians may not treat them against their wishes. However, in the case of a minor child, the court may appoint a guardian who can give consent for the child's procedure.

### Confidentiality

Patients expect that all information and records about their treatment will be kept confidential by the physician and staff. In fact, the Medical Patients Rights Act provides that all patients have the right to have their personal privacy respected and their medical records handled with confidentiality. Any information, such as test results, patient histories, and even the fact that the patient is a patient, cannot be told to another person. A breach of confidentiality is both unethical and illegal. See Chapter 10 for a detailed discussion of confidentiality when using electronic transmission of patient's medical information as mandated by the Health Insurance Portability and Accounting Act of 1996 (HIPAA).

 **MED TIP**  Remember that no patient information can be given over the telephone without that person's permission.

**Privileged communication** refers to confidential information that has been told to a physician (or attorney) by the patient. The physician–patient relationship is considered to be a protected relationship and, as such, keeps the holder of this information from being forced to disclose it on a witness stand.

The American Hospital Association developed a published statement called "A Patient's Bill of Rights," which describes the physician–patient relationship (see Table 5-3). All health care professionals must follow these guidelines when working with patients.

**TABLE 5–3**  A Patient's Bill of Rights

1. The patient has the right to considerate and respectful care.
2. The patient has the right to and is encouraged to obtain from the physicians and other direct caregivers relevant, current, understandable information concerning diagnosis, treatment, and prognosis.
3. The patient has the right to make decisions about the plan of care prior to and during the course of treatment and to refuse a recommended treatment or plan of care to the extent permitted by law and hospital policy and to be informed of the consequences of this action.
4. The patient has the right to have an advance directive (such as a living will, health care proxy, or durable power of attorney for health care) concerning treatment or designating a surrogate decision maker with the expectation that the hospital will honor the intent of that directive to the extent permitted by law and hospital policy.
5. The patient has the right to every consideration of privacy.
6. The patient has the right to expect that all communications and records pertaining to his/her care will be treated as confidential by the hospital, except in cases such as suspected abuse and public health hazards when reporting is permitted or required by law.
7. The patient has the right to review the records pertaining to his/her medical care and to have the information explained or interpreted as necessary, except when restricted by law.
8. The patient has the right to expect that, within its capacity and policies, a hospital will make reasonable response to the request of a patient for appropriate and medically indicated care and service.
9. The patient has the right to ask and be informed of the existence of business relationships among the hospital, educational institutions, other health care providers, or payers that may influence the patient's treatment or care.

*(continued)*

**TABLE 5–3   A Patient's Bill of Rights** *(continued)*

---

10. The patient has the right to consent to or decline to participate in proposed research studies or human experimentation affecting care and treatment or requiring direct patient involvement, and to have those studies fully explained prior to consent.

11. The patient has the right to expect reasonable continuity of care when appropriate and to be informed by physicians and other caregivers of available and realistic patient care options when hospital care is no longer appropriate.

12. The patient has the right to be informed of hospital policies and practices that relate to patient care, treatment, and responsibilities.

---

*Source:* Reprinted with permission of the American Hospital Association, © 1992.

## Patient Self-Determination Acts (Advance Directives)

Several documents executed by the patient, called self-determination documents or advance directives, state the patient's intentions for health care–related decisions and in some cases name another person as **proxy** to make decisions for the patient. An **advance directive** is a written statement in which people state the type and amount of care they wish to receive during a terminal illness and as death approaches. These documents include living wills, durable power of attorney, and organ donation. Self-determination documents provide protection for both the patient and the physician. The patients obtain assurance that their health care wishes will be followed at the point in time when they are unable to express their intent, and physicians have an assurance that they are acting within the guidelines for care set by their patients. Table 5-4 contains a brief summary of advance directives.

### Living Will

A **living will** allows patients to set forth their intentions as to their treatment and care. A patient may request that life-sustaining treatments and artificial nutritional support, such as tube feedings, either be used or not be used to prolong life. The patient may

**TABLE 5–4   Advance Directives**

| Type | Description |
|---|---|
| Living will | Document that a person drafts before becoming incompetent or unable to make health care decisions. |
| Durable power of attorney for health care | A legal document that empowers another person (proxy) to make health care decisions for an incompetent patient. It goes into effect after the person becomes incompetent and only pertains to health care decisions. |
| Uniform Anatomical Gift Act | All states have some form of this law. It allows persons 18 years or older and of sound mind to make a gift of any part of their body for purposes of medical research or transplantation. |
| Do not resuscitate (DNR) order | This is an order placed into a person's medical chart or medical record. It indicates that the person does not wish to be resuscitated if breathing stops. |

also request that no extraordinary medical treatment, such as being placed on a respirator (ventilator), be given. In this case, the physician puts a do not resuscitate (DNR) order in the patient's medical chart in either the hospital or nursing home. This living will document gives patients the legal right to direct the type of care they wish to receive when death is imminent.

Ideally, this process is discussed in the physician's office with patients when they are capable of making the decision. Other family members or significant others can also be part of the discussion and decision process. The living will document must be signed by the patient and witnessed by another person. One copy should be kept in the patient's record. Many patients ask their attorneys to also retain a copy. See Figure 5-3 for a sample of a living will document.

### Durable Power of Attorney

The **durable power of attorney,** when signed by the patient, allows an **agent** or representative to act on behalf of the patient. If the durable power of attorney is for health care only, then the agent may only make health care–related decisions on behalf of the patient.

Because the power of attorney is "durable," the agent's authority continues even if the patient is physically or mentally incapacitated. This document is in effect until canceled by the patient. A copy of the durable power of attorney should also be kept with the patient record. See Figure 5-4 for a sample of a durable power of attorney for health care document.

### Uniform Anatomical Gift Act

The **Uniform Anatomical Gift Act** allows persons 18 years or older and of sound mind to make a gift of any or all body parts for purposes of organ transplantation or medical research. The statute includes two specific safeguards. First, the time of death must be determined by a physician who is not involved in the transplant. Second, no money is allowed to change hands for organ transplantation.

The donor carries a card that has been signed in the presence of two witnesses. In some states, the back of the driver's license has space to indicate the desire to be an organ donor, with space for a signature.

If a person has not indicated a desire to be a donor, the family may consent on the patient's behalf. Generally, if a member of the family opposes the donation of organs, then the physician and hospital do not insist on it, even if the patient signed for the donation to take place. See Chapter 11 for a sample donor card.

Questions that are frequently asked about advance directives include the following:

1. To whom should the advance directives be given? Copies of the advance directives should be given to the personal physician, close relatives, and a close friend. In addition, a copy should be placed in the medical chart if the patient is hospitalized or in a nursing home.
2. Where should advance directives be stored? They should be kept with the patient's personal papers in the home or nursing home setting. It is not recommended that they be stored in a safety deposit box, since they will not be accessible in an emergency.

# Living Will

The Living Will includes the following suggested form:

**Declaration:**

This declaration is made this _____ day of _____ (month, year)

I, _____ being of sound mind, willfully and voluntarily make known my desires that my moment of death shall not be artificially postponed.

If at any time I should have an incurable and irreversible injury, disease, or illness judged to be a terminal condition by my attending physician who has personally examined me and has determined that my death is imminent except for death-delaying procedures, I direct that such procedures which would only prolong the dying process be withheld or withdrawn, and that I be permitted to die naturally with only the administration of medication, sustenance, or the performance of any medical procedure deemed necessary by my attending physician to provide me with comfort care.

In the absence of my ability to give directions regarding the use of such death-delaying procedures, it is my intention that this declaration shall be honored by my family and physician as the final expression of my legal rights to refuse medical or surgical treatment and accept the consequences from such refusal.

Signed _____ Date: _____

City, County and State of Residence _____

The declarant is known to me personally and I believe him or her to be of sound mind. I saw the declarant sign the declaration in my presence, or the declarant acknowledged in my presence that he or she had signed the declaration, and I signed the declaration as a witness in the presence of the declarant. I did not sign the declarant's signature above for or at the direction of the declarant. At the date of this instrument, I am not entitled to any portion of the estate of the declarant according to the laws of intestate succession or to the best of my knowledge and belief, under any will of declarant or other instrument taking effect at declarant's death or directly financially responsible for declarant's medical care.

Witness _____ Date: _____

Witness _____ Date: _____

**FIGURE 5–3**   A living will.

**Power of Attorney** made this _____ day of _____, _____
                                                                (month)              (year)

1. I, _____
   (insert name and address of principal)

hereby appoint _____
(insert name and address of agent)

as my attorney-in-fact (my "agent") to act for me and in my name (in any way I could act in person) to make any and all decisions for me concerning my personal care, medical treatment, hospitalization and health care and to require, withhold, or withdraw any type of medical treatment or procedure, even though my death may ensue. My agent shall have the same access to my medical records that I have, including the right to disclose the contents to others. My agent shall also have full power to make a disposition of any part or all of my body for medical purposes, authorize an autopsy, and direct the disposition of my remains.

2. The powers granted above shall not include the following powers or shall be subject to the following rules or limitations (here you may include any specific limitations you deem appropriate, such as: your own definition of when life-sustaining measures should be withheld; a direction to continue food and fluids or life-sustaining treatment in all events; or instructions to refuse any specific types of treatments that are inconsistent with your religious beliefs or unacceptable to you for any other reasons, such as blood transfusion, electro-convulsive therapy, amputation, psychosurgery, voluntary admission to a mental institution, etc.).

_____

_____

_____

(The subject of life-sustaining treatment is of particular importance. For your convenience in dealing with that subject, some general statements concerning the withholding of life-sustaining treatment are set forth below. If you agree with one of these statements, you may initial that statement, but do not initial more than one):

_____ I do not want my life to be prolonged nor do I want life-sustaining treatment to be provided or
(initialed) continued if my agent believes the burdens of the treatment outweigh the expected benefits. I want my agent to consider the relief of suffering, the expense involved, and the quality as well as the possible extension of my life in making decisions concerning life-sustaining treatment.

_____ I want my life to be prolonged, and I want life-sustaining treatment to be provided or continued
(initialed) unless I am in a coma which my attending physician believes to be irreversible, in accordance with reasonable medical standards at the time of reference. If and when I have suffered irreversible coma, I want life-sustaining treatment to be withheld or discontinued.

**FIGURE 5–4**   Power of attorney for health care.

_____ I want my life to be prolonged to the greatest extent possible without regard to my condition, the (initialed)  chances I have for recovery, or the cost of the procedures.

3. This power of attorney shall become effective on _____

_____

(insert a future date or event in your lifetime, such as a court determination of your disability, when you want this power to first take effect)

4. This power of attorney shall terminate on _____

_____

(insert a future date or event, such as a court determination of your disability, when you want this power to terminate prior to your death)

5. If any agent named by me shall die, become incompetent, resign, refuse to accept the office of agent, or be unavailable, I name the following (each to act alone and successively, in the order named) as successors to such agent:

_____

_____

_____

6. I am fully informed as to all the contents of this form and understand the full import of this grant of powers to my agent,

Signed _____
                                   (principal)

The principal has had an opportunity to read the above form and has signed the form or acknowledged his or her signature or mark on the form in my presence.

_____ Residing at: _____
                  (witness)

**FIGURE 5–4**   Power of attorney for health care *(continued).*

3. How can the advance directive be changed or amended? Any revisions can be made by drawing through the outdated statement in the original document. After a revision is made, it should be dated and signed. An amended copy should be given to the personal physician, family member, and friend.
4. Can the advance directive be revoked? People can revoke their documents by destroying them and asking anyone holding a copy to do the same. Ideally, the request to destroy the advance directive should be sent in writing to all those who hold a copy.
5. What does the law say about advance directives? A federal law, the Patient Self-Determination Act (PSDA) was passed in 1991. Congress has strongly supported a person's right to self-determination before becoming incompetent. However, a patient's request for assisted suicide will not be honored in any state except Oregon.

**MED TIP** It is recommended that all persons place in writing their wishes about what type of treatment they should receive if they become incompetent. The advance directive should be specific about treatments such as CPR, tube feedings, and the use of ventilators.

## RIGHTS OF MINORS

A **minor** is a person who has not reached the age of maturity, which in most states is 18. In most states, minors are unable to give consent for treatment, except in special cases involving pregnancy, request for birth control information, abortion, testing and treatment for sexually transmitted diseases, problems with substance abuse, and a need for psychiatric care. The courts have held that the consent of a minor to medical or surgical treatment is not sufficient. The physician must secure the consent of the parents or someone standing in for the parents (*in loco parentis*) or run the risk of liability. Mature minors and emancipated minors are considered competent and can provide consent for other types of treatment as well. The varying degrees of minors' competency are described in Table 5-5.

**TABLE 5–5** Classification of Minors' Competencies

| Classification | Definition |
|---|---|
| Minor | A person under the age of 18 (termed *infant* under the law.) The signature of a parent or legal guardian is needed for consent to perform a medical treatment in nonemergency situations. |
| Mature minor | A person judged to be mature enough to understand the physician's instructions. Such a minor may seek medical care for treatment of drug or alcohol abuse, contraception, venereal disease, and pregnancy. |
| Emancipated minor | A person between the ages of 15 and 18 who is either married, in the military, or self-supporting and no longer lives under the care of a parent. Parental consent for medical care is not required. Proof of emancipation (for example, marriage certificate) should be included in the medical record. |

## PATIENTS' RESPONSIBILITIES

In addition to the patients' rights, they also have certain obligations. Patients are expected to follow their physician's instructions. They must make follow-up appointments to monitor their treatment and medication use if requested by their physician. Patients must be absolutely honest with the physician about such issues as past medical history, family medical history, and tobacco, drug, and alcohol use. Finally, patients are expected to pay the physician for medical services.

### Consent

**Consent** is the voluntary agreement that a patient gives to allow a medically trained person the permission to touch, examine, and perform a treatment. The two types of consent, informed consent and implied consent, are discussed in the following section.

#### The Doctrine of Informed Consent

**Informed (or expressed) consent** means that the patient agrees to the proposed course of treatment after having been told about the possible consequences of having or not having certain procedures and treatments. See Figure 5-5. The patient's signature on the consent form indicates that the patient understands the limits or risks involved in the pending treatment or surgery as explained by the physician.

The physician, who is solely responsible for providing information to the patient, must carefully explain that in some cases the treatment may even make the patient's condition worse. The Doctrine of Informed Consent requires the physician to explain in understandable language

- the advantages and risks of treatment
- the alternative treatments available to the patient
- potential outcomes of the treatment
- what might occur, both risks and benefits, if treatment is refused

**FIGURE 5–5**   A patient signs a consent form.

In addition, the physician must be honest with the patient and explain the diagnosis, the purpose of the proposed treatment, and the probability that the treatment will be successful. In an emergency situation in which the patient cannot understand the explanation or sign a consent form, the physician providing the care is protected by law.

In a case in Alaska, the court determined that the physician did not fulfill his duty to disclose the risks of breast reduction surgery when he failed to warn the patient about the risk of scarring. In answer to the patient's questions, the physician said that she shouldn't worry and she would be happy with the results. The patient wasn't happy, and she sued the physician and won. (*Korman v. Mallin,* 858 P.2d 1145, Alaska 1993.)

It is very difficult to fully inform a patient about all the things that can go wrong with a treatment. However, the physician must make a reasonable attempt to do so in order for the patient to make an informed decision about treatment. The Canterbury decision is a classic example of two crucial components of informed consent: patients *granting consent* because they have the right to control what is done to their bodies and insisting on *information* so they can make an intelligent decision. For patients to be able to consent in an intelligent manner, they must be given information by the physician that a "reasonable person" in the patient's situation would wish to receive. As such, the amount of information is not based on what the physician believes is relevant but on, what the patient believes he or she needs to hear.

The "reasonable person standard" was used in a 1959 case, *Canterbury v. Spence.* Nineteen-year-old Jerry Canterbury, who suffered from back pain, underwent a surgical procedure to treat a suspected ruptured vertebral disk. On the day following surgery, he fell off the hospital bed while he was trying to urinate and subsequently became paralyzed from the waist down. Emergency surgery reversed some of his paralysis, but he continued to have urological problems. Canterbury sued both the physician (Spence) and the hospital, claiming that he was not fully warned about the risk of falling out of bed and of paralysis. The physician based his defense on a therapeutic privilege claim that he did not think the disclosure of the risk of falling out of bed was necessary. The judge in the district court ordered a directed verdict and told the jury that they must find in favor of the hospital and physician. Upon appeal, a higher court sent the case back to the lower court so that a jury could hear the evidence and make a decision. The court was not clear on whether the fall or the surgery had caused the patient's paralysis. The court also declared that a physician cannot use the therapeutic privilege to justify withholding information the patient requires to make an informed decision. In an unusual decision, the jury also found in favor of the hospital and physician. (*Canterbury v. Spence,* 464 F.2d 772, D.C. 1972.)

 **MED TIP** Except in emergency situations, the process of obtaining consent cannot be delegated by the physician to someone else.

Except in cases of emergency, all patients must sign a consent form before undergoing a surgical procedure. This signed form indicates that the patient has been instructed concerning the risks associated with the procedure. If, after the physician has carefully explained the treatment, the patient acknowledges understanding the explanation and risks and signs the consent form, then, generally, there is some protection from lawsuits. However, patients have sued and won cases in which they were presented the risks of a procedure and signed the form, and then the treatment failed.

A patient's informed consent is limited to those procedures to which the patient has consented. For example, in the case of *Mohr v. Williams,* a woman consented to have an operation on her diseased right ear. After she was unconscious under the anesthetic, the ear surgeon determined that the right ear was not diseased enough to warrant an operation, but the left ear was seriously diseased. He proceeded to operate on the left ear without reviving her to seek permission. The operation was skillfully performed and successful. However, the plaintiff sued for battery and won. The physician appealed that verdict, but the appellate court determined that because the surgery was unauthorized, even though successful, it constituted an assault. (*Mohr v. Williams,* 104 N.W.12, Minn. 1905.)

Procedures in which an informed consent form should be signed include

- minor invasive surgery
- organ donation
- radiological therapy, such as radiation treatment for cancer
- electroconvulsive therapy
- experimental procedures
- chemotherapy
- any procedure with more than a slight risk of harm to the patient

In some circumstances—such as HIV testing, procedures involving reproduction, and major surgical procedures—state laws require that the patient sign an informed consent form. This signed document represents a legal statement in which the patient certifies that the risks, benefits, and alternatives to treatment have been thoroughly explained. The document is an indication that the informed patient enters the treatment through free will and not by means of coercion.

> **MED TIP**   Remember that the patient grants informed consent to the physician. Simply explaining a procedure to the patient does not constitute informed consent. The patient must understand the explanation and agree to the procedure.

Certain categories of patients are judged to be incapable of giving an informed consent. These include minors (other than emancipated minors), the mentally incompetent, and persons who do not understand English.

### Implied Consent

A physician should obtain written consent before treatment whenever possible. However, the law will assume or "imply" a patient's consent. **Implied consent** occurs when patients indicate by their behavior that they are accepting of the procedure. The patient's nonverbal communication may indicate an implied consent for treatment or examination. Because consent means to give permission or approval for something, when a patient is seen for a routine examination, there is implied consent that the physician will touch the person during the examination. Therefore, the touching required for the physical examination would not be considered the crime of battery.

In a famous case involving implied consent, the court declared that a woman had given consent for a vaccination when she extended her arm. (*O'Brien v. Cunard S.S. Co.*, 28 N.E. 266, Mass. 1891.) Implied consent is also assumed in medical emergencies when the patient cannot respond to give consent. In this case, the law assumes that if the patient were able, consent would be given for the emergency procedure. In an Iowa case, the court determined that implied consent existed when a surgeon removed the mangled limb of a patient run over by a train because the procedure was necessary to save the patient's life. (*Jackovach v. A. L. Yocum, Jr.*, 237 N.W. 444, Iowa, 1931.)

> **⊞ MED TIP** Both expressed and implied consent should be informed.

### Exceptions to Consent

There are exceptions to the informed consent doctrine that are unique to each state. Some of the more general exceptions follow:

1. A physician need not inform a patient about risks that are commonly known. For example, physicians need not tell patients that they could choke swallowing a pill.
2. A physician who believes the disclosure of risks may be detrimental to the patient is not required to disclose them. For instance, if a patient has a severe heart condition that may be worsened by an announcement of risks, the physician should not disclose the risks.
3. If the patient asks the physician not to disclose the risks, then the physician is not required to do so.
4. A physician is not required to restore patients to their original state of health, and in some cases, may be unable to do so.
5. A physician may not be able to elicit a cure for every patient.
6. A physician cannot guarantee the successful results of every treatment.

### Refusal to Grant Consent

Adult patients who are conscious and considered to be mentally capable have a right to refuse any medical or surgical treatment. The refusal must be honored no matter what the patient's reasoning: concern about the success of the procedure, lack of confidence in the physician, religious beliefs, or even mere whim. Failure to respect the right of refusal could result in liability for assault and battery. In *Erickson v. Dilgard,* the hospital requested the court to authorize a blood transfusion over the patient's objection. The court held in favor of the patient who refused a blood transfusion, even though the refusal could have resulted in the patient's death. (*Erickson v. Dilgard,* 252 2d 705, N.Y.S. 1962.) The hospital and medical personnel have a responsibility to use reasonable care to protect the patient from touching (assault and battery) when consent has not been granted.

## ROLE OF THE HEALTH CARE CONSUMER

Today's health care consumer is better informed about medicine and treatments than ever before due to an abundance of literature, television programming, and information available on the World Wide Web. However, wise consumers will not self-medicate or offer their medications to family members and friends for their use. Health care personnel must carefully question all patients/consumers about over-the-counter (OTC) medications they may be taking. Many OTC medications, such as aspirin, can have a negative interaction with prescribed medications. Dietary supplements such as herbs and vitamins should also be declared by the patient. The consumer must alert the medical staff to any allergies and adverse reactions to medications.

Health care consumers must be honest with their physicians about prescriptions they may be taking that were prescribed by other doctors. Every patient/consumer should carry a small card listing all medication names and dosages in the event the names are needed for a patient history or in an emergency situation. They should ask questions about their medications and the treatments they are receiving. If they do not understand what they are told, then they should be persistent with the physician or health care professional until they do understand the instructions.

The patient/consumer can assist the physician in prevention of medical errors. Before undergoing any surgical treatment, it is important that the patients, their personal physicians, and their surgeons all are clear on what will be done. Many fail-safe approaches have been instituted by medical professionals to prevent errors. For instance, performing surgery at the wrong site, such as the right knee instead of the left knee, is rare. But to prevent this type of injury to the patient, the American Academy of Orthopedic Surgery urges all its members to sign their initials directly on the site to be operated upon before the surgery.

**MED TIP**   It is important to remember that many patients do not understand medical terminology. They are often ashamed to admit that they either do not understand or cannot hear the instructions. It is the health care professional's duty to make sure that the patient is fully informed.

Errors in taking medications are some of the most problematic concerns for patients. All patient/consumers should be advised to take the following precautions with medications:

■ Carry a list of all medications being taken, including the dosage, along with the name of the pharmacy. List all over-the-counter (OTC) medications, including nutritional supplements and herbal products.
■ Read the label every time a medication is taken.
■ Store medications away from children.
■ Store tubes of ointments or creams away from toothpaste tubes.
■ Never chew, crush, or break capsules unless instructed.
■ Do not share medications with anyone else.

## POINTS TO PONDER

1. Does it surprise you to find out that physicians have the right to select the patients they wish to treat?
2. Can a physician receive a payment from a hospital for referring patients to that particular institution? Why or why not?
3. If a deceased relative signed a statement (Uniform Anatomical Gift Act) requesting that any or all body parts be used for organ transplantation or medical research, can a family member overturn that statement?
4. Do you believe that it is appropriate for a physician to report the unethical conduct of a fellow physician?
5. Do you think that physicians should treat their own family members? Why or why not?
6. Can a nurse obtain consent from a patient for a surgical procedure if the physician is extremely busy handling an emergency case?
7. What can you say to your patient's employer who calls to find out if the employee's medical condition has improved?

## DISCUSSION QUESTIONS

1. Explain what it means when one physician "covers" for another.
2. Describe the three advance directives that a patient can use. When are they appropriate?
3. Jack Black is being treated by Dr. Williams after having fallen off a ladder at work. His employer calls to find out how Jack is doing. Can Dr. Williams discuss Jack's progress with his employer? Why or why not?
4. Dr. Williams is treating a popular performer who has attempted suicide. What statement can Dr. Williams or her staff give to reporters when they call Dr. Williams's office?

## PRACTICE EXERCISES

### Matching

Match the responses in column B with the correct term in column A.

**Column A**

_____ 1. agent
_____ 2. minor
_____ 3. standard of care
_____ 4. implied consent
_____ 5. privileged communication
_____ 6. informed consent

**Column B**

a. commonly known risks
b. consent granted by inference
c. document that allows an agent to represent a patient
d. same skill that is used by other physicians
e. representative acts on patient's behalf

_____ 7. exception to
            consent
_____ 8. right to be informed
_____ 9. durable power
            of attorney
_____ 10.abandonment

f. withdrawing medical care without notice
g. person under 18 years of age
h. "A Patient's Bill of Rights"
i. knowledgeable consent
j. confidential information

## MULTIPLE CHOICE

Select the one best answer to the following statements.

1. A patient rolling up a sleeve to have a blood sample taken is an example of
   a. standard of care
   b. informed consent
   c. implied consent
   d. advance directive
   e. agent

2. A condition in which a patient understands the risks involved by not having a surgical procedure or treatment performed is known as
   a. standard of care
   b. informed consent
   c. implied consent
   d. advance directive
   e. agent

3. The Uniform Anatomical Gift Act is applicable for
   a. persons up to the age of 18
   b. persons 18 years of age and older
   c. persons who are mentally handicapped
   d. very few people
   e. the purpose of selling organs

4. Which of these refers to a physician using the same skill that is used by other physicians in treating patients with the same ailment?
   a. privileged communication
   b. informed consent
   c. implied consent
   d. standard of care
   e. none of the above

5. The physician's rights include
   a. the right to decline to treat a new patient
   b. the ability to receive payment from hospitals for referring patients
   c. the right to protect fellow physicians who are guilty of a deception

d. the right to publish confidential information about a patient if it is in the physician's best interests

e. all of the above

6. In what document are patients able to request the type and amount of artificial nutritional and life-sustaining treatments that should or should not be used to prolong their life?
   a. Uniform Anatomical Gift Act
   b. Medical Patients Rights Act
   c. living will
   d. standard of care
   e. euthanasia

7. The patient's obligations include
   a. honesty about past medical history
   b. payment for medical services
   c. following treatment recommendations
   d. a and c only
   e. a, b, and c

8. Exceptions to informed consent include
   a. telling the patient about the risk involved in not having the procedure
   b. the discussion of sensitive sexual matters
   c. not having to explain risks that are commonly known
   d. all of the above
   e. none of the above

9. The Doctrine of Informed Consent
   a. can be delegated by the physician to a trusted assistant
   b. may have to be waived in the event of an emergency situation
   c. does not have to be signed by every patient
   d. could result in a lawsuit for assault and battery if not performed
   e. b and d only

10. A newspaper reporter seeks information from a receptionist about a prominent personality who has been hospitalized. What information can be given to the reporter?
    a. none
    b. the basic fact that the person is a patient
    c. the name and phone number of the attending physician
    d. a very brief statement about the person's medical condition
    e. there are no restrictions

## PUT IT INTO PRACTICE

Interview someone you know who has recently been a patient. Ask that person to tell you what he or she believes are the patient's responsibilities and the physician's responsibilities. Do these statements agree with those in the textbook? How do they differ?

Search the Web site of the U.S. Department of Health and Human Services (*www.hhs.gov*) and examine "The Patient's Bill of Rights in Medicare and Medicaid." What does the document have to say about the confidentiality of health information?

On the Web site *www.findlaw.com*, click on "Medical Malpractice." Search for an article on "Understanding Informed Consent." According to this article, what are the situations discussed in which informed consent may not be necessary or may be implied?

REFERENCES

American Academy of Orthopaedic Surgeons. 1991. *Advisory statement on orthopaedic surgeons who test positive for human immunodeficiency virus (HIV)*. (March 6).

American Association of Medical Assistants. 1996. *Health care law and ethics*. Chicago.

American Hospital Association. 1992. *A patient's bill of rights*. Chicago.

American Hospital Association. 1985. *Values in conflict: Resolving issues in hospital care: Report of the special committee on biomedical ethics*. Chicago: American Hospital Association, 24.

American Medical Association. 1998. *Code of medical ethics: Current opinions with annotations*. Chicago.

American Medical Association. 1991. *Statement on HIV infected physicians*. (January 17).

Black, H. 2004. *Black's law dictionary*. 8th ed. St. Paul, Minn.: West Publishing.

*CDC National AIDS Clearinghouse*. 1996. Rockville, Md.: CDC National AIDS Clearinghouse.

Cozalos, M. 1978. *Nursing and the law*. Germantown, Md.: Aspen.

Devettere, R. 2000. *Practical decision making in health care ethics*. Washington, D.C.: Georgetown University Press.

Dubler, N., and D. Nimmons. 1992. *Ethics on call*. New York: Harmony Books.

Fletcher, J. 1954. *Morals and medicine*. Boston: Beacon Press.

Flynn, E. 2000. *Issues in health care ethics*. Upper Saddle River, N.J.: Prentice Hall.

Garrett, T., H. Baillie, and R. Garrett. 1993. *Health care ethics*. Upper Saddle River, N.J.: Prentice Hall.

Hackett, T. 1976. Psychological assistance for the dying patient and his family, *Annual review of medicine* 27: 372–3.

Hall, M., and M. Bobinski. 2003. *Health care law and ethics in a nutshell*. St. Paul, Minn.: West Publishing.

Jackson, J. 2001. *Truth, trust and medicine*. New York: Routledge.

Judson, K., and S. Blesie. 1994. *Law and ethics for health occupations*. New York: MacMillan/McGraw.

Kantrowitz, B. 1991. Doctors and AIDS. *Newsweek*. July 1, 48–57.

Lipman, M. 1994. *Medical law & ethics*. Upper Saddle River, N.J.: Prentice Hall.

Lo, B. 1995. *Resolving ethical dilemmas: A guide for clinicians*. New York: Lippincott Williams & Wilkins.

Lo. B., and R. Steinbrook. 1992. Health care workers infected with the human immunodeficiency virus: The next steps. *JAMA*. 267: 1000–1005.

Mangione, C., J. Gerberding, and S. Cummings. 1991. Occupational exposure to HIV: Frequency rates of underreporting of percutaneous and mucocutaneous exposures by medical housestaff. *American Journal of medicine* 90: 85–90.

Mappes, T., and D. DeGrazia. 2001. *Biomedical ethics*. New York: McGraw Hill.

McConnell, T. 1997. *Moral issues in health care: An introduction to medical ethics*. Albany, N.Y.: Wadsworth.

Munson, R. 1996. *Intervention and reflection: Basic issues in medical ethics*. New York: Wadsworth.

National Commission on AIDS. 1992. *Preventing HIV transmission in health care settings*. Washington, D.C.: National Commission on AIDS.

Oken, Donald. 1961. What to tell cancer patients: A study of medical attitudes, *JAMA* 175 (April 1): 1120–1128.

Pallone, N., and J. Hennessy. 1995. *Fraud and fallible judgment.* New Brunswick, N.J.: Transaction Publishers.

Snell, M. 1991. *Bioethical dilemmas in health occupations.* Lake Forest, Ill.: MacMillan/McGraw.

Study: Hospital lapses killing 32,000 yearly. 2003. *Chicago Tribune,* sec. 1 (October 8) 16.

U.S. National Research Council. 1993. *Social impact of AIDS.* Washington, D.C.: National Academy Press.

Veatch, R. 2000. *The basics of bioethics.* Upper Saddle River, N.J.: Prentice Hall.

## CASE STUDY

Dr. Williams has just telephoned Carrie, her medical assistant, explaining that she is behind schedule doing rounds at one of the hospitals. She has asked Carrie to do her a favor and interpret Mrs. Harris's EKG, sign her name, and fax the report to Mrs. Harris's internist, who is expecting the results.

1. Given the scope of Carrie's education and training, would this "favor" fall within her scope of practice? Would it make a difference if Carrie were a nurse?

_____

_____

_____

_____

2. Would any portion of Dr. Williams's request fall within the scope of practice for Carrie?

_____

_____

_____

_____

3. Does Dr. Williams's request violate the physician–patient relationship? Why or why not?

_____

_____

_____

_____

4. What, if anything, should Carrie say to Dr. Williams?

_____

_____

_____

_____

CHAPTER **6**

# Professional Liability and Medical Malpractice

## LEARNING OBJECTIVES

1. Define the glossary terms.
2. Define the four Ds of negligence for the physician.
3. Discuss the meaning of *respondeat superior* for the physician and the employee.
4. Discuss the meaning of *res ipsa loquitur*.
5. Explain the term *liability* and what it means for the physician and other health care professionals.
6. List ten ways to prevent malpractice.
7. State two advantages to arbitration.
8. Discuss three types of damage awards.
9. Describe two types of malpractice insurance.
10. Explain the law of agency.

## KEY TERMS

Affirmative defenses
Alternative dispute resolution (ADR)
Arbitration
Arbitrator
Assumption of risk
Borrowed servant doctrine
Cap
Claims-made insurance
Comparative negligence
Compensatory damages

Contributory negligence
Damages
Dereliction
Direct cause
Duty
Feasance
Fraud
Liable
Malfeasance
Malpractice
Mediation

Misfeasance
Negligence
Nominal damages
Nonfeasance
Occurrence insurance
Proximate
Punitive damages
*Res ipsa loquitur*
*Res judicata*
Rider
Settle

## INTRODUCTION

Health care professionals need to be on constant alert for practices that could result in injury to the patient. Not only is the injury a painful process, it can also be a life-threatening one. All health care professionals must realize that they are responsible for their actions. The physician/employer also assumes responsibility for the employees through the doctrine of *respondeat superior.* While people have always been liable for their own conduct, the courts are now finding that everyone associated with negligent actions is liable for damages (monetary award to the plaintiff). This chapter includes numerous examples of court cases to illustrate the wide variety of lawsuits and negligence cases.

 **MED TIP**   All health care workers are responsible for their actions even though the doctrine of *respondeat superior* states that an employer is also liable for injury to a patient.

## PROFESSIONAL NEGLIGENCE AND MEDICAL MALPRACTICE

Professional misconduct or demonstration of an unreasonable lack of skill with the result of injury, loss, or damage to the patient is considered **malpractice.** It means the physician was negligent or failed to perform professional duties to an accepted standard of care. For example, a physician is held to a higher standard of care than a nurse, medical assistant, or phlebotomist. **Negligence,** which is an unintentional action, occurs when a person either performs or fails to perform an action that a reasonable person would or would not have committed in a similar situation. A jury in a negligence trial would have to determine if a reasonable person would have done the same action. Malpractice is the wrongdoing or negligence committed by a professional person, such as a medical professional.

 **MED TIP**   Health care professionals are expected to use "reasonable skill" when providing care and treatment to patients. This means that not everyone will perform an action in exactly the same way, since each person's skill level will vary by small amounts. However, an "unreasonable lack of skill" is unacceptable, since it demonstrates that a person does not have the required skills or is simply being careless. This lack of skill can result in injury to the patient.

However, for most people, the tort (civil wrong) of negligence and malpractice is often considered to be the same thing. Every mistake or error, however, is not considered malpractice. Therefore, when a treatment or diagnosis does not turn out well, the physician is not necessarily negligent. Rather, physicians must act within the standard of care appropriate for their special field or their particular level of medicine. All health care providers are held to this same standard in their field of practice in their particular locality. Physicians and health care workers who fail to act reasonably in the same circumstances are negligent.

# THE TORT OF NEGLIGENCE

Both actions and inactions (omissions) can be considered negligence. Failure to provide clear instructions regarding treatment or the use of medications is an omission that could result in a disastrous outcome for the patient. Providing incorrect information is also considered negligence.

 **MED TIP** Remember that you can be sued even if you are right. Patients can be injured through no fault of the medical personnel.

Professional liability malpractice claims are classified in three ways: malfeasance, misfeasance, and nonfeasance. These terms all stem from the word **feasance,** which means doing an act or performing a duty.

**Malfeasance** refers to performing a wrong and illegal act. For example, it is malfeasance for a nurse or medical assistant to prescribe a medical treatment or medication over the telephone. Only the physician can prescribe medications and treatments. Medical personnel must be especially aware of malfeasance when they offer advice such as, "Try giving your child aspirin to bring down the fever." The term malfeasance is often used when a public official has done something illegal.

**Misfeasance** is the improper performance of an otherwise proper or lawful act. An example of misfeasance occurs when a poor technique is used by a nurse, medical assistant, or phlebotomist to perform a venipuncture and the patient suffers nerve damage.

**Nonfeasance** is the failure to perform a necessary action. For instance, if a medical assistant or nurse is trained in cardiopulmonary resuscitation (CPR) but does not administer this lifesaving technique when a patient collapses in the physician's waiting room and requires CPR, that would be nonfeasance.

## The Four Ds of Negligence

In order to obtain a judgment for negligence against a physician (defendant), the patient (plaintiff) must be able to show what are called the "four Ds"—duty, dereliction of duty, direct or proximate cause, and damages:

- Duty—takes place when a physician and client relationship is established.
- Dereliction of duty—the physician or health care provider failed to provide a correct standard of care to the patient.
- Direct or proximate cause—the dereliction or breach of duty was the direct cause of the patient's injury.
- Damages—injuries caused by the defendant for which compensation (financial or otherwise) is due.

### Duty

**Duty** is the responsibility established by the physician–patient relationship. The patient must prove that this relationship had been established. When the patient has made an appointment and has been seen by the physician, a relationship has been established. Further office visits and treatment also establish that the physician has a duty or obligation to the patient.

The duty of due care uses the reasonable person standard, which is that everyone owes a duty to act as a reasonable, prudent person of average intelligence would under the same or similar circumstances. Those in special professions, such as physicians, nurses, and medical assistants, are held to a standard of care exercised by similar professionals in the same or similar community. This standard never varies for a particular professional, so a physician is held to the same standard as another reasonable and prudent physician, a nurse is held to the same standards as other nurses, and so on.

The standard of care for physicians and other health care professionals is determined according to what members of the same profession would do in a similar situation within the same geographic area. For example, radiologists are held to the same standard of care or performance that other radiologists in a similar circumstance would perform. Nurses, medical assistants, laboratory technicians, and physician's assistants are all held to a standard of care within their own discipline.

### Dereliction or Neglect of Duty

**Dereliction,** or neglect, of duty is a physician's failure to act as any ordinary and prudent physician (a peer) within the same community would act in a similar circumstance. To prove dereliction or neglect of duty, a patient would have to prove that the physician's performance or treatment did not comply with the acceptable standard of care. For example, if a physician does not properly inform patients about all the risks associated with surgical procedures, then the physician has neglected, or breached, his or her duty to the patients. If the outcome of the procedure is one that the patient did not anticipate or was not informed about, then this may constitute grounds for a lawsuit claiming dereliction of duty.

### Direct or Proximate Cause

**Direct cause** is the continuous sequence of events, unbroken by any intervening cause, that produces an injury and without which the injury would not have occurred. Direct or **proximate** cause means that the injury was proximately or closely related to the physician's (defendant's) negligence. It does not necessarily mean the closest event in time or space to the injury, and it may not be the event that set the injury in motion. Proximate cause means that there were no intervening forces between the defendant's action(s) and the plaintiff's (patient's) injury—hence a cause-and-effect relationship. Proximate cause of injury requires the patient to prove that the physician's or agent's (such as a nurse's) dereliction of duty was the direct cause for the injury that resulted.

An example of proximate cause would be if a medical assistant or laboratory technician, who works under the direct supervision of a doctor, performs a venipuncture on a patient to obtain a blood sample, and subsequently the patient complains of a loss of feeling in the arm that was used for the venipuncture. To prove proximate cause, the plaintiff (patient) would have to prove that there was no intervening cause, such as a tennis injury or damage from an accident, that occurred between the time the blood was drawn and the time the nerve damage happened.

**MED TIP**   Proximate cause refers to the *last* negligent act that contributed to a patient's injury, without which the injury would not have resulted.

*Preponderance of Evidence*   One side of a case must demonstrate a greater weight of evidence than the other side. The plaintiff must prove that it is more likely than not that the defendant, in this case the physician, has caused the injury. If the defendant demonstrates more convincing evidence than does the plaintiff, then the case will be found for the defendant. If both sides demonstrate equally convincing evidence, then the case will also be found in favor of the defendant.

**MED TIP**   To have a preponderance of evidence to find in favor of the plaintiff, the jury believes that it is at least 51 percent likely the defendant caused the injury.

*Res Ipsa Loquitur*   The doctrine of **res ipsa loquitur,** meaning "the thing speaks for itself," applies to the law of negligence. This doctrine tells us that the breach (neglect) of duty is so obvious that it doesn't need further explanation, or it "speaks for itself." For instance, leaving a sponge in the patient during abdominal surgery, dropping a surgical instrument onto the patient, and operating on the wrong body part are all examples of *res ipsa loquitur.* None of these would have occurred without the negligence of someone. *Res ipsa loquitur,* often called *res ipsa* or RIL, is so obvious that expert witnesses are usually not necessary.

Under the doctrine of *res ipsa loquitur,* the burden of proof falls to the defendant, who must prove that the patient's injury was not caused by negligence. The judge decides in pretrial hearings if a case can be tried on the basis of *res ipsa.* Three conditions must be present:

1. The injury could not have occurred without negligence.
2. The defendant had total and direct control over the cause of injury, and the duty had to be within the scope of the duty owed to the patient or injured party.
3. The patient did not, and could not, contribute to the cause of the injury.

For example, a patient under anesthesia when the alleged injury occurred could not have contributed to the cause of the injury. However, if before receiving the anesthetic, the patient neglected to inform the physician about a condition that could be adversely affected by the procedure or anesthesia, such as a diabetic condition or eating a full meal, then this may rule out *res ipsa loquitur,* since the patient may have contributed to the cause.

### Damages

**Damages** refer to any injuries caused by the defendant. Patients seek recovery, or compensation, for a variety of damages:

- permanent physical disability
- permanent mental disability
- loss of enjoyment of life
- personal injuries
- past and future loss of earnings
- medical and hospital expenses
- pain and suffering

 **MED TIP**    If the patient does not receive any injury, then there is no negligence case.

The court may award compensatory damages to pay for the patient's injuries. Other monetary awards fall into the categories of special compensatory, punitive, and nominal damages. Some states have placed a limit, or **cap,** on the amount of money that can be awarded in a medical malpractice case.

**Compensatory damages** are payment for the actual loss of income, emotional pain and suffering, or injury suffered by the patient. These losses are both current and future, and include lost wages and profits. The court will consider the amount of physical disability, loss of earnings to date, and any future loss of earnings to determine the amount of the monetary award.

Special compensatory damages refer to a monetary award to compensate the patient for any losses that were not directly caused by the negligence. For example, the patient might incur additional medical expenses for physical therapy to regain strength after being bedridden due to the original injury.

**Punitive damages,** also called exemplary damages, are monetary awards by a court to a person who has been harmed in an especially malicious or willful way. This monetary award is not related to the actual cost of the injury or harm suffered. Its purpose is to serve as punishment to the offender and a warning to others not to engage in malicious behavior. Punitive damages can result in a large cash amount. The punitive awards have been growing substantially over the past decade and may reach into the millions.

**Nominal damages** refer to a slight or token payment to a patient to demonstrate that, while there may not have been any physical harm done, the patient's legal rights were violated. The award may be as little as one dollar. However, most states currently require actual damages in the form of compensatory payments rather than just nominal damages or payments.

*Wrongful-Death Statutes*   If a patient's death has been caused by the physician's negligence, the deceased person's dependents and heirs may sue for wrongful death. Some states have wrongful-death statutes that allow the deceased person's beneficiaries (estate) and dependents to collect money from the offender to compensate for the loss of future earnings to the estate. A plaintiff in a wrongful-death suit does not have to prove that he or she was completely dependent on the deceased person for support, but only that the death resulted in a financial loss. To win such a case, the plaintiff must prove that the defendant's actions were the "proximate," or immediate, cause of death. Some states, such as Iowa, Missouri, and Pennsylvania, allow the surviving spouse and children of a wrongful-death victim to sue for compensatory damages for the pain and suffering they experienced upon the death of their loved one. However, many states have placed a cap on the amount of money that can be awarded in wrongful-death cases.

The courts do not allow one member of a family to sue another member for wrongful death. In common law practice, a government is also immune from wrongful-death suits, although some state governments now allow suits brought against state employees.

*Fraud*    Contrary to negligence, which is an unintentional action that could lead to patient injury, **fraud** is the deliberate concealment of the facts from another person for unlawful or unfair gain. Fraud in health care includes a wide range of illegal actions: illegal billing for services that may or may not have been rendered; receiving kickbacks for making referrals for Medicare and Medicaid patients; dishonesty when conducting medical research; embezzlement, particularly in the medical office; and the illegal sale of drugs.

Fraud in the health care setting is one of the fastest growing criminal areas. This is especially true in the medical office. Therefore, it is paramount that medical assistants remain vigilant when performing their duties. There have been many cases in which medical assistants were requested by their physician/employers to perform fraudulent acts. In every case, the medical assistant could have refused to perform the actions that were either beyond his or her scope of practice or obviously fraudulent.

In the case of *People v. Gandotra,* Dr. Gandotra hired three medical assistants to provide care for patients in his clinic. One of the medical assistants prescribed controlled substances (Diazepan and Fiorinal with Codeine no. 3) to patients and to undercover federal agents. Dr. Gandotra billed the state of California under his provider number for the medical assistant's unauthorized services. The court stated that the medical assistants were not licensed to practice medicine or write prescriptions. Evidence was also presented that Dr. Gandotra had presented claims for payment for services that were never rendered. His wife, Rita, processed some of the fraudulent claims. As a result of the fraudulent billing practices, Dr. Gandotra and his wife were both charged and convicted of felonies. They paid a fine of $30,000. The medical assistants were not charged with criminal action. (*People v. Gandotra,* 14 Cal. Rptr. 2d 896, 11th Cal. App. 1992.)

In *People v. Scofield,* the Aetna Casualty and Surety Company charged that Scofield, the patient, along with a physician, presented the company with a fraudulent insurance claim. A medical assistant, who handled the overload of medical insurance work for the office, was employed by the physician. The physician instructed her that his patients were to be billed for treatments three times a week, regardless of whether actual treatment was given. A second medical assistant stated during the grand jury hearing that the same physician told her that his personal injury patients were not put in the regular bookkeeping system; these patients had separate cards. She was told to prepare bills for these patients showing treatments that were not reflected on the actual patient records. The physician told her that it was office policy to submit fraudulent bills to insurance companies for at least $100 to $300 worth of treatment, and then the defendant (Scofield), the patient, and "we" (the physician and the medical assistant) would each get $100. The court determined that the medical assistant did prepare the bills with guilty knowledge of their fraudulent nature and purpose. However, she was not convicted of aiding in the actual fraud. In this case, Scofield was sentenced to serve 90 days in the county jail. The physician was not charged in this trial. The significance of this case for medical personnel is that the two medical assistants are clearly named even though they were not charged in the fraud. (*People v. Scofield,* 95 Cal. Rptr, 405, Cal. App. 1971.)

In *United States v. Busse, Dey, Lupulescu, and Failla,* the defendants were charged with participating in a scheme to generate fraudulent billings to Blue Cross and Blue Shield of Michigan from their five medical/chiropractic health clinics. The chiropractors (Busse and Dey) would see the patients and then refer them to the medical side of the clinic, knowing that no physician would be present to examine them. Instead, several medical assistants became involved in the case when they used Dr. Lupulescu's "standing medical orders" (SMOs) to take the patient's medical history, record the patient complaints, and order medical tests, including EKGs, ultrasound, and blood and urinalysis tests. Blue Cross and Blue Shield were then billed for all of these tests. Dr. Lupulescu visited the clinic one afternoon a week to see only the returning patients. His new patients were routinely seen only by the medical assistants, who would then order the tests in conjunction with his SMOs. He was indicted on 68 counts and was convicted on 48 counts. Dr. Lupulescu was sentenced to fifteen concurrent four-year prison terms and fined $6,000. Dr. Dey was sentenced to five concurrent 18-month terms and fined $5,000. Dr. Busse was convicted of aiding in the fraud but was not sentenced to prison or fined. Mr. Failla, the business manager of the clinics, was also convicted of criminal action. The medical assistants were not charged with fraud. (*U.S. v. Busse, Dey, Lupulescu, and Failla,* 833 F.2d 1014, U.S. App. 1987.)

It appears that the medical assistants involved in the above cases were aware of the fraudulent activities taking place in their office or clinic. They were not charged in these cases. However, this is no guarantee that they will always be protected under the doctrine of *respondeat superior.*

## Office of Inspector General

One of the major players in the war against health care fraud, such as false insurance claims, is the Office of Inspector General (OIG). This office was created to protect the programs under the Department of Health and Human Services (HHS), such as Medicare and Medicaid, from fraudulent activities. The OIG reports to the Secretary of State and Congress problems with health care programs and recommendations on how to correct them. The Office of Counsel to the Inspector General

- provides legal services to the OIG.
- represents the OIG in civil cases tried under the False Claims Act.
- imposes money penalties on health care providers found guilty of fraud.
- issues fraud alerts.

The OIG accepts public comments relating to its alerts. The address is Department of Health and Human Services, Office of Inspector General, 330 Independence Avenue, SW., Room 5246, Washington, D.C. 20201.

**MED TIP**    Remember that every person has the ability to say "no" when asked to perform an activity that is unethical, illegal, or against his or her own value system.

## DEFENSE TO MALPRACTICE SUITS

After the plaintiff's case has been presented, the defendant puts forward a defense, called an **affirmative defense,** which allows the defendant (usually a physician or hospital) to present evidence that the patient's condition was the result of factors other than the defendant's negligence. The attorney for the physician will suggest defenses that can be used to support the physician's side in a lawsuit relating to negligence. The most frequently used defense to negligence is denial. Other defenses include assumption of risk, contributory negligence, comparative negligence, borrowed servant, ignorance of the facts and unintentional wrongs, statute of limitations, and Good Samaritan laws.

 **MED TIP**    It is easier to prevent negligence than it is to defend it.

### Denial Defense

The burden of proof, with the exception of *res ipsa loquitur,* is on the plaintiff (patient), who must prove that the defendant (physician) did the wrongful or negligent action. Therefore, the most common defense in a malpractice lawsuit is denial on the part of the physician. It is up to a jury to determine if the plaintiff proved the defendant most likely caused the injury. The physician may bring in expert witnesses to substantiate that the standard of care was met.

### Assumption of Risk

**Assumption of risk** is the legal defense that prevents a plaintiff from recovering damages if the plaintiff voluntarily accepts a risk associated with the activity. For example, when people continue to smoke after reading health warnings found on cigarette packaging, then they accept the risk when they smoke. A medical professional who agrees to treat a person with a communicable disease knows and assumes the risk of contracting the disease. A patient who understands the risks associated with open-heart surgery and signs a consent form has assumed those risks.

In order for this defense to be valid, the plaintiff must know and understand the risk that is involved, and the choice to accept that risk must be voluntary. Patients should be asked to sign an authorization for all procedures indicating that they understand the risks involved, accept that risk, and give their consent for treatment.

**MED TIP**    The physician is responsible for explaining the risks of a treatment or procedure. Physicians can delegate this function to a nurse, medical assistant, or physician's assistant, but the physician still retains overall responsibility.

## Contributory Negligence

**Contributory negligence** refers to conduct on the part of the plaintiff that is a contributing cause of an injury. If it is determined that the patient was fully, or in part, at fault for the injury, the patient is barred from recovering monetary damages.

For example, in *Jenkins v. Bogalusa Community Medical Center,* a patient being treated for arthritis was told not to get out of bed without ringing for assistance. He nonetheless attempted to get out of bed and fell, fracturing his hip; he subsequently died from an embolism following hip surgery. The court ruled that he contributed to his own death by failing to follow instructions. (*Jenkins v. Bogalusa Comm. Medical Ctr.,* 340 So.2d 1065, La. Ct. App. 1976.)

 **MED TIP**    The *Jenkins v. Bogalusa Community Medical Center* case illustrates the importance of specific and timely charting. Instructions given to the patient should always be noted in the patient's record.

## Comparative Negligence

**Comparative negligence** is a defense very similar to contributory negligence in that the plaintiff's own negligence helped cause the injury. However, contrary to contributory negligence, which is a complete bar to recovery (meaning the plaintiff will recover nothing), comparative negligence allows the plaintiff to recover damages based on the amount of the defendant's fault. For instance, if a physician is 60 percent at fault and the patient is 40 percent at fault and the patient suffers $100,000 in damages, the physician will be required to pay $60,000.

A defense of comparative negligence has been used in cases in which the physician may be proven negligent, but the patient, in failing to continue with follow-up care by the physician, was also negligent, which added to the patient's injury.

## Borrowed Servant

The **borrowed servant doctrine** is a special application of *respondeat superior.* This occurs when an employer lends an employee to someone else. The employee remains the "servant" of the employer, but under the borrowed servant doctrine, the employer is not liable for any negligence caused by the employee while in the service of a temporary employer.

For instance, if a hospital (the employer) allows an operating room nurse to assist a surgeon while in the operating room, the surgeon is "the captain of the ship" and directs the work of the operating room nurse. Thus, under the borrowed servant doctrine, the surgeon, not the hospital, is legally responsible for the nurse's actions. However, the employee still maintains responsibility for his or her actions.

## Ignorance of Facts and Unintentional Wrongs

A health care professional should have an understanding of what is right and wrong under the law. Arguing that a negligent act was unintentional is not a defense. If this were a legitimate defense, everyone would use it.

 **MED TIP**   Remember that ignorance of the law is not a defense.

## Statute of Limitations

As discussed in Chapter 3, all states have statutes of limitations, which set a time period for the injured party to file a lawsuit. If too many years have passed since the events causing the injury, it is difficult to gather witnesses; and the witnesses may have difficulty in correctly recalling what happened. In general, the statute of limitations for negligence is from one to three years, depending on the state.

An exception to the statute of limitations is the rule of discovery. The statute of limitations does not begin to "run" until the injury is discovered. In addition, it will not begin to "run" if fraud is involved. In a Michigan case, a patient who had a thyroidectomy suffered paralyzed vocal cords after the surgery. He was told it was due to a calcium deficiency when, in fact, the vocal cords had been accidentally cut during surgery. The statute of limitations would have run out in this case; but since fraud (hiding the presence of the cut vocal cords) was present, the statute did not begin to "run" until the patient discovered the fraud. (*Buchanan v. Kull*, 35 N.W.2d 351, Mich. 1949.)

### Res Judicata

**Res judicata** means "the thing has been decided" or "a matter decided by judgment." Thus, if a court decides a case, then the case is firmly decided between the two parties, and the plaintiff cannot bring a new lawsuit on the same subject against the same defendant.

# PROFESSIONAL LIABILITY

In the largest sense of the term, everyone is legally responsible or **liable** for his or her own actions. Even children have caused injury to others. All homeowners, business owners, and health care employers are responsible for accidents and other harmful acts that take place on their property or premises.

## Civil Liability Cases

As discussed, physicians and other medical professionals may be sued under a variety of legal theories, including negligence and *respondeat superior.* Unfortunately, a fear of such lawsuits has influenced the practice of medicine. Some physicians and hospitals have been reluctant to withdraw or withhold treatment at the specific directive of the patient or family. A clearly stated refusal for continued treatment by an informed patient should relieve the physician and hospital of the duty to continue treatment. In fact, if treatment is continued after it has been refused by the patient, the health care provider could be liable for battery. In a 1990 case, a federal appellate court ruled that a physician who implanted a Hickman catheter into a minor child, based on a court order, could be sued for the death of the child two weeks later from a massive pulmonary embolus. The court ruled the physician committed battery because the court order was not properly obtained and therefore was invalid. The father of the child, who had opposed the Hickman implant, was eventually awarded $2 million.  (*Bendiburg v. Dempsey,* 19 F.3d. 557, 11th Cir. 1994.)

 **MED TIP**   Medical personnel must listen to and respect the patient's wishes.

## Physical Conditions of the Premises

Medical offices, clinics, and hospitals are required to exercise the same standard of care as any other business that has a public facility and grounds. An institution may be liable when regulatory standards have been violated, such as when an accident occurs in a clinic that has not followed regulations for maintaining a safe environment for patients who are disabled. The institution may not be liable, however, if the plaintiff was aware of a situation that could cause an injury and then chose to ignore it. For example, if someone walks on a wet floor in spite of the caution sign, it is at his or her own risk.

Lawsuits involving the physical condition of hospitals and other medical facilities have involved such cases as broken steps, malfunctioning elevators and doors, and defective carpets. Every staff member must take responsibility for reporting and correcting defects that could cause injury.

## Promise to Cure

A promise to cure a patient with a certain procedure or form of treatment is considered under contract law rather than civil law. In a Michigan case, a physician promised to cure a bleeding ulcer, and even though the physician was not negligent in the care of the patient, he was found liable for breach of contract when the treatment was unsuccessful. After this case, many states passed laws requiring that all promises to cure must be in writing.  (*Guilmet v. Campbell,* 385 Mich. 57, 188 N.W.2d 601, 1971.)

 **MED TIP**   Always use caution when speaking to patients. A comment such as "I'm sure you'll be fine" could be taken as a verbal contract.

## Law of Agency

The law of agency governs the legal relationship formed between two people when one person agrees to perform work for another person. For instance, in a medical office, the list of agents for the physician includes nurses, medical assistants, technicians, and even the cleaning staff if they are hired and paid directly by the physician. In order to protect the physician/employer from liability for negligence under the doctrine of *respondeat superior,* the health care professional should

- have a written job description that clearly defines the responsibilities, duties, and skills necessary for the job.
- use extreme care when performing his or her job.
- carry out only those procedures for which he or she is trained.
- be honest about any errors or inability to perform a procedure.

One exception to the law of agency is the relationship between the pharmacist and the physician. A pharmacist is not an agent of the physician because the pharmacist is not hired, fired, or paid directly by the physician. Therefore, the law of agency has not been established.

## Who Is Liable?

Under the doctrine of *respondeat superior,* or "let the master answer," discussed in Chapter 3, the employer is liable for the consequences of the employee's actions committed in the scope of employment. The employer may not have done anything wrong, yet still is liable. For example, if a medical assistant in a physician's office injures a patient while taking a blood sample, the physician/employer can be liable for the action even if the medical assistant was properly selected, well trained, and suitably assigned to the task. *Respondeat superior* does not assign any responsibility to anyone other than the employer. Therefore, the immediate supervisor, if he or she is not the employer, of the medical assistant is not the responsible party.

The doctrine of *respondeat superior* was implemented for the benefit of the patient, not the employee. It is not meant to protect the employee. Thus, the patient can sue both the physician and employee. If both are found liable by the court, the plaintiff may seek to collect money from either party; however, the plaintiff cannot collect twice. The employer, if not at fault but forced to pay the plaintiff, can turn around and sue the employee for those damages (*St. John's Reg. Health Ctr. v. American Cas. Co.,* 980 F.2d 1222, 8th Cir. 1992.)

Because a pharmacist is not an agent of a physician, the doctrine of *respondeat superior* does not apply to injuries a pharmacist causes.

## Liability Insurance

In order to protect against the risk of being sued and ultimately held liable for the plaintiff's injuries, most physicians carry liability and malpractice insurance. Liability insurance is a contract by which one person promises to compensate or reimburse another if he or she suffers a loss from a specific cause or a negligent act. Many insurance plans are contingent on the insured person practicing good safety habits. For example, liability coverage for buildings may be contingent on having a good fire alarm system.

In most cases, employers have a general liability policy to cover acts of their employees during the course of carrying out their duties. Some physicians carry a **rider,** or addition, to the policy that covers any negligence on the part of their assistants. For example, if a patient falls and breaks a bone while getting off the exam table, even though a medical assistant had warned the patient to sit up slowly and use the footstool, the insurance company might **settle,** or come to an agreement about the case, even though negligence was not found.

The two major types of liability insurance are claims-made insurance and occurrence insurance.

- **Claims-made insurance** covers the insured party for only the claims made during the time period the policy is in effect (or policy year). For example, if an injury occurred in one year but the claim for liability insurance coverage was made a year later, then the claim would be denied. It is therefore important with claims-made insurance to file claims reports in a timely manner, especially at the time of the policy's year end.
- **Occurrence insurance** (also called claims-incurred insurance) covers the insured party for all injuries and incidents that occurred while the policy was in effect (policy year), regardless of when they are reported to the insurer or the claim was made. Under this type of policy, if an injury occurred in one year when the policy was in effect, but the claim against the physician was made two years later, the occurrence liability insurance would cover the claim. With occurrence insurance, it is important to clearly document when an event took place.

## Malpractice Insurance

Since physicians treat the human body, not all medical outcomes are predictable or desirable—sometimes through no fault of the physician. Therefore, physicians carry malpractice insurance to cover any damages they must pay if they are sued for malpractice and lose. All licensed medical professionals such as nurses and pharmacists should carry malpractice insurance. Unlicensed health care personnel, such as medical assistants, are usually covered under their physician/employer's policy. However, due to the litigious nature of today's medical practice, many medical assistants also carry their own malpractice insurance coverage.

Malpractice insurance is expensive. Depending on the type of medical practice, it can cost more than $100,000 a year. Coverage for obstetricians and orthopedic surgeons is among the most expensive. Most physicians carry a rider to these policies that covers malpractice suits based on injuries caused by employees and assistants during the course of carrying out their duties. Such coverage is important, again, because of the doctrine of *respondeat superior.*

## ARBITRATION

The process of **arbitration,** which involves submitting a dispute to a person other than a judge, is becoming a popular means for resolving a civil dispute. This third person, called an **arbitrator,** issues a binding decision after hearing both sides present witnesses and facts or evidence relating to their case. However, for the arbitrator's decision to be binding, both parties (the patient and physician) must agree ahead of time to accept the decision of the arbitrator. The selection of an arbitrator must be agreed upon by both sides. This can be a time-consuming process.

Using methods other than going to court to solve civil disputes is called **alternative dispute resolution (ADR).** In addition to arbitration, these methods include **mediation** and a combination of the two methods referred to as med-arb. Mediation involves using the opinion of a neutral third person for a nonbinding decision. The mediator listens to both sides of the dispute and then assists the parties in finding a solution. Using the arbitration, mediation, or med-arb methods for deciding a civil case can save money and time.

## LIABILITY OF OTHER HEALTH PROFESSIONALS

Not all cases of employee negligence are covered under the doctrine of *respondeat superior.* Also, physicians are not the only medical professionals liable for negligence. The following discussion summarizes some cases illustrating negligence lawsuits against other medical professionals.

### Dental Assistant

In a South Carolina case, a patient sued a dental clinic and a dental assistant after the assistant, who was not supervised by the dentist, cut the patient's tongue with a sharp instrument. The court held that the dental assistant performed a breach of duty to the patient. The clinic was also held liable. (*Hickman v. Sexton Dental Clinic*, P.A. 367 S.E.2d. 453, S.C. CT. App. 1988.)

### Laboratory Technician

Medical employees who make repeated errors are not only liable for their errors but also subject to discharge. For instance, in *Barnes Hospital v. Missouri Commission on Human Rights,* a hospital fired a laboratory technician for inferior work performance when he mismatched blood on three occasions. The employee alleged that racial discrimination was the reason for his dismissal. The Supreme Court of Missouri determined that the evidence did not support racial discrimination and upheld the lower court's finding that he was justly discharged. (*Barnes Hospital v. Missouri Commission on Human Rights,* 661 S.W.2d 534, Mo. 1983.)

### Medical Assistant

In the case of *Landau v. Medical Board of California,* Dr. Landau appealed a lower court's decision to remove her medical license. The lower court found her guilty of allowing her medical assistant to evaluate and remove lesions for biopsy from patients. Dr. Landau was found guilty of gross negligence by allowing an untrained and unlicensed medical assistant to remove tissue, such as moles, from patients for biopsy purposes. The court stated that Dr. Landau's failure to follow up with two of the patients constituted an extreme departure from standard of care and had serious consequences—one of the patients died. Dr. Landau's license to practice medicine was revoked. The medical assistant was not charged. (*Landau v. Medical Board of California,* 71 Cal. Rptr. 2d 54, Cal. App. 1998.)

## Nurse

When nurses exceed their scope of practice, they violate their nursing license and may be performing tasks that are reserved by statute for another health care professional, such as a physician. Due to the shortage of nurses, their responsibilities are ever-increasing, which may lead to practices that result in malpractice. However, nurses have not generally been involved in lawsuits for exceeding their scope of practice, or license, unless they also acted negligently.

Nursing supervisors have been found negligent for not establishing procedures for the nursing staff that are designed to protect patients. In an Illinois case, the director of nursing was found negligent for failing to develop standards to prevent accidents involving excessive temperatures while bathing patients. (*Moon Lake Convalescent Center v. Margolis,* 435 N.E.2d 956, Ill. App. Ct. 1989.)

> **MED TIP**    Remember that "nurse" means a person is a registered nurse (R.N.). The general public often gives all persons wearing a white uniform the title "nurse." A person who is not an R.N. must correct anyone who addresses him or her as "nurse."

In *Quinby v. Morrow,* a patient recovered damages against a surgeon, the instrument nurse, and the hospital for a burn suffered when a hot metal gag was placed in the patient's mouth, causing third-degree burns. (*Quinby v. Morrow,* 340 F.2d 584, 2d Cir. 1965.)

A nurse was found negligent in a Florida case when she continued to inject a saline solution into an unconscious patient after she noticed the solution's ill effects on the patient. (*Parrish v. Clark,* 145 So. 848 Fla. 1933.)

A nurse was held liable in a Massachusetts case where a patient who had received a strong sleeping medication fell out of the hospital bed, fracturing her hip. The nurse had left the bedside rails down and thus had failed to exercise due care. (*Polonsky v. Union Hospital,* 418 N.E.2d 620, Mass. App. Ct. 1981.)

## Nursing Assistant

A nursing assistant in a Mississippi nursing home was attempting to lift a patient into a whirlpool bath using a hydraulic lifting device. The seat on the device became disconnected, causing the patient to fall and fracture a hip. The nursing assistant was found negligent for improperly connecting the seat to the lift device. (*Kern v. Gulf Coast Nursing Home, Inc.,* 502 So.2d 1198, Miss. 1987.)

## Paramedic

Most states have statutes that provide civil immunity for paramedics who provide emergency lifesaving care. In *Morena v. South Hills Health Systems*, the Pennsylvania Supreme Court held that paramedics were not negligent when they transported a shooting victim to the nearest hospital rather than a hospital five miles away that had a thoracic surgeon. The court stated that paramedics were not capable of determining the extent of the patient's injury. (*Morena v. South Hills Health Systems*, 462 A.2d 680, Pa. 1983.)

## Pharmacist

A pharmacist in New York violated statutes covering the sale of controlled substances. He was found negligent relating to the sale of codeine cough substances, and his license was revoked to protect the public. (*Heller v. Ambach*, 433 N.Y.S.2d 281, 1979.)

## Physical Therapist

A physical therapist who refused to allow an 82-year-old nursing home resident to use the bathroom before beginning a therapy session was found to be negligent. The therapist appealed the disciplinary process in the nursing home. The state supreme court ruled that a nursing home has a policy of allowing patients to use the bathroom when they wish, and therefore the therapist was negligent of the patient's health and welfare. (*Zucker v. Axelrod*, 527 N.Y.S.2d 937, 1988.)

## Respiratory Therapist

All health care professionals are required to report unusual situations to their supervisors. If they do not, they are negligent in their duties. In an Indiana case involving an inhalation therapist and a nurse, the court found the two negligent in failing to report to their supervisor that an endotracheal tube had been left in a patient longer than the usual three to four days. The patient suffered injury from the tube and needed several surgical procedures to remove scar tissue and open her voice box. Subsequently, the patient required a tracheotomy to breathe and was only able to speak in a whisper at the trial. (*Poor Sisters of St. Francis v. Catron*, 435 N.E.2d 305, Ind. Ct. App. 1982.)

# MALPRACTICE PREVENTION

### General Guidelines

- Always act within your scope of practice.
- Make certain that all staff have a clear understanding of what conduct is unlawful.
- Provide in-service training on what is meant by standard of care and professional conduct.
- Do not make promises of a cure or recovery.
- Treat all patients with courtesy and respect.

- Avoid having patients spend more than 20 minutes in the waiting room. Explain the reason for any delays in treatment.
- Always carefully identify the patient before beginning treatment. When a patient identification bracelet is available, use that to identify the patient as well as to address the patient by name.
- Never attempt to provide care beyond the scope of one's training or experience.
- Physicians should avoid diagnosing and prescribing medications over the telephone whenever possible.
- Provide ongoing continuing education and training for all staff.

## Safety

- Have periodic inspections of all equipment.
- Check electrical cords to make sure they are grounded.
- Keep all equipment in safe condition and ready to use.
- Keep floors clear and clean.
- Open doors carefully to avoid injuring someone on the other side.
- Provide a mechanism to ensure that all doors and windows, and drawers if necessary, are locked.
- Lock up all controlled substances (narcotics).
- Place warning signs regarding wet floors, fresh paint, and other slippery or unsafe conditions.
- Handle biohazardous waste and sharps such as needles by placing them in the correctly labeled containers.
- Know and follow Occupational Safety and Health Administration (OSHA) safety guidelines.
- Have a disaster plan and provide periodic drills for the staff.

## Communication

- Maintain confidentiality concerning all patient information and conversations.
- Return telephone calls to patients as soon as possible.
- Refrain from criticizing other medical professionals.
- Discuss all fees before beginning treatment.
- Provide emergency telephone numbers for patients to use when the office is closed.
- Take all patient complaints seriously.
- Never discuss patient information within hearing distance of other patients.
- Use a coding system, such as the last four digits of the patient's Social Security number, on the patient registration log rather than the patient's name.
- Place all special instructions for the patient in writing.
- Listen carefully to all the patient's remarks. Communicate the patient's concerns to the entire health care team.
- If the physician must withdraw from a case, fully inform the patient of the withdrawal in writing and provide enough notice (30 to 60 days) for the patient to acquire another physician.
- Call patients at home, either the afternoon of outpatient (day) surgery or the following day, to check on their progress. Document this phone call.

■ Follow up on all missed and canceled appointments.

■ Inform patients of all risks associated with any treatment and assure they understand and, in writing, agree to accept the risks.

■ Place all special instructions for patients in writing and maintain one copy for the medical record.

### Documentation

■ Prepare an incident report to document any unusual occurrence in the medical office, clinic, laboratory, or hospital.

■ Maintain an accurate log of all telephone conversations.

■ Carefully document in the patient's medical record all prescription and refill orders.

■ Make sure that signed consent forms are obtained before beginning any treatment or procedure.

■ Document all missed appointments and cancellations in the patient's medical record.

■ Document any occasion when it is necessary to withdraw from caring for a patient.

■ Keep all paperwork current.

■ Make sure that the physician has read and initialed all diagnostic test reports before filing them.

## POINTS TO PONDER

1. Is it true that if a patient is injured through no fault of yours, you could still be sued for negligence?
2. If you are trained in CPR and fail to use it on a patient in your facility, could you be sued for malpractice (nonfeasance)?
3. Do all four Ds of negligence need to be present in order to obtain a judgment of negligence against a physician?
4. Does the doctrine of *res ipsa loquitur* apply to all health care professionals or only to physicians?
5. Can an employee be sued even if the employer (physician) is liable under the doctrine of *respondeat superior*?
6. You accidentally knock a sterile package of gauze on the floor in the nurse's treatment room. What do you do, if anything?

## DISCUSSION QUESTIONS

1. List five ways to prevent malpractice based on good communication.
2. Give examples of malpractice cases involving health care workers, other than physicians, as discussed in this chapter.
3. Name and discuss the four Ds of negligence.
4. Discuss the law of agency and why it is an important concept for the health care worker to understand.
5. Explain the difference between malfeasance, misfeasance, and nonfeasance.

6. What is an exception to the statute of limitations?
7. Why do you need a thorough understanding of the law as it impacts your employer's practice?
8. State ten steps that may protect a physician and staff from liability.

## PRACTICE EXERCISES

### Matching

Match the responses in column B with the correct term in column A.

**Column A**

_____ 1. liable
_____ 2. rider
_____ 3. tort
_____ 4. proximate
_____ 5. misfeasance
_____ 6. nonfeasance
_____ 7. *res ipsa loquitur*
_____ 8. *res judicata*
_____ 9. cap
_____ 10. dereliction

**Column B**

a. "the thing has been decided"
b. improper doing of a lawful act
c. legally responsible for one's actions
d. "the thing speaks for itself"
e. neglect
f. add-on to an insurance policy
g. failure to perform a necessary action
h. limit
i. a civil wrong
j. direct cause of injury

## MULTIPLE CHOICE

Select the one best answer to the following statements.

1. Carl Simon, a pharmacy technician, fills a prescription for Coumadin, a blood-thinning agent, for Beth White. He hands Beth the prescription without giving her any instructions. Beth has been taking large doses of aspirin for arthritis. The aspirin and Coumadin cause excessive bleeding when Beth takes them together. What is the legal term to describe a potential liability that Carl may have committed?
   a. malfeasance
   b. misfeasance
   c. nonfeasance
   d. arbitration
   e. standard of proof

2. Emily King mistakenly administers syrup of ipecac, which causes vomiting, instead of syrup of cola, which soothes the stomach lining, to Jacob Freeman. Jacob immediately begins to vomit. Which term could be used to describe Emily's action?
   a. *res judicata*
   b. *res ipsa loquitur*

    c. nonfeasance

    d. misfeasance

    e. rider

3. Which of the four Ds is violated when a physician fails to inform the patient about the risks of not receiving treatment?

    a. duty

    b. dereliction

    c. direct cause

    d. damages

    e. proximate cause

4. A phlebotomist draws blood from Sam Ford's right arm. Sam experiences pain and numbness in that arm immediately after the blood is drawn. This is an example of what legal doctrine?

    a. duty

    b. feasance

    c. *res judicata*

    d. proximate cause

    e. rider

5. Allan Walker continues to smoke after his physician warns him that smoking carries the risk of lung cancer. His physician documents this admonition in Allan's medical record. When Allan develops lung cancer, he sues his doctor for malpractice. Allan states that he did not know about the risk of continued smoking. What malpractice defense might apply in this case?

    a. denial

    b. assumption of risk

    c. contributory negligence

    d. borrowed servant

    e. b and c both apply

6. Once the court has decided a case and the appeals process is over, there can be no new lawsuit on the same subject between the same two parties. This is referred to as

    a. statute of limitations

    b. *res ipsa loquitur*

    c. *res judicata*

    d. contributory negligence

    e. comparative negligence

7. To cover their employees, some physicians carry additional insurance that is added onto the physician's liability insurance. This is called a

    a. liability

    b. rider

    c. tort

    d. cap

    e. standard of proof

8. In a medical office, the list of agents for the physician includes the
   a. nurse, medical assistant, and LPN
   b. technicians
   c. cleaning staff
   d. a and b only
   e. a, b, and c

9. The doctrine of *respondeat superior* does not apply between the physician and the
   a. nurse
   b. medical assistant
   c. phlebotomist
   d. pharmacist
   e. physical therapist

10. Using a third person to help settle a dispute in a nonbinding decision is called
    a. mediation
    b. arbitration
    c. malpractice lawsuit
    d. civil lawsuit
    e. none of the above

## PUT IT INTO PRACTICE

Call an insurance company that handles malpractice insurance. Inquire about the cost and coverage for someone in your profession. Request an informational brochure. Write a summary of the information and report it back to your class or your instructor.

## WEB HUNT

Using the Web site for the National Association for Healthcare Quality (NAHQ), *www.nahq.org*, discuss the six values (transformational leadership, customer-driven continuous improvement, team work, diversity, integrity, and professional development) they list as they relate to your chosen profession.

Use the Web site for Health Care Providers Service Organization (HPSO), *www.hpso .com*, to get information regarding health care professionals' insurance services information. Click on "More Sites About Medical Malpractice Insurance." Look under "Allied Healthcare Professionals Insurance Center" to determine if your field of study is included in their coverage. Look under "Nurses Service Organization" to find out what the yearly malpractice insurance premium would be for $1,000,000 coverage for a registered nurse with more than one year of experience and who works full-time.

Using the Web site *www.findlaw.com*, click on "Medical Malpractice" and summarize the article on *res ipsa loquitur.*

## REFERENCES

Black, H. 2004. *Black's law dictionary.* 8th ed. St. Paul, Minn.: West Publishing.

Fremgen, B. 1998. *Essentials of medical assisting: Administrative and clinical competencies.* Upper Saddle River, N.J.: Prentice Hall.

Hall, M., and M. Bobinski. 2003. *Health care law and ethics in a nutshell.* St. Paul, Minn.: West Publishing.

Havinghurst, C. 1988. *Health care law and policy: Readings, notes, and questions.* Westbury, N.Y.: Foundation Press.

Lipman, M. 1994. *Medical law & ethics.* Upper Saddle River, N.J.: Prentice Hall.

Miller, R. 1996. *Problems in health care law.* Gaithersburg, Md.: Aspen.

Oran, D. 1985. *Law dictionary for nonlawyers.* New York: West Publishing.

Posgar, G. 1993. *Legal aspects of healthcare administration,* Gaithersburg, Md.: Aspen.

Tucker, E., and B. Henkel. 1992. *The legal & ethical environment of business.* Homewood, Ill.: Irwin.

## CASE STUDY

Jessica Mass, a phlebotomist, drew a blood sample from Glenn Ross, a 30-year-old patient of Dr. Williams, to test for AIDS. As Glenn was leaving the office, his friend Harry came in and they greeted each other. Jessica took Harry into an exam room, and in the course of making conversation, he told her that he was a good friend of Glenn's. He asked Jessica why Glenn was seeing the doctor. Jessica responded that it was just for a routine test for AIDS.

When Harry arrived back home, he called Glenn and told him what the phlebotomist had said. Glenn called Dr. Williams and complained about Jessica's action and said that he planned to sue Dr. Williams. Dr. Williams dismissed Jessica. She told Jessica that if Glenn did bring a lawsuit against her, then she would sue Jessica.

1. What should Jessica have done or said when Harry asked about Glenn's reason for being in the office?

_____

_____

_____

2. Did Dr. Williams have a legal right to sue Jessica if she was sued?

_____

_____

_____

3. What important right did Jessica violate?

_____

_____

_____

CHAPTER 7

# Public Duties
# of the Physician

## LEARNING OBJECTIVES

1. Define the glossary terms.
2. Describe the public duties of a physician.
3. Discuss the guidelines that should be used when completing a legal record or certificate.
4. List the information that must be included in a death certificate.
5. Describe the cases in which a coroner or health official would have to sign a death certificate.
6. List ten reportable communicable diseases.
7. Discuss the Child Abuse Prevention and Treatment Act of 1974.
8. Describe eight signs that indicate a child, spouse, or elderly person may be abused.
9. Discuss the federal legislation of controlled substances.
10. List and explain the five schedules of drugs.
11. Discuss Good Samaritan laws.
12. Explain how an Employee Assistance Program (EAP) can help troubled employees.

## KEY TERMS

Addiction

Autopsy

Bureau of Narcotics and
   Dangerous Drugs
   (BNDD)

Controlled Substances
   Act of 1970

Coroner

Data

Drug Enforcement
   Administration (DEA)

Employee Assistance
   Program (EAP)

Food and Drug
   Administration (FDA)

Habituation

Inquest

Postmortem

Public duties

Vital statistics

## INTRODUCTION

In order to protect the health of all citizens, each state has passed public health statutes that require certain information to be reported to state and federal authorities. These statutes help protect the public from unsanitary conditions in public facilities such as restaurants and restrooms, and they require the examination of water supplies. Physicians and other health care workers must inform the government when a situation may affect public health, such as in the case of communicable diseases.

## PUBLIC HEALTH RECORDS AND VITAL STATISTICS

Vital events, or **vital statistics,** in a person's life, such as birth and death dates, are used by the government, public health agencies, and other institutions to determine population trends and needs. The reporting agencies and services include the Department of Health and Human Services, Center for Disease Control and Prevention, the National Center for Health Statistics, and the Public Health Service.

The physician's duty to report these events is a duty owed the public—**public duties.** These duties include reports of births, stillbirths, and deaths; communicable illnesses or diseases; drug abuse; certain injuries, such as rape, gunshot, and knife wounds; animal bites; and abuse of children, spouses, and older adults. Additional information includes data such as marriages, divorces, and induced termination of pregnancies.

Many of these duties may be carried out by office personnel such as nurses, medical assistants, and school nurses. The collection of this information should be taken seriously. The **data**—or facts, figures, and statistics—represent information about the individual patient's life. In addition, some of the data is of a highly sensitive nature, such as the facts concerning rape, abuse, and death.

 **MED TIP** Even though office staff may actually perform the paperwork requirements of the law, the ultimate responsibility for reporting health statistics and abuse remains with the physician.

Recommendations for completing legal records such as birth and death certificates are summarized in Table 7-1.

### Births

Physicians, primarily those assisting at births, issue the certificate of live birth that will be maintained during a person's life as proof of age. A valid birth certificate is required to receive many government documents such as a Social Security card, passport, driver's license, and voter registration.

A physician must sign the certificate of live birth. For a hospital birth, the certificate is filed by the hospital at the county clerk's office in the state in which the birth took place. If the delivery occurs at home, the midwife or person in attendance at the birth can file the birth certificate at the county clerk's office. Some states impose a criminal penalty if the birth and death certificates are not properly completed and handled.

**TABLE 7–1**    Recommendations for Completing Legal Records and Certificates

1. Request information from the state registrar for specific requirements on completing certificates.
2. Type all documents when possible. If the record is completed manually, then print using black ink.
3. Make sure that all blank spaces are completed.
4. Verify all names for correct spelling.
5. Use full original signature, not rubber stamps.
6. File original certificates or reports with the appropriate registrar. Copies or reproductions are not acceptable.
7. Avoid abbreviations.
8. Do not alter the certificate or make erasures.
9. Keep a copy in the patient's file.

## Deaths

Physicians sign a certificate indicating the cause of a natural death. The Department of Public Health in each state provides the specific requirement for that state. For example, in the case of a stillbirth before the twentieth week of gestation, in some states the physician must file both a birth and death certificate. In other states, neither is required if the fetus has not reached the twentieth week of gestation. In the case of a live birth with a subsequent death of the infant, both a birth certificate and a death certificate are necessary in all states.

The physician who had been attending the deceased person usually signs the death certificate, stating the time and cause of death. The physician must include the following information on the certificate:

- the date and time of death
- the cause of death: diseases, injuries, or complications
- how long the deceased person was treated for the disease or injury before dying
- the presence or absence of pregnancy (for female decedent)
- if an autopsy took place

In most states, a death certificate must be signed within 24 to 72 hours after the patient's death. After the physician has signed the certificate, it is given to the mortician, who files it with the state or county clerk's office.

 **MED TIP**   Since funeral arrangements and burial cannot take place until the death certificate is signed, it is important that the physician sign as soon as possible.

The death certificate provides proof that a death has occurred. It is often required to confirm information concerning veteran's benefits, Internal Revenue Service information, insurance benefits, and other financial information when settling an estate.

In some deaths, a coroner or health official must sign a certificate. These cases include

- no physician present at the time of death
- a violent death, including homicidal, suicidal, or accidental
- death as a result of a criminal action
- an unlawful death such as assisted suicide
- death from an undetermined cause (unexpected or unexplained)
- death resulting from chemical, electrical, or radiation injury
- death caused by criminal abortion, including self-induced
- death occurring less than 24 hours after hospital admission
- no physician attending the patient within 36 hours preceding death
- death occurring outside of a hospital or licensed health care facility
- suspicious death
- death of a person whose body is not claimed by friends or relatives
- death of a person whose identity is unknown
- death of a child under the age of two years if the death is from an unknown cause or if it appears the death is from Sudden Infant Death Syndrome (SIDS)
- death of a person in jail or prison

A coroner or medical examiner completes the death certificate if the deceased has not been under the care of a physician. A **coroner** is the public health officer who holds an investigation, or **inquest,** if the death is from an unknown or violent cause. In some states, the coroner will also investigate an accidental death, such as one resulting from a fall. A medical examiner is a physician, usually a pathologist, who can investigate an unexplained death and perform autopsies. An **autopsy,** which is a **postmortem** examination of the organs and tissues of the body, may have to be performed to determine the cause of death.

## Communicable Diseases

Physicians must report all diseases that can be transmitted from one person to another and are considered a general threat to the public. The report can be made to the public health authorities by phone or mail. The communicable report should include the following:

- name, address, age, and occupation of the patient
- name of the disease or suspected disease
- date of onset of the disease
- name of the person issuing the report

The list of reportable diseases differs from state to state, but all states require reports of tuberculosis, rubeola, rubella, tetanus, diphtheria, cholera, poliomyelitis, AIDS, meningococcal meningitis, and rheumatic fever. In addition, some diseases, such as influenza, need to be reported if there is a high incidence within a certain population. Sexually transmitted diseases (STDs) or venereal diseases, such as syphilis, gonorrhea, and genital warts, must also be reported to protect the public. Employees in food service, day care, and health care occupations are more carefully monitored for contagious diseases by public health departments.

The following childhood vaccines and toxoids are required by law (the National Childhood Vaccine Injury Act of 1986):

- diphtheria, tetanus toxoid, pertussis vaccine (DPT)
- measles, mumps, rubella (MMR)
- poliovirus vaccine, live
- poliovirus vaccine, inactivated
- hepatitis B vaccine
- tuberculosis test

Many pediatricians also recommend that every child receive *H. influenzae* type b vaccine (HiB), hepatitis A vaccine, varicella (chicken pox) vaccine, and pneumococcal (pneumonia) vaccine (PCV7).

The National Childhood Vaccine Injury Act, passed by Congress in 1986, requires a physician or health care administrator to report all vaccine administrations and adverse reactions to vaccines and toxoids. The physician must report information directly relating to the vaccine and toxoid such as the manufacturer and lot number. In addition, the name and address of the person administering the vaccine and the date of administration should be documented in the patient's record.

## Child Abuse

The Child Abuse Prevention and Treatment Act of 1974 requires reporting of all child abuse cases. All states have statutes that define child abuse and require that all abuse must be reported. Many states list personnel who are required by law to make an immediate report of any suspected child abuse. These personnel include teachers, health professionals such as physicians and emergency room staff, law-enforcement personnel, day-care personnel, and social service workers. Questionable injuries of children, including bruises, fractured bones, and burns, must be reported to local law-enforcement agencies. See Figure 7-1. Signs of neglect such as malnutrition, poor growth, and lack of hygiene are reportable in some states. In a Minnesota case, the court ruled that the Minnesota Board of Psychology acted correctly when it revoked the license of a psychologist who failed to report the sexual abuse of a child (*In re Schroeder*, 415 N.W.2d 436, Minn. Ct. App. 1987).

Physicians have been held liable if they do not report cases of child abuse. For example, in *Landeros v. Flood*, the state Supreme Court ruled that the physician should not have returned a battered child to the parents after he treated the child for intentionally inflicted injuries. The court held that the "battered child syndrome" was a legitimate medical diagnosis and the physician should have suspected that the parents would inflict further injury on the child. (*Landeros v. Flood*, 551 P.2d 389, Cal. 1976.)

Any person who suspects that child abuse is taking place can report the abuse to local authorities without fear of liability. It can sometimes be difficult to determine if a child's injury is accidental or intentional. The persons reporting these cases, acting in the best interests of the child, are protected by law from being sued by parents and others. In the case of *Satler v. Larsen*, a pediatrician reported a case of possible child abuse concerning a four-month-old comatose infant to the Bureau of Child Welfare. There was not enough evidence to demonstrate that the parents were at fault, and they subsequently sued the physician for defamation. The defamation lawsuit was

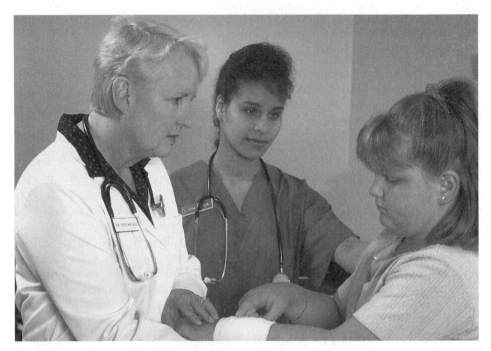

**FIGURE 7–1** A young child explains her injury to a physician.

 dismissed, since the physician reported the suspected abuse in good faith. (*Satler v. Larsen*, 520 N.Y.S.2d 378, App. Div. 1987.)

Most state statutes require that an oral report of suspected abuse be made immediately, followed by a written report. The written report should include

- name and address of the child
- child's age
- person(s) responsible for the care of the child
- description of the type and extent of the child's injuries
- identity of the abuser, if known
- photographs, soiled clothing, or any other evidence that abuse has taken place

**MED TIP** The person reporting a suspected case of child abuse is protected from civil and criminal liability unless that person is the abuser. However, failure to report a suspected case of child abuse may result in a charge of misdemeanor.

## Elder Abuse

Elder abuse is defined in the amendment to the Older Americans Act (1987). It includes physical abuse, neglect, exploitation, and abandonment of adults 60 years and older, and is reportable in most states. The reporting agency varies by state but generally includes social service agencies, welfare departments, and nursing home personnel. As in the case of child abuse, the person reporting the abuse is, in most states, protected from civil and criminal liability.

Residents of nursing home facilities must be protected from abusive health care workers. To do so, some states have made "resident abuse" a crime. In the case of *Brinson v. Axelrod,* a nurse's aide was prosecuted for resident abuse for causing injuries to the hands and face of an elderly resident. (*Brinson v. Axelrod,* 499 N.Y.S.2d 24, App. Div. 1986.) Another medical employee in a New York case was found guilty of resident abuse when she "held the patient's chin and poured the medication down her throat" after the patient had refused medication. (*In re Axelrod,* 560 N.Y.S.2d 573, App. Div. 1990.)

The elderly are also protected by the Older Americans Act from financial abuse or exploitation. This is considered a crime in many states.

## Spousal Abuse

Laws governing the reporting of spousal abuse vary from state to state. The local police may have to become involved when spousal abuse is suspected, and in some cases a court will issue a restraining or protective order prohibiting the abuser from coming into contact with the victim.

## Signs of Abuse

Health care workers, social workers, day-care personnel, and nursing home staff should all be on the lookout for victims of abuse. However, physical signs in children, spouses, the elderly, and the mentally incompetent vary. These signs may include

- repeated injuries
- bruises such as blackened eyes and unexplained swelling
- unexplained fractures
- bite marks
- unusual marks, such as those occurring from a cigarette burn
- bruising, swelling, or pain in the genital area
- signs of inadequate nutrition, such as sunken eyes and weight loss
- venereal disease and genital abrasions and infections
- makeup used to hide bruises
- sunglasses worn inside a building or hospital to hide blackened eyes

Health care workers must do everything possible to gain the victim's confidence. However, it is not possible to assure the victim that all information will be held in confidence, since abuse cases are reportable by law. This should be clearly explained to the victim at the time of the initial visit.

It is difficult to discuss the abuse with the victim when the suspected abuser is present. Always attempt to speak to the victim in private. If possible, have another health care professional present during the interview to act as a witness.

 **MED TIP** Those persons who are unable to protect themselves, such as children and the elderly, must be protected by health care workers and caregivers who become aware of abusive situations.

## Substance Abuse

Abuse of prescription drugs is reportable immediately, according to the law. Such abuse can be difficult to determine, since the abuser may seek prescriptions for the same drug from different physicians. A physician will want to see a patient before prescribing medication. A violation of controlled substances laws is a criminal offense.

 **MED TIP**   All physicians and health care workers should be familiar with the laws relating to controlled substances. Violation of the laws can result in fines, imprisonment, and a loss of license to practice medicine.

## Gathering Evidence in Cases of Abuse

Gathering evidence from abuse victims usually takes place in a hospital or emergency room setting. However, a physician may see an abused patient in the office. Precise documentation of all injuries, bruises, and suspicious fluid deposits in the genital areas of children is critical. The court may subpoena these records at a later date. The physician may also be asked to testify in court and offer observations.

Evidence in abuse cases includes the following:

- photo of bruises and other signs of abuse
- female child's urine specimen (containing sperm)
- clothing
- body fluids, such as semen, vomitus, or gastric contents
- various samples, such as blood, semen, and vaginal or rectal smears
- foreign objects such as bullets, hair, and nail clippings

Evidence should be handled as little as possible, and by only one employee, to prevent damaging the evidence. All evidence in abuse cases should be protected with sealed plastic bags or covers.

### Chain of Custody for Evidence

It is important to maintain a clear chain of custody for evidence to verify that the specimen has been handled correctly. All evidence must be clearly labeled with the name of the patient, date, and time when the specimen was obtained, and all information regarding evidence should be carefully documented in the patient's medical record. In addition to the time and date, the medical record should include complete documentation of the patient's condition as well as the treatment that was provided. All photographs and x-rays should be carefully labeled with the patient's name, patient registration number, time, and date. Items such as clothing, including underwear, must be retained as evidence and not handled excessively or washed. All evidence should be kept in a locked storage area until it is required.

Care must be taken when turning evidence over to a third party. Always request identification and authorization of the person as well as a receipt, which can then be placed into the medical record.

## Other Reportable Conditions

Many states require physicians to file a report of certain medical conditions in order to maintain accurate public health statistics. These conditions include cancer, epilepsy, and congenital disorders such as phenylketonuria (PKU) of the newborn that can cause retardation if untreated. Because the testing for many of these conditions occurs in the hospital, the reporting responsibility rests on the hospital.

## CONTROLLED SUBSTANCES ACT AND REGULATIONS

The **Food and Drug Administration (FDA),** an agency within the Department of Health and Human Services, ultimately enforces drug (prescription and over-the-counter) sales and distribution. The FDA came into existence with the passage of the Food, Drug, and Cosmetic Act of 1938, which sought to ensure the safety of those items sold within the United States.

Drugs that have a potential for **addiction, habituation,** or abuse are also regulated. The **Drug Enforcement Administration (DEA)** of the Department of Justice controls these drugs by enforcing the Comprehensive Drug Abuse Prevention and Control Act of 1970, more commonly known as the **Controlled Substances Act of 1970.** This act regulates the manufacture and distribution of the drugs that can cause dependence and places controlled drugs into five categories: I, II, III, IV, and V. The **Bureau of Narcotics and Dangerous Drugs (BNDD)** is the agency of the federal government authorized to enforce drug control.

Physicians who administer controlled substances, also called narcotics, must register with the DEA in Washington, D.C., and the registration must be renewed every three years. A DEA registration number is assigned to each physician. A physician who leaves the practice of medicine must return the registration form and unused narcotic order forms to the nearest DEA office.

An accurate count of all narcotics must be kept in a record such as a narcotics log, and all narcotics records must be kept for two years. The date and person to whom the drug was administered, along with the signature of the person administering the drug, are recorded. In some states, physicians who prescribe narcotic drugs but do not administer them are also required to maintain narcotics logs and inventory records.

Most states limit the administration of narcotics to physicians and nurses. States may be more restrictive, but not less, than the federal government when regulating the administration of controlled substances. For example, a state may require physicians to keep controlled substances records for a longer period of time than the federal regulations require.

All narcotics must be kept under lock and key. If a controlled (narcotic) drug needs to be "wasted," or destroyed, it should be poured down a drain or flushed down a toilet. Two people should be present when controlled substances are destroyed.

Some commonly controlled substances are

| | | |
|---|---|---|
| anabolic steroids | chloral hydrate | diazepam |
| APC with codeine | cocaine | heroin |
| butabarbital | codeine | LSD |

marijuana                opium                secobarbital
morphine                 phenobarbital

The controlled drugs are classified into five schedules based on the potential for abuse, which are summarized in Table 7-2.

A violation of the Controlled Substances Act is a criminal offense that can result in a fine, loss of license to practice medicine, and a jail sentence. Medical office personnel can assist the physician in maintaining compliance with the law by

- alerting the physician to license renewal dates
- maintaining accurate inventory records
- keeping all controlled substances in a secure cabinet
- keeping prescription blanks and pads locked in a secure cabinet, office, or physician's bag

**TABLE 7–2    Schedule for Controlled Substances**

| Level | Description | Comment |
|---|---|---|
| Schedule I | Highest potential for addiction and abuse. Not accepted for medical use. May be used for research purposes. Example: marijuana, heroin, and LSD | Cannot be prescribed. |
| Schedule II | High potential for addiction and abuse. Accepted for medical use in the United States. Example: codeine, cocaine, morphine, opium, and secobarbital | A DEA-licensed physician must complete the required triplicate prescription forms entirely in his or her own handwriting. The prescription must be filled within seven days, and it may not be refilled. In an emergency, the physician may order a limited amount of the drug by telephone. These drugs must be stored under lock and key if they are kept on the office premises. The law requires that the dispensing record of these drugs be kept on file for two years. |
| Schedule III | Moderate-to-low potential for addiction and abuse. Example: butabarbital, anabolic steroids, and APC with codeine | A DEA number is not required to prescribe these drugs, but the physician must handwrite the order. Five refills are allowed during a six-month period, and this must be indicated on the prescription form. Only a physician may telephone the pharmacist for these drugs. |
| Schedule IV | Lower potential for addiction and abuse than Schedule III drugs. Example: chloral hydrate, phenobarbitol, and diazepam | The prescription must be signed by the physician. Five refills are allowed over a six-month period of time. |
| Schedule V | Low potential for addiction and abuse. Example: cough medications containing codeine, lomotil | Inventory records must be maintained on these drugs. |

## Prescriptions of Controlled Drugs

Only those persons with a Drug Enforcement Administration (DEA) registration number may issue a prescription for narcotics. The registration number must appear on all prescriptions for controlled substances. Schedule I drugs require approval by the Food and Drug Administration (FDA) and the DEA for use in research. The sale of these drugs is forbidden. Schedule II drugs require a special DEA order form that is completed in triplicate. One copy is kept in the physician's records, one copy is sent to the narcotics supplier, and one copy is sent to the DEA. Because there is a high potential for abuse and addiction with these drugs, the prescription cannot be refilled. Physicians must take a written inventory of their drug supply every two years. All narcotics-dispensing records must be kept for a two-year period. It requires careful communication between the physician and patient to assure that the patient is not seeking narcotics prescriptions from multiple physicians. In some instances, pharmacies that maintain careful records have been able to pinpoint abuse.

 **MED TIP**   A violation of the Controlled Substances Act is a criminal offense. The penalties range from a fine to a long prison sentence.

# PROTECTION OF THE EMPLOYEE AND THE ENVIRONMENT

## Employee Assistance Programs (EAPs)

An Employee Assistance Program (EAP) is a service provided by many institutions, such as hospitals and corporations, for all of their employees and employees' family members. An **Employee Assistance Program (EAP)** may be defined as a management-financed and confidential counseling and referral service designed to help employees and/or their family members assess a problem, such as alcoholism or marital strife, develop a plan to resolve personal problems, and determine the appropriate resources to assist in the resolution process. The EAP is geared toward helping employees maintain their job performance while attempting to resolve the difficulty. It is generally administered and staffed by experienced professionals who are trained to understand personal problems and their relation to job performance.

It is estimated that personal problems cost the American economy $70 billion annually. Nearly half of this cost, $30.1 billion, is related to alcohol and/or drug abuse and the resulting loss of productivity. The Department of Health and Human Services estimates that

- 4.0 percent of the employed population use some form of illegal drugs daily.
- 5 to 10 percent of the workforce suffer from alcoholism. These substance-abusing employees are absent from work 16 times greater than average, have four times more home accidents, use a third more sickness benefits, and have five times more compensation claims.

A "troubled" employee also means a supervisor will have a problem, and productivity may decline for both employees. The types of problems that an EAP can help with are substance abuse (alcoholism and drug abuse), stress-related (depression and anxiety), family and marital, psychological, and job-related (interpersonal and burnout). See Table 7-3 for a description of symptoms related to employee problems.

 **MED TIP** It is important to remember that only trained, objective professionals should counsel employees regarding their personal problems.

**TABLE 7–3**  Visible Symptoms Related to Employee Problems

Substance Abuse

Alcoholism

- casual or lethargic attitude about work
- decreased productivity
- personal appearance deteriorates
- misses job-related appointments or deadlines
- absenteeism, especially on Mondays
- personality and attitude changes
- blames others for problems
- fierce denial of problem
- off-the-job family disturbances
- off-the-job auto accidents
- odor of alcohol at work
- increasingly long absences from work
- hospitalizations

Drug Abuse

- may have more accidents than other employees
- may cause security problems such as missing drugs at work
- more health claims than other employees

Stress-Related Problems

- depression
- anxiety
- increased susceptibility to physical illness
- reduced energy levels
- reduction in the ability to concentrate, remember, make decisions, think clearly
- changes in behavior that involve sleeping, eating, smoking, drinking alcohol, taking medication

*(continued)*

**TABLE 7-3** Visible Symptoms Related to Employee Problems *(continued)*

Family and Marital Problems

- inability to concentrate at work
- frequent personal phone calls
- continuous discussion of personal problems with other employees
- physical evidence of abuse such as bruises
- use of more sick days than other employees

Job-Related Problems

- increased feelings of emotional exhaustion in a job that was previously pleasurable
- generalized negative, cynical attitude
- feelings of unhappiness and sense of dissatisfaction with accomplishments
- over-bonding with coworkers, boredom, depression, sense of feeling trapped, sense of hopelessness
- frequent job changes
- increased illness or inability to handle minimum illness

Interpersonal

- inability to carry his or her load of work
- conflicts with coworkers

Without an effective way to deal with employee problems, a health care supervisor may confront the employee, accept continued excuses, provide inadequate counseling, reassign tasks, give verbal warnings, demote or transfer the employee, give a final warning, and eventually resort to termination of the employee. By using an effective EAP, the supervisor

- continues to supervise the employee's job performance
- receives feedback of the first appointment from the EAP (subsequent appointment counseling sessions are not reported back to the supervisor due to confidentiality issues)
- notes improved performance or states the consequences of poor performance
- consults the EAP for suggestions of how to work with a difficult employee
- does not diagnose
- follows disciplinary documentation procedures
- is free to focus on job performance
- continues to talk with the employee, but does not provide counseling

See Table 7-4 for warning signs that an employee needs EAP.

Confidentiality is essential for the success of any EAP. Employees who have confidence in the medical staff may discuss personal problems with physicians and nurses. Many of these problems are those that an EAP staff is especially trained to handle, such as alcoholism, drug abuse, and marital problems. If it is necessary for a medical

TABLE 7–4   Warning Signs That an Employee Needs EAP

| | |
|---|---|
| • Attitude changes | • Prolonged lunch hours or breaks |
| • Decrease in output | • Mysterious absences from work station |
| • Inability to carry his/her load | • Decline in personal appearance |
| • Persistent lateness in completing tasks | • Mood changes |
| • Lowered quality of work | • Conflicts with coworkers |
| • Increase in accidents or near accidents | • Increase in personal phone calls |
| • Repeated safety violations | • Increased use of medical service |
| • Excessive tardiness | • Calls from creditors |
| • Repeated early departures | • Garnishments of wages |
| • Excessive absenteeism | |

unit, such as in a hospital setting, to receive feedback on the employee's condition, then the employee must sign a release allowing the EAP counselor to communicate with the medical unit.

## Medical Waste

Hospitals, dental practices, veterinary clinics, laboratories, nursing homes, medical offices, and other health care facilities generate 3.2 million tons of hazardous medical waste each year. Much of this waste is dangerous, especially when it is potentially infectious or radioactive. There are four major types of medical waste: solid, chemical, radioactive, and infectious.

Solid waste is generated in every aspect of medicine, including administration, cafeterias, patient rooms, and medical offices. It includes trash such as used paper goods, bottles, cardboard, and cans. Solid waste is not considered hazardous, but can pollute the environment. Mandatory recycling programs have assisted in reducing some of the solid waste in the United States.

Chemical wastes include germicides, cleaning solvents, and pharmaceuticals. This waste can create a hazardous situation—a fire or explosion—for the institution or community. It can also cause harm if ingested, inhaled, or absorbed through the skin or mucous membranes. Medical personnel have a duty to refrain from pouring toxic, flammable, or irritating chemicals down a drain. These chemicals should be placed in sturdy containers or buckets and then removed by a licensed removal facility. Chemical wastes must be documented on the Materials Safety Data Sheet (MSDS), which also provides specific information on handling and disposing of chemicals safely.

Radioactive waste is any waste that contains or is contaminated with liquid or solid radioactive material. This waste must be clearly labeled as radioactive and never placed into an incinerator, down the drain, or in public areas. It should be removed by a licensed removal facility.

Infectious waste is any waste material that has the potential to carry disease. Between 10 and 15 percent of all medical waste is considered infectious. This waste includes laboratory cultures as well as blood and blood products from blood banks, operating rooms, emergency rooms, doctor and dentist offices, autopsy suites, and patient rooms. All needles and syringes must be placed in a specially designed medical waste container. The three most dangerous types of infectious pathogens (microorganisms) found in medical waste are hepatitis B virus (HBV), hepatitis A virus (HAV), and the human immunodeficiency virus (HIV), which causes Acquired Immune Deficiency Syndrome (AIDS).

Infectious waste must be separated from other solid and chemical waste at the point of origin such as the medical office. It must be labeled, decontaminated onsite, or removed by a licensed removal facility for decontamination.

 **MED TIP** Physicians and health care personnel have an ethical responsibility to protect the public from harm caused by medical waste.

## POINTS TO PONDER

1. Is it only the responsibility of the physician to report child abuse cases? To whom, in your community, should such a report be made?
2. How soon after death does a death certificate have to be signed?
3. Does a woman have to report a stillbirth if it happens at home?
4. Who signs a death certificate in a death resulting from a fall from a window?
5. Does the physician have to report a case of genital warts, or can this information be kept confidential?
6. Is the "battered child syndrome" a legitimate medical diagnosis?
7. Can a physician who reports a suspected case of child abuse be sued by parents?
8. Can a "wasted" controlled substance be poured down a sink?
9. Wouldn't it be better for a person who has personal problems to be counseled by a supervisor or employer who knows him or her than to be counseled by a stranger in EAP? Why or why not?

## DISCUSSION QUESTIONS

1. What drugs fall under each of the five categories of controlled substances?
2. To what does the term *public duties* refer?
3. What are the physician's public duties?
4. What records must physicians keep if they dispense or administer controlled substances?
5. What are the four categories of medical waste?
6. What is the health care worker's responsibility with medical waste?
7. What are some conditions surrounding death that require an autopsy?

## PRACTICE EXERCISES

### Matching

Match the responses in column B with the correct term in column A.

**Column A**

_____ 1. data
_____ 2. coroner
_____ 3. Schedule II drug
_____ 4. postmortem
_____ 5. Schedule I drug
_____ 6. addiction
_____ 7. inquest
_____ 8. DPT
_____ 9. STDs
_____ 10. public duty

**Column B**

a. after death
b. statistics
c. physical dependence
d. diphtheria, tetanus toxoid, pertussis vaccine
e. public health official who investigates cause of death
f. report child abuse
g. LSD
h. codeine
i. sexually transmitted diseases
j. investigation to determine cause of death

## MULTIPLE CHOICE

Select the one best answer to the following statements.

1. Vital statistics from a person's life include all of the following except
   a. pregnancies
   b. marriages and divorces
   c. animal bites
   d. sensitive information such as rape and abuse
   e. all of the above are considered to be vital statistics

2. A coroner does not have to sign a death certificate in the case of
   a. suicide
   b. death of elderly persons over the age of 90
   c. death occurring less than 24 hours after hospital admission
   d. death from electrocution
   e. death of a prison inmate

3. All of the following vaccines and toxoids are required for children by law except
   a. measles
   b. polio
   c. hepatitis
   d. a and b only
   e. a, b, and c are all required

4. The Controlled Substances Act is also known as the
   a. Drug Enforcement Administration Act
   b. Food and Drug Administration Act
   c. Comprehensive Drug Abuse Prevention and Control Act
   d. Bureau of Narcotics and Dangerous Drugs Act
   e. none of the above

5. Schedule III drugs
   a. can be refilled by an order over the phone from the office assistant
   b. are allowed only five refills during a six-month period
   c. require the DEA number of the physician on the prescription
   d. require the order to be typed on the prescription form
   e. all of the above

6. An EAP program may help an employee cope with
   a. marital problems
   b. alcoholism and drug abuse
   c. criminal charges
   d. a and b only
   e. a, b, and c

7. Infectious waste
   a. should be separated from chemical waste at the site of origin
   b. can be safely removed by a licensed removal facility
   c. consists of blood and blood products
   d. may contain the HIV and hepatitis A and B viruses
   e. all of the above

8. Phenobarbital is an example of a
   a. Schedule I drug
   b. Schedule II drug
   c. Schedule III drug
   d. Schedule IV drug
   e. Schedule V drug

9. The best method to "waste," or destroy, a narcotic is to
   a. place it in a medical waste container that is clearly marked
   b. return it to the pharmaceutical company
   c. flush it down a toilet
   d. do it without any witnesses
   e. none of the above

10. Elder abuse is clearly defined in the
    a. Food and Drug Administration Act
    b. Controlled Substances Act of 1970
    c. amendment to the Older Americans Act of 1987
    d. amendment to the Older Americans Act of 1974
    e. none of the above

## PUT IT INTO PRACTICE

Ask some hospital employees if they have an EAP in their facility. Have them describe what services their EAP covers.

## WEB HUNT

Search the Web site of the Centers for Disease Control (*www.cdc.gov*). Provide a definition for the morbidity tables and mortality tables using the CDC's definition as stated on its Web site.

Search the Web site *www.findlaw.com* to find information on your state's child abuse laws. Summarize them.

## REFERENCES

American Association of Medical Assistants. 1996. *Health care law and ethics*. Chicago: American Association of Medical Assistants.

*Code of medical ethics: Current opinions and annotations*. 1998. Chicago: Council on Ethical and Judicial Affairs of the American Medical Association.

Fremgen, B. 1998. *Essentials of medical assisting: Administrative and clinical competencies*. Upper Saddle River, N.J.: Prentice Hall.

Hitner, H., and B. Nagle. 2005. *Basic pharmacology for health occupations*. New York: Glencoe.

Lipman, M. 1994. *Medical law & ethics*. Upper Saddle River, N.J.: Prentice Hall.

Miller, R. 1990. *Problems in hospital law*. Rockville, Md.: Aspen.

*Physician's desk reference*. 2004. 58th edition. New York: Three Rivers Press.

Pozgar, G. 1993. *Legal aspects of health care administration*. Gaithersburg, Md.: Aspen.

*Prescription drugs*. 1995. Lincolnwood, Ill.: Publications International.

*Professional guide to drugs*. 1991. Horsham, Pa.: Intermed Communications.

Rybacki, J., and J. Long. 2000. *The essential guide to prescription drugs*. New York: Harper.

*Taber's cyclopedic medical dictionary*. 2001. 19th ed. Philadelphia: F. A. Davis.

U.S. Department of Justice. 1990. *Drug enforcement administration: Physician's manual*. Washington, D.C.: U.S. Department of Justice.

Veatch, R. 1989. *Medical ethics*. Boston: Jones & Bartlett.

## CASE STUDY

A pharmaceutical salesperson has just brought in a supply of nonprescription vitamin samples for the physicians in your practice to dispense to their patients. These vitamins are a new, expensive variety that is being given away to patients who are on a limited income and cannot afford to buy them. The other staff members all take the samples home for their families' personal use. They tell you to do the same, since the samples will become outdated before the physicians can use all of them. It would save you money.

1. What do you do?

_____

_____

_____

2. Is your action legal? Why or why not?

_____

_____

_____

3. Is your action ethical? Why or why not?

_____

_____

_____

4. Does your physician/employer have any responsibility for the dispensing of these free nonprescription vitamins? Explain your answer.

_____

_____

_____

**CHAPTER 8**

# Federal Regulations Affecting the Medical Professional

## LEARNING OBJECTIVES

1. Define the glossary terms.
2. Describe the employment-at-will concept.
3. Discuss the regulations concerning equal employment opportunity and employment discrimination.
4. Describe the regulations affecting employee health and safety.
5. Discuss the regulations affecting employee compensation and benefits.
6. Give examples of regulations affecting consumer protection and collection practices.
7. Define and explain the federal labor acts.
8. Discuss the antitrust laws and why they are important for the medical practice.
9. List several rights of labor. List several rights of management.
10. List several questions that may be legally asked during an employment interview. List several questions that are illegal to ask during the interview.
11. Discuss guidelines for good hiring practices.

## KEY TERMS

| | | |
|---|---|---|
| **Bloodborne pathogens** | **Debtor** | **Parenteral** |
| **Cease and desist order** | **Discrimination** | **Preempt** |
| **Creditor** | **Garnishment** | **Vesting** |

## INTRODUCTION

The employer (physician) and employee (staff) relationship is regulated by both state and federal laws. In some cases, local laws in a particular city or county may also regulate a medical practice. Therefore, health care facilities and medical practices must remain current on regulations affecting employment practices, such as health, safety, compensation, worker's compensation, unions, and discrimination laws. It is always wise to seek advice from legal counsel or a corporate attorney, if the organization has one on staff, concerning specific cases.

In most situations, federal laws **preempt,** or overrule, state laws. However, there are some exceptions. One occurs when there is not a federal law relating to a topic, in which case the states can then regulate it. A second exception occurs if the court has already ruled that state law does not conflict with federal law, in which case the state law is enforced. Another exception is called a complete preemption, in which Congress prohibits states from regulating a particular area of law. An example of this is the Employment Retirement Income Security Act (ERISA), which is discussed later in this chapter.

The major categories of federal laws regulating the employer–employee relationships include equal employment opportunity and employment discrimination; employee health and safety; compensation and benefits regulations; consumer protection and collection practices; antitrust laws; and federal labor acts. In discussing these regulations, many of the legal terms, such as a law and an act, are interchangeable. The cases discussed in this chapter illustrate the variety of lawsuits relating to these regulations.

# EQUAL EMPLOYMENT OPPORTUNITY AND EMPLOYMENT DISCRIMINATION

The government regulates many aspects of the employment relationship, including laws affecting recruitment, placement, pay plans, benefits, penalties, and terminations. The basis of the law is that people must be judged primarily by their job performance. A discussion of these laws should be prefaced with a look at the historical doctrine of employment-at-will.

## Employment-at-Will Concept

The common-law doctrine of employment-at-will has historically governed the employment relationship. Employment-at-will means that employment takes place at the will of either the employer or the employee. Thus, the employment may be terminated at will at any time for no reason. Conversely, the employee may quit at any time. The exception to this occurs when there is a specific employment contract between the employer and employee, specifying the duration and terms of employment. Then the relationship cannot be terminated during the contract period. The only protection of an at-will employment is that employees cannot be fired for an illegal reason—for example, due to the color of their skin or their age.

This concept of termination for any reason without incurring liability had been widely accepted. However, in the late 1900s, it began to lose favor. Wrongful-discharge lawsuits have become more common. Statistics indicate that some states, such as California, are more inclined to favor the rights of the employee, while other states, such as New York, have been more employer-oriented in their lawsuit outcomes. Even if employers win a wrongful-discharge lawsuit, they may ultimately be the losers due to the negative publicity and effect on employee morale.

Statements in employee handbooks have been interpreted as "implied contracts" in a court of law. In *Watson v. Idaho Falls Consolidated Hospitals, Inc.,* a nurse's aide

**TABLE 8–1**    Equal Employment Opportunity and Employment Discrimination Laws

- Title VII of the Civil Rights Act of 1964
- Equal Employment Opportunity Act (EEOA) of 1972
- Pregnancy Discrimination Act of 1978
- Civil Rights Act of 1991
- Age Discrimination in Employment Act of 1967
- Americans with Disabilities Act of 1990

claimed wrongful discharge and sued her employer, a hospital, for violating provisions in the employee handbook when it terminated her. Employees had been asked to read and sign a revised handbook to show that they understood the hospital policies regarding counseling, discipline, and termination. The court stated that management and the employees were under an obligation to follow the policies stated in the handbook. Because the hospital violated the stated policy, Watson won her suit. (*Watson v. Idaho Falls Consol. Hosp., Inc.,* 720 P.2d 632, Idaho 1986.)

In another case, a Minnesota court held in a wrongful-discharge suit that the hospital's employee handbook was clearly an employment contract. The handbook contained detailed statements on conduct and procedures for discipline, which the hospital violated when it fired the plaintiff. (*Harvet v. Unity Medical Ctr.,* 428 N.W.2d 574, Minn. Ct. App. 1988.)

These cases indicate that employee handbooks must be examined for any erroneous or misleading statements. See Table 8-1 for a listing of equal employment opportunity and employment discrimination laws.

## Title VII of the Civil Rights Act of 1964

Title VII prohibits **discrimination,** or unfair treatment, in employment based on race, color, religion, sex, or national origin. This proposal, which came from the Kennedy administration, is considered one of the most important pieces of all legislation, since it affects employment opportunity and discrimination.

However, Title VII includes several exceptions. For instance, religious discrimination is permitted in certain religious-affiliated colleges such as Brigham Young University in Salt Lake City, Utah, in which faculty are required to be of the Mormon faith. Title VII also does not apply to public officials and their staff.

Title VI of the Civil Rights Act of 1965 also forbids discrimination in all aspects of patient care in institutions that receive federal financial assistance, such as Medicare and Medicaid. Most claims, though, are filed under Title VII, not under this statute.

The Equal Employment Opportunity Commission (EEOC) monitors Title VII, and the Justice Department enforces the statute. In some cases, the EEOC defers enforcement to local and state agencies. Employees must exhaust all administrative remedies offered from the EEOC before they can sue their employer under Title VII. This act has been further amended by the Equal Employment Opportunity Act, the Pregnancy Discrimination Act, and the Civil Rights Act of 1991.

Title VII also makes sexual harassment a form of unlawful sex discrimination. Sexual harassment is defined as "unwelcome sexual advances, requests for sexual favors, and other verbal or physical conduct of a sexual nature." An employee who quits a job because sexual harassment created an offensive or hostile work environment may sue the employer for damages.

### Who Is an Employee Under Title VII?

Title VII only prohibits employers from discriminating against employees. If an employer withholds employment taxes from a person's income, then that person is considered an employee. While some cases are less clear, in general, if the employer can control the details of that person's work, the person is an employee. In some cases, physicians who have lost medical staff memberships and thus hospital admitting privileges, have been able to sue the hospital under Title VII. An example of this is a federal case in which Dr. Pardazi sued the Cullman Medical Center. The federal case was tried in the 11th Circuit Court, and Title VII was the federal law that won the case.  (*Pardazi v. Cullman Med. Ct.*, 838 F.2d 1155, 11th Cir. 1988.)

### Who Is an Employer Under Title VII?

A person who employs the services of another and provides payment for those services is considered an employer. In addition, an employer has the right to control the physical conduct of the employee in performing the service. The statute only applies to employers who have more than ten employees, and it does not apply to independent contractors. A coworker is not an employer and thus is not liable under Title VII. The courts have also found that a parent company of the employer is not liable as the employer under Title VII.  (*Garcia v. Elf Atochem*, N. Am., 28 F.3d 446, 5th Cir. 1994.)

## Equal Employment Opportunity Act (EEOA) of 1972

This act authorizes the Equal Employment Opportunity Commission (EEOC) to sue employers in federal court on behalf of a class of people or an individual whose rights under Title VII have been violated.

## Pregnancy Discrimination Act of 1978

Under this law, employers must treat pregnant women as they would any other employee, providing they can still do the job. This act has saved jobs for women and allowed them to advance even if they became pregnant or had to take a short leave for childbirth. An employer cannot force a woman to quit her job because she is pregnant. In addition, under this law, a woman cannot be refused a job because she has had an abortion. The pregnant woman is assured of equal treatment in such areas as disability, sick leave, and health insurance. The employer's medical plan must cover pregnancy in the same way it would cover other medical conditions. If the worker is unable to work because of the pregnancy, then she qualifies for sick leave on the same basis as all the other employees.

If the employer offers employee leaves for disabilities, then a similar leave must be offered for pregnancy. Mandatory maternity leaves violate Title VII, since the Pregnancy Discrimination Act of 1978 is an amendment to that statute. In addition, the employer's health plan must provide coverage for the dependent spouses of employees.

A federal district court found that a hospital had violated the Pregnancy Discrimination Act when it fired an x-ray technician upon learning that she was pregnant. The court felt that while it was necessary for the x-ray technician to avoid working in some areas of the x-ray department due to her condition, there were less discriminatory alternatives that the hospital could have used. (*Hayes v. Shelby Memorial Hosp.*, 726 F.2d 1543, 11th Cir. 1984.)

This statute has many aspects that require special considerations. For instance, one federal court held that an employee who had job absences due to infertility treatments was not protected under this act. (*Zatarain v. WDSU-Television, Inc.*, WI 16777 E.D.La. 1995.) In a 1994 case, a federal appellate court ruled that a pregnant home-health nurse who refused to treat an AIDS patient could be discharged under this statute. (*Armstrong v. Flowers Hosp.*, 33 F.3d 1308, 11th Cir. 1994.)

## Civil Rights Act of 1991

Congress again amended Title VII by passing the Civil Rights Act of 1991. Wrongful-discharge suits fall under this law. The law permits the court to award both compensatory damages (for loss of income or emotional pain and suffering) and punitive damages (to punish the defendant) to mistreated employees. Punitive damages are awarded to deter others from committing this action. Prior to this amendment, only compensatory damages were awarded.

## Age Discrimination in Employment Act of 1967

This act protects persons 40 years or older against employment discrimination because of age. This law applies to employers who have 20 or more persons working for them. The employer will not be liable for violation of this law if there are extenuating circumstances, such as if the person does not have the ability to perform the job. If two people are up for hiring or a promotion and one of them is over 40, then the employer must be able to show (in writing) why the younger person, if hired or promoted, is more qualified. Education and performance, in addition to other factors, count toward qualification. Mandatory retirement is prohibited under this law except for certain exempt executives.

 **MED TIP**    Note that women over 40 are protected by both Title VII and this act.

Employers must be cautious about what they say or put into writing in the event that they must terminate a person's employment. For example, in a 1985 age discrimination suit, a 62-year-old supervisor nurse resigned and then sued the hospital because its administration had told her "new blood" was needed and made comments about her "advanced age." She believed these statements made working conditions intolerable. The nurse supervisor won the suit. (*Buckley v. Hospital Corp. of America, Inc.*, 758 F.2d 1525, 11th Cir. 1985.)

## Rehabilitation Act of 1973

This act prohibits discrimination based on disability in any institution that receives federal financial assistance. Therefore, a hospital or agency that receives Medicare and Medicaid reimbursement must comply with this law. However, courts have held in favor of plaintiffs, such as hospitals and nursing homes, that are not equipped to care  for a special-needs patient such as a violent or aggressive patient who abuses the staff. (*Grubbs v. Medical Facilities of America, Inc.,* 879 F. Supp. W.D., Va. 1995.)

## Americans with Disabilities Act (ADA) of 1990

There are 43 million disabled persons in the United States. The ADA prohibits employers who have more than 15 employees from discriminating against such individuals. Persons with Acquired Immune Deficiency Syndrome (AIDS) are also covered under this act. In order to comply with this act, the employer must make reasonable accommodations, such as lowering telephones, installing ramps, and making elevator floor numbers accessible to wheelchair-bound persons. The exception to this occurs if the accommodations would be an undue hardship for the employer, such as the significant difficulty of installing an elevator in an old building. The term undue hardship has caused problems, since there is no clear definition of the term *hardship* or a dollar amount that constitutes hardship. There is a two-year implementation window for employers who must comply with this law.

Patients are also protected under this statute. Title III of the ADA prohibits discrimination based on disability "in the full enjoyment of the goods, services, facilities, privileges, and accommodations of any privately owned place of public accommodation, including hospitals and professional offices."

Private physicians can be held liable under the ADA for acts that take place in their offices. For example, in 1995 a federal appellate court upheld a lower court decision that an HIV-positive patient could sue his primary care physician for allegedly  failing to treat or refer him to another physician. (*Woolfolk v. Duncan,* 872 F. Supp. 1381, E.D. Pa. 1995.)

In *Tugg v. Towney,* a federal court ruled that the ADA requires a state to provide counselors who use sign language to counsel deaf patients in state mental facilities. According to the court, the facility did not satisfy the ADA statute by merely providing mental health services through the use of interpreters. (*Tugg v. Towney,* 864 F. Supp. 1201, S.D. Fla. 1994.)

# EMPLOYEE HEALTH AND SAFETY

Both state and federal laws regulate issues affecting an employee's health and safety. While the state law may be stricter than the federal law, it cannot be more lenient. See Table 8-2 for a list of employee health and safety laws.

## Occupational Safety and Health Act (OSHA) of 1970

Under OSHA, an employer is required by law to provide a safe and healthy work environment: the employer must protect the worker against hazards. OSHA regulations preempt all other state and local regulations regarding employee safety

**TABLE 8–2**    Employee Health and Safety Laws

• Occupational Safety and Health Act (OSHA) of 1970

• Health Maintenance Organization (HMO) Act of 1973

• Consolidated Omnibus Budget Reconciliation Act (COBRA) of 1985

• Drug-Free Workplace Act of 1988

and health, meaning that states may not pass any laws concerning the working environment.

Many jobs are dangerous by their very nature. OSHA regulations seek to protect workers in these jobs by, for instance, having workers wear special equipment. For example, workers who are spray painting must wear respiratory masks. Laboratory employees working with toxic chemicals must have adequate ventilation systems in the work area. Hospitals have been cited for OSHA violations for failing to protect employees from tuberculosis or from patient violence.

Employers and office managers should become familiar with OSHA regulations as they apply to their specific fields, not only to protect employees but to avoid fines for OSHA violations, which can be severe. In addition, the poor publicity and public relations resulting from a serious OSHA violation can damage an office or company's reputation.

In 1991, OSHA developed rules to protect health care workers from bloodborne diseases. These are known as OSHA Occupational Exposure to Bloodborne Pathogens Standards. OSHA also established severe penalties of up to $7,000 for each violation of these standards by employers. These standards apply to any employee who has occupational exposure, which is defined as a reasonable anticipation that the employee's duties will result in skin, mucous membrane, eye, or **parenteral** (a medication route other than rectal or oral) contact with **bloodborne pathogens** (disease-producing microorganisms) or other potential infectious material. Physicians, nurses, medical assistants, laboratory workers, and housekeeping personnel have occupational exposure. The OSHA standards mandate that each employee with occupational exposure must be offered the hepatitis B vaccination at the expense of the employer.

 **MED TIP**    Note that an employee may decline, in writing, to receive the hepatitis B vaccine.

Potential infectious materials include

■ body fluid contaminated with blood
■ saliva in dental procedures
■ amniotic fluid
■ cerebrospinal fluid
■ tissues, cells, or fluids known to be HIV-infected
■ microbiological waste (kits or inoculated culture media)
■ pathologic waste (human tissue)
■ any unidentified body fluid

The OSHA standards refer to urine, stool, sputum, nasal secretions, vomitus, and sweat only if there is visible evidence of blood.

**MED TIP**    OSHA guidelines are available from the U.S. Department of Labor, Washington, D.C.

OSHA regulations now provide right-to-know standards that apply to all employers that produce or import chemicals. These employers must provide their workers and customers—such as hospitals, medical offices, and laboratories—with detailed instructions that identify the chemicals and the appropriate safety precautions.

**MED TIP**    In a medical workplace, additional safety issues may arise that are not found elsewhere, including protecting individuals against bloodborne pathogens.

### Health Maintenance Organization (HMO) Act of 1973

The Health Maintenance Organization Act requires any company with at least 25 employees to provide an HMO alternative to regular group insurance for their employees if an HMO is available in the area.

Many new HMOs were formed in response to this law. HMOs have been able to cut health care costs in some areas by focusing on wellness. An HMO may pay for procedures such as mammograms and well-baby physicals because these tests and examinations may prevent a major illness. Under an HMO, the patient does not have the same wide choice of doctors as under a traditional health care plan. In addition, a patient may have to get a second opinion and permission from the HMO before having a major procedure performed.

### Comprehensive Omnibus Budget Reconciliation Act (COBRA) of 1985

As of January 2001, 45 million Americans were left without any health care coverage, many due to job loss. COBRA has helped to decrease the number of uncovered Americans. Under COBRA, a company with 20 or more employees must provide extended health care insurance to terminated employees for as long as 18 months—usually, but not always, at the employee's expense. This insurance may be costly, but some people would be unable to obtain insurance any other way.

### Drug-Free Workplace Act of 1988

Employers have become increasingly aware of how expensive drug-using employees are in terms of decreased productivity, workplace accidents, and increased health care costs. Even under the best security conditions, the nature of some health care organizations, such as hospitals, medical offices, and clinics, allows for employee access to various drugs.

**MED TIP**    To prevent drug abuse, some organizations, such as hospitals, require drug testing as a condition of employment.

Under the Drug-Free Workplace Act, employers contracting to provide goods or services to the federal government must certify that they maintain a drug-free workplace. The employer must inform the employee of the intent to maintain a drug-free workplace and of any penalties that the employee would incur for violation of the policy.

## COMPENSATION AND BENEFITS REGULATIONS

These laws influence the compensation (salary) and benefits provided to employees. See Table 8-3 for a listing of compensation and benefits laws.

### Fair Labor Standards Act (FLSA) of 1938

This is the main statute regulating employee benefits. The FLSA establishes the minimum wage, requires payment for overtime work, and sets the maximum hours employees covered by the act may work. The act covers all nonmanagement employees in for-profit and not-for-profit institutions.

The employer must pay one and one-half times the regular hourly pay rate for any work the employee performs over 40 hours in a seven-day (one week) period. FLSA uses the single workweek to compute the hours of overtime. The law does not permit averaging hours over two or more weeks. Thus, an employee who works 35 hours one week and 45 hours the next—for a weekly average of forty hours for the two weeks—must still be paid the overtime rate for five hours.

One exception allows hospitals to negotiate an agreement with their employees to establish a work period of 14 days. In this case, overtime pay would go into effect for employees who work more than 80 hours in the 14-day period. It is also acceptable to require fewer than forty hours a week to qualify for overtime payment or a higher rate than one and one-half times the regular hourly pay, but the employer cannot require more hours or pay less than the law requires.

This law affects only full-time hourly employees. Some workers, such as management or salaried employees, are exempt from the minimum wage and overtime requirement of the FLSA. Part-time employees and employees who are part of a time-sharing program generally do not benefit from this law. In addition, outside sales personnel and many professional employees are exempt because Congress holds that these workers are in a position to protect themselves financially.

**TABLE 8-3**   Compensation and Benefits Law

- Fair Labor Standards Act (FLSA) of 1938
- Social Security Act of 1935
- Equal Pay Act of 1963
- Federal Insurance Contribution Act (FICA) of 1935
- Workers' Compensation Act
- Employee Retirement Income Security Act (ERISA) of 1974
- Family and Medical Leave Act (FMLA) of 1994

## Unemployment Compensation

The Social Security Act of 1935 was the origin of the current unemployment insurance program. Nowadays, employers pay taxes into a state unemployment compensation plan that covers employees who are unable to work through no fault of their own. The unemployment compensation laws provide for temporary weekly payments for the unemployed worker.

In order to receive unemployment insurance, the employee must have worked for an employer who has paid or was required to pay unemployment compensation taxes. In general, the law requires such payment from any employer who has one or more employees for 20 or more weeks in a calendar year and who pays at least $1,500 in wages in any calendar quarter. However, certain types of employers are exempt, such as employers for religious, educational, or charitable organizations; employers for small farming operations; employers of family members; and employers of federal government labor.

While state unemployment insurance law provides temporary payments for those who lose their jobs, if an employee is fired for good cause, the employee is not entitled to unemployment benefits. In the case of *Love v. Heritage House Convalescent Center,* the court found that a nursing assistant was properly denied unemployment benefits because she was terminated for poor work attendance. According to the employee's personnel record, the convalescent center had already shown great tolerance in allowing the employee to continue working as long as it had. (*Love v. Heritage House Convalescent Ctr.,* 463 N.E.2d 478, Ind. Ct. App. 1983.)

Unemployment compensation was also denied in a case in which a nurse's aide was discharged for leaving a resident unattended and unrestrained on a commode, and for using the medication of one patient (a medicated cream) on another patient. (*Starks v. Director of Div. of Employment Section,* 462 N.E.2d 1360, Mass. 1984.)

## Equal Pay Act of 1963

This act, an amendment to the FLSA, makes it illegal for an employer to discriminate on the basis of gender in the payment to men and women who are performing the same job. Equal work means work that requires equal skill, responsibility, and effort under the same or similar working conditions. For example, male orderlies cannot be paid more than female orderlies. (*Odomes v. Nucare, Inc.,* 653 F.2d 6th Cir. 1981.)

This act has helped many female professionals in the medical, legal, and accounting fields. Some employers have tried to avoid meeting the requirements of this law by changing the job description, but that practice is also illegal under this law.

The Equal Pay Act applies to the same employees covered by the FLSA, but also includes executive, administrative, professional, and labor union employees, and employees of federal, state, and local governments.

## Federal Insurance Contribution Act (FICA) of 1935

The Federal Insurance Contribution Act of 1935 is the oldest act relating to compensation. Under FICA, employers are required to contribute to Social Security plans for their employees. There is a severe fine if the payment by the employer is not made on time. This act also requires detailed record-keeping to document the employer's payment. The key to the proper implementation of this act is to hire a trusted office manager.

## Workers' Compensation Act

Workers' compensation statutes protect workers and their families from financial problems resulting from employment-related injury, disease, and even death. Under the law, employers must pay into a fund to help cover costs when an employee is hurt or injured, such as a back injury, or has a work-related disease, such as carpal tunnel syndrome from improper or prolonged computer keyboard usage.

The goal of workers' compensation is to get the employee back to work as soon as possible. If there is a health problem within the first three months of employment on a new job, the previous employer may have to pay the workers' compensation, since most of the benefits were paid into the employee's fund by that employer. Some practices only handle patients with workers' compensation injuries.

Under the Workers' Compensation Act, an employee must submit a written notice of the injury to the employer. Generally, an employee will receive only a partial salary, such as two-thirds of salary, as compensation.

Workers' compensation benefits are generally available even if the employee is at fault for his or her injury, but an employee who has violated hospital policy is not eligible to receive benefits. In *Fair v. St. Joseph's Hospital,* the hospital employee was disqualified from receiving compensation because he violated the policy by fighting with a coworker. (*Fair v. St. Joseph's Hosp.,* 437 S.E.2d 875, N.C. App. 1933.)

Almost every state has enacted mandatory workers' compensation laws that define terms such as *employee* and *injury* and that include required schedules of payment in the event of an injury. However, New Jersey, South Carolina, and Texas have adopted voluntary plans, allowing employers to decide whether to be covered by workers' compensation or be sued for common-law negligence. Employers who adopt workers' compensation coverage must pay an injured employee the state-set amount whether or not the employer was at fault. The injured employee cannot recover any additional amounts. On the other hand, if the employer does not opt for workers' compensation coverage, the employer will be liable only if at fault or negligent. In this case, the employer, in the three states mentioned above, may be required to pay substantially more than under the workers' compensation statute.

Even if an employee is covered by workers' compensation, the employee may still sue and recover for injuries caused by nonemployees. For example, in a 1994 case in California, a psychiatric nurse sued a psychiatric patient who kicked her in the abdomen, causing injury to her unborn child. The court ruled that the workers' compensation law did not bar this lawsuit. (*Agnew-Watson v. County of Alameda,* 36 Cal. Rptr. 2nd 196, CT. App. Cal. 1994.)

## Employee Retirement Income Security Act (ERISA) of 1974

ERISA regulates employee benefits and pension plans. Prior to the passage of ERISA, widespread abuse of pension plans led to their collapse, leaving retired employees without the pension benefits their companies had planned. ERISA responded to this problem by requiring employers to put aside money that can be used only to pay future benefits. ERISA also guarantees vesting of pension plans.

**Vesting** refers to a certain point in time, such as after ten years of employment, when an employee has the right to receive benefits from a retirement plan. Under ERISA, employees who stay with a company for ten years are entitled to 50 percent of the employer's retirement plan even if they leave the company and take another job. The employee is entitled to 100 percent of the employer's pension contribution after 15 years of employment, when they become fully vested. In some cases, employees have been laid off just before they become vested. ERISA prohibits this practice.

## Family and Medical Leave Act (FMLA) of 1994

This law allows both the mother and father to take a leave of absence of up to 12 weeks, in any 12-month period, when a baby is born. The employee's job, or an equivalent position, must be available when he or she returns to work. In almost all cases, the leave is without pay. The FMLA also requires employers to provide unpaid leave for up to 12 weeks to employees who request leave for their own or a family member's medical or family-related situation, such as birth, death, or adoption.

In order to be eligible, the employee must have worked for the employer for at least one year; worked 1,250 hours in the previous 12 months; and work in a locality where there are at least 50 company employees within 75 miles. Thirty days' advance notice is required when the leave is foreseeable, such as in the case of a birth.

The company must maintain the employee's health coverage while the employee is on a family medical leave. The employee must be returned to the original or equivalent position he or she held before going on the leave. In addition, there cannot be any loss of employment benefits that accumulated prior to the start of the leave.

# CONSUMER PROTECTION AND COLLECTION PRACTICES

The consumer protection and practices laws serve to protect the consumer from unfair practices. See Table 8-4 for a listing of these laws.

## Fair Credit Reporting Act of 1971

This act establishes guidelines for use of an individual's credit information. If a patient has been denied credit based on a poor rating from a credit agency, the patient must be notified of this fact and given the name and address of the reporting agency. The agency must disclose the credit information to the consumer, who may correct and update this information.

**TABLE 8–4** Protection and Collection Practices

- Fair Credit Reporting Act of 1971
- Truth in Lending Act (Regulation Z) of 1969
- Fair Debt Collection Practices Act of 1978
- Federal Wage Garnishment Law of 1970

### Equal Credit Opportunity Act of 1975

This act prohibits businesses, including hospitals and medical offices, from granting credit based on the applicant's race or sex—unfair treatment referred to as discrimination. This law mandates that women and minorities must be issued credit if they qualify for it, based on the premise that if credit is given to one person, it should be given to all persons who request it and are qualified.

### Truth in Lending Act (Regulation Z) of 1969

The Truth in Lending Act requires a full written disclosure about interest rates or finance charges concerning the payment of any fee that will be collected in more than four installments. This is also called Regulation Z of the Consumer Protection Act. Installment payments are often used for orthodontia, obstetrical care, and surgical treatment. It is legal to include a finance charge if a patient pays the bill in installments. However, few physicians and dentists do this.

### Fair Debt Collection Practices Act of 1978

This act prohibits unfair collection practices by **creditors** (institutions or persons who are owed money). For example, the Federal Communications Commission (FCC) has issued guidelines for the specific times that credit collection phone calls can be made. The FCC prohibits telephone harassment and threats. Under this law, telephone calls for purposes of collections must be made between the hours of 8:00 A.M. and 9:00 P.M., with no weekend calls. See Figure 8-1.

**FIGURE 8–1**   Collection calls are made between 8:00 A.M. and 9:00 P.M.

## Using a Collection Agency

Medical offices and hospitals would not be able to remain in business if patients didn't pay their bills for medical care. Fair collection practices must be honored. Table 8-5 provides some guidelines for collection efforts.

Professional collection agencies are available when all other attempts to collect unpaid bills fail. The account should always be reviewed with the physician or head of the medical practice before turning it over for collection.

Collection agencies should be chosen carefully. Reputable agencies will have references that can be checked. These agencies charge for their service either by a flat fee per account or a percentage of the amount collected. The patient's diagnosis should not be included when sending financial information to the agency.

Once the patient is told the account is going to a collection agency, it must, by law, go. After the account has been turned over, no further collection attempts can be made by the physician's office or hospital; that would be considered harassment. If the patient should contact the office or hospital after the account has been turned over for collection, the patient should be referred to the collection agency.

**TABLE 8–5**    Guidelines for Collection Efforts

1. Establish policies and procedures relating to collections and instruct all staff on these procedures.
2. Have a list of the established fees available for patients and staff.
3. Discuss the fee and when the fee is due with the patient prior to treatment.
4. Prepare written material for patients that includes general information about the office, such as office hours and emergency numbers to call when the office or facility is closed. Include information about the billing process and how insurance claims are handled.
5. Request payment, whenever possible, before the patient leaves the office or health care facility.
6. Be consistent in all billing practices. This includes sending statements to arrive on the first of each month and sending a follow-up letter on delinquent accounts when they reach a certain date, such as one month overdue.
7. Use care when making telephone collection calls:
   a. Always use courtesy when speaking to patients.
   b. Always introduce yourself. Make sure the patient understands the reason for the call. Do not misrepresent yourself by implying you are someone other than who you are.
   c. Make all calls on weekdays between 8:00 A.M. and 9:00 P.M., observing the time difference for patients living in another time zone.
   d. Protect the patient's privacy. Carefully identify the person accepting the telephone call. Do not discuss a delinquent account with anyone except the patient (debtor). Do not leave a message on a telephone answering machine.
   e. Never threaten an action that you do not intend to take. For example, do not tell the patient that the account will be handed over to a collection agency if payment is not received by this afternoon. It is also never a good idea to threaten a patient.
   f. Try to establish a payment plan. Try to get a commitment from the patient on when a full or partial payment can be made.
   g. Do not harass or intimidate the patient (debtor).

**MED TIP**   Personnel involved in the billing and collections operations of any facility must have a full understanding of the laws regulating the collection process.

## Bankruptcy

When patients become unable to pay their debts, they may file for bankruptcy. Bankruptcy is a legal method for providing some protection to **debtors** and establishing a fair method for distribution of the debtor's assets to all the creditors. If a patient files for bankruptcy, the patient's assets are placed in a special fund by a court-appointed trustee. The trustee then distributes the funds according to a predetermined method. Once a debtor files for bankruptcy, a **creditor,** such as a physician, who has an outstanding debt owed by the patient, may no longer seek payment from the patient but must instead file a claim in bankruptcy court at a later date.

 **MED TIP**   A creditor who fails to comply with bankruptcy laws can be cited for contempt of court.

## Federal Wage Garnishment Law of 1970

**Garnishment** refers to a court order that requires an employer to pay a portion of an employee's paycheck directly to one of the employee's creditors until the debt is resolved. The Federal Wage Garnishment Law restricts the amount of the paycheck that can be used to pay off a debt.

## Claims against Estates

When a patient dies, a bill should be sent to the estate of the deceased. Contact the probate court or the next of kin to find out who the administrator of the estate is. It is important to follow up with the collection of bills to prevent the impression that the physician was at fault in the patient's death. There is generally a specific time limit allowed when filing a claim against an estate. The probate department of the superior court in the county that is handling the estate can provide information on the time limits and the name of the administrator of the estate.

## The Statute of Limitations

This statute defines how long a medical practice has to file suit to collect on a past-due account. Since the time limit varies from state to state, an attorney should be consulted to determine the particular state's law. If an aging account is more than three years old, the creditor should investigate the state's statute of limitations before spending time, effort, and money to collect the debt. Because there is a statute of limitations on collecting a debt, it is important to attempt any debt collection as soon as possible.

## ANTITRUST LAWS

Antitrust laws represent a major concern for health care institutions and hospitals. These laws seek to preserve the private competitive market system by prohibiting activities that are anticompetitive. Mergers, exclusive contracts, exchanges of price information, denial of medical staff privileges, actions that bar or limit new entrants into the field, preferred provider arrangements, and other actions must all be considered within the framework of antitrust laws. Hospitals that limit the number of physicians admitted to their medical staff can effectively limit competition from other physicians and medical groups. For example, a surgeon in Oregon claimed that another physician had conspired to terminate the surgeon's staff privileges at the only hospital in town and, in doing so, drove him out of practice. He won a $2 million jury

 verdict that was upheld by the United State Supreme Court. (*Patrick v. Burget,* 486 U.S. 94, 1988.)

The primary antitrust laws that affect the medical industry are the Sherman Antitrust Act, the Clayton Act, and the Federal Trade Commission Act. These laws prohibit a variety of anticompetitive behavior, as discussed in the following sections. See Table 8-6 for a listing of these laws.

### The Sherman Antitrust Act

This act seeks to eliminate restraints of trade and to prevent the formation of monopolies. If a person or practice is "injured" economically due to a violation of the Sherman Act, the plaintiff can receive three times, or treble, damages in a civil lawsuit. In an Ohio lawsuit, 1,800 physicians brought a class action suit against an HMO. The jury determined that the HMO had been engaged in price-fixing and other violations that caused $34 million in damages. Based on the treble principle, the jury awarded $100 million to the plaintiffs. Rather than appealing the decision, the parties ulti-

 mately settled this suit with the HMO for $37.5 million. (*Thompson v. Midwest Found. Indep. Physicians Ass'n.,* 124 F.R.D. 154, 1988.)

**TABLE 8–6**    Antitrust Laws

- The Sherman Antitrust Act
- The Clayton Act
- The Federal Trade Commission (FTC) Act

## The Clayton Act

The Clayton Act forbids price discrimination and prohibits acquisitions and mergers where the effect may be to substantially lessen competition or create a monopoly. One of the sections in the law provides for treble damages for person(s) injured by the Clayton Act.

## The Federal Trade Commission (FTC) Act

The FTC Act prohibits unfair methods of competition and deceptive practices affecting commerce, such as false advertising. The FTC has the power to enforce the Sherman or Clayton acts. Therefore, the FTC may issue a **cease and desist order** requiring the violator to immediately stop the unlawful behavior and not attempt any further violation.

## FEDERAL LABOR ACTS

Union activity in the health care field was minimal before the 1950s. Since then, unions have become more active in areas beyond their origins. Many professional organizations, such as state nurses' organizations, have become active in collective bargaining on behalf of their members. See Table 8-7 for a listing of federal labor laws.

## The National Labor Relations Act (NLRA) of 1935

The National Labor Relations Act, also called the Wagner Act, gives employees the right to form and join unions, to bargain collectively, and to strike for better benefits and working conditions. The purpose of this law is to protect employees. The National Labor Relations Board (NLRB), created under this act, oversees compliance. This act stimulated the growth of unions.

The NLRA establishes rights for both employers and employees, and also defines some prohibited acts by employers, called unfair labor practices. The NLRB publishes booklets on this topic. Any manager who supervises union employees should obtain a copy.

In supervising union employees, employers should take the following precautions:

1. Do not threaten or interfere with any employees who exercise their rights under the NLRA. Employers should not even give a subtle indication that they are unhappy with union activity.
2. An employer cannot discriminate because of an employee's union activity.

**TABLE 8–7**   Federal Labor Acts

* The National Labor Relations Act (NLRA) of 1935
* Labor Management Relations Act (LMRA)

3. The employer cannot refuse to bargain in good faith with the union officials.
4. The employer cannot attempt to control or interfere with union affairs.

## Labor Management Relations Act (LMRA)

Also known as the Taft-Hartley Act of 1947, the LMRA seeks to protect employers and employees by balancing the power fairly between unions and management. It includes the National Labor Relations Act of 1935, which defines the conduct of the employer and the employee and designates what are considered unfair labor practices.

In general, health care facilities are subject to the provisions of the NLRA. Several groups of health care workers are exempt from this law, including independent contractors, some students, supervisors, confidential employees, and managerial employees.

Under this law, unions cannot

- refuse to bargain in good faith
- threaten or restrain employees who wish to exercise their rights to join or not to join a union
- force employers to discriminate against employees who are not union members
- charge discriminatory dues or entrance fees
- coerce employees to engage in secondary boycotts for illegal purposes
- force an employer to pay for work not performed
- picket to coerce unionization without seeking an election by workers

# LABOR RIGHTS

## Elections

The NLRA determines the procedures employees use when selecting a union as the collective bargaining unit to negotiate with a health care employer or facility. If the employer and employees determine that a formal procedure will be used, an election is held under the supervision of the NLRB. If the majority of employees vote for a particular union, then it becomes their bargaining representative. Labor and management rights are summarized in Table 8-8.

## Effective Hiring Practices

As indicated in earlier examples of lawsuits, it is important for an employer to operate within the confines of the law. Fairness is one of the most important elements when supervising employees. In addition, employers can improve the quality of their employees by using an effective screening process before the actual hiring takes place. It is imperative to perform thorough background checks on applicants in the health care field because they may not confess to a criminal record on an application form. Employers are at risk of lawsuits when they hire employees who are a foreseeable danger to others. Some recommendations for good hiring practices are presented in Table 8-9.

**TABLE 8–8   Summary of Labor and Management Rights**

Labor Rights

Employees have certain rights that management must respect. These include

1. the right to organize and bargain collectively

2. the right to have the employer bargain in good faith

3. the right to have one or more persons picket peacefully

4. the right to solicit and distribute union information during nonworking hours, including mealtimes and breaks

5. the right to strike

There are certain restrictions that apply to where employees may picket. In addition, there are new requirements that attempt to reduce the disruption that a strike causes to health care services.

Management Rights

Management has certain rights and responsibilities also. These include

1. the right to hire replacement workers

2. the right to restrict union activity to a specific area to avoid interference with health care services

3. the right to receive a ten-day notice of an impending strike from the collective bargaining unit

4. the right to deny union activity during working hours

5. the right to prohibit supervisors (or persons in positions of authority) from participating in union activity

**TABLE 8–9   Recommendations for Good Hiring Practices**

Develop clear policies and procedures on hiring, discipline, and termination of employees.

Effectively screen potential employees' backgrounds.

Clearly state in all written materials such as employee handbooks, memos, and manuals, that an employee handbook is not a contract.

Use a two-tier interview screening process. It is always appropriate to include trained human resource or personnel department employees in the screening and hiring process.

Carefully assess the applicant's skill level.

Develop an application form that provides accurate information about the applicant's qualifications.

Provide a job description to every employee.

Develop a progressive disciplinary procedure and make the policy known to all employees and supervisors.

Provide in-service training to supervisors on how to conduct job interviews and motivate and discipline employees.

Become familiar with the legal and illegal questions that can be asked in an employment interview.

## Legal and Illegal Interview Questions

The Equal Employment Opportunity Commission (EEOC) has strict guidelines on the types of questions that can be asked during a job interview. Questions that may be interpreted as discriminatory cannot be asked. In some cases, a question may be legal but still inadvisable for the interviewer to ask. For example, while it is legal under the law to ask if an applicant is married, it is inadvisable because it may be discriminatory. Marriage has nothing to do with job performance. If an unmarried applicant is hired, a married applicant may believe that he or she was not given the job based on marital status. Table 8-10 contains a list of questions you can and cannot ask during an interview.

 **MED TIP** A smooth-running medical office, clinic, or hospital requires attention to many factors, including employment practices and careful screening of all candidates before hiring takes place. It is especially important in a health care setting to make careful background checks—especially relating to drug use—before hiring an individual.

**TABLE 8–10** Legal and Illegal Interview Questions

| Questions | Legal/Illegal |
| --- | --- |
| Age? | Legal to ask applicants if they are between the ages of 17 and 70, but not to ask their specific age. If their age falls outside these boundaries, then it is legal to ask their birth date. |
| Birthplace? | Legal, but it is inadvisable to ask where the applicants, their parents, spouse, or children were born. It is illegal to ask about their national heritage or nationality or that of their spouse. |
| Address? | Legal to ask, along with how long the applicant has lived there. Illegal to ask if they rent or own their home. |
| Married? | Legal to ask, but inadvisable. |
| Children? | Illegal to ask. It is also illegal to ask any questions relating to child-care arrangements. |
| Height and weight? | Illegal to ask unless it relates to the job requirements. |
| Race or color? | Illegal to ask. |
| Religion or creed? | Illegal to ask, but it is legal to ask if working on a particular day, such as a Saturday or Sunday, would interfere with applicant's religious practice. |
| Ever been arrested? | Illegal to ask because an arrest does not indicate guilt. It is legal to ask if the applicant has ever been convicted of a crime. For example, "Have you been convicted within the past year on drug-related charges?" |
| Citizenship? | Legal to ask, "Are you a citizen of the United States?" |
| Handicaps? | Illegal to ask if an applicant has a handicap or a disease. It is legal to ask if the applicant has any physical impairment that would affect the ability to do the job. |

*(continued)*

TABLE 8–10   Legal and Illegal Interview Questions *(continued)*

| Questions | Legal/Illegal |
|---|---|
| Organizations you belong to? | Legal to ask applicants if they belong to any organizations. Illegal to ask about membership in any specific organization or to require applicants to list the organizations to which they belong. |
| Languages? | Legal to ask what languages a person can speak or write. However, it can be perceived as discriminatory and a method to determine a person's national origin. |
| Education and experience? | Legal to ask. |
| Military experience? | Legal to ask if they have been a member of the armed forces, the type of training they had, and when they were discharged. It is illegal to ask what type of discharge they received (honorable, dishonorable, medical, etc.). |

## POINTS TO PONDER

1. Why did the federal government enact laws such as Title VII, the ADA, and COBRA?
2. How do you respond to an illegal interview question?
3. Isn't it important for an employer to know if a potential employee has a disability? Why or why not?
4. Should all health care employees be tested for HIV? Why or why not?
5. Does an employer have any rights when hiring union employees?
6. Should health care employees be unionized? Why or why not?
7. In your opinion, does the Family and Medical Leave Act of 1994 discriminate against working persons who do not have children or elderly parents?
8. Are you entitled to take off a couple of days to re-energize yourself if you do not use up all of your sick days during the year?

## DISCUSSION QUESTIONS

1. Identify the principal kinds of illegal discrimination that result in unequal employment opportunities.
2. What amendments to Title VII are discussed within this chapter?
3. What are considered potential infectious materials under OSHA guidelines?
4. What regulation assists terminated employees in obtaining extended health care coverage?
5. What does the Fair Labor Standards Act of 1938 control?
6. What purpose does the Sherman Antitrust Act serve?
7. Who is eligible to receive a leave of absence under the Family and Medical Leave Act of 1994?
8. What does ERISA control?
9. Discuss the two major federal labor acts.

## PRACTICE EXERCISES

### Matching

Match the responses in column B with the correct term in column A.

**Column A**

_____ 1. creditor
_____ 2. preempt
_____ 3. vesting
_____ 4. discrimination
_____ 5. cease and desist
order
_____ 6. employment-at-
will
_____ 7. OSHA
_____ 8. ADA
_____ 9. Title VII
_____ 10. debtor

**Column B**

a. Civil Rights Act of 1964
b. Occupational Safety and Health Act
c. court order to stop an activity
d. overrule
e. one who owes money to another
f. to whom a debt is owed
g. unfair treatment
h. employee gains the rights to receive benefits
i. Americans with Disabilities Act of 1990
j. employment can be terminated

## MULTIPLE CHOICE

Select the one best answer to the following statements.

1. In most cases, federal laws
   a. are better than state laws
   b. are not followed as closely as state laws
   c. preempt state laws
   d. are used when state laws are not effective
   e. none of the above

2. Title VII of the Civil Rights Act of 1964 prohibits discrimination based on
   a. color, race, and national origin
   b. religion
   c. sex
   d. income level and education
   e. a, b, and c only

3. The following acts are covered as amendments under Title VII with the exception of the
   a. Pregnancy Discrimination Act of 1978
   b. Drug-Free Workplace Act of 1988
   c. Equal Employment Opportunity Act of 1972
   d. Civil Rights Act of 1991
   e. Age Discrimination in Employment Act of 1967

4. The Occupational Safety and Health Act (OSHA) developed standards in 1991 stating that infectious materials include all of the following except
   a. any unidentified body fluid
   b. amniotic fluid
   c. saliva in dental procedures
   d. cerebrospinal fluid
   e. all of the above are included under OSHA

5. The most important act covered under compensation and benefits regulations is said to be the
   a. Workers' Compensation Act
   b. Social Security Act of 1935
   c. Federal Insurance Contribution Act of 1935
   d. Fair Labor Standards Act
   e. Family and Medical Leave Act of 1994

6. Regulation Z of the Consumer Protection Act is also referred to as
   a. Equal Credit Opportunity Act of 1975
   b. Fair Credit Reporting Act of 1971
   c. Truth in Lending Act of 1969
   d. Employee Retirement Income Security Act of 1974
   e. Workers' Compensation Act

7. When making a claim for payment after a patient has died, the claim (or bill) must be
   a. sent in the name of the deceased person to his or her last known address
   b. sent to the administrator of the estate of the deceased person
   c. sent to a collection agency with specific instructions to collect the payment from the next of kin
   d. waived
   e. none of the above

8. When using a collection agency to collect outstanding debts (unpaid bills) from a patient,
   a. allow the collection agency to take a tough, aggressive attitude with patients who owe money
   b. stay closely involved in the process and make frequent follow-up phone calls to the delinquent patient
   c. it is wise to first threaten the patient that you will send the unpaid account to a collection agency and then give the patient a second chance
   d. review the delinquent account with the physician or office manager before turning over the account to the agency
   e. all of the above

9. ERISA
   a. controls employee benefit plans
   b. controls employee pension plans
   c. determines eligibility

    d. determines vesting

    e. all of the above

10. Under the Workers' Compensation Act,

    a. employers must pay into a fund to help cover costs when an employee is hurt

    b. every state, without exception, has enacted mandatory laws regarding schedules of payment for injured workers

    c. a worker who accepts a workers' compensation payment may still sue the employer for the injury

    d. employees may not sue nonemployees

    e. there is a guarantee of receiving a full salary while on workers' compensation

## PUT IT INTO PRACTICE

Write a letter of application for a position you may wish to seek upon graduation from your program of study. Submit this letter, along with an updated resume, to your instructor for comments. Using Table 8-10 as a guide, review the personal information you provided in your cover letter and resume. Have you given any information that is not required? Are there any gaps in your employment record? If so, why? How will you answer any of the questions in Table 8-10 if you are asked them during an interview?

## WEB HUNT

Searching the Web site of the Occupational Safety and Health Act (*www.osha.org*), find an article that relates to OSHA or workers' compensation. Summarize the article.

Search the Web site *www.findlaw.com*. Under the title of "U.S. State Laws, Cases, Codes, Statutes, and Regulations," find information on unemployment compensation in your state.

## REFERENCES

Fremgen, B. 1998. *Essentials of medical assisting: Administrative and clinical competencies.* Upper Saddle River, N.J.: Prentice Hall.

Havinghurst, C. 1988. *Health care law and policy: Readings, notes, and questions.* Westbury, N.Y.: Foundation Press.

Miller, R. 1996. *Problems in health care law.* Gaithersburg, Md.: Aspen.

Pozgar, G. 1993. *Legal aspects of health care administration.* Gaithersburg, Md.: Aspen.

Sanbar, S., A. Gibofsky, M. Firestone, and T. LeBland. 1995. *Legal medicine.* St. Louis: Mosby.

Soltis, M. 1998. Hiring the right person for your medical office. *PMA* (July/August).

Steingold, F. 1999. *The employer's legal handbook.* Berkeley, Calif.: Nolo Press.

Tucker, E., and B. Henkel. 1992. *The legal and ethical environment of business.* Homewood, Ill.: Irwin.

## CASE STUDY

Nancy Moore, a registered nurse, is assisting Dr. Brown while he performs a minor surgical procedure. Dr. Brown is known to have a quick temper, and he becomes very angry if a surgical procedure is delayed for any reason. As Nancy is handing a needle with suture thread to Dr. Brown, she feels a slight prick in her sterile gloves. She tells Dr. Brown about this and explains that she will have to be excused from the procedure for a few minutes while she changes gloves. He becomes angry and tells her to "forget about it and help me finish."

1. Will it be harmful to anyone if Nancy wears the gloves during the rest of the procedure, since it was just a slight prick and the patient's wound does not appear to be infected?

_____

_____

_____

2. Who is at fault if the patient does develop an infection?

_____

_____

_____

3. What recourse does Nancy have if she develops a bloodborne pathogen infection, such as hepatitis, from the small hole in her gloves?

_____

_____

_____

4. Is this an ethical or a legal issue, or both?

_____

_____

_____

5. Are there any federal regulations that might help Nancy in the event of an injury or infection?

_____

_____

_____

## CHAPTER 9

# The Medical Record

## LEARNING OBJECTIVES

1. Define the glossary terms.
2. List five purposes of the medical record.
3. List seven requirements for maintaining medical records as recommended by the Joint Commission on Accreditation of Healthcare Organizations.
4. Discuss eleven guidelines for effective charting.
5. Discuss what is meant by timeliness of charting and why it is important in a legal context.
6. Define the Privacy Act of 1974.
7. Describe seven ways to protect patient confidentiality that relate to the use of fax, copiers, e-mail, and computers.
8. Discuss the time periods for retaining adults' and minors' medical records, fetal heart monitor records, and records of birth, death, and surgical procedures.
9. Explain eleven guidelines to follow when *subpoena duces tecum* is in effect.

## KEY TERMS

Disclosed

Doctrine of professional
   discretion

Joint Commission on
   Accreditation of
   Healthcare
   Organizations (JCAHO)

Problem-oriented medical
   record (POMR)

SOAP

Subpoenaed

## INTRODUCTION

Medical records consist of all written documentation relating to a patient. They include past history information, current diagnosis and treatment, and correspondence relating to the patient. Billing information is often maintained in a separate accounting record. It is important to remember that the medical record is a legal document. Various laws cover the reporting, disclosure, and confidentiality of medical records.

Thus, medical record management requires attention to accuracy, confidentiality, and proper filing and storage. Proper management is also necessary because the records may be **subpoenaed,** ordered by the court, during a malpractice case.

## THE MEDICAL RECORD

Each patient's medical record contains essentially the same categories of material but with information unique to each patient. For example, not every patient has a consultation report from another physician or a surgical report.

The format for the medical record reflects the physician's specialty. An obstetrician, for instance, uses a format that includes questions pertaining to the mother's prenatal and postnatal periods.

## PURPOSE OF THE MEDICAL RECORD

Medical records serve multiple purposes. They provide a medical picture and record of the patient from birth to death. The record is an important document for the continual management of a patient's health care. Medical records provide data and statistics on health matters such as births, deaths, and communicable diseases. A physician can track the ongoing patterns of the patient's health through the medical record. See Figure 9-1.

In addition, since this record documents a patient's medical condition and treatment, either the patient or the physician in a malpractice suit may use this informa-

**FIGURE 9-1**    A medical records filing system.

tion. Finally, the medical record is a legal document and, as such, should not contain flippant or unprofessional comments such as "The patient is very annoying."

 **MED TIP**  The medical record is a document that records both the care and treatment that a patient did and did not receive.

## CONTENTS OF THE MEDICAL RECORD

The medical record contains both personal information about the patient and medical or clinical notations supplied by the physician and other health care professionals caring for the patient. Personal patient information includes full name, address, telephone number, date of birth, marital status, employer, and insurance information. The clinical data or information includes all records of medical examinations, including x-rays, laboratory reports, and consent forms.

As a legal document, the medical record can be used by both the defendant (physician) and plaintiff (patient) in a lawsuit. Because of its importance, some states have passed statutes that define what must be contained in the record. Many of these statutes reflect the accreditation requirements of the Joint Commission on Accreditation of Healthcare Organizations (JCAHO) or Medicare requirements as the minimum standard. Under these requirements, the medical record must include

- admitting diagnosis
- evidence of a physician examination, including a health history, not more than seven days before admission or 48 hours after admission to a hospital
- documentation of any complications such as hospital-acquired infections or unfavorable medication reactions
- signed consent forms for all treatments and procedures
- consultation reports from any other physicians brought in on the case
- all physicians' notes, nurses' notes, treatment reports, medication records, radiology and laboratory reports, and any other information used to monitor the patient
- discharge summary, with follow-up care noted

The components of a standard medical record are listed in Table 9-1.

Because of the need to keep accurate and detailed medical records, health care professionals have adopted various procedures or methods for tracking a patient's care. Two common forms are the chronological record and the problem-oriented medical record (POMR). The chronological record uses a blank form with the patient's name stamped or written on each page. The date of each visit, vital signs, and the physician's comments are added at the time of each visit. This type of chronological documentation may span a period of several years in the patient's record. As a result, some medical problems, such as borderline hypertension, may go undiscovered unless the medical professional reads the entire chronology. The problem of this patient's hypertension could more easily be caught using the **problem-oriented medical record (POMR)** method of documentation, which focuses on a patient's problems and not just on the diagnosis. One of the most frequently used methods for charting

**TABLE 9–1**   Standard Medical Record

Patient's complete name, address, home and work telephone numbers, social security number, birth date, and marital status

Patient's past medical history

Dates and time of all medical appointments and treatments

History of present illness

Review of symptoms, reason for appointment

Chief complaints (CC)

Results of physical examination performed by physician

Physician's assessment, diagnosis, and recommendations for treatment

Progress notes from past visits and treatments

Family medical history

Personal history

Medication history with notations of all refill orders

Treatments

X-ray reports

Laboratory test results

Consultation reports (referrals) diagnosis

Other patient-related correspondence:

   Informed consent documentation, when appropriate

   Signature for release of information

   Copy of living will

Documentation of all prescriptions and authorization for refill orders

Documentation of dates when the medical record (or portions) is copied, including to whom it was sent

Documentation of any missed appointments and the subsequent action taken, such as follow-up telephone calls

Instructions concerning diet, home care, exercise, and follow-up appointments

Hospital clinical records will also include

   Nurses' notes (observations by the nursing staff)

   Operative report

   Delivery record

   Anesthesia reports

   Medication and treatment records

   Social service reports

   Physical therapy notes and reports

   Dietary notes and reports

   Fluid intake and output (I & O) charts

   Discharge summary

in the POMR is called **SOAP (subjective, objective, assessment, plan)** charting. Using the SOAP method of charting, the nurse, medical assistant, or other health care professional documents the subjective (S) statements of the patient and records the objective (O) data, such as laboratory results and vital signs. The physician may add objective (O) data and determine the assessment (A) or diagnosis and the plan (P) of treatment. General guidelines for medical charting are found in Table 9-2.

 **MED TIP** Document patient comments such as "I'm all alone" or "I just feel I can't go on." Any comments of this nature should be relayed to the physician because they may indicate an emotional problem in addition to the physical one for which the patient is seeking treatment.

## Corrections and Alterations

Some medical record errors are unavoidable. These might include errors in spelling, transcription, or inadvertently omitted information or test results. All corrections should be made by drawing one line through the error, writing the correction above the error, dating the change, and then initialing it. Do not erase or use correction fluid.

Falsification of medical records is grounds for criminal indictment. In a New York case, two orthopedic surgeons performed a procedure on a patient that required implanting a prosthetic device into the hip joint. The salesman of the prosthetic device was in the operating room when the patient had to be reopened in order to correct the placement of the device. One of the surgeons left the operating room to return to

### TABLE 9–2    Guidelines for Charting

1. Double check to make sure you have the correct patient medical record.
2. Use dark ink, preferably black, and write legibly. Printing is preferred if your handwriting is difficult to read. The record must be legible.
3. The patient's name should appear on each page of the medical record. Medical offices and hospitals have a device that will stamp the patient's name and identification number onto paper.
4. Every entry must be dated and signed or initialed by the person writing the entry. The full name of the person initialing the document should be either in the medical record or on file in the physician's office, clinic, or hospital. No one can sign a medical record for anyone else.
5. Entries should be brief but complete.
6. Use only accepted medical abbreviations known by the general staff, and correctly spell all medical terms.
7. Never erase or in any way remove information from a medical record.
8. Document all telephone calls and other correspondence relating to the patient.
9. Document any action(s) taken as a result of telephone conversations.
10. Document all missed appointments.
11. Charting notations should not be derogatory or defensive.

his office and agreed that the salesman could assist the remaining surgeon. The salesman assisted by removing the prosthesis from the patient and preparing it for the surgeon to re-implant. The surgeon who left the operating room was sued for malpractice because the surgical record did not show that he had been replaced with a nonphysician during the surgery. The hospital and surgical nurse were also indicted for violating a duty imposed on them by the nature of their profession. (*People v. Smithtown Gen. Hosp.* 736, 402 N.Y.S.2d 318, Sup. Ct. 1978.)

 **MED TIP**   Use only black or blue ink when charting in a medical record. Never use pencil or colored ink pens.

## Timeliness of Documentation

Medical records must be accurate and timely. All entries should be made as they occur or as soon as possible afterward. Federal reimbursement guidelines mandate that all medical records should be completed within 30 days following the patient's discharge from a hospital. The **Joint Commission on Accreditation of Healthcare Organizations (JACHO),** an agency that oversees hospital accreditation standards, also has issued guidelines for timeliness in charting.

Late entries into the medical chart mean that, even for a brief period of time, the medical record is incomplete. This can cause a serious problem if the incomplete record is subpoenaed for a malpractice suit. Any entry made into a medical record after a lawsuit is threatened or filed is suspect. Also, if the medical record is not updated promptly, there could be a lapse of memory about what actually occurred.

## Completeness of Entries

The medical record may be the most important document in a malpractice suit because it documents the type and amount of patient care that was given. If the medical record is incomplete, the physician or other health care provider may be unable to defend allegations of malpractice, even if there was no negligence. For instance, in a 1985 Missouri case, a physician ordered that a patient be turned every two hours. The attending nurses, however, failed to note in the patient's record when they turned her. The patient claimed that she had not been turned as ordered and that this caused her to develop serious bedsores, which led to the amputation of one leg. The nurses presented an expert witness who testified that in some instances nurses become so busy that they place the needs of the patient, such as turning, before the need to document. The court eventually dismissed this case. However, not all such cases are dismissed. (*Hurlock v. Park Lane Med. Ctr. Inc.*, 709 S.W.2d 872, Mo. Ct. App. 1985.)

 **MED TIP**   The medical record is a legal document and as such can be subpoenaed into court as evidence in a malpractice case.

In a California case, an appeals court ruled that the physician's inability to provide the patient's medical record created the inference of guilt. (*Thor v. Boska,* 113 Cal. Rptr. 296, Ct. App. 1974.) This is an example of a situation in which the physician may not have been at fault. However, the fact that he was unable to provide any documentation about his treatment of the patient meant that even at the appeals court level, he did not win his case.

 **MED TIP** Remember that in the eyes of the court, if it's not documented, it wasn't done.

## CONFIDENTIALITY

To protect patient confidentiality, medical records should not be released to third parties without the patient's written consent. If an attorney obtains a subpoena for the medical records, only the specific records that are requested, such as the surgical notes, should be copied and sent. For example, the fact that a patient is HIV-positive or has been seen in an emergency room after an auto accident may have no bearing on a malpractice suit relating to a surgical procedure.

Taking photographs or other visual images of patients, such as videotapes, without the proper patient consent is an invasion of the patient's privacy. The patient must sign an authorization form in order for photos and films to be used or released outside of the medical facility. Guidelines for maintaining patient confidentiality when using a fax machine, copy machine, e-mail, or computer are listed in Table 9-3.

**TABLE 9–3** Maintaining Patient Confidentiality When Using Fax (facsimile) Machines, Copy Machines, E-mail, or the Computer

**Fax Machines**
1. Make sure the intended receiver is there before sending confidential records by fax.
2. Shred confidential papers that are no longer needed. Do not place them in the trash.
3. Use a fax cover sheet that states "Confidential."
4. Send patient information via fax only when absolutely necessary.
5. Only fax the specific document requested, not the entire medical record.
6. Ideally the fax machine should be located in a restricted access area.

**Copy Machines**
1. Never leave medical records unattended on a copy machine where others may read them.
2. Shred all discarded copies.

**E-mail and the Computer**
1. Avoid using e-mail to send confidential information.
2. Do not allow other patients or unauthorized staff members to view a computer screen with confidential patient information.

## OWNERSHIP

State statutes may establish who owns the medical records. In most states, the general rule is that the physician or owners of a health care facility, such as a hospital, own the medical records, but patients have the legal right of *privileged communication* and access to their records. Therefore, patients must authorize release of their records in writing. Patients also have a right to access their records and to request a copy of those records. Since some records are large and require duplicating time and expense, the physician may charge for this service.

Patients have the right to expect that accurate medical records will be recorded and maintained in a safe manner. In some cases, such as for a patient with mental health problems, it may cause harm to patients if they read their own records. Under the **doctrine of professional discretion,** a physician may determine, based on his or her best judgment, if the patient with mental or emotional problems should view the medical record.

**MED TIP**   An original copy of a medical record should never be sent. A copy should be made of the original, and the copy sent to a patient who has requested the record in writing. In the case of x-ray film, the physician may allow the original to be sent, with the stipulation that it be returned. Medical information should never be given over the telephone.

### Release of Information

Records should not be released to the patient without the physician's permission. The information contained in the record can be upsetting to some patients without the proper explanation. Insurance companies often have a desire to examine the medical records before they issue a reimbursement for a procedure. The patient must sign a release form for this as well.

State hospital licensing regulations typically stipulate that the medical record is the property of the hospital and should not be removed from the premises unless there is a court order. Under the law, access to mental health records is more limited than to general medical records. See Chapter 10 for a further discussion of release of patient information under HIPAA regulations.

**MED TIP**   Never send the entire medical chart unless it is requested. Send out only the exact material, or portion of the medical record, that is requested.

### Privacy Act of 1974

The Privacy Act of 1974 provides private citizens some control over information that the federal government collects about them by limiting the use of information for unnecessary purposes. Under this 1974 law, an agency may maintain only the information that is relevant to its authorized purpose. Additionally under this law, citizens have the right to gain access to their records and to copy any of the records if necessary.

The Privacy Act only applies to federal agencies and government contractors. However, hospitals that are operated by the federal government, such as Veterans' Administration hospitals, are bound by the act to make their records available for public disclosure.

## State Open-Records Laws

Some states have freedom of information laws that grant public access to records maintained by state agencies. These are called open-records laws. However, medical records are generally exempt from this statute, so the public cannot obtain such information. In some cases, though, if the private patient's interest in confidentiality is outweighed by the benefit of disclosure for the public interest, then disclosure is allowed. For example, in the case of *Child Protection Group v. Cline,* the court allowed personal information about a bus driver's psychiatric records to be **disclosed,** or made known, to parents of schoolchildren when there was a concern that he would not be able to drive the school bus safely. (*Child Protection Group v. Cline,* 350 S.E.2d 541, W. Va. 1986.)

## Alcohol and Drug Abuse Patient Records

The Public Health Services Act protects patients who are receiving treatment for drug and alcohol abuse. Any person or program that releases confidential information relating to these patients is subject to criminal fines. Hospitals maintain a patient registry at their switchboard or front desk, but they cannot divulge that a patient with drug or alcohol abuse problems is even a patient there.

An exception to this disclosure of information law would be if the patient should require emergency care that would necessitate divulging the abuse problem.

# RETENTION AND STORAGE OF MEDICAL RECORDS

Each state varies on the length of time for which medical records and documents must be kept. Legally, all medical records should be stored for ten years from the time of the last entry. However, most physicians store medical records permanently because malpractice suits can still be filed within two years from the date that the occurrence or malpractice event became known.

Using the statute of limitations as a guide for retaining records, the medical record of a minor would be kept until the patient reaches the age of maturity plus the period of the statute. As an example, in a state where the age of maturity is 21 and the statute of limitations for torts is two years, the retention period for a newborn's record would be 23 years.

Table 9-4 describes time period recommendations for retaining medical records as adopted by the American Health Information Management Association (AHIMA).

Due to limited storage space, medical records may have to be destroyed after a period of time has elapsed. State laws should always be checked before destroying any records.

**TABLE 9–4**    Time Periods for Retaining Medical Records

| | |
|---|---|
| Adult patient records | ten years after the most recent encounter |
| Minor's health records | age of maturity plus statute of limitations |
| Fetal heart monitor records | ten years after infant reaches maturity |
| Medicare and Medicaid records | five years |
| Register of birth | permanently |
| Register of death | permanently |
| Register of surgical procedures | permanently |
| Immunization records | permanently |
| Chemotherapy records | permanently |

The courts take the requirement to retain records seriously. An Illinois appeals court declared that a patient could sue when a hospital failed to retain her x-rays. (*Rodgers v. St. Mary's Hospital,* 556 N.E.2d 913, Ill. App. Ct. 1990.) In a Florida case, a woman whose husband died during the administration of anesthesia was unable to present expert testimony because her husband's anesthesiology records were missing. The court ruled that she could sue the hospital because it was the hospital's duty to make and maintain medical records. (*Bondu v. Gurvich,* 473 So. 2d 1307, Fla. Dist. Ct. App. 1984.)

## Storage

Records of current patients are usually kept within the physician's office for easy access. See Figure 9-2. Older records of former patients do not need to be kept in the office where they will take up valuable space. Physicians often rent storage space. It is important to use a clean, dry warehouse space for storage. If records that are needed in court have been destroyed in a warehouse fire or flood, the court may believe that it was a deliberate attempt by the physician to avoid the truth. Some physicians hire a service to place all their records on microfilm.

## Computerized Medical Records

Many medical offices, clinics, and hospitals have fully computerized methods of record keeping. Data and patient records can be created, modified, authenticated, stored, and retrieved by the computer. While this has made record maintenance and retrieval much more efficient and effective, it has also caused some problems, particularly in the area of patient confidentiality.

Legal confidentiality obligations apply to all methods of record keeping. With a computer-based system, it is even more important to be diligent in protecting the patient's rights because generally more people have access to the computerized records. Special safety measures should be taken, such as establishing personal identification and user verification codes for access to records. Computer-based records should be accessed only on a need-to-know basis. Not everyone in a health care facility should have authorization to pull up patient records on the computer screen.

**FIGURE 9–2**     Medical records storage unit.

## REPORTING AND DISCLOSURE REQUIREMENTS

State laws require the disclosure of some confidential medical record information without the patient's consent. These items are discussed in Chapter 7 under public duties of the physician.

### Duty to Report AIDS, HIV, and ARC Cases

All states have statutes or regulations that require health care providers to report cases of acquired immune deficiency syndrome (AIDS) to the local or state department of health. Most states also require that human immunodeficiency virus (HIV) and AIDS-related complex (ARC) cases be reported as well. Who should report the cases varies. In some states, it is the duty of the attending physician or the laboratory that performs the test. Other states may require hospitals, clinics, blood banks, and other facilities to report positive cases.

To date, Minnesota is the only state that has a self-reporting provision requiring health care workers who are diagnosed with HIV to report that fact to the health department or commissioner of health within 30 days of learning the diagnosis. In addition, the Minnesota law requires health care workers to report, within ten days, other health care workers who are infected. (*Minn. Stat.,* § 214.18(2),(4).)

Many states have confidentiality statutes that allow notification of an HIV patient's spouse, needle-sharing partner, or other contact person who is at risk of the infection. (California Health and Safety Code 121015.) A physician who wishes to notify a contact person under one of these laws should always discuss such plans with the patient first. The physician may wish to remind the patient of the moral obligation to others. Patients should also be informed that there are some statutes that impose criminal liability on someone who is an HIV carrier and knowingly engages in activities that could spread the virus to others. (*Fla. Stat. § Ann.* 384.24.)

> **MED TIP** Laws regarding medical records vary from state to state. Health care professionals who have any involvement with the medical record should learn what the statutes in their own state require.

## USE OF THE MEDICAL RECORD IN COURT

### Improper Disclosure

Health care providers and institutions such as hospitals and clinics may face civil and criminal liability for releasing medical records without the proper patient authorization. Private citizens can institute a civil lawsuit to recover damages if their records are released inappropriately. Wisconsin statutes provide for compensatory as well as punitive damages for improper disclosure. (*Wis. Stat. § 252.15(8).*) Many of the cases that have been tried for improper disclosure relate to HIV and AIDS patients.

While disclosure of a patient's HIV and AIDS status to the health department is required by state statute, disclosure to any other person or organization is not allowed.

### Subpoena Duces Tecum

A *subpoena duces tecum* is a written order requiring a person to appear in court, give testimony, and bring the particular records, files, books, or information that are described in the subpoena. The court issues a subpoena for records that document patient care and, in some instances, billing and insurance records.

A subpoena is often served by a local sheriff or federal marshal, but many state statutes allow anyone over the age of 18 to serve a subpoena. The subpoena may be served either by certified mail or in person, depending on the state requirement.

If a medical record has been **subpoenaed,** or requested by the court, certain guidelines should be followed.

1. Notify the physician that a subpoena has been received.
2. Notify the patient that his or her record has been subpoenaed.
3. Notify the physician's attorney that a subpoena has been received.
4. Verify that all the information on the subpoena is correct. Pay particular attention to identification numbers such as the Social Security number. In some cases, patients may have the same name, and a subpoena is sent to a physician in error.
5. Carefully make sure that the requesting attorney's name and phone number as well as the court case (docket) number are listed on the subpoena.

6. Review the records to make sure that all the records requested are available. No attempt should be made to alter or add any information to the record.
7. Photocopy the original record and number all the pages. Place the total number of pages on the front of the file folder. Prepare a cover list of the contents and place that in the file folder along with the medical documents.
8. Turn over only the specific materials that have been requested.
9. After the medical record materials relating to the subpoena have been compiled, lock the file in a secure place.
10. Turn the records directly over to the judge on the due date. The materials should not be left with a clerk or receptionist.
11. The health care professional who takes the records to court should be prepared to be sworn in to make the records admissible as evidence.

All the copying costs associated with subpoenaed records must be borne by the attorney requesting the subpoena.

## POINTS TO PONDER

1. How do you respond when a patient says, "Please give me my medical record, since I own it"?
2. Do you agree with the statement, "If it's not documented, it wasn't done"? Why or why not?
3. In order to protect your physician–employer, should you "hide" to avoid receiving a *subpoena duces tecum*? Why or why not?
4. As a health care professional, are you able to read the medical record of a person you know? Why or why not?
5. Would it be helpful to other health care professionals who will be using the same patient's medical record to document that patient's poor attitude by including a statement such as "bad attitude"? Why or why not?
6. Can you be liable if you or your staff lose a patient's medical record?
7. A patient requests her physician's office to change her diagnosis in her medical record from R/O (rule out) bladder infection to "bladder infection," since her insurance will not pay for an R/O diagnosis. Should the record be changed?

## DISCUSSION QUESTIONS

1. What is the significance of the medical record for the physician? For the health care professional? For the patient?
2. Describe the steps to follow when preparing a *subpoena duces tecum*.
3. Discuss the confidentiality issues that relate to the patient who is HIV-positive or has AIDS.
4. What laws affect patient privacy issues?
5. Who owns the medical chart?

## PRACTICE EXERCISES

### Matching

Match the responses in column B with the correct term in column A.

**Column A**

_____ 1. subpoenaed
_____ 2. POMR
_____ 3. disclosed
_____ 4. chronological record
_____ 5. falsification of
     records
_____ 6. *subpoena duces tecum*
_____ 7. SOAP
_____ 8. timeliness
_____ 9. Privacy Act of 1974
_____ 10. JCAHO

**Column B**

a. made known
b. provides control over release of information
c. subjective, objective, assessment, plan
d. when something has been requested by the
   court
e. in the order of occurrence
f. Joint Commission on Accreditation of
   Healthcare Organizations
g. problem-oriented medical record
h. grounds for criminal indictment
i. no late entries on medical chart
j. written order to bring materials to court

## MULTIPLE CHOICE

Select the one best answer to the following statements.

1. Medicare and Medicaid records should be retained for
   a. one year
   b. five years
   c. ten years
   d. for the lifetime of the patient
   e. for an indefinite period of time

2. The contents of the medical record include all of the following except
   a. past medical problems
   b. informed consent documentation
   c. patient's income level
   d. family medical history
   e. a, b, c, and d are all correct

3. Medical record entries should be made
   a. within 60 days of the patient's discharge
   b. at the physician's discretion
   c. after the patient gives consent
   d. as soon as possible
   e. ten days after the procedure

4. The patient
    a. has the legal right of privileged communication
    b. owns the medical record
    c. cannot have any portion of the medical record
    d. a and c
    e. a, b, and c

5. When correcting a medical error, one should
    a. use a professional brand of error correction fluid to make the correction
    b. erase the error and make the correction
    c. draw a line through the error, write the correction above the error, and initial the change
    d. never make any corrections on the medical record
    e. none of the above

6. The medical record is legally owned by the
    a. patient
    b. physician
    c. state
    d. lawyer
    e. no one

7. Medical records
    a. provide a record from birth to death
    b. provide statistics on health matters
    c. are legal documents
    d. a and c only
    e. a, b, and c

8. All of the following are guidelines to use when sending medical records by fax except
    a. make sure there is a receiver waiting for the fax
    b. use a cover sheet marked "confidential"
    c. send the entire medical record via fax
    d. do not place the original fax in a trash container
    e. all of the above are correct

9. An exception to the open-records laws in some states is/are
    a. psychiatric history
    b. confidential medical record information such as HIV test results
    c. safety and criminal records of persons involved in the education of children
    d. all of the above
    e. none of the above

10. The records of all adult patients should be kept a minimum of
    a. two years
    b. five years
    c. ten years
    d. twenty years
    e. permanently

## PUT IT INTO PRACTICE

Request a copy of your medical record from your primary care physician. Examine the contents to determine how well they document your medical history.

## WEB HUNT

Using the Web site of the American Health Information Management Association (*www.ahima.org*), provide a description of the organization. Go into the Patient Resource Center of this site and summarize the statement concerning who owns the medical record.

Using *www.findlaw.com*, look up your state statute regarding the statute of limitations for medical records in your state.

## REFERENCES

Fremgen, B. 1998. *Essentials of medical assisting: Administrative and clinical competencies.* Upper Saddle River, N.J.: Prentice Hall.

Joint Commission on Accreditation of Healthcare Organizations. 1995. *1995 comprehensive accreditation manual for hospitals.* Chicago: JCAHO.

Miller, R. 1996. *Problems in health care law.* Gaithersburg, Md.: Aspen.

Neubauer, M. 1990. Careful charting—Your best defense. *RN* 53:11.

Posgar, G. 1993. *Legal aspects of health care administration.* Gaithersburg, Md.: Aspen.

Roach, W. 2001. *Medical records and the law.* Gaithersburg, Md.: Aspen Publishers.

*Taber's cyclopedic medical dictionary.* 2001. 19th ed. Philadelphia: F. A. Davis.

# CASE STUDY

Mary Smith has been a patient of Dr. Williams from 1985 to the present time. During that time, she has had three children and been treated for a variety of conditions, including depression in 1986 and herpes in 1990. Mary and her husband, George, have filed for divorce. George wants custody of the children and is claiming that Mary has a medical condition that makes her an unfit mother. An attorney, acting on George's behalf in the divorce proceedings, has obtained a subpoena for Mary's medical records for the years 1995 to the present. Dr. Williams's assistant, who is a medical records technician, copies Mary's entire medical record from 1985 to the present and sends it to the attorney.

1. What negative effects for Mary might this error cause?

_____

_____

_____

2. Is there a violation of confidentiality? Why or why not?

_____

_____

_____

3. Do you believe that this is a common or uncommon error?

_____

_____

_____

4. Was it appropriate for the assistant to make a copy of any part of Mary's medical record?

_____

_____

_____

CHAPTER **10**

# Confidentiality in Medical Practice

## LEARNING OBJECTIVES

1. Define the glossary terms.
2. Identify the problems associated with patient confidentiality.
3. Discuss the purpose of the Health Insurance Portability and Accountability Act (HIPAA) of 1996.
4. Describe the information to which the Privacy Rule refers.
5. List which entities are affected by HIPAA.
6. Discuss the penalties for noncompliance with HIPAA.
7. List the patients' rights under the Privacy Standards.
8. Discuss the ethical issues concerning information technology.

## KEY TERMS

Clearinghouse
Covered entities
Employer Identification
  Number (EIN)
Employer Identifier
  Standard
Health care plan
Healthcare Integrity
  and Protection Data
  Bank (HIPDB)

Health Insurance
  Portability and
  Accountability Act
  of 1996 (HIPAA)
Medical informatics
Minimum necessary
  standard
Office of Civil Rights
  (OCR)
Privacy Rule

Protected Health
  Information (PHI)
Sanctions
Telemedicine
Wireless Local Area
  Networks (WLANs)

## INTRODUCTION

Patients have two major expectations when they visit a physician's office or other medical facility: quality care and confidentiality. They have a right to expect both. However, with the advent of modern technology, including the Internet, e-mail, fax machines, and computers, the number of people who have access to patient information has increased at a rapid rate. In order to address the concern for patients' privacy, especially via electronic transmissions, Congress mandated that the Health Insurance Portability and Accountability Act of 1996 (HIPAA) enforce its privacy provision by April 14, 2003. This law, while somewhat complicated and expensive for physicians to implement, has meant more careful attention to issues of patient privacy.

## CONFIDENTIALITY

One version of the Hippocratic Oath states, "What I see or hear in the course of the treatment . . ., which on no account must be spread abroad, I will keep to myself . . ." Historically, physicians were expected to maintain all confidences concerning their patients, and patients took this confidentiality for granted. However, the image of one patient sharing his or her medical information with only one physician is no longer applicable in today's modern world. A dozen or more physicians may be involved in a patient's care along with multiple institutions, including hospitals, MRI testing centers, rehabilitation centers, and skilled-nursing facilities. Today there is widespread use of computerized record keeping and transmission of medical records. For example, information needs to be transmitted to third-party providers, such as insurance companies, to arrange for payment of the patient's medical services.

Modern medicine and technology have meant that patient privacy issues have become of paramount concern among patients, medical professionals, and ethicists. In many cases, patients have become fearful of admitting to what could be embarrassing information, such as past drug use, abortions, homosexuality, and mental health problems. When patients fail to convey this information to their physicians, it creates a difficult environment for the physicians who are treating the patients without benefit of complete medical information.

Confidentiality about sensitive information is necessary to preserve the patient's dignity. However, in order to receive payment from third-party payers such as insurance companies, Medicare, and Medicaid, the patient's diagnosis may have to be revealed, no matter how embarrassing it is for the patient.

The medical community has been conscientious about having patients sign an approval form granting permission for the release of their medical records. See Figure 10-1 for a copy of an approval form for release of medical information. However, patients' confidentiality and privacy have become more difficult with the advent of technologies such as fax transmission, the Internet, and computers in every medical office. Unfortunately, the creation of new laws has become necessary as a result of the unethical violation of patients' privacy.

## HEALTH INSURANCE PORTABILITY AND ACCOUNTABILITY ACT (HIPAA) OF 1996

The **Health Insurance Portability and Accountability Act (HIPAA)** was signed into law on August 21, 1996, regulating the privacy of patient health information. This law was an effort to reduce costs of health care and streamline the fragmented and

AUTHORIZATION FOR RELEASE OF MEDICAL INFORMATION

Date: _____

I, _____,
        (print patient's name)

authorize: _____
        (physician, hospital or other)

to release medical information from my medical record

[ ] entire record
[ ] specific information (inclusive dates) _____
[ ] other (specify) _____

to:

_____
        (name of physician, hospital, other)

_____
        (address)

_____
        (city, state, zip code)

Signature: _____ Date: _____
                (Patient)

Address of patient: _____
_____

Telephone number: _____

Witness: _____ Date: _____

**FIGURE 10–1**    Approval Form for Release of Medical Information complicated health care system. HIPAA is a sweeping reform law that affects virtually everyone in the U.S. health care system—patients, providers, payers, and intermediaries, such as pharmacies and medical device companies. The four objectives are to

- improve the portability of health insurance
- combat fraud, abuse, and waste in health care
- promote the expanded use of medical savings accounts
- simplify the administration of health insurance

Five major categories are covered under HIPAA.

Title I: Insurance Portability
Title II: Administrative Simplification
Title III: Medical Savings and Tax Deduction
Title IV: Group Health Plan Provisions
Title V: Revenue Offset Provisions

Title II, Administrative Simplification, is the section of HIPAA that affects most health care providers, insurance companies, and clearinghouses. Within this law, the Title II provisions were meant to make it easier and cheaper to electronically transmit health information. However, Congress realized that widespread electronic transmission of a patient's health information could affect a patient's privacy. Subsequently, Congress mandated that the Department of Health and Human Services (HHS) was responsible for developing detailed privacy standards. The **Privacy Rule** went into effect on April 14, 2001, and required that all "covered entities" must be in compliance with the privacy, security, and electronic-data provisions by April 14, 2003. These rules are meant to ensure

- standardization of electronic patient health records; administrative and financial data, including health care claims, health care payment, and remittance advice; health claim status; enrollment and disenrollment in a health care plan; eligibility in a health care plan; and health care premium payments
- unique identifying codes for all health care providers, health care plans, employers, and individuals
- security of electronic health information with standards protecting the confidentiality and integrity of individually identifiable health information, past, present, or future

 **MED TIP**  Many of the privacy provisions under HIPAA have caused confusion for the medical community. The original document began as a 337-word guideline, but the final regulation expanded to 101,000 words, or more than 500 pages.

The costs associated with compliance of HIPAA can be extremely high depending on the size of the organization. Blue Cross estimates that the cost of complying with the privacy law will be several billion dollars over a five-year period. This is needed to cover new staffing, computer software, and expanded paperwork.

## The Privacy Rule

The Privacy Rule applies to **Protected Health Information (PHI),** which refers to any individually identifiable information that relates to all past, present, and future physical or mental conditions or the provision of health care to an individual. For example, information such as a patient's name, age, gender, and medical diagnosis are all PHI. This information can be oral or recorded in any form or medium, such as with electronic transmission.

HIPAA requires the covered entities to limit the disclosures to only the *minimum* information necessary to carry out the medical treatment. Under HIPAA, this information can be conveyed to vendors, such as health insurance carriers, if they have obtained a written assurance (contract) from the vendor that the information will be protected. These standards to protect the PHI are in effect even if the patient is deceased.

Under HIPAA, patients must grant written consent or permission to disclose their PHI for treatment, payment, and other health care reasons. See Figure 10-2 for an example of a notice of the privacy practices for a private physician.

## Denial of the Request for Privacy

Some health care institutions, such as nursing homes, may have to deny access to a patient's medical information in order to provide protection to the patient. Table 10-1 lists reasons a nursing home may declare for denying a request for access to protected information.

## Who Is Affected?

Public health authorities, health care clearinghouses, and self-insured employers, as well as life insurers, information systems vendors, various service organizations, and universities are all included under HIPAA. These organizations are referred to as **covered entities.** A health care **clearinghouse** is a private or public entity that processes or facilitates the processing of nonstandard electronic transactions into HIPAA transactions. Thus, a clearinghouse may refer to a billing service. Covered entities include

- physicians
- hospitals
- skilled-nursing facilities
- comprehensive outpatient rehabilitation facilities
- home health agencies
- hospice programs
- ambulance companies
- clinical laboratories
- pharmaceutical companies
- medical device companies

Under HIPAA, a **health care plan** is an individual or a group plan that provides or pays for medical care. Health care plans include group health plans, health

NOTICE OF PRIVACY PRACTICES

(As required by the Privacy regulations created as a result of the Health Insurance Portability and Accountability Act of 1996 (HIPAA)

THIS NOTICE DESCRIBES HOW HEALTH INFORMATION ABOUT YOU (AS A PATIENT OF OUR PRACTICE) MAY BE USED AND DISCLOSED, AND HOW YOU CAN GET ACCESS TO YOUR INDIVIDUALLY PROTECTED HEALTH INFORMATION.

PLEASE REVIEW THIS NOTICE CAREFULLY

### A. Our commitment to your privacy

This practice is dedicated to maintaining the privacy of your individual protected health information (PHI). In conducting our business, we will create records regarding you and the treatment and services we provide to you. Federal and state laws require that we maintain the confidentiality of health information that identifies you. We are also required by law to provide you with this notice of our legal duties and the privacy policies that we maintain in our practice concerning your Protected Health Information. By federal and state law, we must follow the terms of the notice of privacy practices that we have in effect at the time.

**The terms of this notice apply to all records containing your Protected Health Information (PHI) that are created or retained by our practice. We reserve the right to revise or amend this Notice of Privacy Practices. Any revision or amendment to this notice will be effective for all your records that our practice has created or maintained in the past, and for any of your records that we may create or maintain in the future. Our practice will post a copy of our current Notice in our offices in a visible location at all times, and you may request a copy of our most current Notice at any time.**

### IF YOU HAVE QUESTIONS ABOUT THIS NOTICE, PLEASE CONTACT:

**Our practice Privacy Officer, _____ _____, at (000) 000-0000**

### B. We may use your Protected Health Information (except as it relates to psychotherapy notes) for the following purposes without obtaining your written consent:

1. **To Provide Treatment.** This relates to coordination and planning for your care and discussions between caregivers. For example, we may ask you to have laboratory tests and use the results to help us reach a diagnosis. We might use your health information in order to write a prescription for you, or we might disclose your information to a pharmacy when we order a prescription for you. Many of the people who work for our practice—including, but not limited to, our doctors and nurses—may use or disclose your information in order to treat you or to assist others in your treatment. Additionally, we may disclose such information to others who may assist in your care, such as another health care provider or your spouse, children or parents.

2. **For Payment.** Our practice may use and disclose your Protected Health Information in order to bill and collect payment for the services and items you may receive from us. For example, we may contact your health insurer to certify that you are eligible for benefits (and for what range of benefits), and we may provide your insurer with details regarding your treatment to determine if your insurer will cover, or pay for, your treatment. We may also use and disclose your Protected Health Information to obtain payment from third parties that may be responsible for such costs, such as family members. Also, we may use your Protected Health Information to bill you directly for services and items.

**FIGURE 10–2**  Notice of Privacy Practices for a Private Physician

3. **In Health Care Operations.** Our practice may use and disclose your Protected Health Information to operate our business. As examples of the ways in which we may use and disclose your information for our operations, our practice may use your information to evaluate the quality of care you received from us, or to conduct cost-management and business planning activities for our practice.

**Unless you object or specifically request to restrict use, other ways we may use your Protected Health Information (PHI) are:**

4. **Appointment Reminders.** Our practice may use and disclose your PHI to contact you and remind you of an appointment.

5. **Treatment Options.** Our practice may use and disclose your PHI to inform you of potential treatment options or alternatives.

6. **Release of Information to Family/Friends.** Our practice may release your PHI to a friend or family member that is involved in your care, or who assists in taking care of you. For example, a parent or guardian may ask that a babysitter or relative take his or her child to the pediatrician's office for treatment of a cold. In this example, the babysitter may have access to this child's information.

7. **Disclosures As Required By Law.** Our practice will use and disclose your Personal Health Information when we are required to do so by federal, state, or local law.

C. **SPECIAL CIRCUMSTANCES. Unless the Protected Health Information is protected by state confidentiality laws (Drug, Alcohol, Psychiatric or HIV-related information), we may use and disclose your Protected Health Information without your consent or without providing you the opportunity to object as follows:**

1. **Public Health Risks.** Our practice may disclose your PHI to public health authorities that are authorized by laws to collect information for the purpose of:

   • maintaining vital records, such as births and deaths

   • reporting child abuse or neglect

   • preventing or controlling disease, injury or disability

   • notifying a person regarding potential exposure to a communicable disease

   • notifying a person regarding a potential risk for spreading or contracting a disease

   • reporting reactions to drugs or problems with products or devices

   • notifying individuals if a product or device they may be using has been recalled

   • notifying appropriate government agencies/authorities regarding the potential abuse or neglect of an adult patient (including domestic violence); however, we will only disclose this information if the patient agrees or we are required or authorized by law to disclose this information

2. **Health Oversight Activities.** Our practice may disclose your PHI to a health oversight agency for activities authorized by law. Oversight activities can include, for example, investigations, inspections, audits, surveys, licensure and disciplinary actions; civil, administrative, and criminal procedures or actions; or other activities necessary for the government to monitor government programs (Medicare and Medicaid), compliance with civil rights laws, and the health care system in general.

3. **Lawsuits and Similar Proceedings.** Our practice may use and disclose your PHI in response to a court or administrative order if you are involved in a lawsuit or similar proceeding. We also may disclose your PHI in response to a discovery request or lawfully issued subpoena.

4. **Law Enforcement.** We may release PHI if asked to do so by a law-enforcement official:

   • regarding a crime victim in certain situations

   • concerning a death we believe has resulted from criminal conduct

**FIGURE 10–2** Notice of Privacy Practices for a Private Physician *(continued)*

- regarding criminal conduct at our office

- in response to a warrant, summons, court order, subpoena, or similar process

- to identify/locate a suspect, material witness, fugitive, or missing person

- in an emergency, to report a crime (including the location or victim(s) of the crime, or the description, identity, or location of the perpetrator)

5. **Deceased Patients.** Our practice may release Personal Health Information to a medical examiner or coroner to identify a deceased individual or to identify the cause of death. We also may release information for funeral directors to perform their jobs.

6. **Organ and Tissue Donation.** Our practice may release your PHI to organizations that handle organ, eye, or tissue procurement or transplantation, including organ donation banks, as necessary to facilitate organ or tissue donation and transplantation if you are an organ donor.

7. **Serious Threats to the Health or Safety.** Our practice may use and disclose your PHI when necessary to reduce or prevent a serious threat to your health and safety or the health and safety of another individual or the public. Under these circumstances, we will only make disclosures to a person or organization able to help prevent the threat.

8. **Military.** Our practice may disclose your PHI if you are a member of U.S. or foreign military forces (including veterans) and if required by the appropriate authorities.

9. **National Security.** Our practice may disclose your PHI to federal officials for intelligence and national security activities authorized by law. We also may disclose your PHI to federal officials in order to protect the President, other officials, or foreign heads of state, or to conduct investigations.

10. **Inmates.** Our practice may disclose your PHI to correctional institutions or law-enforcement officials if you are an inmate or under custody of a law-enforcement official. Disclosure for these purposes would be necessary: (a) for the institution to provide health care services to you, (b) for the safety and security of the institution, and/or (c) to protect your health and safety or the health and safety of other individuals.

11. **Workers' Compensation.** Our practice may release your PHI for workers' compensation and similar programs.

**ALL OTHER DISCLOSURES WILL BE MADE ONLY WITH YOUR SPECIFIC WRITTEN AUTHORIZATION, WHICH MAY BE REVOKED, EXCEPT TO THE EXTENT IT HAS ALREADY BEEN RELIED UPON.**

### D. Organized Health Care Arrangement (OHCA)

The physicians/practitioners at _____ and _____ Hospital and its medical staff operate as an Organized Health Care Arrangement, which means that for purposes of compliance with Federal Privacy Standards, you will be receiving a joint Notice of Privacy Practices from the hospital and its staff for services provided at the hospital.

### E. YOUR RIGHTS REGARDING YOUR PROTECTED HEALTH INFORMATION:

1. **Confidential Communications.** You have the right to request that our practice communicate with you about your health and related issues in a particular manner or at a certain location. For instance, you may ask that we contact you at home rather than at work. In order to request a type of confidential communication, you must make a written request to our privacy officer, specifying the requested method of contact, or the location where you wish to be contacted. Our practice will accommodate **reasonable** requests.

**FIGURE 10–2**   Notice of Privacy Practices for a Private Physician *(continued)*

2. **Requesting Restrictions.** You have the right to request a restriction in our use or disclosure of your PHI for treatment, payment or health care operations. Additionally, you have the right to request that we restrict our disclosure of your PHI to only certain individuals involved in your care, such as family members and friends. **We are not required to agree with your request;** however, if we do agree, we are bound by our agreement except when otherwise required by law, in emergencies, or when the information is necessary to treat you. In order to request a restriction in our use or disclosure of your PHI, you must make your request in writing. Your request must describe in a clear and concise fashion the information you wish restricted and to whom this will apply.

3. **Inspection/Copies.** You have the right to inspect and obtain a copy of the PHI that may be used to make decisions about you, including patient medical records and billing records, but not including psychotherapy notes. You must submit your request in writing in order to inspect and/or obtain a copy of this information. Our practice may charge a fee for the costs of copying, mailing, labor and supplies associated with your request. Our practice may deny your request to inspect and/or copy in certain limited circumstances; however, you may request a review of our denial. Another licensed health care professional chosen by us will conduct reviews.

4. **Amendment.** You may ask us to amend your health information if you believe it is incorrect or incomplete, and you may request an amendment for as long as the information is kept by or for our practice. To request an amendment, your request must be in writing. You must provide us with a reason that supports your request for amendment. Our practice will deny your request if you fail to submit your request (and the reason supporting your request) in writing. Also, we may deny your request if you ask us to amend information that is in our opinion: (a) accurate and complete, (b) not part of the PHI kept by or for the practice, (c) not part of the PHI which you would be permitted to inspect and copy, (d) not created by our practice, unless the individual or entity that created the information is not available to amend the information.

5. **Accounting of Disclosures.** All of our patients have the right to request an "accounting of disclosures." An accounting of disclosures is a list of certain nonroutine disclosures our practice has made of your PHI for nontreatment or operations purposes. Use of your PHI as part of the routine patient care in our practice does not need to be documented. (For example, the doctor sharing information with the nurse or the billing department using your information to file your insurance claim.) In order to obtain an accounting of disclosures, you must submit your request in written form. We have 60 days to provide you with the accounting. All requests for an "accounting of disclosures" must state a time period, which may not be longer than six (6) years from the date of disclosure and may not include dates before April 14, 2003.

6. **Right to File a Complaint.** If you believe your privacy rights have been violated, you may file a complaint with our practice or with the Secretary of the Department of Health and Human Services. All complaints must be submitted in writing. You will not be retaliated against for filing a complaint.

**For any requests, contact our privacy officer in writing:**

**Privacy officer** _____ **Address** _____

Our practice will obtain your written authorization for uses and disclosures that are not identified by this notice or permitted by applicable law. Any authorization you provide to us regarding the use and disclosure of your PHI may be revoked at any time in writing. Please note, we are required to retain records of your care.

**You are entitled to receive a paper copy of our current notice of privacy practices. You may ask us to give you a copy of this notice at any time.**

**FIGURE 10–2** Notice of Privacy Practices for a Private Physician *(continued)*

**TABLE 10–1**   Reasons Given by a Nursing Home for Denial of Access to Information

We may deny a request for access to protected health information if

(a) a licensed health care professional has determined, in the exercise of professional judgment, that the access requested is reasonably likely to endanger your life or physical safety or that of another person;

(b) the protected health information makes reference to another person (unless such other person is a health care provider) and a licensed health care professional has determined, in the exercise of professional judgment, that the access requested is reasonably likely to cause substantial harm to such other person; or

(c) the request for access is made by the individual's personal representative and a licensed health care professional has determined, in the exercise of professional judgment, that the provision of access to such personal representative is reasonably likely to cause substantial harm to you or another person.

If we deny a request for access for any of the three reasons described above, then you have the right to have our denial reviewed in accordance with the requirements of applicable law.

You have the right to request an amendment to your protected health information, but we may deny your request for amendment if we determine that the protected health information or record that is the subject of the request

(a) was not created by us, unless you provide a reasonable basis to believe that the originator of protected health information is no longer available to act on the requested amendment;

(b) is not part of your medical or billing records or other records used to make decisions about you;

(c) is not available for inspection as set forth above; or

(d) is accurate and complete

In any event, any agreed-upon amendment will be included as an addition to, and not a replacement of, already existing records. In order to request an amendment to your health information, you must submit your request in writing to _____, our privacy officer, along with a description of the reason for your request.

maintenance organizations (HMOs), the Medicare program parts A and B, the Medicaid program, and employee welfare benefit plans. Thus, there are few, if any, health care providers that are not affected by this law.

In addition, certain businesses and individuals, such as employers who sponsor health plans, lawyers, accountants, consultants, and other professionals working for the covered entities, are affected by HIPAA in an indirect manner. The covered entity must make sure that the businesses it works with comply with the Privacy Rule. There are severe penalties for violations for both the covered entity and the indirect supplier.

## Unique Identifiers for Health Care Providers

In the past, health care organizations used multiple identification formats when doing business with each other. This resulted in confusion and errors. Standard identifiers are now being used in an attempt to reduce these problems. The **Employer Identifier Standard,** which was published in 2002, uses an employer's tax ID number or their **Employer Identification Number (EIN)** as the standard code number for all electronic transmissions.

An individual's Social Security number is still used for insurance identification purposes, since most Americans have a Social Security number and identification card. HIPAA has added the EIN for purposes of electronic transmission by health care providers.

## Can Public Health Information (PHI) Be De-identified?

There are many reasons for obtaining health information in which the patient does not need to be identified. For instance, health statistics relating to communicable diseases can be obtained by de-identifying the patient. In order to "de-identify" patient information, the following forms of identity must be removed from the data:

- patient's name
- address, including e-mail
- telephone and fax numbers
- all dates, including birth (except year), admission, discharge, and death
- Social Security number
- medical records numbers
- health care insurance numbers
- license numbers
- facial photographs such as found on a driver's license
- other identifying numbers or characteristics

## What Are the Obligations to the Patient Under HIPAA?

The health care provider, such as a physician, has several confidentiality obligations to the patient. These include obligations to obtain patient consent and authorization for any disclosures of medical information, and permitting patient access to medical information. In addition, the provider must obtain patient authorization prior to disclosing PHI for purposes other than medical treatment, such as payment collection or a disclosure of psychotherapy notes.

The provider has a requirement to provide only the **minimum necessary standard** for any disclosure about the patient. This standard means that the provider must make a reasonable effort to limit the disclosure of patient information to only the minimum that is necessary to accomplish the purpose of the request. The minimum necessary standard does not apply when a provider is submitting information to the patient, the HHS, or another provider, such as a physician or hospital, for the purpose of treatment.

The minimum necessary standard requirements do not apply to any health information disclosures that are required by law. For example, a physician, as a covered entity, is still required to disclose PHI that is requested in a subpoena.

 **MED TIP**   The minimum necessary standard is important to remember when supplying a request for patient information. Never send a copy of the patient's entire medical record when only specific information is requested.

## What Are the Penalties for Noncompliance with HIPAA?

Noncompliance with HIPAA can result in serious penalties for health care providers such as physicians and hospitals. The penalties for violating HIPAA range from civil penalties of up to $100 per person per incident for minor improper disclosures of health information, and up to $25,000 for multiple violations of the same standard in a calendar year. Federal criminal liability for improper disclosure of information or for obtaining information under false pretenses carries **sanctions** (fines) of $50,000 and one year in prison. The liability for obtaining protected health information under false pretenses with the intent to sell, transfer, or use the information for personal gain or for a malicious action, such as Medicare fraud, carries penalties of $250,000 and/or up to ten years in prison. Severe penalties are in effect if lax security allows health information to be stolen. There is also a risk of a class action suit as well as public relations damage to the institution's or physician's image.

Health care fraud, especially relating to the Medicare and Medicaid programs, has been increasing during the past decade. Fraud alerts issued by the Inspector General's office of the Department of Health and Human Services (HHS) concerning suspicious practices can alert providers and the public to the potential for medical privacy abuse.

Another provision under HIPAA is the establishment of the **Healthcare Integrity and Protection Data Bank (HIPDB).** This is a national data bank that collects reports and disclosures of actions taken against health care practitioners, providers, and vendors for noncompliance and fraudulent activities. This extensive data bank is not available to the general public but can be accessed by federal and state government agencies and various health plans.

## What Are the Patients' Rights Under the Privacy Standards?

Patients have many rights under HIPAA. Health care providers have the additional responsibility of alerting patients to their own rights under this law. For example, patients have a right to

- a copy of the privacy notice from the health care provider
- access their medical records, and the right to restrict access by others, request changes, and learn how their records have been accessed
- ask the provider to limit the way in which health care information is shared and to keep disclosures to the minimum needed for treatment and business operations
- ask for an accounting of to whom the health care information was given
- ask to be contacted in a special way such as by mail or at work
- examine and copy the health information the provider has recorded
- complain to the covered entity and the Department of Health and Human Services if the patient believes there is a violation of his or her privacy

## Special Rules Relating to Research

HIPAA regulations also relate to medical information that is compiled and used for research purposes. Providers and other covered entities that wish to use individually identifiable patient information that is related to treatment, such as for cancer patients, must perform a very detailed authorization form. The researchers must obtain

- a patient authorization that complies with the rules set by HIPAA, or
- a waiver of authorization from a privacy board or an Institutional Review Board, such as is found in a teaching hospital or university. The waiver must include extensive documentation as required by HIPAA.

This regulation also covers information used for research from deceased patient records.

## Problems Relating to Implementation of HIPAA's Privacy Rules

HIPAA regulations have made many health care agencies, such as hospitals, reluctant to release any information about their patients due to fear of civil or criminal penalties under HIPAA. This is particularly true when a patient refuses to be listed on the hospital's patient directory. In certain situations, some health care providers, trying to avoid any error under HIPAA by disclosing PHI inappropriately, refuse to provide medical records to anyone except the patient. For instance, state workers' compensation programs, which are exempted under HIPPA, have difficulty receiving the medical information they require in order to provide financial assistance for the patient.

Reports of problems with accessing patient information have been filed by nonmedical persons. For example, human resource departments often require medical information in order to administer the Family Medical Leave Act (FMLA), facilitate return-to-work policies, assist in Americans with Disabilities Act (ADA) accommodation discussions, and obtain results from drug testing. In addition, lawyers working with workers' compensation claims, medical malpractice, and personal injury litigation need access to medical records.

The reason for many of these problems is that some health care providers, trying to avoid any error under HIPAA by disclosing PHI inappropriately, refuse to provide medical records to anyone except the patient. For example, members of the clergy complain that the privacy rules keep them from visiting the sick members of their congregations when they are hospitalized. They complain that the law is being too narrowly interpreted.

Police are also confronting problems as a result of HIPAA. The law requires hospitals to report to the police when a patient comes in with a gunshot wound or there is a suspected case of child abuse or neglect. According to some police officials, compliance with HIPAA is slowing police investigations and even impeding the prosecution of crimes. Police officers complain that they are being denied access to anyone, including crime victims and missing persons, who have opted not to be listed in hospital directories. Although HIPAA makes exceptions for criminal investigations, some hospitals, concerned with violating the law, err on the side of caution and refuse to release any information. Under HIPAA, hospitals must allow police to interview patients and must provide information about their condition when a serious crime has been committed.

 **MED TIP**   A violation of HIPAA, a federal law, is a criminal offense. Therefore, fear of violating this law has caused an overreaction to it among many health care professionals.

## Misconceptions About HIPAA

The Department of Health and Human Services (HHS) states that the law requires "reasonable safeguards" to be taken in order to protect patient privacy. The privacy provision applies to physicians, pharmacists, and insurers. It was originally intended to protect computerized medical records and billing. An additional purpose of HIPAA was to allow patients easier access to their own medical records. However, the purpose has been interpreted much more broadly. According to the HHS, many misconceptions about HIPAA are slowly being cleared up. The privacy law

- does not prevent physicians or hospitals from sharing patient information with other physicians or hospitals in order to treat patients.
- does not prevent hospitals from disclosing names of patients to clergy or from keeping patient directories. It does not require that patients sign in to be included in the hospital directory of patients, only that they can opt out and not be included.
- allows hospitals or physicians to share information with the patient's spouse, family members, friends, or anyone whom the patient has identified as involved in their care.
- does not apply to most police or fire departments. The hospital may release names and information about homicides, accident victims, and other incidents. However, HIPAA does limit the information that emergency medical technicians (EMTs) may disclose.

Office personnel, acting on behalf of physicians and dentists, can still send out reminders about appointments and leave messages on patients' answering machines.

 **MED TIP** The HIPAA law, as currently written, prohibits patients/consumers from suing over privacy violations. Instead, patient/consumers must register their complaints to the government.

## Recommendations

Following are some practical recommendations for physicians and physician groups to follow when implementing HIPAA:

- Appoint and train a privacy officer to receive complaints and provide information concerning the provider's privacy notice materials.
- Conduct an internal assessment of existing policies, procedures, and practices for collecting and handling medical records and patient information to determine where the gaps may be.
- Enter into agreements with all nonemployee service providers who may have access to PHI.
- Adopt procedures for handling patient requests.
- Implement a notice of privacy practices.
- Revise employee manuals regarding HIPAA standards. These personnel policies must reflect the organization's handling of employees who use or disclose PHI in

violation of HIPAA. The **Office of Civil Rights (OCR)** would likely ask for a copy of these policies during an investigation of violations.

■ Train all employees on policies and procedures regarding HIPAA.
■ Retain signed authorizations, copies of notices of privacy practices, and any agreements with patients restricting disclosure of PHI. This documentation should be retained for a period of six years from the date they were created or the date when they were last in effect.
■ Implement and enforce sanctions (penalties) for violations of provider policies and procedures.
■ Establish a complaint process for noncompliance with the privacy regulation.

# ETHICAL CONCERNS WITH INFORMATION TECHNOLOGY (INFORMATICS)

**Wireless local area networks (WLANs)** are used by physicians and nurses to access patient records from central databases while they are conducting patient rounds (bedside visits), adding observations and patient assessments to the databases, checking on medications, and completing a variety of other functions. The use of wireless networks by health care professionals presents ethical challenges and dilemmas. There can be a tradeoff between quick access to the patient's medical records and security of that record. Decisions relating to the use of WLANs must take into account the impact they have on the patient's privacy as mandated by HIPAA. HIPAA requires that there be safeguards in place to protect the privacy of electronic and nonelectronic protected health information. The HIPAA security rules that were issued in final form on February 20, 2003, apply to PHI in electronic form only.

 **MED TIP** Since the amount of medical information available is said to double every five years, computerized systems have become indispensable.

**Medical informatics** is the application of communication and information to medical practice, research, and education. Many hospitals and health care institutions are able to link together diverse areas such as pharmacy, laboratory, administrative, and medical records through the use of informatics.

**Telemedicine,** or the use of communications and information technologies to provide health care services to people at a distance, is seen as the future of medicine. Modern technology has the ability to provide health services for homebound and rural patients via telephone, fax, Internet, and even real-time television. All of these methods have been used to provide continuing medical education for the past decade.

Some of these methods for treatment are still in the developmental stage. For example, Virginia Mason Medical Center, a large multi-specialty group practice in Seattle, has telemedicine sites in rural Washington and Alaska. This center uses telemedicine to consult on diagnosis and treatment, transmit radiological studies, and conduct presurgical and postsurgical exams. It has telemedicine projects in radiology, cardiology, neurology/neurosurgery, psychiatry, dermatology, oncology, rheumatology, and rehabilitation medicine.

Health Partners, a Minneapolis-based health plan, uses a 24-hour two-way video conferencing method to link the nurses with the home care patients. Ordinary phone lines are used in this system. The nurses are able to inspect wound care and healing over this video link.

A multitude of medical information is currently available over the Internet—in varying degrees of usefulness. Health care consumers can use the Internet to research their disease and treatment options. Many health care plans and institutions have their own Web sites with current information about services and medical information (see Appendix C for a listing of useful medical Web sites).

Telemedicine raises legal issues, such as concerns about practicing medicine across state lines, that must be addressed. Physician reimbursement for these types of consultations is uncertain. Also, the credentials of the person giving medical advice over the Internet are open to both legal and ethical discussion.

Informatics presents a multitude of ethical issues, especially with the use of the Internet by physicians and patients. Health care providers have expressed concern about security when patient data, such as that contained in medical records, is transmitted via the Internet. A report on confidentiality and security issues by the Computer-Based Patient Record Institute, based in Schaumburg, Illinois, states, "Breaches of confidentiality can lead to loss of employment and housing, health and life insurance problems, and social stigma. . . . Formal information security programs must be established by each organization entrusted with health care information."

## POINTS TO PONDER

1. Will it be possible to balance the wealth of medical information available to the patient via the Internet with the loss of a personal relationship between the patient and caregiver?
2. How can a patient's PHI be maintained when medical information is being faxed from one location to another?
3. Is the high cost of implementing HIPAA in a small medical practice worth the expense?
4. In your opinion, will HIPAA make it more or less difficult for public services such as police, fire, and ambulance services to administer to patients? Explain your answer.

## DISCUSSION QUESTIONS

1. Why has patient confidentiality become more difficult in the present health care environment?
2. Why is the implementation of the new Privacy Rule so expensive?
3. Should family members, and even friends, have access to a patient's medical record? Why or why not?
4. Should patients be treated via the Internet? Why or why not?

## PRACTICE EXERCISES

### Matching

Match responses in column B with the correct term in column A.

**Column A**

_____  1. privacy rule
_____  2. WLANs
_____  3. HIPAA
_____  4. EIN
_____  5. clearinghouse
_____  6. health care plan
_____  7. PHI
_____  8. telemedicine
_____  9. employer identifier
          standard
_____  10. HHS

**Column B**

a. number assigned to an employer
b. individually identifiable information
c. wireless system to send and receive data
d. based on employer's tax ID or on their EIN
e. all covered entities must be in compliance
f. Department of Health and Human Services
g. a billing service
h. use of information technologies to treat people at a distance
i. Health Insurance Portability and Accountability Act of 1996
j. individual or group that provides or pays for medical care

## MULTIPLE CHOICE

Select the one best answer to the following statements.

1. The Privacy Rule is meant to ensure
   a. standardization of health data
   b. standardization of financial data
   c. standardization of medical care
   d. a and b only
   e. a, b, and c

2. An example of a clearinghouse is
   a. PHI
   b. skilled nursing facility
   c. a billing service
   d. a government regulation
   e. EIN

3. The government organization that investigates a violation of a patient's medical privacy
   a. OSHA
   b. OCR
   c. PHI
   d. HIPAA
   e. none of the above

4. A network of wireless communication systems used to access patient records is
   a. HIPAA
   b. PHI
   c. WLANs
   d. EIN
   e. ADA

5. The privacy law
   a. prevents hospitals from sharing medical information with other facilities
   b. prevents hospitals from sharing registered patient names with the clergy
   c. does not apply to most police and fire departments
   d. allows unlimited information to be shared by EMTs
   e. none of the above

6. A violation of HIPAA
   a. is a criminal offense
   b. does not carry any financial penalty at present
   c. is not reportable
   d. does not affect a physician's reputation, since it is just a document
   e. may have a fine of under $100 for all offenses

7. When implementing HIPAA, physicians and physician groups should
   a. hire a privacy officer
   b. implement a notice of privacy practices
   c. retain signed authorizations for at least six years
   d. enter into agreements with nonemployee service providers
   e. all of the above

8. Covered entities include all of the following except
   a. hospice programs
   b. medical device companies
   c. clinical laboratories
   d. police departments
   e. skilled-nursing facilities

9. Patient's rights under HIPAA include the ability to
   a. examine their medical record
   b. have a full copy of their medical record
   c. complain to the HHS if they believe there is a violation of privacy
   d. a and c only
   e. a, b, and c

10. When patient information is requested via a subpoena, you must
    a. comply and send the entire record immediately
    b. provide only the minimum necessary standard even if more is requested in the subpoena
    c. provide all PHI that is requested in the subpoena
    d. provide PHI only with the consent of the patient
    e. none of the above are correct

## PUT IT INTO PRACTICE

Request a copy of a Notice of Privacy Practice from your physician's office. Compare it to the privacy notice in Table 10-2. How do they differ?

## WEB HUNT

Look under the patient/consumer Web site *www.healthfinder.gov* to find consumer information on complaints. Click on "all topics"; under C, click on "complaints"; click on "Bureau of Consumer Protection: Online Complaint Form." Do you believe the information is accurate? Why or why not? Do you believe the information is useful? Why or why not? Rate the information on a scale of 1 to 10 with 1 = low usefulness and 10 = high usefulness.

Look under the official government Web site relating to HIPAA, *www.hhs.gov/ocr/hipaa*, to find the answers to frequently asked questions about HIPAA. Describe five questions and answers that you believe all health care professionals should know.

## REFERENCES

American Association of Medical Assistants. 1996. *Health care law and ethics.* Chicago: American Association of Medical Assistants.

Associated Press. 2004. Privacy keeps clergy from sick. *Hartford Courant.* April, 12, B2.

Beauchamp. T., and J. Childress. 1983. *Principles of biomedical ethics.* New York: Oxford University Press.

Garrett, T., H. Baillie, and R. Garrett. 1993. *Health care ethics: Principles and problems.* Upper Saddle River, N.J.: Prentice Hall.

Hall, R. 2000. *An introduction to healthcare organizational ethics.* Oxford, England: Oxford University Press.

McConnell, T. 1997. *Moral issues in health care: An introduction to medical ethics.* Albany, N.Y.: Wadsworth.

Parker, L. 2003. Medical-privacy law creates wide confusion. *USA Today.* October 17, 1, 2.

Rae, S., and P. Cox. 1999. *Bioethics.* Grand Rapids, Mich.: William B. Eerdmans.

Schiff, M. 2003. *HIPAA: The questions you didn't know to ask.* Upper Saddle River, N.J.: Prentice Hall.

Somma, A. 2003. Privacy rules stymie police. *Hartford Courant,* August 7, 1, 10.

Veatch, R. 1989. *Medical ethics.* Boston: Jones & Bartlett.

## CASE STUDY

Mary Smith has just reported for duty and is reviewing the patients she will have during the evening shift. One of them, Ida Monroe, a recovering alcoholic, is in the hospital for some liver function tests. Dr. Jerome comes into the nursing station around 9:00 P.M. after making hospital rounds to see his patients. He tells Mary that he noticed that one of his neighbors, Ida Monroe, is a patient, and he would like to review her medical chart. Mary starts to give him the chart and then realizes that Dr. Jerome is not Ida's physician. Dr. Jerome says not to worry about that, since he has taken care of the rest of Ida's family for years and is sure that Ida will want him to consult on her case. When Mary hesitates to give him the chart, Dr. Jerome says that he will report her to her nursing supervisor. He walks over to pick up the chart.

1. Should Mary give Ida's medical chart to Dr. Jerome? Why or why not?

_____

_____

_____

2. What should Mary say to Dr. Jerome?

_____

_____

_____

3. What should Mary do if Dr. Jerome continues to insist on seeing Ida's chart?

_____

_____

_____

4. What ethical principles are involved in this case?

_____

_____

_____

5. What legal regulations are involved in this case?

_____

_____

_____

# MEDICAL ETHICS

CHAPTER **11**

# Ethical and Bioethical Issues in Medicine

## LEARNING OBJECTIVES

1. Define the glossary terms.
2. List and discuss at least ten bioethical issues the modern physician and health care professional faces.
3. Describe how an ethical decision-making model can be used when confronted with difficult ethical dilemmas.
4. Discuss the importance of ethics committees.
5. Define medical etiquette.
6. Summarize the ethical issues of organ transplantation.

## KEY TERMS

Allege
Censure
Double-blind test
Euthanasia
Expulsion
Institutional Review Board (IRB)

Medical etiquette
National Organ Transplant Law of 1984
Nontherapeutic research
Posthumous
Revocation

Social utility method of allocation
Therapeutic research
United Network for Organ Sharing (UNOS)

## INTRODUCTION

Health care ethics, bioethics, and medical law are intertwined out of necessity. When ethical principles are violated, a civil lawsuit often follows. Ethics, that branch of philosophy relating to morals or moral principles, involves the examination of human character and conduct, the distinction between right and wrong, and a person's moral duty and obligations to the community.

Ethics, as discussed in the health care professions, is applied ethics. In other words, while theoretical concepts involving ethics are important for the student to know, the basis for study involves applying one's moral and value system to a career in health care.

Ethics involves more than just common sense, which is an approach for making decisions that most people in society use. Ethics goes way beyond common sense: it requires a critical-thinking approach that examines important considerations such as fairness for all consumers, the impact of the decision on society, and the future implications of the decision.

The dignity of the individual, whether it is the patient, employee, or physician, must always be of paramount concern when discussing ethics and bioethics. Bioethics concerns ethical issues discussed in the context of advanced medical technology. The somewhat new field of bioethics requires the health care professional to ask whether a practice such as gene therapy or harvesting embryo organs can be morally justified. In addition, physicians must ask themselves if these practices are compatible with the character traits of a good physician.

 **MED TIP**   An illegal act, or one that is against the law, is always unethical. However, an unethical act may not be illegal. For instance, providing medical treatment, such as an organ transplant, to a celebrity and denying the same treatment for an indigent "street person," while legal, is clearly unethical.

## EARLY HISTORY

Ethics has been a part of the medical profession since the beginning of medical practice. The earliest code of ethics, or principles to govern conduct of those practicing medicine, is the Code of Hammurabi, which dates back to around 1800 B.C.

In 400 B.C., Hippocrates, a Greek physician referred to as "the father of medicine," wrote a statement of principles for his medical students to follow that is still important in medicine. Called the Hippocratic Oath, the code reminds students of the importance of their profession, the need to teach others, and the obligation they have to act in a way so as to never knowingly harm a patient or divulge a confidence. The principles stated in the oath are found today in many of the professional codes of ethics, such as that of the American Medical Association (AMA). The Hippocratic Oath is found in Appendix A.

## ETHICAL STANDARDS AND BEHAVIOR

Ethical behavior, according to the AMA, refers to moral principles or practices, the customs of the medical profession, and matters of medical policy. Unethical behavior would be any action that does not follow these ethical standards. For example, physicians who accept payment for referring patients to another physician are guilty of a practice called fee splitting, which is unethical.

A physician who is accused of unethical behavior or conduct in violation of these standards can be issued a warning or **censure** (criticism) by the AMA. The AMA Board of Examiners may recommend the **expulsion** (being forced out) or suspension of a physician from membership in the medical association. Expulsion is a severe penalty because it limits the physician's ability to practice medicine. Even if the AMA censors its members, it does not have authority to bring legal action against the physician for unethical behavior. However, not all physicians belong to the AMA.

If someone **alleges,** or declares without proof, that a physician has committed a criminal act, the AMA is required to report it to the state licensing board or governmental agency. Violation of the law, followed by a conviction for the crime, may result in a fine, imprisonment, or **revocation** (taking away) of the physician's license.

 **MED TIP** The loss of a physician's license, as required by law in serious cases of fraud, could also mean the loss of the physician's reputation.

## CODES OF ETHICS

People's behavior must match their set of values. For example, it is not enough to believe that patient confidentiality is important if one then freely discusses a patient's personal information with a coworker or friend. In this case, the health care professional's values and behavior are at odds. Professional organizations have developed codes of ethics that summarize the basic principles and behavior that are expected of all practitioners in that discipline. These codes are meant to govern the conduct of members of a given profession, such as medicine.

Some codes of ethics were developed as a direct response to atrocities that occurred during wartime, especially in response to the medical experimentation in Nazi concentration camps. These codes—including the Declaration of Geneva and the Declaration of Helsinki, authored by the World Medical Association (see Appendix A)—provide guidance to present-day medical researchers.

Concern for the human subject in medical experimentation is the theme of the Nuremberg Code. Public awareness of the ethical and legal problems associated with medical research on human subjects gained prominence in the post–World War II trials at Nuremberg, Germany. In these trials, more than 25 medical personnel were accused of committing war crimes against involuntary human subjects. What became known as the Nuremberg Code developed after these trials made public what the Nazis had done under the guise of medical research. This code became a forerunner for the subsequent codes and guidelines that were adopted by medical and research organizations and agencies. The Nuremberg Code, which is reprinted from Trials of War Criminals before the Nuremberg Military Tribunals, is found in Appendix A.

Due to advances in medical science and technology, and changes in the medical profession, physicians have developed modern codes of ethics that serve as a moral guide for the health care professional. The AMA has taken a leadership role in setting standards for the ethical behavior of physicians in the United States. The first Code of Ethics of the AMA was formed in 1847, shortly after the organization was founded.

### American Medical Association (AMA) Principles of Medical Ethics

The AMA Principles of Medical Ethics—which appear in Chapter 5—discuss human dignity, honesty, responsibility to society, confidentiality, the need for continued study, patient autonomy, and a responsibility of the physician to improve the community.

### Judicial Council Opinions of the AMA

The Council on Ethical and Judicial Affairs of the AMA is comprised of nine members who interpret the Principles of Medical Ethics. The council's interpretation or clarification is then published for AMA members. All members of the medical team are expected to cooperate with the physician in upholding these principles. A few of the opinions of the Council on Ethical and Judicial Affairs are adapted and summarized in Table 11-1.

## CODES OF ETHICS FOR OTHER MEDICAL PROFESSIONALS

Other professional organizations have developed codes of ethics that assist to guide members' behavior. Two such groups of professionals include nurses and medical assistants.

### Nurses' Code of Ethics

Nurses have a code of ethics developed by the International Council of Nurses. This code discusses the role of nurses as they relate to people, their practice, society, their coworkers, and their profession. In addition, the American Nurses Association (ANA) has developed a code for nurses that discusses the nurses' obligation to protect patients' privacy, respect patients' dignity, maintain competence in nursing, and assume responsibility and accountability for individual nursing judgments.

### Code of Ethics of the American Association of Medical Assistants (AAMA)

Medical assistants may not be faced with the life-and-death ethical decisions that face the physician, but they will encounter many dilemmas regarding right and wrong on an almost daily basis. For example, how does the medical assistant handle a situation in which another employee violates confidentiality or uses foul language in front of a patient? How is the patient whose body smells of urine and alcohol treated? These are issues involving ethics and doing the right thing at the right time. To provide

**TABLE 11–1**  Summary of Opinions of the Council on Ethical and Judicial Affairs of the AMA

| Issue | Opinion |
|---|---|
| Abuse | Physicians who are likely to detect abuse in the course of their work have an obligation to familiarize themselves with protocols for diagnosing and treating abuse and with community resources for battered women, children, and elderly persons. If it were not reported, it might mean further abuse or even death for the victim. |
| Accepting patients | A physician may decline to accept a patient if the medical condition of the patient is not within the area of the physician's expertise and practice. However, a physician may not decline a patient due to race, color, religion, national origin, or any other basis for discrimination. |
| Allocations of health resources | Physicians have a duty to do what they can for the benefit of the individual patient. Physicians have a responsibility to participate and to contribute their professional expertise in order to safeguard the interests of patients in decisions made at the societal level regarding the allocation or rationing of health resources. The treating physician must remain a patient advocate and therefore should not make allocation decisions. |
| Artificial Insemination | Artificial insemination—the insertion of semen by the physician into a woman's vagina from the woman's husband, partner, or a donor by means other than sexual intercourse—requires the consent of the woman and her husband. Artificial insemination husband (AIH) refers to a procedure in which sperm from the woman's husband or partner is used. Artificial insemination donor (AID) refers to a procedure in which sperm from a donor is used. If artificial insemination is from a donor, the physician is ethically bound to carefully screen the donor for any defects. The physician or physician's staff may not reveal the identity of the donor to anyone. |
| Confidential care of minors | Physicians who treat minors have an ethical duty to promote the autonomy of minor patients by involving them in the medical decision-making process to a degree equal with their abilities. |
| Euthanasia | Euthanasia is the administration of a lethal agent by another person to cause the patient's death and thereby relieve the patient's intolerable and incurable suffering. Instead of engaging in euthanasia, physicians must aggressively respond to the needs of patients at the end of life. Patients should not be abandoned once it is determined that a cure is impossible. |
| Fee splitting | The practice of a physician accepting payment from another physician for the referral of a patient is known as fee splitting and is considered unethical. |
| Financial incentives for organ donation | The voluntary donation of organs in appropriate circumstances is to be encouraged. However, it is not ethical to participate in a procedure to enable a donor to receive payment, other than for the reimbursement of expenses necessarily incurred in connection with removal, for any of the donor's nonrenewable organs. In addition, the death of the donor must be decided by a physician other than the donor patient's physician. |

*(continued)*

**TABLE 11–1**   Summary of Opinions of the Council on Ethical and Judicial Affairs of the AMA *(continued)*

| Issue | Opinion |
|---|---|
| Gene therapy | The Council's position is that gene therapy, the replacement of a defective or malfunctioning gene, is acceptable as long as it is used for therapeutic purposes and not for altering human traits. |
| Ghost surgery | A surgeon cannot substitute another surgeon to perform a procedure without the consent of the patient. |
| HIV testing | Physicians should ensure that HIV testing is conducted in a way that respects patient autonomy and assures patient confidentiality as much as possible. |
| Mandatory parental consent to abortion | Physicians should ascertain the law in their state on parental involvement in abortion to ensure that their procedures are consistent with their legal obligations. |
| Physician-assisted suicide | Instead of assisting patients in committing suicide, physicians must aggressively respond to the patients at the end of life. |
| Quality of life | In making decisions for the treatment of the seriously disabled newborns or of other persons who are severely disabled by injury or illness, the primary consideration should be what is best for the individual patient and not the avoidance of a burden to the family or to society. Quality of life, as defined by the patient's interests and values, is a factor to be considered in determining what is best for the individual. |
| Withholding or withdrawing life-prolonging treatment | Patients must be able to make decisions concerning their lives. Physicians are committed to saving lives and relieving suffering. When these two objectives are in conflict, the wishes of the patient must be given preference. |

Adapted from the American Medical Association, Code of Medical Ethics, © 1998.

guidance for this category of allied health professional, the AAMA has developed a Code of Ethics for Medical Assistants.

Other professional organizations, including the American Dietetic Association, the American Health Information Management Association (AHIMA), the American Society for Medical Technology, and the American Society of Radiologic Technologists, have developed codes of ethics. All of these codes can be found in Appendix A.

 **MED TIP**   Know the code of ethics that relates to your professional practice. Many health care professionals keep a framed copy near their place of work to remind them of this responsibility.

## ETHICS COMMITTEES

Hospitals and many other health care organizations and agencies have active ethics committees that examine ethical issues relating to patient care. This type of oversight committee consists of a variety of members from many health care disciplines, including physicians, nurses, clergy, psychologists, ethicists, lawyers, health care administrators, and family and community members. The ethics committee can serve in an advisory capacity to patients, families, and staff for case review of difficult ethical issues, especially when there is a lack of agreement as to what is in the patient's best interest. They also develop and review health policies and guidelines regarding ethical issues such as organ transplantation. After examining the facts surrounding the ethical issue, the committee often determines a recommendation based on predetermined criteria. This criteria might include the severity of the patient's medical condition, the age of the patient, and the chance for ultimate health recovery.

The ethics committee may examine issues such as when hospitalization or treatment needs to be discontinued for a patient. For example, a hospital ethics committee will assist in determining the best action to take for a terminally ill patient who is on a respirator. In some cases, the committee may be asked to examine if a patient received the appropriate care.

## BIOETHICAL ISSUES

Bioethical issues, resulting from advances in medical technology, are reported in newspapers and journals almost daily. Debates about cloning, harvesting embryos, and in-vitro fertilization were unknown a decade or two ago. Table 11-2 illustrates a wide variety of medical issues relating to bioethics.

### The Ethics of Transplant Rationing

One of the most discussed bioethical issues today relates to whom shall receive an organ transplant. The issue of organ transplantation adds a strong ethics component to medical ethics. These procedures are some of the most expensive of all medical procedures. Liver transplants cost about $250,000. In addition, the follow-up care to aid the transplant by suppressing the immune system can cost another $20,000 to $30,000 a year.

The criteria for rationing of transplants are controversial. The problem began back in the 1960s when kidney dialysis machines and centers were scarce. The centers had to establish screening committees to determine who should be allowed to have kidney dialysis. At a Seattle, Washington, dialysis center, a screening committee was composed of a lawyer, a physician, a housewife, a businessman, a minister, a labor

**TABLE 11–2**   Medical Issues Relating to Bioethics

| | |
|---|---|
| Abortion | In-vitro fertilization |
| Allocation of scarce health resources | Organ donation and transplantation |
| Determination of death | Quality-of-life issues |
| Euthanasia: active and passive | Random clinical trials |
| Fetal tissue research | Sterilization |
| Genetic counseling | Surrogate parenthood |
| Harvesting of embryos | Withdrawing treatment |
| HIV, AIDS, and ARC | Withholding lifesaving treatment |

leader, and a state government official. This committee became known as the "God squad." One of the lay members of this committee recalled voting against a woman who was a known prostitute and a playboy ne'er-do-well. An observer to this process claimed that committee members were measuring patients according to their own middle-class, suburban standards.

Many believe that there is an element of "playing God" with the moral issues of removing human body parts from one person and placing them into another person's body. In many, if not most, cases, the donors are still alive when the discussions are held concerning the harvesting of their organs, adding another dilemma.

In some countries, it is legal to remove organs from a deceased person unless the person has made an objection. However, the United States and Great Britain are among the countries still committed to the donation model for organs. Under the donation model, organs may be taken (harvested) only with the consent of the donor (or the donor's surrogate representative). The Uniform Anatomical Gift Act, which has been adopted in all states, permits competent adults to either allow or forbid the **posthumous** (after death) use of their organs through some type of written document, including a donor card. See Figure 11-1.

---

**Organ Donor Card**

I, _____, hereby make the following anatomical gift, if medically acceptable, to take effect upon my death.

_____Any organs or parts    _____Entire body

Only the following specific organs or parts:

_____

Limitations or special wishes if any:

_____

(Signatures of donor and witnesses appear on reverse side.)

Front of card

---

**Organ Donor Card** (side two)

Signed by the donor and the following two witnesses in the presence of each other.

Donor Signature: _____

Date of Birth: _____ Date signed: _____

City and State: _____

Witness Signature: _____

Witness Signature: _____

This is a legal document under the Uniform Anatomical Gift Act or similar laws.

Back of card

FIGURE 11–1   Organ donor card.

Problems still arise over the allocation of scarce organs. By some estimates, more than 64,000 people are waiting for organs in the United States each year. Many ethicists and others believe that since there is a fixed supply of transplant organs, especially livers and hearts, clearly defined standards should be used by all transplant committees. One basis for determining the allocation of organs is to give them to patients who will benefit the most. This is the **social utility method of allocation.** It is based on careful screening and matching of the donor with the recipient to determine if there is a strong chance of the recipient's survival. Another favored approach is one of justice, which gives everyone an equal chance to the available organs.

Other methods used to allocate scarce transplant organs include a seniority (first-come, first-served) basis and a lottery method. Both of these methods cause concern because they may result in providing a scarce resource, such as a heart, to a patient whose need is not as great as a patient further down the seniority list. The lottery method may result in a patient with little chance for recovery, such as someone suffering from terminal cancer, receiving a scarce organ. When other criteria for selection are added, such as age, social status, or ability to give back something to the community, there is the suspicion that this is not a just system for all persons.

A combination approach using basic "medical suitability," which measures the medical need and medical benefit to the individual patient, may be used first. After a decision is reached, then a seniority (first-come, first-served) basis is most often used.

The **United Network for Organ Sharing (UNOS)** is the legal entity in the United States responsible for allocating organs for transplantation. UNOS has developed an allocation formula that gives half the weight to considerations of medical utility, or need, and the other half to considerations of justice.

Most people agree that selling organs is morally objectionable. The **National Organ Transplant Law of 1984** forbids the sale of organs in interstate commerce. This law seeks to protect the poor from being exploited, since they may be tempted to earn money by selling what they believe to be an unneeded organ, such as a kidney. There is also a concern addressed by this legislation that the donor organs should be located as close to the patient's locale as possible.

Medicare has been expanded to fully fund kidney transplants, and most insurance plans will now fund heart transplants. A number of courts have questioned or even reversed decisions by Medicaid to not fund liver transplants. In a Michigan case, the court required the state to fund a liver transplant for an alcoholic patient. The court found in favor of the patient in spite of documentation that the patient's alcoholism most likely resulted in the need for the transplant. (*Allen v. Mansour,* 681 F. Supp. 1232, E.D. Mich. 1986.) See the case study "Mantle's New Liver," at the end of this chapter.

# ETHICAL ISSUES AND PERSONAL CHOICE

In some cases, the health care professional may have a personal, religious, or ethical reason for not wishing to be involved in a particular procedure, such as artificial insemination husband (AIH) or artificial insemination donor (AID). Ideally, this preference should be stated before one is hired. If a situation arises after an employee is hired, it should be discussed openly with the employer. The employee can request permission to refrain from participating in a procedure, such as a therapeutic abortion, if that procedure would violate the employee's values or religious beliefs. However, in some situations, the inability of an employee to assist the physician may jeopardize the health and safety of the patient. In these cases, it may be necessary for the employee to resign.

There are still many areas of medical ethics for which there are no conclusive answers. When should life support be withdrawn? When does a life begin? Is **euthanasia** ever permissible? Should a baby's life be sacrificed to save the life of the mother? Scientific discoveries continue to present new medical possibilities and choices—but with these possibilities come more complicated ethical issues that must be addressed before choices can be made.

For example, the advent of fertility treatments and drugs has allowed many previously infertile couples to conceive. The fertility drugs, when effective, often result in multiple births. There have been instances where a mother has been carrying as many as seven or eight embryos after taking fertility drugs. Doctors have begun to "harvest," or remove and discard, some of the developing embryos from within the mother's body so that the remaining embryos have a better chance for life. Many believe that this harvesting of embryos is the same as killing.

The ethical implications of these issues and dilemmas must be thought through by the health care professional. The ethics of the employer must be in agreement with the ethics of the health care professional.

# THE ETHICS OF BIOMEDICAL RESEARCH

## Ethics of the Biomedical Researcher

The relief of pain and suffering, the restoration of body functions and health, and the prevention of disability and death are all aims of health care. Human experimentation is considered necessary for medical progress to occur. Both animal testing and human testing have been used successfully to further medical knowledge and conquer disease.

Medical research almost always carries with it some degree of risk. Human beings cannot be used for testing purposes unless they consent to participate. Obtaining informed consent is particularly important in **nontherapeutic research,** or research that will not directly benefit the research subjects. The justification for all medical research is that the benefits must outweigh the risks. Merely increasing knowledge is not considered an adequate justification for taking a risk with a human life. The medical researcher must abide by the standards for testing that have been established by the medical associations, such as the AMA and the ANA.

Government standards for research are implemented by the Department of Health and Human Services (HHS). The government requires that all institutions that receive federal research funds, such as hospitals and universities, establish an **Institutional Review Board (IRB)** that oversees any human research in that facility.

## Consent

Informed consent (as discussed in Chapter 5) is necessary when a patient is involved in therapeutic research. **Therapeutic research** is that form of medical research that may directly benefit the research subject. The research subject must be made aware of all the risks involved with the research. In addition, the subject must be informed about the type of research design that is used: control group with no treatment, randomized study in which the subject is assigned at random to either the control or experimental treatment group, or a placebo group in which an inactive substance or an alternative type of treatment is given. The physician conducting the research must explain all the facts relating to the research, even if this means that the patient may decide not to participate.

**MED TIP**   The physician is responsible for explaining to the patient all the risks involved in a research project. However, other health care professionals, such as nurses, pharmacists, and medical assistants, may become aware of information relating to a research project that needs to be conveyed to the attending physician. An example would be a patient who tells the nurse that he is taking a medication prescribed by another attending physician at the same time that he is taking an experimental drug from a medical researcher.

## Conflicts of Interest

A conflict of interest can arise in medical research if the researcher's interests are placed above the interests of the patient. For example, medical researchers fearful of losing financial backing for research projects may state incorrect data or test results in order to have the research appear more successful than it is. If physicians engaged in drug-testing research for pharmaceutical companies own stock in those companies, it is a conflict of interest. In both examples, the physicians may be improperly placing their own interests before the patient's interests.

## Ethics of Randomized Test Trials

Many ethicists believe that it is unethical to use a control group when conducting medical experiments, since this group has no hope of benefiting from the experimental drug. A race-based control group may produce an additional ethical dilemma. For example, many years ago, the Public Health Service used members of the black population who had untreated syphilis as a control group. These patients were not given an effective treatment for syphilis that was available at the time. A race-based selection of research patients is unethical unless there is evidence that they will benefit by the therapy. There are some diseases that affect only a particular portion of the population, such as Tay-Sachs disease that affects the Jewish population. In this instance, research participants in a study to eradicate Tay-Sachs disease would be drawn from the Jewish population.

## Problems with the Double-Blind Test

In a **double-blind test,** neither the experimenter nor the patient knows who is getting the research treatment. This is considered to be an objective means of gathering test data because it eliminates any bias the researcher may have toward a specific research method or treatment. An ethical question arises with double-blind tests about the process of informed consent. Are the patients fully aware that they may not be receiving any treatment whatsoever? In some research situations, where the physicians discover an immediate positive effect of an experimental drug on the test group, the project will be adjusted so that the control group can also receive the treatment.

## MEDICAL ETIQUETTE

There are certain rules of **medical etiquette,** or standards of professional behavior, that physicians practice in their relationships or conduct with other physicians. These are general points of behavior and are not considered to be medical ethics issues. For instance, physicians expect that their telephone calls to fellow physicians will be taken promptly and that they will be seen immediately when visiting a physician's office.

 **MED TIP**   The outdated medical courtesy practice of physicians providing free medical care to their colleagues is not advisable. If their colleagues were to need further treatment, their insurance coverage may be in jeopardy because of the initial "free" care they had received.

### POINTS TO PONDER

1. Why do students still learn about codes of ethics such as the Nuremberg Code and the Hippocratic Oath?
2. Why do some health care professionals ignore the code of ethics in their particular discipline?
3. Do all physicians follow the guidelines relating to euthanasia as discussed in the Opinions of the Council on Ethical and Judicial Affairs of the AMA? If not, why not?
4. What would you do if you knew that a patient suffering from cancer was part of a control group of research patients who were not receiving a drug that could benefit them?
5. What do you do when you observe unethical behavior by a coworker?
6. What do you do when you make a mistake?
7. In your opinion, what criteria should be used for selecting the recipient of a scarce organ such as a heart or liver? Would you include such factors as the patient's medical need, chance for success of the procedure, and the patient's responsibility for causing the illness? Why or why not?

## DISCUSSION QUESTIONS

1. Explain what the AMA Principles of Medical Ethics statement on "improved community" means.
2. Discuss the freedom of choice that a physician has about accepting patients, as stated in the AMA's Principles of Medical Ethics.
3. Discuss the AMA's opinion on euthanasia.
4. What should health care professionals do if their ethical values differ from those of their employer? Discuss several options.
5. Describe several bioethical issues that modern-day health care professionals have to face.
6. Why are bioethical issues discussed in codes of ethics?

## PRACTICE EXERCISES

### Matching

Match the responses in column B with the correct term in column A.

**Column A**

_____ 1. revocation
_____ 2. expulsion
_____ 3. censure
_____ 4. allege
_____ 5. posthumous
_____ 6. fee splitting
_____ 7. euthanasia
_____ 8. ghost surgery
_____ 9. double-blind test
_____ 10. medical etiquette

**Column B**

a. condemn
b. standards of professional behavior
c. after death
d. research design
e. take away; recall
f. one physician substituting for another
g. force out
h. illegal referral payment
i. to assert
j. aiding in the death of another person

## MULTIPLE CHOICE

Select the one best answer to the following statements.

1. Nontherapeutic research
   a. will always benefit the research subject
   b. does not directly benefit the research subject
   c. is unethical
   d. should be justified with the benefits outweighing the risks
   e. b and d only

2. A double-blind test means that
   a. the control group may not receive any benefit from the experimental drug
   b. the participants are visually impaired
   c. the results will not be gained from an objective method for testing
   d. the control group will eventually benefit from being in the experiment
   e. there is an unethical practice taking place

3. Many professional codes of ethics are based on
   a. current laws
   b. mandates from the government
   c. early writings of Hippocrates
   d. outdated value systems
   e. none of the above

4. The practice of fee splitting
   a. is legal but unethical
   b. is both unethical and illegal
   c. results in benefit for the patient
   d. is advised by the American Medical Association
   e. is addressed in the code for nursing

5. The Declaration of Helsinski and the Declaration of Geneva are
   a. authored by the World Medical Association
   b. meant as guidelines for medical researchers
   c. a response to Nazi experimentation during World War II
   d. a and c only
   e. a, b, and c

6. The Summary of Opinions of the Council on Ethical and Judicial Affairs of the AMA
   a. describes fee splitting as an acceptable practice
   b. admonishes the surgeon against "ghost surgery"
   c. admonishes the physician to be sensitive to the need to assist patients in suicide
   d. describes gene therapy as acceptable as long as it is for the purpose of altering human traits
   e. all of the above

7. Taking away a license to practice medicine is called
   a. revocation
   b. censure
   c. expulsion
   d. a and c only
   e. a, b, and c

8. Medical issues relating to bioethics include
   a. harvesting embryos
   b. DRGs
   c. withdrawing treatment
   d. HMOs
   e. a and c only

9. Conflicts of interest occur
   a. when there are financial interests present
   b. if stock is owned by the physician in the company that sponsors the research
   c. if the researcher can control the results of the research
   d. if the patient's needs are not considered
   e. all of the above

10. A model for making ethical decisions requires that
    a. the potential consequences are not revealed in order to provide objectivity
    b. the alternative of "not doing anything" is not an appropriate consideration
    c. the ethical issues be defined in vague terms in order to look at all the dimensions of the problem
    d. the facts be determined by asking who, what, where, when, and how
    e. all of the above

## PUT IT INTO PRACTICE

Select a newspaper article relating to a medical ethics or bioethical issue. Summarize the article. Discuss the people who could be adversely affected by this issue.

## WEB HUNT

Using the Web site of the National Association for Healthcare Quality (*www.nahq.org*), discuss the Code of Ethics for Healthcare Quality Professionals.

Using the Web site of the Department of Health and Human Services (*www.hhs.gov*), examine the statement on "National Organ and Tissue Donation Initiative." Click on the site for organ donation and discuss the steps that you would need to take in order to become an organ and tissue donor.

Using information on the Web site of the United Network for Organ Sharing (UNOS) (*www.unos.org*), summarize the purpose of this organization.

## REFERENCES

American Association of Medical Assistants. 1996. *Health care law and ethics.* Chicago: American Association of Medical Assistants.

American Medical Association. 1998. *Code of medical ethics: Current opinions on ethical and judicial affairs of the American Medical Association.* Chicago: American Medical Association.

Arras, J. 1999. *Ethical issues in modern medicine.* Mountain View, Calif. Mayfield.

Flynn, E. 2000. *Issues in health care ethics.* Upper Saddle River, N.J.: Prentice Hall.

Fremgen, B. 1998. *Essentials of medical assisting: Administrative and clinical competencies.* Upper Saddle River, N.J.: Prentice Hall.

Garrett, T., H. Baillie, and R. Garrett. 1993. *Health care ethics: Principles and problems.* Upper Saddle River, N.J.: Prentice Hall.

Gorner, P., and P. Baniak. 1995. "Mantle's new liver: A question of ethics," *Chicago Tribune*. June 9, Sec.1, 3.

Hall, M., and M. Bobinski. 2003. *Health care law and ethics: A nutshell*. St. Paul, Minn.: West Publishing.

McConnell, T. 1997. *Moral issues in health care: An introduction to medical ethics*. New York: Wadsworth.

Miller, R. 1990. *Problems in hospital law*. Rockville, Md.: Aspen.

Sanbar, S., A. Gibofsky, M. Firestone, and T. LeBlang. 1998. *Legal medicine*. St. Louis: Mosby.

*Trials of war tribunals criminals before the nuremberg military*. 1948. Washington, D.C.: U.S. Government Printing Office.

Veatch, R. 2000. *The basics of bioethics*. Upper Saddle River, N.J.: Prentice Hall.

## HISTORICAL CASE STUDY

Mickey Mantle, Baseball Hall of Fame center fielder for the New York Yankees, received a liver transplant in 1995 after a six-hour operation. It took only two days for the Baylor Medical Center's transplant team to find an organ donor for the 63-year-old former baseball hero when his own liver was failing due to cirrhosis and hepatitis. Mantle was a recovering alcoholic who also had a small cancerous growth that was not believed to be spreading or life-threatening.

There is usually a waiting period of about 130 days for a liver transplant in the United States. A spokesperson for the United Network for Organ Sharing located in Richmond, Virginia, stated that there had been no favoritism in this case. She based her statement on the results of an audit conducted after the transplant took place. However, veteran transplant professionals were surprised at how quickly the transplant liver became available.

Doctors estimated that due to Mantle's medical problems, he had only a 60 percent chance for a three-year survival. Ordinarily, liver transplant patients have about a 78 percent three-year survival rate. There are only about 4,000 livers available each year, with 40,000 people waiting for a transplant of this organ. According to the director of the Southwest Organ Bank, Mantle was moved ahead of others on the list due to a deteriorating medical condition. The surgery was uneventful, and Mantle's liver and kidneys began functioning almost immediately. His recovery from the surgery was fast.

There were mixed feelings about speeding up the process for an organ transplant for a famous person. However, Kenneth Micetich, an ethicist at Loyola University in Chicago, stated, "People should not be punished just because they are celebrities." The ethics of giving a scarce liver to a recovering alcoholic was debated in many circles. University of Chicago ethicist Mark Siegler said, "First, he had three potential causes for his liver failure. But he also represents one of the true American heroes. Many people remember how he overcame medical and physical obstacles to achieve what he did. The system should make allowances for real heroes."

Mickey Mantle died a few years later from cancer.

1. As in the case of the liver transplant for Mickey Mantle, should the system make allowances for "real heroes"? Why or why not?

_____

_____

_____

*(continued)*

2. Analyze the Mickey Mantle case using the seven-step model found in Chapter 1 for examining ethical dilemmas.

    I.  Determine the facts.

_____

_____

_____

    II.  Define the precise ethical issue.

_____

_____

    III.  Identify the major principles, rules, and values.

_____

_____

_____

    IV.  Specify the alternatives.

_____

_____

_____

    V.  Compare values and alternatives.

_____

_____

_____

    VI.  Assess the consequences.

_____

_____

_____

    VII.  Make a decision.

## CHAPTER 12

_____

_____

_____

# Ethical Issues Relating to Life

## LEARNING OBJECTIVES

1. Define the glossary terms.
2. Discuss the ethical considerations relating to artificial insemination.
3. Describe the Baby M case.
4. Discuss the ethical considerations relating to surrogate motherhood and contraception.
5. List several ethical issues surrounding sterilization and contraception.
6. Explain the importance of *Roe v. Wade*.
7. Explain what is meant by a conscience clause and its importance for health care professionals.
8. Discuss ethical issues relating to genetic testing.
9. Describe the advances in human stem cell research.

## KEY TERMS

Amniocentesis
Artificial insemination
Artificial insemination
  donor (AID)
Artificial insemination
  husband (AIH)
Conscience clause
Contraception
Embryo

Eugenic (involuntary)
  sterilization
Eugenics
Fetus
Gene therapy
Genetics
Gestational period
Human genome
Human Genome Project

Induced abortion
In-vitro fertilization (IVF)
Spontaneous abortion
Sterilization
Surrogate mother
Therapeutic sterilization
Viable

## INTRODUCTION

Issues relating to birth and life are especially difficult because they carry the extra burden of one's own personal values. There is widespread disagreement on when life begins and ends. However, all health care professionals must be willing to understand the topics and issues discussed by patients, physicians, and the federal court system.

# FETAL DEVELOPMENT

## When Does Life Begin?

An issue that causes great controversy is the question of when life begins. Many people and various religions believe that life takes place at the moment of conception; therefore, any interference with this process, such as abortion or a morning-after pill, is the wrongful taking of another's life.

Others believe that life does not begin until 14 days after the egg and sperm unite to form an embryo. The **embryo** stage is the stage of development between the second and twelfth week. During this time, the embryo is attached to the uterine wall. Some claim that life begins when the **fetus,** which is the term used when the embryo reaches the third month of development, starts to develop organs and has a pronounced heartbeat and a functioning brain. This occurs around 24 weeks after conception. Still others claim that life does not begin for the fetus until birth occurs. There are perhaps as many claims about when life begins as there are weeks in the time before birth occurs, or the **gestational period,** which is usually around 40 weeks.

This controversy has created an ethical dimension for many medical professionals. Physicians and other health care workers whose religious or personal beliefs lead them to oppose abortion cannot counsel women on ending a pregnancy, assist at abortions, or in any way terminate a pregnancy. Their religious beliefs must be respected by coworkers.

# ASSISTED OR ARTIFICIAL CONCEPTION

Some couples desire children and have viable reproductive organs, but are unable to achieve pregnancy. These couples often seek medical assistance through their own physician or a fertility expert. Three of the most recent methods for assisted conception are artificial insemination, in-vitro fertilization (IVF), and surrogate motherhood.

## Artificial Insemination

**Artificial insemination (AI)** is the injection of seminal fluid that contains male sperm into the female's vagina from her husband or partner **(artificial insemination husband, AIH),** or donor (AID) by some means other than sexual intercourse.

 **MED TIP** Do not confuse the abbreviation for artificial insemination donor (AID) with the abbreviation for the disease Acquired Immune Deficiency Syndrome (AIDS).

Artificial insemination has become a very common practice, resulting in thousands of babies being conceived. There are few legal problems if the husband's semen is used. However, in some cases, women have used their deceased husband's semen, which has caused problems concerning the child's rights in relation to the father. For instance, should the child be entitled to receive Social Security benefits from the deceased father's Social Security account? In a 1995 case, a federal administration law judge ruled that a child conceived from frozen sperm and born more than 11months after her father's death was entitled to receive Social Security benefits.

### Consent for Artificial Insemination Donor (AID)

An **artificial insemination donor (AID)** is a man who donates his semen for insemination of a woman who is not his wife. Because the donor is unrelated to the woman, many legal difficulties can arise. In response, many states have passed laws to address such issues, but none of these laws have prohibited the use of a donor's sperm.

Oklahoma was the first state to pass AID legislation that provides guidelines for both the physician and the hospital regarding the issue of consent. The 1967 Oklahoma statute specifies that both the husband and wife must consent in writing to the procedure. The reasons for this strict mandate are twofold. First of all, if the physician touches the woman without her consent, it could result in a charge of battery. Second, the husband might claim that the wife had committed adultery because the semen was not his.

**MED TIP** Even if your state does not have a statute regulating AID, it is always wise to require consent in writing from both the husband and wife.

### Legal Status of Offspring

The most common legal and ethical concern relates to the legitimacy of the child and the determination of who is responsible for the child's support. Several state statutes suggest that a child is legitimate if the husband consents to the AID. These statutes also state that the donor is not responsible for the child's support.

The Oklahoma statute also clarifies that a child conceived through artificial insemination is legitimate and entitled to all the rights of a naturally conceived child. Thus, a child born as a result of AID must receive support from the nondonor husband. Similarly, California holds the husband responsible for child support, as if he were the natural father, if he consented in writing to the AID procedure.

### Ethical Considerations in Artificial Conception

Many moral and ethical problems surround the issue of AID. AID records, which contain the identity of the sperm donor, are considered confidential and handled in the same manner as adoption papers: they are not made a part of a public record.

While most states require that only a licensed physician should perform artificial insemination, this does not guarantee that it will be done in an ethical manner. In one famous case, a fertility physician was convicted for using his own sperm. (*James v. Jacobson,* 6 F.3d 233, 4th Cir. 1993.)

Assisted conception can cause future problems for both the couple and the child. The husband may resent his wife and the child if his sperm was not used. The child may question his or her parentage. Even though the husband signs the consent before the AID procedure, there is no guarantee that he will treat the child as his own once it is born.

## In-Vitro Fertilization

Some couples have viable reproductive cells (ovum and sperm), but conception does not occur for them using the natural means of sexual intercourse. Some couples in this situation turn to **in-vitro fertilization (IVF).** In this process, ovum and sperm cells are combined outside of the woman's body. These cells are grown in a laboratory and later implanted into the woman's uterus. Until the early 1990s, this procedure was considered experimental. This attitude has changed, and several insurers now pay for the procedure.

The physician needs to carefully explain the entire procedure to the couple, including what happens to the unused cells. In most cases, the unused cells, even when they are fertilized embryos, are destroyed. There are moral and ethical issues involved in destroying, or what many people believe to be "killing," these embryos.

In some cases, the fertilized cells are not destroyed but frozen for possible future implantation. While several babies have been born using frozen embryos, this procedure has created legal and ethical problems. Custody battles have challenged the "ownership" of the frozen embryos. In a 1989 divorce case, a Tennessee couple contested the ownership of frozen embryos in their divorce proceedings. The trial judge ruled that the embryos were children, and he awarded custody to the mother. However, the appellate court granted joint custody. The case then went to the Supreme Court in Tennessee, which ruled that if the parties did not agree, the embryos should be destroyed. In this case, the couple did not agree, and the embryos were destroyed. *(Davis v. Davis,* 842 S.W.2d 588, Tenn. 1992.)

## Surrogate Motherhood

An infertile couple who does not wish to adopt a child may use a surrogate or gestational mother who agrees to bear the child for them. Conception usually takes place by means of artificial insemination using the husband's viable sperm. In-vitro fertilization can also be accomplished without using the surrogate mother's genes; instead, the ovum of the wife, if she is fertile, or another woman is combined with the husband's sperm and then implanted into the **surrogate mother.** A contract is established between the couple wanting the child and the surrogate mother, who must give up the child at birth. The couple may pay as much as $10,000 for the medical expenses of the surrogate mother; however, because of the U. S. Constitution's prohibition on slavery, the baby cannot be bought. Currently, few, if any, laws regulate surrogate motherhood, and it is legal in most states.

Many surrogate cases end up in court because either the surrogate mother or the contractual parents changed their mind. This often occurs when the baby is born with a health problem or defect. In a Washington, D.C., surrogate case, both the surrogate mother and the contracting couple refused to claim an HIV-positive baby.

A problem arises, too, if the surrogate mother changes her mind when the baby is born, as occurred in the famous Baby M case.

### The Baby M Case

The Baby M case resulted from a surrogate parenting contract between Mary Beth Whitehead and Mr. and Mrs. Stern. Initially, Mrs. Whitehead had agreed to a surrogate motherhood arrangement—in which she would give up the child at birth—with the Sterns in return for $10,000. A Michigan attorney and a New York infertility clinic handled this agreement. Mrs. Whitehead was then inseminated with Mr. Stern's sperm in 1985. On March 7, 1986, Baby M was born. She was named Sarah Elizabeth by the Whiteheads and Melissa Elizabeth by the Sterns. The baby was turned over to the Sterns on March 30. The next day, the Sterns temporarily returned the baby when Mrs. Whitehead threatened suicide. On May 5, Mr. Stern went to the Whitehead residence with a court order to return the baby to his custody. However, Richard Whitehead had escaped to Florida with the child. Three months later, both the Whiteheads and the child were located by a private detective. Baby M was returned to the Sterns on July 31. Mrs. Whitehead was allowed visitation rights pending the outcome of the trial.

The New Jersey Supreme Court eventually granted parental rights to the natural mother, who had since remarried. However, the court granted the Sterns continuing custody of the baby, saying it was in the best interests of the child. The decision allowed overnight stays and vacations with the natural mother. The Sterns did not appeal this decision. (*In re Baby M,* 537 A.2d 1227, N.J. 1988.)

### Ethical Considerations with Surrogate Motherhood

Many ethical and legal problems surround surrogate motherhood. Is it right to ask a surrogate mother to give up all rights to a baby she has carried for nine months? Does, or should, the child have an emotional or physical link to the surrogate mother? Will the relationship between the husband and wife be altered if the husband's sperm is implanted into another woman? What is the sibling relationship toward the surrogate baby? Can the contract between the surrogate mother and the couple be enforced?

There have also been "compassionate" cases such as the situation in which a 48-year-old grandmother carried triplets for her daughter who was unable to bear children. However, many religions oppose this procedure, claiming it is being immoral.

Other ethical dilemmas relating to surrogate motherhood include

- potential court battles over custody of a child conceived outside of marriage
- potential embarrassment for the gestational (surrogate) mother, whose actions some people have likened to prostitution
- potential harm to the surrogate mother's own children when they learn she has given one child away and received money in return
- future emotional distress when the child learns that he or she was deliberately taken away from the natural mother
- reducing birth to a legal arrangement and the exchange of money

## Fertility Drugs

One of the more recent advances in the treatment of fertility problems, or the inability of the female to conceive, is the use of fertility drugs. These drugs increase female hormones and the production of ova, thus enhancing the ability to conceive a pregnancy.

However, the use of fertility drugs increases the woman's chance of having a multiple birth. While the birth of twins to a woman who has taken fertility drugs is not unusual, there is also a chance that she may conceive as many as eight embryos at a time. These babies are all underweight and usually are born prematurely. The "baby boom" resulting from aggressive fertility treatments has resulted in thousands of miscarriages, stillbirths, infant deaths, and disabled children. While there have been many advances in premature care allowing tinier babies to survive, the statistics relating to the survival of babies in multiple births is ominous. Even if all the babies live, they often suffer severe life-long medical problems. Table 12-1 lists the statistics relating to septuplet and octuplet births during the past 13 years.

Because there is little chance that all seven or eight babies of a multiple pregnancy will survive, physicians may recommend that some of the embryos be "harvested." This procedure is performed by entering the uterus and removing some of the embryos, leaving only two or three. The embryos removed are usually destroyed, although there have been some attempts to freeze discarded embryos for later use in stem cell research. Another method for embryo reduction consists of performing a vaginal ultrasound after a fertility drug such as Clomid is administered and counting the number of mature egg follicles. If the count finds three to five follicles of mature size, the patient is injected with Human Chorionic Gonadatropin (HCG). Then, insemination, either artificial or natural, is attempted. If too many eggs are found or they appear to be too small, then the couple is advised to wait and try the procedure

### TABLE 12–1  Statistics of Septuplet and Octuplet Births

- Six girls and two boys born to Nkem Chukuw, 27, of Houston, Texas, on December 8, 1998. All eight survived.
- Three girls and four boys born to Hasna Mohammed, 40, of Saudi Arabia, on January 14, 1998. All seven survived.
- Four boys and three girls born to Bobbi McCaughey, 29, of Carlisle, Iowa, on November 19, 1997. All seven survived, a first for septuplets.
- Five girls and two boys born to Maria Rocio Diaz Carrillo, 28, of Mexico, on January 21, 1997. None survived.
- Four boys and two girls born to Roasario Clavijo, 31, in Spain, on December 5, 1996. Those six babies survived, but two other fetuses were stillborn.
- Six boys and two girls born to Mandy Allwood, 32, of England, on September 30, 1996. All died.
- Three boys and four girls born to Lidia Santartia, 23, of Italy, on October 23, 1992. At least two died.
- Three boys and four girls born to Susan Halton, 27, of England, on August 15, 1987. All died.
- Five boys and three girls born to Sevil Capan, 25, of Turkey, on December 20, 1985. All died.
- Four boys and three girls born to Patti Frustaci, 30, of Orange, California, on May 21, 1985. One child was stillborn; three died after birth; two boys and a girl survived.

again after another menstrual cycle. However, problems develop when couples either ignore their physician's advice or do not seek medical care and attempt to regulate their drug intake on their own. Ethical issues surround this procedure. Any time the uterus is invaded, there is some risk to the mother and babies. Also, removing some of the embryos results in their death, so many religions and people oppose harvesting embryos.

Many ethicists speak out against the widespread practice of using fertility drugs. They have concerns that the result is often some very damaged babies. Thomas Murray, an ethicist at Case Western Reserve University, states, "I think it's yet another wake-up call that calls into question the relatively unregulated practice of fertility treatment in the United States." While most physicians believe that it is up to the couples to decide if they wish to have a multiple birth, many physicians believe that the indiscriminate use of fertility drugs is in danger of becoming reckless.

# CONTRACEPTION

**Contraception** stems from two words—*contra,* or against, and *conception,* meaning the union of the male sperm and the female ovum. Therefore, contraception is any action taken to prevent pregnancy from occurring. Birth control drugs, condoms, a tubal ligation of the female, and a vasectomy of the male are all forms of contraceptive techniques. Abstinence from sexual intercourse and noncoital sex are also means of avoiding pregnancy.

It is important to bear in mind that Christianity has, as a tradition, condemned contraception. Many Christian churches still maintain this belief. In addition, several states still have laws that prohibit selling contraceptives to minors.

However, many people do not consider contraception and sterilization to be moral issues. In fact, many ethicists and moral philosophers only address these issues when discussing the subject of a coerced sterilization, such as the sterilization of criminals, the mentally retarded, or irresponsible mothers.

In 1965, Connecticut's law banning contraceptives was challenged in a case known as *Griswold v. Connecticut.* Prior to 1965, Connecticut imposed a criminal penalty on any physician who prescribed contraceptives for a married woman who the physician believed would be harmed by a pregnancy. The U.S. Supreme Court struck down the Connecticut law, declaring that it was the woman's constitutional right to privacy to use contraceptives if she wished. (*Griswold v. Connecticut.* 381 U.S. 479, 1965.) Eight years later, this ruling had a major effect on the *Roe v. Wade* decision, which concluded that a woman's right to privacy included the right to abortion. (*Roe v. Wade,* 410 U.S.113, 1973.)

# STERILIZATION

**Sterilization** is the process of medically altering reproductive organs so as to terminate the ability to produce offspring. It may be the result of surgical intervention such as a vasectomy in the male or a tubal ligation in the female. While sterilization is usually considered an elective or voluntary procedure, it can also be therapeutic, incidental, or an involuntary action. Sterilization can be incidental if the procedure is performed for another purpose, such as in the case of a hysterectomy for uterine carcinoma. It can also be a side effect of treatments such as chemotherapy.

## Voluntary Sterilization

Voluntary or elective sterilization of competent persons presents few legal problems—although there are many religions that oppose sterilization. Sterilization is becoming the most popular method of contraception, or birth control, in the United States. However, the failure of sterilization procedures to prevent births is the most common reason for "wrongful conception" or "wrongful pregnancy" cases.

Sterilization is sought for a variety of reasons: economic, personal, therapeutic, and genetic. Some couples, for economic reasons, do not want to assume the additional expense of raising a child. Other couples just do not want any more children. Therapeutic sterilization is sought if the mother's health is in danger. Genetic reasons include the fear of having a child with a genetic defect.

Currently, no state prohibits the voluntary sterilization of a mentally competent adult. The sterilization patient receiving Medicaid payments must sign a special consent thirty days prior to having the procedure. Written consent should always be given before a sterilization procedure is performed. Implied consent is not sufficient.

## Consent for Sterilization

In an early case relating to sterilization, *Skinner v. Oklahoma,* the court held that a law permitting sterilization of habitual criminals violates the equal protection clause of the Fourteenth Amendment. The court stated that the right to bear children is one of the basic civil rights of man and is fundamental to the very existence of the human race. (*Skinner v. Oklahoma,* 316 U.S. 535, 1942.) As a result of the case, a patient, even though a criminal, must grant consent for the surgical procedure of sterilization.

For most surgical operations, the patient's written consent is all that is necessary. Without consent, this procedure, or operation, could be considered battery. In cases of sterilization, many hospitals and physicians also require the consent of the spouse. Spousal consent should always be encouraged. However, in most cases, performing sterilization without spousal consent has presented very little legal risk. In a case in Oklahoma, a husband sued his wife's physician for performing a sterilization without his consent. The court dismissed the suit and stated that he had not been legally harmed, since his marital rights do not include a childbearing wife. (*Murray v. Vandevander,* 522 P.2d 302, Okla. Ct. App. 1974.)

Currently, no federal law requires consent from one spouse for another spouse's sterilization. Because sterilization procedures are permanent, consenting individuals must be at least 21 years of age.

### Voluntary Sterilization of Unmarried Minors

The voluntary sterilization of unmarried minors poses special problems. Some state statutes authorize such sterilization if a parent or guardian will also consent. However, many state statutes forbid sterilization of an unmarried minor. Therefore, most physicians are very reluctant to sterilize a minor without a court order. In addition, most physicians do not want to perform this procedure on a young person unless there is a medical reason.

## Therapeutic Sterilization

**Therapeutic sterilization** may be necessary if the mother's life or mental health is threatened. In some cases, it is necessary to remove a diseased organ, such as in cancer of the uterus or ovaries, in order to preserve the patient's life. This operation would result in sterilization, but it would be incidental and thus would not be classified as a sterilization procedure.

## Eugenic Sterilization

**Eugenic (involuntary) sterilization** is the sterilization of certain categories of persons, such as those who are insane, feeble-minded, or epileptic, in order to assure that they won't pass on the defective gene to their children. Some states still authorize the involuntary sterilization of wards of the state who are genetically retarded. The procedure must be proven to the courts to be in the best interests of the mentally disabled person. However, this practice is no longer as common as it once was. Recent research demonstrates that most forms of mental retardation are not hereditary.

Some state statutes allow sterilization without the consent of the patient or the patient's agent. Several states have included categories of persons, such as sexual deviates and habitual criminals, who may also be sterilized for the purpose of preventing procreation. Those procedures include providing a notice to the person or the person's representative, guardian, or nearest relative; a hearing by a board designated by statute to perform a review; and an opportunity to appeal to a court. For instance, in a civil lawsuit brought by a single, deaf-mute mother of two, the mother alleged that  several social workers and physicians conspired to sterilize her against her will. The court decided in her favor. (*Downs v. Sawtelle*, 574 F.2d 1, Cir. 1978.)

 **MED TIP** It is important to remember that anyone who castrates or sterilizes another person without following the procedures required by law is personally liable (civilly or criminally) for assault and battery.

## Negligence Suits Related to Sterilization

Many negligence claims involve cases where a woman has become pregnant after a sterilization procedure. In an Oklahoma case, a physician assured his patient that she was sterile after he performed such a procedure in August 1980. She subsequently became pregnant and delivered a baby in October 1981. She successfully argued that because of the physician's negligence in performing the operation, she incurred $2,000 in medical expenses and would require $200,000 to raise the child. This case went to an appeals court, which ruled that parents could not recover the expenses for raising  a healthy child, but they were entitled to the expenses resulting from the unplanned pregnancy. (*Goforth v. Porter Med. Assoc., Inc.*, 755 P.2d 678, Okla. 1988.)

In some cases, the negligence occurs during the sterilization procedure. For example, in *McLaughlin v. Cooke,* a physician was found negligent for mistakenly cutting an artery while performing a vasectomy. This error resulted in excessive bleeding and tissue necrosis, and the testicle eventually had to be removed. The physician was found to be negligent because he did not intervene soon enough to prevent the necrosis from happening. (*McLaughlin v. Cooke,* 774 P.2d 1171, Wash. 1989.)

## Ethical Issues Surrounding Sterilization and Birth Control

Regardless of one's religious beliefs, health care professionals must realize that sterilization and birth control present ethical issues because of the risks surrounding these procedures. The ethical issues surrounding contraception and sterilization include the following:

1. Eugenic sterilization is particularly abhorrent to many people. It carries a stigma of attempting to determine who shall live and who shall die. **Eugenics** is the science that studies methods for controlling certain characteristics in offspring.
2. Is it morally acceptable for public schools, receiving federal and state funding, to dispense contraceptive devices, such as condoms and birth control pills, and information?
3. Some courts suggest that habitual and violent sex offenders should be ordered to undergo sterilization. Is this morally and ethically acceptable?
4. Some people believe that women who receive public funds such as Medicaid should not continue to have children by unknown fathers and thus increase the welfare rolls. Is it ethical and morally acceptable to require these women to seek sterilization before they are allowed welfare money?
5. Many hospitals refuse to allow sterilization procedures on their premises. What is the ethical implication of this restriction if this is the only hospital in the area?
6. Some people believe that mentally incompetent women should be sterilized to prevent a pregnancy from occurring if a man takes advantage of them.
7. Are children being treated as property?
8. Is human life being destroyed to achieve birth (for example, by harvesting of embryos)?
9. Some people believe that issues of contraception can interfere with the relationship between husband and wife.

These are some of the questions and issues that patients, physicians, other health care professionals, and policymakers are considering. There are no easy answers. Some people refuse the use of any contraceptive device for any reason, based on their religious beliefs. However, not all people, and thus patients, hold identical beliefs regarding the ethics of using contraceptives.

# ABORTION

Abortion has become a major issue in the United States. Even though the number of abortions declined somewhat during the 1990s, about 1.2 million legal induced abortions are performed every year.

Abortion is the termination of a pregnancy before the fetus is **viable,** or able to survive outside the uterus. (There have been some cases of viable aborted fetuses with birth defects who were allowed to die.) An abortion may be spontaneous or induced. A spontaneous abortion is one that occurs naturally without any interference. It is also referred to by the layperson as a miscarriage. A **spontaneous abortion** can result from an illness or injury of the mother, her physical inability to bear a child, or many other causes. An **induced abortion,** or one that is caused by artificial means such as medications or surgical procedures, is used to save the life of the mother. An induced abortion is also used to destroy life. The laws have focused on induced abortions performed for the purposes of killing the fetus.

Under common law in the nineteenth century, abortions performed prior to the first fetal movements, which occur at or about six weeks, were not illegal. However, legal and illegal abortions were being performed that were painful and often resulted in the mother's death. The AMA adopted an anti-abortion position in 1959, which was quite influential and resulted in political action to control abortions. States began passing statutes that made induced abortions a crime, whether they occurred before or after fetal movements, unless they were performed to save the mother's life.

In the 1960s and 1970s, states amended these laws to permit induced abortion only if the physical or mental health of the mother was threatened, if the child was at serious risk of congenital defects, or when the pregnancy was the result of a rape or incest. More laws continued to be passed, and in 1973, the major case affecting abortion, *Roe v. Wade,* was tried.

## Roe v. Wade

In *Roe v. Wade,* the United States Supreme Court declared a Texas criminal abortion law that prohibited all abortions not necessary to save the life of the mother to be a violation of the woman's right to privacy under the Fourteenth Amendment of the Constitution. (*Roe v. Wade,* 410 U.S. 113, 1973.) This 1973 case gave strength to the argument that a woman should be allowed the right to have privacy over matters that relate to her own body, including pregnancy. While the Supreme Court refused to determine when life begins, it did recognize that states would have an interest in protecting the potential lives of their citizens. Therefore, the Court tried to clarify the extent to which states can regulate and even prohibit abortion. To set up guidelines, the Supreme Court adopted a three-step process relating to the three trimesters of pregnancy.

1. First trimester—During the first three months of pregnancy, the decision to have an abortion is between the woman and her physician. The state may, however, require that this physician be licensed in that state. During the first trimester, the fetus is generally not viable, or able to live outside of the uterus.
2. Second trimester—During the second three months of pregnancy, the court determined, "the State, promoting its interest in the health of the mother, may, if it chooses, regulate the abortion procedure in ways that are reasonably related to maternal health." Therefore, during the fourth to sixth months of pregnancy, the state may regulate the medical conditions under which an abortion is performed. If the fetus is viable, which occurs at around six months, the Supreme Court

believes the states have a compelling interest in the life of the unborn child, and so abortions could be prohibited at this stage except when necessary to preserve the life or health of the mother.

3. Third trimester—The Supreme Court determined that by the time the final stage of pregnancy has been reached, the state has a compelling interest in the unborn child. This interest would override the woman's right to privacy and therefore justify stringent regulation of and even prohibit abortions. So, during the third trimester, the state may prohibit all abortions except to save the life of the mother or to protect maternal health.

Under the Supreme Court's decision in *Roe v. Wade*, as the pregnancy progresses toward term (birth), the state's legislative powers increase. Several recommendations coming from this decision include the following:

1. First trimester abortions should be performed in hospitals.
2. The approval process for abortions should include other physicians in addition to the woman's attending physician.
3. Viability of the fetus needs to be carefully defined.
4. The woman should wait for a designated period of time before having the abortion and should receive counseling.
5. Certain medical procedures, such as partial-birth abortion, cannot be used.
6. The father's consent should be obtained.

## Historical Progression of Cases Affecting Abortion

Since *Roe v. Wade*, a steady progression of abortion cases has reached the Supreme Court to challenge that ruling. The following briefly summarizes some of the cases that resulted in major changes to the *Roe v. Wade* decision.

In a 1976 case, the Supreme Court ruled it unconstitutional to require a pregnant woman to obtain her husband's consent or if she was a single minor under the age of eighteen to obtain parental consent in writing before she could obtain an abortion. However, the Court failed to determine any guidelines for obtaining parental consent if the minor is too immature to understand the nature of the procedure. (*Planned Parenthood of Central Missouri v. Danforth*, 428 U.S. 52, 1976.)

The following year, the Supreme Court examined a Connecticut statute that denied Medicaid payment for first-trimester, medically necessary abortions. In this case, the Court considered the argument that because Medicaid covered pregnancy and childbirth expenses, states were obligated to subsidize nontherapeutic abortions. However, the Supreme Court voted six to three that states may refuse to spend their public funds to provide nontherapeutic abortions. (*Maher v. Roe*, 432 U.S. 464, 1977.)

In 1980, the Supreme Court upheld the Hyde Amendment, which prohibits the use of federal funds to pay for Medicaid abortions. The Court ruled that the states are not compelled to pay for Medicaid recipients' medically necessary (therapeutic) abortions. However, the Court allowed states to fund these abortions if they wished to do so. (*Harris v. McRae*, 448 U.S. 297, 1980.)

The next year, the Supreme Court upheld a Utah statute requiring the physician to notify, if possible, the parents or guardian before an abortion is performed on a minor. In *H. L. v. Matheson*, a physician had advised the minor patient that an abortion would be in her best interests, but that he would not perform the procedure without her parents' consent. The Court ruled that a state statute could require a parental notice, when possible, and that this did not violate the constitutional rights of the immature minor. However, the Court also declared in this case that a state may not legislate a blanket power for parents to veto their daughter's abortion. (*H. L. v. Matheson*, 450 U.S. 398, 1981.)

In 1990, the Supreme Court upheld the federal statute that prohibited federally funded family planning clinics from giving abortion advice. (*Rust v. Sullivan*, 500 U.S. 173, 1991.)

The most significant case was the 1992 *Planned Parenthood of Southeastern Pennsylvania v. Casey*, in which the Supreme Court examined Pennsylvania's law that restricted a woman's right to abortion. This case was important because it rejected the trimester approach used in *Roe v. Wade*, which limited the regulations states could issue on abortion based on the stage of the fetus's development. Instead of the trimester approach, the Court looked at the abortion rules in terms of whether they placed "an undue burden on the mother." In this case, undue burden meant placing a substantial obstacle in the path of a woman seeking an abortion before viability of the fetus. The Court ruled that it is an undue burden to require spousal consent. (*Planned Parenthood of Southeastern Pennsylvania v. Casey*, 50 U.S. 833, 1992.) This ruling has been upheld in several subsequent cases in which the husband could not prevent the mother from aborting the child.

**MED TIP**    It is always wise to remember that it is not the duty of anyone, except the physician, to advise the patient concerning such topics as sterilization and abortion.

## Partial Birth Abortion

Currently, as a result of *Roe v. Wade*, the law states that a woman may terminate a pregnancy for any reason until the fetus is viable (able to survive outside the womb). After that point, which is about 24 weeks, or toward the end of the second trimester, an abortion is permitted by law only if the mother's health or life is at risk. Many people are uncomfortable allowing late-term abortions, since there is a very narrow margin at this stage between a fetus and a baby. Due to advanced treatment of premature infants, many survive when the delivery takes place at a very early stage during the pregnancy. In a few cases, a late-term abortion has resulted in the delivery of a live baby.

A partial birth abortion is performed in one of several ways. One method is a two-day process in which absorbent fibers are inserted into the mother's cervix to gradually dilate it overnight. If she is 20 or more weeks pregnant, she also receives an injection of digoxin, a heart medication, into her amniotic fluid, which stops the fetus's heart. The next day, the fetus is removed by using forceps and suction. This procedure, known as dilation and evacuation (D&E), is used for second-trimester pregnancies. Another procedure involves allowing the fetus to enter the birth canal while still alive, and then removing the brain contents with suction. Many state legislatures oppose procedures that allow the fetus to enter the birth canal while still alive (partial birth abortion).

Many women wait until the second trimester to have an abortion because they do not have the money to pay for one any earlier. They cannot use Medicaid, which would ordinarily pay for medical care for the poor. Rep. Henry Hyde (R-Ill.) sponsored the Hyde Amendment, a law stating that federal funds cannot be used for an abortion except to save the life of the mother or in the case of incest or rape. As expected, there is a great deal of controversy about late-term abortions.

## Incompetent Persons and Abortion

Difficult ethical issues surround situations in which incompetent persons may be subjected to unplanned or unwanted pregnancies. Many believe that if the incompetent person were able to speak for herself, she would not wish to be pregnant as a result of incest or rape. In some of these cases, abortions have been performed using a welfare agency as the *guardian ad litem* (a guardian appointed by the court to speak on behalf of the incapacitated party). In a 1987 case, a profoundly retarded woman became pregnant as a result of a sexual attack while she was a resident in a group home. The attacker was unknown. In this case, the *guardian ad litem,* rather than the girl's mother, spoke on behalf of the patient, since the mother and daughter had little contact. The family court authorized an abortion in this case. (*In re Doe,* 533 A.2d 523 R.I., 1987.)

## Opposition to Abortion

People have very strong, and often differing, viewpoints about abortion. Many people, because of their religious and moral beliefs, believe that *Roe v. Wade* protects the "personhood" of the mother and neglects the "personhood" of the fetus. According to this viewpoint, abortion is killing a human being and thus constitutes murder. The opponents of abortion believe that while *Roe v. Wade* protected a woman's right to choose an abortion under the 14th Amendment, the fetus was not covered under this amendment. *Roe v. Wade* does not declare when human life begins. An initiative is underway in some state legislatures to include a definition of a person as human life from the time of conception.

In 1999, the House of Representatives passed a resolution called the Unborn Victims of Violence Act. This bill is designed to provide legal penalties for any harm that is done to an unborn child at federal facilities such as military bases or in crimes that cross state lines. This bill treats all unborn life as a person.

Almost forty states have statutes that grant varying degrees of legal standing to a fetus. These are statutes that relate to criminal matters, murder and homicide, and permit civil wrongful-death suits. Both Louisiana and South Dakota define "personhood" as beginning with fertilization. In Illinois, killing a fetus is not murder, but the intentional killing of a fetus is considered a homicide. This decision, not to make the killing of a fetus an act of murder, was related to a court case in which a man was convicted of killing a woman who was eight and one-half months pregnant. The court ruled that in that case the death of the child was not murder, since the child died before a live birth took place. The current Illinois law now states that an "unborn child" exists from the moment of fertilization until birth.

## Employee's Right to Refuse to Participate in Abortions

Hospital employees have the right to refuse to participate in performing an abortion, and a hospital cannot dismiss the employee for insubordination. An employee can abstain from assisting in an abortion procedure as a matter of conscience or religious conviction.

**MED TIP**  Heath care professionals must keep in mind that people have very strong, and often differing, viewpoints about abortion. Their viewpoints must be respected even when they differ from the employee's viewpoint. However, no one should be required to participate in an action, such as abortion, if it is against his or her beliefs.

## Funding for Abortion

Funding for abortion procedures has been another area of great controversy. Under the Hyde Amendment, the U.S. Congress limited the types of medically necessary abortions for which Medicaid monies may be spent.

There are many arguments both for and against abortion. Pro-choice advocates argue that women have the right to choose what to do with their bodies. They argue that legalized abortions are safer for the woman. They cite statistics showing that deaths from illegal abortions—and there were thousands of deaths before *Roe v. Wade*—have diminished to just a few deaths when they are performed correctly in a hospital or clinic. They further argue that a woman has the right to an abortion when she is the victim of rape or incest.

The right-to-life advocates argue that no one has the right to deny a life. They believe that the embryo, no matter how young, is a human life; that it is morally wrong to take a human life; and that the right of the unborn child should take precedence over the right of the mother not to be pregnant. They also argue that those who carry out an abortion diminish humanity for everyone involved, including the mother, the physician, and the health care professionals.

## Ethical Issues Surrounding Abortion

Abortion raises a multitude of ethical issues, even for those who believe abortion, in general, should be legal.

1. One of the most vocal opponents of induced abortion is the Catholic Church, which believes that abortion, performed at any time from conception of the fetus to a full-term baby, is immoral. The Church condemns the action as the deliberate taking of a life, or "killing" the unborn child. It is considered morally wrong for anyone of the Catholic faith to have an abortion or to assist in the procedure.
2. Many private citizens do not wish their tax money to be spent on funding abortions for women on Medicaid. They cite both moral and economic reasons for their opposition.

3. Is it a violation of the rights of an incompetent person to have to submit to an abortion for eugenic reasons?
4. Is it appropriate for the government to deny spousal consent for abortion?
5. Abortion is always a moral decision, since it results in the loss of a human life.
6. Should abortion be used as a means for gender selection of children?

## CONSCIENCE CLAUSES

Because many employees in a variety of health care settings have religious or moral objections to assisting with procedures such as sterilization and abortion, several states have enacted legislation called a **conscience clause.** These clauses state that hospitals may choose not to perform sterilization procedures and that physicians and hospital personnel cannot be required to participate in such procedures or be discriminated against for refusing to participate. In 1979, a Montana nurse-anesthetist was awarded payment (damages) from a hospital that violated the Montana conscience clause. The hospital had fired her for refusing to participate in a tubal liga-  tion. (*Swanson v. St. John's Lutheran Hosp.*, 597 P.2d 702, Mont. 1979.)

On the other hand, there have been situations in which employees do not wish to leave their work setting even though they are morally unable to assist with sterilization or abortion procedures. In one New Jersey case, a court held that a hospital could transfer a nurse from the maternity ward to the medical-surgical staff because the nurse refused to assist in sterilization and abortion procedures. The court ruled that the transfer was not illegal because the nurse did not lose her seniority and it did not  alter her pay or work shift. (*Jeczalik v. Valley Hosp.*, 434 A.2d 90, N.J. 1981.)

## GENETIC COUNSELING AND TESTING

### Genetic Counseling and Testing

The science of **genetics,** discovered by Austrian botanist and priest Gregor Mendel, is the study of heredity and its variations. It describes the biological influence that parents have on their offspring.

> **MED TIP**   The study of genetics should not be confused with eugenics. Eugenics, the science that studies methods for controlling certain characteristics in offspring, is also called selective breeding. Hitler practiced eugenics when he tried to eliminate the Jewish population in favor of an Aryan one.

Genetic counseling is usually performed by geneticists who have a master's or higher degree, or by physician geneticists who are medical doctors with special training in genetics. Genetic counselors meet with the couple, usually one-on-one, before pregnancy occurs to discuss the potential for passing on a defective gene.

Genetic counseling has emerged as a legitimate means to identify couples who are at risk of passing on a genetic disease to their offspring. Over 2,000 human diseases have been identified as having a genetic factor, including Tay-Sachs disease, sickle-cell anemia, and cystic fibrosis. In these recessive gene diseases, each parent must pass on a copy of the defective gene in order for the disease to be produced in the child. Therefore, persons who carry the recessive gene for these disorders can be tested before marriage, with the option of making a decision to remain childless. Other conditions for which genetic testing is available include Huntington's chorea, retinoblastoma, Down syndrome, and phenylketonuria (PKU). These and other hereditary disorders are explained in Table 12-2.

## Prenatal Testing

There are ethical dilemmas associated with genetic testing. For example, should we or should we not test for genetic disorders in the fetus for conditions that may only show up late in life, such as Huntington's disease (a severe late-onset neurological disorder)? At one time, physicians felt it was wrong to burden the patient with disturbing news when there was nothing that could be done to solve the problem. In addition,

**TABLE 12–2**   Hereditary Disorders

| Disorder | Characteristics |
| --- | --- |
| Cooley's anemia | Rare form of anemia or reduction of red blood cells. More common in people of Mediterranean origin. |
| Cystic fibrosis | Disorder of exocrine glands causing an excessive production of thick mucus. Affects organs such as the pancreas and respiratory system. |
| Down syndrome | Moderate to severe retardation. Child may have a sloping forehead, flat nose, lowset eyes, and general dwarfed physical growth. More commonly seen when the mother is over 40. However not all forms of Down syndrome are hereditary. |
| Duchenne's muscular dystrophy | A progressive wasting away of muscles. May also have heart and respiratory problems. Caused by a recessive gene and is more common in boys. |
| Hemophilia | Bleeding disorder in which there is a deficiency in one factor necessary for blood to clot. The mother carries the recessive gene and passes it on to the males. Found almost exclusively in boys. |
| Huntington's chorea | A condition in which there are bizarre involuntary movements. May have progressive mental and physical disturbances. |
| Phenylketonuria (PKU) | A metabolic disorder in infants that, if untreated, can result in mental retardation. Is treated with a special diet. Most states require a screening test for PKU. Affects mainly Caucasians. |
| Retinoblastoma | A cancerous tumor of the eye that is fatal if untreated. |
| Sickle-cell anemia | Severe, chronic, incurable disorder that results in anemia and causes joint pain, chronic weakness, and infections. Occurs more commonly in people of Mediterranean and African heritage. |
| Tay-Sachs disease | A deficiency of an enzyme leading to mental and physical retardation and blindness. Transferred by a recessive gene and more commonly found in families of Eastern European Jewish descent. Death generally occurs before the age of four. |

physicians felt that the patient really didn't want to know any "bad news," and further-more, they would not understand the diagnosis. However, this medical paternalistic approach is no longer in favor. Patients believe they have a right to be informed of their medical conditions. A better educated public with greater access to medical in-formation via the Internet is now demanding to know the results of testing.

The most common means of genetic testing during a pregnancy is through **am-niocentesis.** In this test, the physician uses a needle to withdraw from the uterus a small amount of amniotic fluid that surrounds the fetus. This fluid is tested for the presence of genetic defects such as Tay-Sachs disease and Down syndrome. The physi-cian carefully introduces the needle into a portion of the uterus in which there is the least likelihood of touching the fetus. Prior to the procedure, physicians must discuss all the risks with the patient, such as the risk of damage to the fetus and of causing early labor. A consent form must be signed, since the procedure is invasive.

**MED TIP** Genetic testing is not always performed for the purpose of termina-tion of a pregnancy. In many cases, parents are better able to plan for the care of the child if they have advance information about a potential for genetic defects.

## Genetic Testing of Newborns

It is estimated that between 3 and 5 percent of all newborns have a hereditary or con-genital disorder, and one-fourth of all hospitalizations and deaths among babies are due to these disorders. Routine genetic screening on newborns has become standard in many hospitals.

Almost all states have passed laws requiring phenylketonuria (PKU) testing on in-fants immediately after birth so that treatment, such as dietary restrictions, can begin right away. Without this treatment, PKU babies face mental retardation and even death. In addition, federally funded voluntary screening centers exist to screen for sickle-cell anemia. Due to the growing use of artificial insemination, donors of semen are routinely screened to rule out genetic diseases.

## Ethical Questions Regarding Genetic Testing

Genetic testing and counseling has provided assistance for parents who wish to make rational decisions regarding their family planning. Many parents want to avoid the birth of children with crippling impairments such as Huntington's disease. If all people who are carriers of diseases caused by a dominant gene, such as Huntington's disease, produced no children with the disease, then the disease would become eradicated. However, many ethical and moral questions arise when examining these issues:

1. Do parents have the right to be informed of all the results of a genetic test? The duty of the physician is to inform the patient of all the results of testing. This is es-pecially difficult for some physicians who oppose abortion, since they know that there is a likelihood the parents may seek an abortion if the testing indicates a de-fective baby. Another more common problem is the case of "misidentified pater-nity" in which genetic testing indicates that the biological father is someone other

than the man who believes he is the father. Some genetic researchers believe that if a result of the genetic test is not medically relevant, such as in the case of a misidentified father, then there is no need to confront the father with the results, since it would just cause trouble. However, the mother is usually quietly told about the misidentified paternity. It is now almost routine to tell patients that genetic testing might uncover unexpected unpleasantness, such as the discovery that they might be at risk for Alzheimer's disease, but that they will be given all the information if they ask. It is estimated by researchers at the University Hospital of Cleveland that 1 to 10 percent of all people may have misidentified paternity.

2. Does a person have a right to have children who are likely to be impaired? For example, after having a series of tests, including an amniocentesis, a woman may be informed that the baby she is carrying will be born with a neural tube defect such as spina bifida. Since this child will have a difficult life, including painful surgeries, the mother may be advised to abort. However, many people who are opposed to abortion would elect to deliver the baby and spend the time during pregnancy preparing to care for a handicapped child. There is no legal sanction either for or against abortion in this case. Each decision must be based on the free choice of the parents.

3. Is society ever justified in requiring people to submit to genetic screening and counseling? And, if so, what diseases should they be screened for? Many people in favor of prenatal screening believe that children born with genetic diseases and defects require the expenditure of large amounts of public funds. A tendency for diseases such as Tay-Sachs disease, which primarily affects the Jewish population, and sickle-cell anemia, which primarily affects the African-American population, can be determined before birth. With prenatal screening for these diseases, the parents can be prepared before birth to find effective treatment. There is mandatory screening for PKU, which was the first mass testing program required by state laws. PKU is a relatively rare (5.4 per 100,000 infants) metabolic disease that accounts for only about 0.8 percent of all mentally retarded institutionalized people.

4. Does a small number of people with the potential for a disease or genetic condition justify the expense of testing all babies?

5. Should public funds be used to pay for genetic testing when the parents are unable to pay? Many people believe that indigent patients should have the same access to genetic testing that the rest of the population has. However, if genetic problems are discovered, according to the Hyde Amendment, public funds cannot be used to pay for an abortion.

These and other difficult questions face the parents and physicians every time genetic testing is performed.

# WRONGFUL-LIFE SUITS

## Wrongful Life

In some cases, a baby is born with severe defects that greatly affect the quality of life for the child. A wrongful-birth claim or lawsuit is often brought against a physician or laboratory by the parent(s) of a child born with these genetic defects. The parents may claim that they were not informed in a timely fashion that their child may have defects. They believe that this lack of information meant that they did not have the option of deciding whether to abort the child.

Some lawsuits are also brought when sterilization has failed. Parents have brought lawsuits against a physician or laboratory for breach of duty when they negligently failed to inform the parents of an unfavorable genetic test result or a failed sterilization. In general, the courts have rejected wrongful-life lawsuits brought against hospitals or physicians by children with genetic defects who claim they were injured by the action of being born. The courts reason that it is impossible to assess a dollar amount of damages for being alive as opposed to being dead.

*Smith v. Cote* is an example of such a case. The court awarded damages for wrongful birth but not for wrongful life. The court ruled that the physician was negligent by failing to test for the mother's exposure to rubella and to inform her of the potential for birth defects. Rubella in pregnant women during the first trimester can cause defects, such as deafness, in the fetus. In this case, the mother claimed that she may have sought an abortion if she had known all the facts surrounding her pregnancy. However, the court refused to award the child damages for the "wrong" of being born. (*Smith v. Cote,* 513 A.2d 341 N.H., 1986.)

**MED TIP**   It is important for all health care workers to take the issue of their own health seriously. They need to alert their employer if they contract a disease such as rubella, which could cause serious complications for a pregnant patient or coworker.

## Wrongful Conception/Wrongful Pregnancy

A 1991 case in New Mexico presented many ethical concerns. In this case, the parents of a healthy baby were awarded the cost of raising the child to adulthood when they conceived a child after an unsuccessful tubal ligation (sterilization). The physician ligated only one of the mother's tubes and failed to inform her of this negligence. (*Lovelace Medical Ctr. v. Mendez,* 805 P.2d 603, N.M. 1991.)

**MED TIP**   The best method to avoid wrongful conception/wrongful pregnancy is for the physician to advise the parents, in writing, that there is always a small number of failures in these procedures.

# HUMAN GENOME PROJECT

The **Human Genome Project** was begun in the early 1990s as a research program by the federal government. The purpose was to determine or "map" and sequence, the total number of genes, estimated at 100,000, within the 23 pairs of human chromosomes. This complete set of genes is known as the **human genome.** It resembles a set of blueprints for the human being that is stored in the nucleus of each cell.

The goal of the Human Genome Project, which is supported by scientists in several countries, is to provide a map of where each gene is located on the 23 pairs, or 46 chromosomes. The U.S. portion of the genome project was divided between scientists in nine centers at both national laboratories and universities. This important project was estimated to cost between $3 and $5 billion and take 15 to 20 years to complete. However, the project was completed ahead of time in the year 2000 and has provided important information for both biological and medical researchers.

The Human Genome Project provides a better understanding of the process of human evolution. The most important information for medical researchers relates to an improved understanding of the relationship between certain genes and particular diseases. The hope is that this genome information will result in the eventual elimination or control of genetic diseases. Ultimately, a test for a gene could actually diagnose a medical condition before any symptoms even appear. The maps that have been created by this project make it ten times quicker to locate a particular gene on a linkage map.

 **MED TIP**    A genome linkage map is similar to a roadmap in that it provides the location of where a particular gene (genetic material) is located on the chromosomes. Chromosomes are threadlike structures within the nucleus (center) of a cell that transmit genetic information.

There is currently an astonishing list of genes identified as gene markers that are responsible for disease. Some of these gene markers for disease are for colon cancer, amyotrophic lateral sclerosis (ALS), Type II (adult onset) diabetes, Alzheimer's disease, Huntington's disease, and achondroplastic dwarfism.

## GENETIC ENGINEERING

The ability to alter the basic structure of life to correct a malfunction is the goal of genetic engineering. It has increased the prospect of curing genetic diseases and enhancing the genetic code of children. The new trait, as developed through genetic engineering, would then be passed along to succeeding generations.

### Cloning

Moral and ethical concerns are raised by critics who say that manipulating the human genetic code is "playing God." One of the most controversial examples of genetic engineering is in the area of human cloning. A clone is a group of genetically identical cells that come from a single common cell. Thus, cloning makes an exact replication of a parent or a cell. In 1997, a sheep named Dolly was cloned by a Scottish scientist who found a new way to reproduce sheep by fusing the nucleus of a cell taken from the udder of a six-year-old sheep with the ovum from another sheep after the nucleus was removed. This resulted in the lamb receiving the chromosomes from only one parent, not two. Dolly was then a clone, or twin, of her six-year-old mother. The birth of Dolly caught the public's attention. There was widespread speculation about the ability for human cloning. Shortly after Dolly was cloned in February 1997, President Clinton banned the use of federal funds for research on cloning human beings.

Researchers claim that one major reason for developing cloning in animals is to permit the study of genetic development and genetic diseases. It has been claimed that studying cloning in humans might eventually enable infertile couples to have children that are genetically related to them. Further claims state that cloning could also reduce the risk of passing along some diseases that are caused by defective genes, since only nondefective chromosomes would be used in the cloning process. There has been speculation that cloning could be used to create "spare parts" by growing stem cells for particular areas of the body. It is not yet clear if there would be major advantages to human cloning.

One of the strongest arguments against human cloning is the effect it might have on human dignity. There is a concern that if we are able to control the creation of human beings, then we might also have the ability to limit the creation of defective human beings. The definition of "defective" could have very different meanings depending upon who supplies the definition. For example, a child born with crossed eyes or a club foot might be considered to be "defective" even though these are relatively easy-to-repair disorders. There are three reasons that are most frequently given to oppose cloning:

1. health risks from the mutation of genes
2. emotional risks
3. the risk of abusing the technology

Several early attempts at cloning produced disfigured animals with many abnormalities. Additionally, there is a concern about the emotional pressure of knowing that a person is perhaps the twin of a long dead brother, or even the notion a person's mother is actually his or her sister. Finally, the abuse of this technology causes some people to equate cloning with a Hitler-like attempt to create only "perfect" human beings—in the case of Hitler, these would be members of the Aryan race.

The anti-abortion lobby promotes a ban on therapeutic cloning used for medical purposes, since four-day-old embryos are destroyed in this process. This group believes that this practice is the same as taking a life.

## Gene Therapy

**Gene therapy,** in which a needed gene is spliced onto the DNA of body cells to control the production of a particular substance, is still in its infancy. The opportunities are limitless. For example, diseases such as PKU, that are caused by the absence of a single enzyme, might be corrected by altering a person's genes to manufacture that enzyme. Many diseases involve dozens, or even hundreds, of genes and are more difficult to correct.

However, scientists are investigating many unanswered questions about gene therapy. The biotechnology companies, in particular, are expecting to earn millions with the development of their new medical techniques and products for gene therapy. But they are also raising troubling ethical and moral problems. Should gene therapy be used to create healthier fetuses? Should these companies develop tests to predict mental illness? Fertility clinics are interested in testing their embryos for the newly discovered cancer gene, which would then allow parents to pick a child without that risk. Religious leaders have criticized scientists for patenting genes they discover, saying that no one can "own" genes.

Many people are concerned that gene therapy, performed to save lives, will eventually become gene enhancement to augment a desirable feature in our appearance or body function. For example, a wish for tall, blond children is an example of a misplaced use of gene therapy. Other ethical issues include whether it is right to provide a therapy to fight dwarfism, but not let other children take it to add a few inches to their height. What about engineering hormones to turn average-sized children into basketball players? What are the implications for a society of people seven feet tall? Biotechnology's societal implications are becoming more complex as scientific discoveries increase.

## Human Stem Cell Research

Stem cells are considered the master cells in the body that can generate specialized cells. In 1998, Dr. James A. Thomson, a University of Wisconsin researcher, became the first person to isolate stem cells. These cells, which can grow into any cell or tissue in the body, are extracted from the inner mass of an embryo. They are composed of 100 to 300 cells that are small enough to fit on the head of a needle. These cells are regarded by scientists as the building blocks of a new era of regenerative medicine in which the body can eventually heal itself. According to scientists, the stem cells can be used to treat a variety of diseases, including Parkinson's disease, Alzheimer's disease, stroke, and diabetes. For example, in the case of diabetes in which the pancreatic cells are ineffective, researchers can produce healthy pancreatic cells from embryonic stem cell lines which are then transplanted into a diabetic patient.

The controversy surrounding human stem cell research is not about the ability to end disease, since most people agree that this should be the purpose of medical research, but rather the use of frozen embryos to conduct the research. Cells are removed from frozen embryos, which are obtained in a variety of ways, including those that would be discarded by in-vitro fertilization clinics. Some of the embryos are grown in the laboratory especially for the purpose of stem cell research, some are obtained from terminated pregnancies, and a few are donated by couples who have excess embryos as a result of IVF.

This research has resulted in intense criticism from several fronts, including religious groups and abortion opponents, because the embryos used in this research are destroyed. These groups believe that the embryo is a living human being, and destroying them is therefore the same as killing a person. The issue is so controversial that Congress has banned all federal financing for stem cell research. However, this ban does not affect private stem cell research. In addition, the Food and Drug Administration (FDA), which oversees research therapy tested on people, presently has little jurisdiction over embryonic research.

Many states have opposing views on the research. For instance, a Massachusetts law enacted in 1974 prohibits using any live human fetus in experiments. On the other hand, Pennsylvania has introduced legislation to allow government-financed scientists to derive stem cells from embryos. A representative from South Dakota, Jay Duenwald, who introduced legislation to ban stem cell research, likened it to Nazi experiments. His legislation passed, and embryonic stem cell research is now a crime in South Dakota, punishable by as much as a year in jail and a $1,000 fine.

Many state spokespersons are not opposed to studies using frozen embryos to treat diseases like diabetes, but they fear what they consider negative uses, such as for cloning. President George W. Bush restricted federally financed research to cells that already existed before August 9, 2001, but no new embryonic cells could be used after that date.

A more noncontroversial approach to stem cell research is offered by the researchers who use sources other than embryos. For example, blood stem cells can regenerate specialized cells to treat blood disorders such as leukemia. These blood stem cells are found in adult bone marrow, in umbilical cord blood, and in small amounts in the circulating blood stream. The hope is that these stem cells can be used in new ways to produce other types of cells such as neural and liver cells. This is far less controversial than embryonic stem cell use.

The recent discovery of a self-renewal gene, called Bmi-1, makes it possible to enable the body's stem cells to constantly renew themselves. This gene was originally identified in brain stem cells but is now found in other cells. The hope is that it can become a universal regulator that controls self-renewal in all stem cells. The Bmi-1 gene works by blocking the activity of other genes as they turn cancerous and divide uncontrollably. Scientists warn that while the use of this gene therapy appears to have fewer ethical and moral dilemmas associated with it, any therapies designed to use stem cells must be carefully regulated to avoid uncontrolled cell growth.

## POINTS TO PONDER

1. What do you say to a patient who asks for family planning advice?
2. How would you react to a coworker who tells you she has recently had an abortion?
3. Can you relate to the dilemma faced by a surrogate mother who is giving up her baby to the contractual parents? Why or why not?
4. What would you say to a person who does not share your religious or moral views concerning abortion?
5. What are some of the daily issues faced by parents who have children born with hereditary disorders?

## DISCUSSION QUESTIONS

1. Discuss the ethics of minors having the same access to contraceptives as adults.
2. Should there be mandatory testing for genetically transmitted diseases? Why or why not?
3. Discuss whether eugenics should be permissible in any circumstances.
4. List and describe six hereditary disorders as discussed in this chapter.
5. Discuss the history of U.S. Supreme Court decisions relating to abortion since *Roe v. Wade.*
6. What are the ethical implications relating to abortion?
7. Discuss some of the ethical implications relating to sterilization.

8. What are some of the ethical implications relating to fertility drugs?
9. Discuss the ethical implications relating to artificial insemination donor (AID).
10. Do you feel that abortion is an appropriate method to use for birth control?
11. What are some of the ethical implications of cloning?
12. How is the traditional notion of family challenged by the new reproductive technologies?

## PRACTICE EXERCISES

### Matching

Match the responses in column B with the correct term in column A.

**Column A**

_____ 1. fetus
_____ 2. embryo
_____ 3. in-vitro fertilization
_____ 4. eugenics
_____ 5. genetics
_____ 6. AID
_____ 7. AIH
_____ 8. surrogate
_____ 9. gestation period
_____ 10. viable

**Column B**

a. time before birth during the development of the fetus
b. artificial insemination by husband
c. controlling certain characteristics in offspring
d. able to survive
e. biological influence of parents on their offspring
f. second to twelfth week of development
g. artificial insemination by donor
h. ovum and sperm combined outside of the mother's body
i. substitute
j. third month of development until birth

## MULTIPLE CHOICE

Select the one best answer to the following statements.

1. The current laws relating to artificial insemination
   a. do not forbid artificial insemination
   b. state that the donor father must provide a portion of the child's support
   c. provide for the records that relate to the donor to remain open
   d. clarify the child's illegitimacy
   e. all of the above

2. The Baby M case is an example of
   a. problems encountered with fertility drugs
   b. problems relating to the practice of eugenics
   c. problems encountered as a result of the use of a surrogate

  d.  problems encountered due to involuntary sterilization
  e.  problems encountered as a result of genetics

3.  Ethical issue(s) relating to contraception is/are
  a.  dispensing contraceptives in schools receiving federal funds
  b.  requiring sex offenders to undergo sterilization
  c.  providing contraceptives for women on Medicaid
  d.  sterilization of mentally incompetent women
  e.  all of the above

4.  A miscarriage is the same thing as a/an
  a.  induced abortion
  b.  spontaneous abortion
  c.  drug-induced abortion
  d.  conscience clause
  e.  eugenics

5.  A genetic disorder that causes severe joint pain, chronic weakness, and infections and is more prevalent in people of African heritage is
  a.  Tay-Sachs disease
  b.  hemophilia
  c.  cystic fibrosis
  d.  sickle-cell anemia
  e.  Cooley's anemia

6.  Genetic testing of the newborn is required by law for
  a.  Tay-Sach's disease
  b.  phenylketonuria
  c.  retinoblastoma
  d.  Down syndrome
  e.  Cooley's anemia

7.  A disease that could cause serious birth defects for an unborn child if the pregnant mother is exposed to it during her pregnancy is
  a.  Down syndrome
  b.  Huntington's Disease
  c.  cystic fibrosis
  d.  rubella
  e.  retinoblastoma

8.  A policy or regulation that allows health care employees to refrain from assisting with an abortion if they have a moral or religious objection to the procedure is
  a.  genetic counseling
  b.  eugenics
  c.  conscience clause
  d.  *Roe v. Wade*
  e.  Hyde amendment

9. A person appointed by the court to defend a lawsuit on behalf of an incapacitated person is a/an
   a. conscience clause
   b. surrogate
   c. AID
   d. AIH
   e. *guardian ad litem*

10. Tay-Sachs disease
    a. results from an enzyme deficiency
    b. is more common among people of Eastern European descent
    c. is curable if diagnosed early
    d. a, b, and c
    e. a and b only

## Put It into Practice

Contact your local chapter of Planned Parenthood and a right-to-life organization and request information on their organization and services. Compare the philosophies and missions of the two organizations as stated in their printed materials. What do they have in common? What are the differences?

## Web Hunt

Using the Web site of the National Institute of Health (*www.nih.gov*), find information on the National Human Genome Research Institute. What is the ELSI program?

Using this same site, click on the Office of Rare Diseases heading. Using the list provided by the office, determine which of the hereditary disorders in Table 12-1 are considered rare diseases.

## References

American Association of Medical Assistants. 1996. *Health care law and ethics.* Chicago: American Association of Medical Assistants.

Arras, J., and B. Steinbock. 1999. *Ethical issues in modern medicine.* Mountain View, Calif.: Mayfield.

Devettere, R. 2000. *Practical decision making in health care ethics: Cases and concepts.* Washington, D.C.: Georgetown University Press.

Dwyer, S., and J. Feinberg. 1997. *The problem of abortion.* New York: Wadsworth.

Flynn, E. 2000. *Issues in health care ethics.* Upper Saddle River, N.J.: Prentice Hall.

Garrett, T., H. Baillie, and R. Garrett. 1993. *Health care ethics: Principles and problems.* Upper Saddle River, N.J.: Prentice Hall.

Kiernan, L., and B. Brotman. 1997. Inside a late-term abortion clinic. *Chicago Tribune.* March 23, 1, 18.

Kotulak, R. 2003. Gene may be the trigger to arouse stem-cell renewal. *Chicago Tribune.* October 23, 14.

Kuhse, H., and P. Singer. 1999. *Bioethics.* Malden, Mass.: Blackwell.

Lachman, V. 2004. Frontiers of biomedicine. *Advance for Nurses.* King of Prussia, Pa.: Merion.

Lipman, M. 1994. *Medical law and ethics.* Upper Saddle River, N.J.: Prentice Hall.

McConnell, T. 1997. *Moral issues in health care: An introduction to medical ethics.* Belmont, Calif.: Wadsworth.

Miller, R. 1996. *Problems in health care law.* Gaithersburg, Md.: Aspen.

Munson, R., 1992. *Intervention and reflection: Basic issues in medical ethics.* Belmont, Calif.: Wadsworth.

Painter, K. 1998. Octuplets fight for life and reignite ethics debate. *USA Today,* December 22, 1, 2.

Pozgar, G. 1993. *Legal aspects of health care administration.* Gaithersburg, Md.: Aspen.

President's Council on Bioethics. 2003. *Stem cells: The administration's funding policy: Moral and political foundations.* Retrieved March 29, 2004 from the World Wide Web: http://bioethics/transcripts/sep03/session2.html.

Sanbar, S., A. Gibofsky, M. Firestone, and T. LeBlang. 1995. *Legal medicine.* St. Louis: Mosby.

Schodolski, V. 2000. When exactly do human cells become a person? *Chicago Tribune.* May 10, 1, 14.

Wade, N. 1998. Scientists cultivate cells at root of human life. *New York Times.* November 6, 1, A24.

Zuckman, J. 2001. House OKs bill on fetus as a victim. *Chicago Tribune.* April 27, 1, 28.

## CASE STUDY

A physician was recently convicted of using his own sperm for artificially inseminating his patients. He told the court that he didn't see anything wrong with this practice because these women came to him wanting to have a child. However, his patients were unaware that he was using his own sperm for the procedure. Some of his office staff became suspicious of the physician's methods, but failed to report their suspicions immediately. Many children were conceived as a result of this physician's sperm having been implanted into the mothers.

1. Is this a legal, ethical, or bioethical issue? Explain your answer.

_____

_____

_____

2. Was the office staff at fault?

_____

_____

_____

3. What is the potential long-term effect for this physician's patients and members of the surrounding community?

_____

_____

4. What should happen to this physician?

_____

_____

_____

## CHAPTER 13

# Death and Dying

## LEARNING OBJECTIVES

1. Define the glossary terms.
2. Discuss the difference between cardiac and brain-oriented death.
3. Describe the Harvard Criteria for a Definition of Irreversible Coma.
4. Discuss the pros and cons of euthanasia.
5. Provide examples of ordinary versus extraordinary means used in the treatment of the terminally ill.
6. List and discuss the five stages of dying as described by Dr. Kubler-Ross.
7. Discuss 11 treatments that might be ordered for the critically or terminally ill.
8. Discuss the items that must be included on a death certificate.

## KEY TERMS

Active euthanasia
Brain death
Cardiopulmonary
Comatose
Electroencephalogram
  (EEG)

Expired
Hypothermia
Mercy killing
Palliative care
Passive euthanasia
Rigor mortis

Terminally ill
Viatical settlements
Withdrawing life-
  sustaining treatment
Withholding life-
  sustaining treatment

## INTRODUCTION

Issues relating to death and dying are especially sensitive, since they are topics that are ultimately faced by everyone. There are no definitive agreements within the medical profession on many of the issues relating to death and dying. The one point of agreement is that the dying patient must be treated with dignity.

## THE DYING PROCESS

Death is inevitable for everyone. Modern medicine has enabled people to live longer and survive diseases such as pneumonia that once caused the elderly to die quickly. Infections can be treated and eliminated. The elderly, who may welcome death at the end of a long life or illness, can now be kept alive by medical technology. This has caused ethical and moral dilemmas for the health care profession. It is important to remember that professional codes of ethics (see Appendix A) usually include a statement about the health care professional's duty to preserve life. For example, the American Medical Association (AMA) and the International Code of Nursing Ethics both discuss the need to respect human dignity and life.

## LEGAL DEFINITION OF DEATH

Determining when a person has died is important for a variety of reasons. Obviously, the most important reason is that no one wants to make the mistake of treating living patients as though they were dead. A person who has died, or is said to have **expired,** is no longer treated the same way as a living human. This in no way means that the body of a deceased person, also known as a corpse, can be handled in a disrespectful way.

The actual determination of death has also become critical in the past few decades due to advances in medicine such as organ transplantation and life-support systems. Life-support systems allow medical practitioners to sustain for additional weeks, months, or even years a person who, according to all traditional standards, has died. The classic case is that of Karen Ann Quinlan.

### Karen Ann Quinlan Case

On April 15, 1975, 21-year-old Karen Ann Quinlan was admitted to a New Jersey hospital after becoming unconscious from a combination of a prescription drug and alcohol. She suffered cardiopulmonary (heart and breathing) arrest and was placed on a respirator after her pulse was restored. She received a tracheotomy, a surgical incision into the trachea to assist in ventilation, had a nasogastric tube inserted to receive nourishment, and was considered to be in a **comatose,** or permanently vegetative, condition. Her **electroencephalogram (EEG),** which measured brain activity, was abnormal, but a brain scan showed her brain activity to be within normal limits. Months passed with no change in Quinlan's comatose condition, but her physical condition continued to deteriorate. She lost weight, dropping from 115 pounds to 70 pounds by September, and her body became rigid.

Karen's father appealed to the court to appoint him guardian, which it ultimately did. He requested that the extraordinary procedures, such as the respirator, be discontinued. The Superior Court denied this request. Many other legal battles took place, and eventually the respirator was discontinued. However, Quinlan continued to breathe on her own even after the respirator was discontinued. The hospital continued to feed Karen by artificial means, and she lived in a coma for ten years before she died on July 11, 1985. The Quinlan case was groundbreaking because it represented the first time a family had requested a court to approve the removal of a respirator from a permanently comatose patient and won the case. (*In re Quinlan*, 355 A.2d 647, N.J. 1976.)

## Criteria for Death

Certain criteria or standards assist in the determination that death has occurred. Some indications, in addition to the loss of a heartbeat, include a significant drop in body temperature, loss of body color, **rigor mortis** (stiffness that occurs in a dead body), and biological disintegration. However, these symptoms may not appear until several hours after death, or not at all if life-support equipment is used.

While the criteria for death vary, this becomes problematic when a general consensus for the definition of *death* is needed. For instance, because a deceased person's organs can be removed for transplantation into a living body, if permission has been granted by the deceased prior to death or by the deceased's relatives, it is important to determine if and when death has occurred.

There is a continuing controversy over whether to use a cardiac definition of death or a brain-oriented definition of death. Even then, in some cases it is difficult to determine if someone is alive or dead.

## Cardiac Death

Traditionally, death was defined as cardiac death, or death in which the heart has stopped functioning. A person who suffered an irreversible cessation of respiratory and circulatory function was considered dead. Medically trained personnel can easily make this determination based on lack of pulse or breathing. A cardiac death is considered a legal death.

In most situations, the cardiac determination of death is effective. However, using only the cardiac definition of death creates some problems. In fact, there is documentation of cases in which people lived even when their hearts stopped functioning. Several years ago, a heart patient at the University of Utah, named Barney Clark, lived for four months with an artificial heart while he waited for a heart transplant. He was able to be partially active while connected to the artificial heart, although his own heart was no longer beating.

The definition for a cardiac death means that there is an irreversible loss of all cardiac function. In some cases, the cessation of breathing and pulse are reversible, such as in a drug overdose or **hypothermia** (the state in which body temperature is below normal range). This prolonged absence of oxygen can result in neurological damage. A patient who has suffered a cardiac arrest and is "clinically dead" may successfully be resuscitated with CPR. This person cannot be considered dead because the cessation of breath and pulse is not irreversible.

 **MED TIP** The terms *cardiac* and **cardiopulmonary,** referring to the heart and the lung function, are interchangeable as a legal definition of death.

Another serious problem with using only the cardiac-oriented definition of death involves organ transplantation. In many cases, if the surgeon waits until all cardiac function has ceased, many of the potential donor's organs are useless as transplants. Obviously, it is not ethical or moral to change the definition of death in order to increase the number of organs available for transplant. However, many people believe that a cardiac-oriented definition of death is inadequate.

## Brain-Oriented Death

The whole-brain-oriented definition of death has gained favor in many countries, including the United States. Under this definition, death occurs when there is irreversible cessation of all brain function. It is based on the premise that the brain is responsible for all bodily functions, and once the brain stops functioning, all other bodily functions will stop. Most states accept this definition of death. One exception is New Jersey, which uses the traditional cardiac criteria to determine death.

 **MED TIP** Modern technology has made it possible to maintain heart and lung function for hours, and even days, after all brain function has stopped.

In most states, if the whole brain is dead, then the person is considered deceased. A dilemma occurs in the case of a patient whose heart and respiratory functions are maintained by mechanical means, such as a ventilator, but who has no brain activity. The patient's brain is dead, but since technology is sustaining cardiopulmonary functioning, the body is still alive. Discontinuing the ventilation support for a patient would result in the cardiac death of the patient. A moral dilemma confronts physicians when they have to definitely determine whether such a person has died.

The issue of death becomes extremely complex when a patient is comatose. In 1968, the Harvard Medical School published a report that outlined criteria for determining when a patient was in an irreversible coma, which, according to the study, meant the patient was brain-dead. The Harvard Criteria for a Definition of Irreversible Coma includes consideration of whether the patient

1. is unreceptive and unresponsive, with a total unawareness of externally applied, and even painful, stimuli
2. has no spontaneous movements or breathing, as well as an absence of response to stimuli such as pain, touch, sound, or light
3. has no reflexes, has fixed dilated pupils, lack of eye movement, and lack of deep tendon reflexes

The Harvard Criteria also specified the required tests, including an electroencephalogram (EEG), to determine the absence of brain activity. Harvard recommended that these tests should be repeated again after 24 hours.

In the years since setting the criteria, there have been no known patients who have recovered after being declared in an irreversible coma using the Harvard Criteria. This irreversible coma is known as **brain death.**

To protect against malpractice suits, a physician should seek an outside medical opinion before terminating a life-support system. This issue has actually had a bearing in a criminal case. In Arizona, a murder defendant argued that it was not his criminal action that caused the death of the victim, but rather the actions of the physician who discontinued the life-support system. In this case, the court rejected the defendant's argument, holding that brain death was the valid test for death in Arizona. The court found that the victim's brain function had ceased as a result of the defendant's criminal action before the life-support was discontinued. (*State v. Fierro*, 603 P.2d 74, Ariz. 1979.)

## Uniform Determination of Death Act

In the 1980s, a Uniform Determination of Death Act (UDDA) was approved by the American Bar Association, the American Medical Association, the Uniform Law Commissioners, the American Academy of Neurology, and others. This law was adopted by a number of states. It says

> An individual who has sustained either (1) irreversible cessation of circulatory and respiratory functions, or (2) irreversible cessation of all functions of the entire brain, including the brain stem, is dead.

Many groups, such as Orthodox Jews, many Catholics, and right-to-life proponents, object to the brain-death criterion. These groups believe acceptance of the brain-death criterion in all circumstances would legitimize practices they consider immoral, such as euthanasia and abortion.

> **MED TIP**   Many phrases are used to refer to a deceased person, such as *passed away, passed on, departed,* and *left this world.* It is important to know which one is used in a particular family so as to be as compassionate as possible when discussing the death of a family member or loved one.

In caring for the critically ill or those patients who are considered to be **terminally ill,** where death is inevitable, there are several ethical considerations: (1) withdrawing versus withholding treatment, (2) active euthanasia versus passive euthanasia, (3) direct versus indirect killing, and (4) ordinary versus extraordinary means.

## Withdrawing Versus Withholding Treatment

**Withdrawing life-sustaining treatment,** such as artificial ventilation, means to discontinue it after it has been started. **Withholding life-sustaining treatment** means never starting it. Health care practitioners often find it more difficult to withdraw treatment after it has been started than to withhold treatment. However, many people believe that both are ethically wrong.

Starting a life-sustaining treatment, even on a temporary basis, allows the physician more time to evaluate the patient's condition. The physician may believe that if the treatment is ineffective, it can be stopped. However, in some cases, it has been necessary to get a court order to discontinue a treatment, such as a respirator, that has already been started.

Patients have the legal right to refuse treatment as well as food, even if they are not terminally ill. In a 1986 California case, a young woman with cerebral palsy, who had no use of her voluntary muscles, was unable to take her own life as she wished to do. She hospitalized herself and then stated her intent to refuse any food and to have her nasogastric (feeding) tube removed so that she could eventually die of starvation. The California Court of Appeals held that she had the right to refuse nutrition and hydration in order to end her life. She won her lawsuit and had the nasogastric tube removed. As recently as 1997, she continued to live and be cared for at home without the use of a feeding tube. (*Bouvia v. Superior Court,* 225 Cal. Rptr. 287, Cal. App. 1986.)

## Active Euthanasia Versus Passive Euthanasia

Most people believe that there is a distinction between actively killing a patient (active euthanasia) and allowing a patient to die by foregoing treatment (passive euthanasia). This moral distinction is approved by the AMA, Roman Catholic moral theology, and the President's Commission for the Study of Ethical Problems in Medicine and Biomedical and Behavioral Research. It is not accepted by Orthodox Judaism.

**Active euthanasia,** the intentional killing of the terminally ill such as by injection of a lethal dose of medication, is illegal in all jurisdictions in the United States, with the possible exception of Oregon. The voters in Oregon have twice voted to give terminally ill patients, under carefully limited circumstances, the right to ask for a doctor's prescription to end their lives. The Oregon law requires a second medical opinion and the determination that the patient is in fact terminally ill and not just depressed. There has not been a stampede demanding death by prescription in Oregon, however. From 1997 to 2001, only 70 people in Oregon used this law. This law in Oregon is still being challenged and allows physician-assisted suicide (PAS) but not homicide.

Rather than directly killing a patient, some physicians have sought to engage a patient-assisted suicide. In this type of assistance, a physician provides a patient with the medical know-how or the means (a prescription) to enable a patient to end his or her own life.

Jack Kevorkian first gained notoriety in June 1990 when he assisted in the suicide of Janet Adkins, a Michigan woman who was in the early stages of Alzheimer's disease. Since that time, he has assisted in the suicides of many other patients. In response to Kevorkian's actions, the state of Michigan enacted a law making assisted suicide a felony punishable by up to four years in prison. Kevorkian, however, ignored this law and went on to assist several more people with their suicides. He is currently serving a sentence in a Michigan prison.

While active euthanasia is illegal, **passive euthanasia,** or allowing a patient to die naturally, is legal everywhere. Passive euthanasia includes withholding basic needs such as hydration (supply of fluids) and nutritional feeding. However, the treatment must be reconsidered if it is considered futile and burdensome to the patient.

 **MED TIP** The term *passive euthanasia* is falling out of favor by organizations such as the Roman Catholic Church. The phrase "allow to die" is used instead.

### Arguments in Favor of Euthanasia

People who favor euthanasia offer the following justifications:

- Respect for patient self-determination. Individuals should have the right to determine the outcome of their lives.

- Euthanasia provides a means for harvesting viable organs.
- It provides relief for the family of a patient with an irreversible condition or terminal disease.
- It provides a means to end a terminally ill person's suffering.

### Arguments in Opposition to Euthanasia

Many people oppose euthanasia in any form (active or passive) for several reasons, including the following:

- There is no certainty regarding death. Many terminally ill patients have been known to recover.
- Modern technology may find a cure for a terminal disease.
- Families who are undergoing stress due to the financial burden of a dying relative may be examining euthanasia just to relieve that burden.
- If euthanasia is allowed, then it might be used indiscriminately.
- It is not good for society to have physicians kill patients or for patients to kill themselves.
- There is value and dignity in every human life.
- When physicians and other health care professionals become involved in any form of euthanasia, it erodes the very ethical basis of the professions.
- The sick and dying may have a fear of involuntary euthanasia if euthanasia is legalized.
- Only God has domination over life.

Individual health care professionals must remember that active euthanasia violates the medical profession's ethics and is against the law. The Nancy Cruzan case is an example of a situation in which the removal of a feeding tube was a form of active euthanasia within the law.

### The Nancy Cruzan Case

On January 11, 1983, 25-year-old Nancy Cruzan was involved in an automobile accident that left her in a vegetative state until her death eight years later. A feeding tube was implanted in her in a Missouri hospital. Three years after the accident, her parents, who had been granted guardianship, realized that she would never regain consciousness. The family sought legal assistance from the American Civil Liberties Union and requested that the feeding tube be removed. The judge ruled in favor of the Cruzans, but the case was appealed. The U.S. Supreme Court overturned the judge's decision and ruled against the Cruzans because under Missouri law, hydration or nutritional support could not be withdrawn from an incompetent patient unless clear evidence demonstrated that this is what the patient would have requested. Several years later, new evidence became known when two of Cruzan's former coworkers came forward. They both stated that she had said she would not wish to be maintained like Karen Quinlan. In December 1990, a judge complied with the Cruzans' wish to have their daughter's feeding tube removed. In reaction to this verdict, right-to-life protestors demonstrated outside the rehabilitation center where Cruzan was being kept alive. The feeding tube was removed and she was pronounced dead on December 26, 1990. (*Cruzan v. Director, Missouri Dep't. of Health,* 497 U.S. 261, 1990.)

**MED TIP**  Patients often ask for advice from health care workers on what course of action they should take for a dying loved one. Remember that the physician is the only health care professional who can advise the patient on a course of medical treatment.

## Direct Versus Indirect Killing

In some situations, an action can lead to two effects: one that is intended and even desirable, and another that is unintended and undesirable.

A person's death may result from another person's intended action or inaction. For instance, if a nurse intentionally ignores a patient who is choking because she or he wants the patient to die, the nurse has killed the patient.

However, death may be an unintentional result of another person's action. For example, if a high-risk patient dies from an anesthetic, the patient's death was not intended or desired. A surgeon who is morally opposed to abortion may have to remove a cancerous uterus in a pregnant woman; the death of the fetus is not intended or desired, but is the indirect result of treating the disease. The death, in this case, would be morally tolerable, even by members of religions opposed to abortion, because death of the fetus was not the intended purpose of the surgery.

These actions fit within the double-effect doctrine, which recognizes that an action may have two consequences: one desired (and intended) and one undesired (and unintended). Groups such as the AMA and the Catholic Church oppose direct killing but accept undesired and unintended deaths. The courts generally make the same distinctions.

## Ordinary Versus Extraordinary Means

Another important distinction concerns the difference between ordinary and extraordinary means. This distinction is important for determining which treatments are morally required. To do this, we cannot simply separate common means, such as fluids and feeding tubes, from uncommon means, such as respirators, because in some situations even common procedures or treatments may be considered extraordinary. Many believe that it is inappropriate to use the complexity of the technology to determine what treatment to use or not use. For example, is it morally right to force a nasogastric feeding tube into a 90-year-old pneumonia patient who does not wish to have this treatment? In other situations, it may be considered an ordinary means of treatment to use a respirator on a 90-year-old woman who is recovering from a choking episode.

The term *ordinary* refers to a treatment or procedure that is morally required, such as fluids and comfort measures. *Extraordinary measures* refer to those procedures and treatments that are morally expendable. Some professionals use the terms *appropriate* and *inappropriate* instead of *ordinary* and *extraordinary*. A treatment is considered morally expendable, or inappropriate, if it does not serve any useful purpose. For example, a common-sense judgment would determine that chemotherapy would be useless in the final days of a cancer patient's life.

Even if a treatment may serve the useful purpose of prolonging life, it may not be morally justified if it involves a grave burden. This was discussed in the President's Commission for the Study of Ethical Problems in Medicine and Biomedical and Behavioral Research. In addition, Pope Pius XII issued the following statement on prolonging life:

> Normally one is held to use only ordinary means—according to circumstances of persons, places, times, and culture—that is to say, means that do not involve any grave burden for oneself or another.

These are difficult issues to encounter. The administration of fluids, nutrition, and routine nursing procedures such as turning a patient may result in what the patient believes is a grave burden. These treatments may cause further pain and discomfort. In addition, they may actually be useless to recovery. However, these are all considered to be ordinary means of care.

### Right to Die Legislation or Right to Refuse Treatment

Patients have the right to refuse treatment. In extreme cases in which the patients' refusal places their lives in danger, legal action sometimes results. The following is an example of such a case.

In January 1978, the Tennessee Department of Human Services filed suit seeking to have a *guardian ad litem* appointed to care for 72-year-old Mary Northern, who had no living relatives and suffered from gangrene of both feet. This condition required removing both her feet in order to save her life. During the court hearings, even though she was alert and lucid, Northern did not have the capacity to understand the severity or the consequences of her disease process, as demonstrated by her insistence that her feet were black because of dirt and that her physicians were incorrect about the seriousness of her infection. The court determined that she was in imminent danger of death without the amputation and authorized the state's commissioner of human services to act on her behalf in consenting for the surgery. However, on May 1, 1989, before Mary could be stabilized for surgery, she died of a blood clot  from the gangrenous tissue. (*State Dep't. of Human Services v. Northern*, 563 S.W.2d 197, Tenn. Ct. App.1978.)

## STAGES OF DYING

Dr. Elizabeth Kubler-Ross devoted much of her life to the study of the dying process. She divided the dying process into five stages that she believes the patient, family members, and caregivers all go through. The five stages are denial, anger, bargaining, depression, and acceptance. According to Kubler-Ross, these stages overlap and may not be experienced by everyone in the stated order, but all are present in the dying patient. The five stages of dying or grief are summarized in Table 13-1.

**TABLE 13–1**   Five Stages of Dying (or Grief)

| | |
|---|---|
| Denial | A refusal to believe that dying is taking place. This may be a time when the patient (or family member) needs time to adjust to the reality of approaching death. This stage cannot be hurried. |
| Anger | The patient may be angry with everyone and may express an intense anger toward God, family, and even health care professionals. The patient may take this anger out on the person closest to them, usually a family member. In reality, the patient is angry about dying. |
| Bargaining | This involves attempting to gain time by making promises in return. Bargaining may be done between the patient and God. The patient may indicate a need to talk at this stage. |
| Depression | There is a deep sadness over the loss of health, independence, and eventually life. There is an additional sadness of leaving loved ones behind. The grieving patient may become withdrawn at this time. |
| Acceptance | This stage is reached when there is a sense of peace and calm. The patient makes such comments such as, "I have no regrets. I'm ready to die." It is better to let the patient talk and not to make denial statements such as, "Don't talk like that. You're not going to die." |

## QUALITY-OF-LIFE ISSUES

*Quality of life* refers to more than just what a person experiences at a moment in time. It includes many dimensions such as physiological status, emotional well-being, functional status, and satisfaction with life in general. A medical procedure or intervention, such as aggressive treatment for a terminal illness, will have an impact on the physical, social, and emotional well-being of the patient. This impact can be measured to assess the intangible costs and consequences of the disease or illness. These quality-of-life measurements can assist with making health care decisions based not only on clinical factors and costs, but on issues that the patient believes are important. Measures used to assess quality of life include

- general health
- physical functioning
- role limitations, such as within the family structure
- pain
- social function
- vitality
- mental health

Questions are asked relating to each of these dimensions by the health care professional to create a patient's health profile. Two useful quality-of-life measurement instruments are the Functional Living Index: Cancer (FLIC) and the Arthritis Impact Measurement Scale (AIMS). The results of these measurement tests can aid the practitioner and the patient in making quality-of-life decisions, such as whether to extend life with the use of support systems.

## USE OF MEDICATIONS

A four-year study of over 8,000 dying patients was published in the *Journal of the American Medical Association* in November 1995. Families reported that half of the patients who were able to communicate in their last days spent most of the time in moderate or severe pain. Physicians often have a reluctance to over-prescribe pain medications for patients out of a fear that the patient may become addicted to the drug. However, in the case of a dying patient, who may not live long enough to become addicted, there is a belief among many physicians that the patient's pain and suffering should be controlled with the use of adequate medications. The Hippocratic tradition of medicine stated that it is a fundamental responsibility of physicians to relieve pain.

Currently, 9 million Americans live with cancer, and about 60 percent of those patients will eventually die of the disease. Surveys indicate that one-third of patients receiving active therapy, such as chemotherapy, and two-thirds of patients with an advanced disease have significant pain. Yet only about half of the patients receive adequate pain control.

 **MED TIP** Even though a nurse may believe that a dying patient requires more pain medication, she or he cannot increase the dosage or administration times without a physician's order.

## HOSPICE CARE

The hospice movement, which originated in France, has a commitment to keep patients as pain-free as possible. Our modern-day hospice is modeled after Saint Christopher's Hospice in London, which was started by Dr. Cicely Saunders in 1966. She established a facility with a home-like atmosphere where terminally ill patients, both young and old, find comfort until death. Hospices, based on Dr. Saunders's model, are found throughout the world. The hospice service is available both in a facility such as Dr. Saunders's model and also in the patient's own home, where a hospice worker provides daily care if needed. In an interview when she was 80 years old, Dr. Saunders was asked, "What did you learn from your early patients?" She replied,

> I said to a patient, a lady called Mrs. Hinson, "tell me about your pain," and without any more prompting, she just said, "Well doctor, it began in my back but now it seems that all of me is wrong." She described her symptoms and then said, "I could have cried for pills and the injections, but I knew that I mustn't. Nobody seemed to understand how I felt, and it seemed as if the world was against me, and my husband and son were marvelous but they were having to stay off work and lose their money, and it's wonderful to just feel safe again." So she has described what I started talking about as total pain.

**FIGURE 13–1**   An elderly hospice patient.

Hospice care is focused on providing comfort measures, emotional support, and a final environment as pain-free as possible for the patient. Additional services, such as pastoral and respite care for the family, are part of the hospice philosophy. Extraordinary procedures and tests such as chemotherapy and MRIs are not ordinarily used. The staff consists of specially trained personnel who have experience and interest in caring for the dying patient. The patient is usually only hospitalized in a hospice unit during the final weeks of life. Most of the hospice care is provided in the patient's home. This can be a burden on the patient's family and the family may therefore need respite care. See Figure 13-1.

## PALLIATIVE CARE

**Palliative care** is the total care of patients whose disease is no longer responsive to curative therapy. This type of care, consisting of comfort measures, is meant to provide a relief of pain and suffering so the patient can die with dignity. Comfort measures include frequent turning and bathing, gentle massage, providing oral fluids, and listening to the patient. Palliative care emphasizes symptom control, such as for pain, shortness of breath, and supportive therapy for depression. Palliative care is not euthanasia, nor do the health care professionals giving this type of care passively allow people to die.

Palliative care, which is the opposite of curative care in which we attempt to cure the patient's disease, requires health care professionals who understand the need for compassion rather than surgical or medical interventions. What palliative care can do is make the end-of-life period a meaningful experience for the patient and not something to be frightened of.

# VIATICAL SETTLEMENTS

**Viatical settlements** allow people with terminal illnesses, such as AIDS, to obtain money from their life insurance policies by selling them. The term *viatical* comes from the Latin term *viaticum*, which were the money and supplies given to Roman officials before taking on a risky journey for the empire. (Viaticum is also the Roman Catholic sacrament given to the dying patient.) A viatical settlement means that in exchange for a 20 to 50 percent discount on the face value of the patient's insurance policy, he or she can have immediate access to the money. The patient names the settlement company as the recipient of the death benefit. In return, the viatical settlement company assumes complete responsibility for the insurance policy, including making all the premium payments. The owner then receives no further benefits from the insurance. At the time of the patient's (viator's) death, the viatical settlement company receives the death benefit from the policy.

Many terminally ill patients have used the money to provide for medical and nursing care during their final illness. However, others have used the money to enjoy a vacation with family members or to pay for experimental medical treatments that health insurance companies will not cover.

There are problems with viatical settlements, including tax liabilities and a potential loss of means-based entitlements such as Medicaid. Since the payment to the patient is less than the face value of the insurance policy, the patient could be "giving away" a significant amount of money to the settlement company. In addition, terminally ill patients often live much longer than they expected with their illness, and the small payment by the settlement company may not be enough to help them.

# ADVANCE DIRECTIVES

The federal Patient Self-Determination Act of 1991 mandates that adult patients admitted into any health care facility that receives funding from either Medicare or Medicaid must be asked if they have an advance directive or wish to have information about these self-determination directives. Ideally, people make decisions about advance directives before they are in a situation in which they are being admitted to a hospital or nursing home. If these documents—such as a living will, durable power of attorney for health care, Uniform Anatomical Gift Act, or do not resuscitate (DNR) order—have to be drawn up after a patient has entered a facility, then it should be done in a nonstressful manner.

Advance directives are popularly known as living wills. These documents became popular about thirty years ago when medical technology made it possible for people to be kept alive in unpleasant and fragile conditions for long periods of time. Advance directives limit the type and amount of medical care and treatment that patients will receive if they should become incompetent and have a poor prognosis. It is important that directives be placed in writing; it is not sufficient for a person to just tell someone what his or her wishes for treatment are. The courts typically enforce written advance directives. For additional discussion about advance directives, see Chapter 5.

**MED TIP**  All health care professionals should be aware that it is also acceptable for a patient to write an advance directive asking to receive maximum care and treatment for as long as possible.

According to Eileen Flynn in *Issues in Health Care Ethics,* there are four situations in which a person cannot exercise the fundamental right to self-determination:

1. Persons with a head injury who are conscious but incoherent or in a coma from which they may not recover.
2. Persons in an irreversible coma or vegetative state with no possibility of recovery. They suffer from permanent destruction of critical brain functions, lack awareness, and are incapable of self-care and interaction with others.
3. People who suffer irreversible brain damage but are otherwise healthy, such as patients with Alzheimer's disease or stroke patients.
4. Persons with a degenerative brain disease but who have also developed a terminal disease such as cancer.

Treatments that might be ordered for patients falling in one of these four categories include CPR, mechanical breathing or respirator, tube feedings, kidney dialysis, chemotherapy, intravenous therapy, surgery, diagnostic tests, antibiotics, transfusions, pain medications, and palliative care.

1. Cardiopulmonary resuscitation (CPR)—CPR, which consists of applying chest compressions and breaths, is applied when a person stops breathing or the heart stops beating. This procedure can be a lifesaving technique for accident and heart attack victims. CPR is used for all hospital and nursing home patients who stop breathing, unless there is a do not resuscitate (DNR) order in their medical chart. A DNR order means that no attempt will be made to revive a patient who stops breathing or whose heart stops. The only health care professional who can place a DNR order on the medical chart is the physician. Physicians write the orders at the explicit direction of the patients or their families. DNR orders are issued when a patient's condition or course of illness will result in death. Many elderly patients do not wish to be resuscitated and then placed on artificial ventilation.

    Current opinions of the Council on Ethical and Judicial Affairs of the American Medical Association include guidelines on DNR orders. They state that efforts should be made to resuscitate patients who suffer cardiac or respiratory arrest, except when the circumstances indicate that CPR would be futile or not in accord with the desires and best interests of the patient. High-risk patients should be encouraged to express in advance their preferences regarding the use of CPR, which should be documented in the patient's medical record.
2. Mechanical breathing or respirator—A respirator, also called a ventilator, is a mechanical device used for artificial ventilation of the lungs. This machine breathes for patients who cannot breathe by themselves. Patients who do not wish to be resuscitated usually also refuse the assistance of a respirator.
3. Tube feedings—This type of artificial nutritional support consists of placing a tube into the patient's stomach either through the nose or directly into the

gastrointestinal system. The general practice in hospitals and nursing homes is to feed patients via tubes if they are unable to eat normally. The patient who is unresponsive or in a vegetative state would have this treatment. If a person does not wish to have tube feedings, then he or she must make this directive known to his or her physician or proxy (representative) ahead of time.

4. Kidney dialysis—This is a medical treatment in which impurities (waste matter) are removed from the patient's blood when the kidneys fail to function. The patient may believe that the benefits of dialysis do not outweigh the burdens of this treatment.

5. Chemotherapy—This is the use of chemicals that have a toxic effect on disease-producing organisms, such as cancer. Some patients object to the strong side effects of chemotherapy.

6. Intravenous therapy—Fluids are administered by inserting a tube into the vein. It is often a standard procedure used when caring for a comatose patient.

7. Surgery—In some situations, an incompetent patient may need surgery such as a heart bypass. The patient's proxy must make this decision on behalf of the patient.

8. Diagnostic tests—Some diagnostic tests, such as magnetic resonance imaging (MRI) and invasive tests in which intravenous dyes are administered, may cause additional stress and discomfort for a comatose patient.

9. Antibiotics—Medications used to fight disease are often administered to ward off illnesses such as pneumonia. Many people issue an advance directive about receiving antibiotics if they become incompetent.

10. Transfusions—Ailments such as severe anemia and hemorrhage may require replacing blood by transfusion. Some persons have religious-based objections to receiving blood transfusions. The right to refuse a blood transfusion can be stated in an advance directive.

11. Pain medications and palliative care—Palliative care used to relieve pain and discomfort is not administered with the intention of curing the patient. It includes care such as turning the patient and keeping the mouth and lips moist. While most people would not issue an advance directive against receiving palliative care, some people refuse pain medications. Clear instructions about these measures should be placed in writing.

**MED TIP** It is recommended that all persons place in writing their wishes about what type of treatment they should receive if they become incompetent. The advance directive should be specific about treatments such as CPR, tube feeding, and ventilators.

## CHOICES IN LIFE AND DEATH

### Suicide

Is it morally permissible to allow competent persons to consent to their own deaths? Voluntary euthanasia and suicide are considered to be morally different. Voluntary euthanasia, or **mercy killing,** is the action (or inaction) of a second person to help or hasten the death of the person who wishes to die. Suicide involves only the actions of the person seeking death. Suicide is considered to be morally wrong and is illegal in most states. However, no state currently punishes people who attempt suicide, although they may be placed in psychiatric care if they present a danger to themselves. Many religions condemn suicide and euthanasia.

## The Case of the Conjoined Twins

A marathon 50-hour operation to separate 29-year-old Iranian twins joined at the head resulted in their deaths during the surgical procedure in July 2003. The twins, Ladan and Laleh Bijani, made a desperate plea to surgeons to give them a chance at living independent lives. The twins knew that the operation carried deadly risks, but knowingly accepted the risks, according to their physicians. Many of their physicians and relatives tried to talk the twins out of having the procedure. The women gave instructions to their next-of-kin that they wished to be separated under all circumstances, no matter what the surgeons encountered during the surgery. Dr. Benjamin Carson, who was a part of the neurosurgical team to separate the twins, said that he was persuaded to proceed with the operation based on the medical evidence and the strong desire of the twins to be separated. He stated, "These were individuals who were absolutely determined to be separated. The reason I felt compelled to become involved is because I wanted to make sure they had their best chance."

However, during the operation, the surgeons found that contrary to their first impression, the twins' brains were fused together, and a vein graft failed, causing the twins to hemorrhage and die. After the death of the twins, Dr. Carson said that in hindsight he believes it was unwise for the medical team to tacitly agree to continue with the surgery to separate the twins no matter what they encountered during the surgery.

There have been many ethical debates about the separation of conjoined twins, such as Ladan and Laleh, who have little chance of both surviving such a surgery. Michael Grodin, director of medical ethics at the Boston University School of Medicine stated, "The key issue is that they were adults and could understand the risks and benefits and make decisions on their own." He went on to say, "Obviously, if the chances were 100 percent that the twins were going to die, then the surgeons shouldn't have offered it. To do so would have been akin to participating in an assisted suicide." Grodin and other ethicists agree that no one knows exactly where the ethical cut-off point should be for an operation or procedure in which the odds for recovery are poor.

## Mechanical Heart Recipient

The first implanted mechanical heart, a grapefruit-sized plastic and titanium four-pound heart called an AbioCor, was implanted into a 59-year old man, Robert Tools, in July 2001. This patient did quite well with his mechanical heart until he suffered a severe stroke from a blood clot that was believed to be caused by the mechanical device. Mr. Tools was unable to take anticoagulant medications to reduce the risk of blood clots forming. He spent the final days of his life partly paralyzed and breathing through a ventilator. Before he had the mechanical heart transplant, Mr. Tools had been on the brink of death with end-stage heart failure and had been given little chance of surviving more than thirty days. Up until the time of his stroke, he expressed gratitude after the surgery and said that he had no regrets. Robert Tools lived for five months with his mechanical heart. The manufacturers of the mechanical heart said the success of the AbioCor is measured by how well it extends life and restores life's quality.

## DEATH CERTIFICATE

After a patient has been pronounced dead by an authority such as a physician or coroner, the attending physician should prepare the required information for a death certificate. This certificate includes the following:

1. name and address of decedent
2. age
3. place and date of birth
4. names of parents (including mother's maiden name)
5. birthplace of parents
6. race
7. decedent's occupation

This information is maintained for statistical and epidemiological purposes. The physician also indicates on the death certificate the length of time the patient was treated, when a physician last saw the patient alive, and the immediate and contributing cause of death. In some cases, the immediate cause of death is not always the actual mechanism for the death. For example, a cardiac arrest could be caused by the condition of a myocardial infraction (heart attack from a blood clot) with arrhythmia (abnormal heart rhythm).

After the physician has completed this information, the mortician types the final death certificate and the physician signs and dates it. If the patient dies while hospitalized, the hospital becomes the temporary custodian of the body and releases the body according to the laws in that state. Most states do not allow burial to take place until the death certificate is signed.

## MEDICAL EXAMINER CASES

Every state provides for a legal investigation by a medical examiner or coroner in cases of suspicious death. A physician reports any suspicious deaths to the medical examiner. Suspicious cases include death

- of a violent nature, including homicide, suicide, or accident
- caused by criminal abortion
- related to contagious or virulent diseases that may cause a public hazard
- of a person confined to jail or other correctional institution
- resulting from an unexplained or unexpected cause
- caused by electrical, radiation, or chemical injury
- of a person who had not had a physician in attendance within 36 hours of death
- of any person whose body is not claimed by a friend or relative
- of a child under the age of two years if death results from an unknown cause
- of a person of unknown identity

## POINTS TO PONDER

1. What do you say to a dying patient who asks you, "Why me?"
2. What are some major concerns of family members of a dying patient?
3. Does an individual have the right to determine when he or she wishes to die? Why or why not?
4. What are the benefits of hospice care for the terminally ill?
5. What is your opinion regarding Jack Kevorkian's behavior?
6. Why is the ability to determine when death has occurred so critical in today's health care environment?
7. What is cardiac death?
8. Can a patient write an advance directive requesting maximum care?

## DISCUSSION QUESTIONS

1. Explain the statement, "Health care practitioners often find it more difficult to withdraw treatment after it has started than to withhold treatment."
2. What attributes do you think a *guardian ad litem* should possess?
3. Describe a situation in which passive euthanasia might be acceptable.
4. Discuss reasons against the practice of euthanasia.
5. How would you describe the following advance directives to a patient: durable power of attorney for health care, Uniform Anatomical Gift Act, and a DNR order?
6. What is the purpose of an ethics committee?
7. What are the pros and cons of a viatical settlement?

## PRACTICE QUESTIONS

### Matching

Match the responses in column B with the correct term in column A.

**Column A**

_____ 1. proxy
_____ 2. expired
_____ 3. mercy killing
_____ 4. comatose
_____ 5. rigor mortis
_____ 6. hypothermia
_____ 7. stages of dying
_____ 8. cardiac death
_____ 9. brain death
_____ 10. active euthanasia

**Column B**

a. body temperature is below normal
b. person acting on behalf of an-other person
c. legal definition of death
d. euthanasia
e. stiffness that occurs in death
f. vegetative condition
g. legal term for killing a patient
h. died
i. irreversible coma
j. Kubler-Ross's reflection on the dying process

## MULTIPLE CHOICE

Select the one best answer to the following statements.

1. The practice of allowing a terminally ill patient to die by foregoing treatment is called
   a. active euthanasia
   b. passive euthanasia
   c. mercy killing
   d. a and c
   e. b and c

2. An electroencephalogram is used to
   a. reverse a coma patient's condition
   b. measure cardiopulmonary function
   c. measure brain function
   d. reverse the condition of hypothermia
   e. reverse the condition of rigor mortis

3. The Uniform Determination of Death Act
   a. provides a definition of active euthanasia
   b. provides a definition of brain death
   c. is also called the doctrine of double effect
   d. mandates that everyone entering a nursing home must provide a written document stating the care he or she wishes to receive
   e. discusses the treatments that might be used for a comatose patient

4. Criteria or standards for death include
   a. rigor mortis
   b. hypothermia
   c. loss of body color
   d. biological disintegration
   e. all of the above

5. What is the ethical term that is used to morally justify the removal of a cancerous uterus from a pregnant patient?
   a. mercy killing
   b. extraordinary means
   c. ordinary means
   d. doctrine of double effect
   e. advance directive

6. Another term meaning death is
   a. comatose
   b. expired
   c. proxy
   d. terminally ill
   e. hypothermia

7. A hospice provides for
   a. palliative care
   b. pain medications
   c. in-patient care
   d. home care
   e. all of the above

8. Extraordinary care means that when caring for a comatose patient, one should include
   a. CPR and mechanical breathing
   b. chemotherapy
   c. turning and hydration
   d. a and b only
   e. a, b, and c

9. The Karen Ann Quinlan case involved
   a. mercy killing
   b. removal of hydration from a comatose patient
   c. removal of a respirator from a comatose patient
   d. a heart transplant
   e. court order for a surgical procedure on an incompetent patient

10. Terms referring to heart and pulmonary function include
    a. cardiac
    b. comatose
    c. hypothermia
    d. cardiopulmonary
    e. none of the above

## PUT IT INTO PRACTICE

Call a local hospice unit in your area and ask for information regarding their service. If possible, visit the hospice and discuss their philosophy with the director.

## WEB HUNT

Search the Web site of the American Medical Association, *www.ama-assn.org*. Click on the heading Health Professionals from the side menu and examine the topic of ethics. Summarize the purpose of the Institute for Ethics that is discussed under that topic.

Using the Web site *www.iom.edu*, search for the report "Improving Palliative Care for Cancer." This is a report by the National Cancer Policy Board of the Institute of Medicine and National Research Council. Summarize the report findings.

Search the Web site of the National Hospice and Palliative Care Organization (*www.nhpco.org*), and look under "find a hospice program." Using this listing, find a hospice in your area.

## References

Altman, L. 2001. Artificial-heart patient is bleeding in the brain. *New York Times.* November 21, 14.

American Medical Association, Council on Ethical and Judicial Affairs. 1996. *Code of medical ethics: Current opinions with annotations, 1996–1997* edition. Chicago: American Medical Association.

Arras, J., and B. Steinbock. 1999. *Ethical issues in modern medicine.* Mountain View, Calif.: Mayfield.

Beauchamp, T., and J. Childress. 1994. *Principles of biomedical ethics.* New York: Oxford University Press.

Brown, D. 2001. Surgeon in doomed operation on twins speaks out. *Hartford Courant.* July 12, A5.

Chanen, J. 1995. Source of comfort: Viatical deals turn insurance into cash for terminally ill. *Chicago Tribune.* July 13, sec. 6, 1, 15.

Cundiff, D. 1992. *Euthanasia is not the answer.* Totowa, N.J.: Humana.

Devettere, R. 2000. *Practical decision making in health care ethics: Cases and concepts.* Washington, D.C.: Georgetown University Press.

Flynn, E. 2000. *Issues in health care ethics.* Upper Saddle River, N.J.: Prentice Hall.

Foley, K. 2001. Pioneer in the battle to avert needless pain and suffering. *New York Times.* November 6, F5.

Garrett, T., H. Baillie, and R. Garrett. 1993. *Health care ethics: Principles and problems.* Upper Saddle River, N.J.: Prentice Hall.

McConnell, T. 1997. *Moral issues in health care: An introduction to medical ethics.* Belmont, Calif.: Wadsworth.

Meisel, A. 1991. *The right to die.* New York: John Wiley and Sons.

Miller, R. 1996. *Problems in health care law.* Gaithersburg, Md.: Aspen.

Munson, R., ed. 1992. *Intervention and reflection: Basic issues in medical ethics.* Belmont, Calif.: Wadsworth.

Pope Pius XII. 1958. The prolongation of life: An Address of Pope Pius XII to the International Congress of Anesthesiologists. *The Pope speaks* 4 (Spring): 393–398.

President's Commission for the Study of Ethical Problems in Medicine and Biomedical and Behavioral Research. 1983. *Deciding to forego life-sustaining treatment: Ethical, medical, and legal issues in treatment decisions.* Washington, D.C.: U.S. Government Printing Office.

Quill, T. 1993. *Death and dignity.* New York: Norton.

Stolberg, S. 1999. Her life's work is caring for the dying. *New York Times.* June 2, 24.

The Support Principal Investigators. 1995. A controlled trial to improve care for seriously ill hospitalized patients. *JAMA,* November 22–29, 274:20, 1591–1598.

## CASE STUDY

Glenn Ross, an alert 55-year-old man, was diagnosed with inoperable pancreatic cancer. His prognosis was poor; he was given about six months to live. He underwent several series of chemotherapy treatments, but they were of no benefit. He continued to lose weight, suffer from nausea, and become weaker. After three months of chemotherapy treatments, he stated that he wanted no further treatment. He became bedridden and was admitted into a nursing home for terminal care. Glenn's son, who lived in another state, arrived at the nursing home and demanded that his father's physician be called immediately. The son wanted his father to be hospitalized and placed on chemotherapy immediately. When the physician explained that there was little hope for the father's recovery, the son threatened to sue the physician for withdrawal of care.

1. Identify the ethical issues in the case.

_____

_____

_____

2. In your opinion, does the son have a legitimate reason to sue the physician? Why or why not?

_____

_____

_____

3. What are the possible solutions to this case?

_____

_____

_____

4. What might the physician have done to prevent the confrontation with Glenn's son?

_____

_____

_____

5. Using Dr. Kubler-Ross's five stages of dying or grief, what stage is Glenn in? What stage is his son in?

_____

_____

_____

# Codes of Ethics

## HIPPOCRATIC OATH[1]

I swear by Apollo Physician and Asclepius and Hygieia and Panaceia and all the goddesses, making them my witness, that I will fulfill according to my ability and judgment this oath and this covenant:

To hold him who has taught me this art as equal to my parents and to live my life in partnership with him, and if he is in need of money to give him a share of mine, and to regard his offspring as equal to my brothers in male lineage and to teach them this art—if they desire to learn—without fee and covenant; to give a share of precepts and oral instruction and all other learnings to my sons and to the sons of him who has instructed me and to pupils who have signed the covenant and have taken an oath according to medical law, but to no one else.

I will apply dietetic measures for the benefit of the sick according to my ability and judgment; I will keep them from harm and injustice.

I will neither give a deadly drug to anybody if asked for it, nor will I make a suggestion to that effect. Similarly I will not give to any woman an abortive remedy. In purity and holiness I will guard my life and my art.

I will not use the knife, not even on sufferers from stone, but will withdraw in favor of such men as are engaged in this work.

Whatever houses I may visit, I will come for the benefit of the sick, remaining free of all intentional injustice, of all mischief and in particular of sexual relations with both female and male persons, be they free or slaves.

What I may see or hear in the course of treatment or even outside of the treatment in regard to the life of men, which on no account one must spread abroad, I will keep to myself holding such things shameful to be spoken about.

[1]Reprinted from *Ancient Medicine: Selected Papers of Ludwig Edelstein,* O. Temkin, and C. Temkin, eds. (Boston, MA: Johns Hopkins University Press, 1967) 6.

If I fulfill this oath and do not violate it, may it be granted to me to enjoy life and art, being honored with fame among all men for all time to come; if I transgress and swear falsely, may the opposite of all this be my lot.

## DECLARATION OF GENEVA[2]

Medical vow adopted by the Second General Assembly of the World Medical Association at Geneva, Switzerland, September 1948; amended by the Twenty-Second World Medical Assembly, Sydney, Australia, August 1968; the Thirty-Fifth World Medical Assembly, Venice, Italy, October 1983; and the Forty-Sixth WMA General Assembly, Stockholm, Sweden, September 1994.

At the time of being admitted as a member of the medical profession:
I solemnly pledge myself to consecrate my life to the service of humanity.
I will give to my teachers the respect and gratitude which is their due;
I will practice my profession with conscience and dignity;
The health of my patient will be my first consideration;
I will respect the secrets which are confided in me; even after the patient has died;
I will maintain by all the means in my power, the honor and the noble traditions of the medical profession;
My colleagues will be my sisters and brothers;
I will not permit considerations of age, disease or disability, creed, ethnic origin, gender, nationality, political affiliation, race, sexual orientation, or social standing to intervene between my duty and my patient.
I will maintain the utmost respect for human life from its beginning, even under threat and I will not use my medical knowledge contrary to the laws of humanity; I make these promises solemnly, freely and upon my honor.

## DECLARATION OF HELSINKI[3]

Recommendations guiding medical doctors in biomedical research involving human subjects, adopted by the Eighteenth World Medical Assembly, Helsinki, Finland, 1964; and revised by the Nineteenth World Medical Assembly, Tokyo, Japan, 1975; Thirty-Fifth World Medical Assembly, Venice, Italy, October 1975; Forty-First World Medical Assembly, Hong Kong, September 1989; and the Forty-Eighth General Assembly, Somerset West, Republic of South Africa, October 1996.

### Introduction

It is the mission of the physician to safeguard the health of the people. His or her knowledge and conscience are dedicated to the fulfillment of this mission.

The Declaration of Geneva of the World Medical Association binds the physician with the words, "The health of my patient will be my first consideration," and the

---

[2]Reprinted with permission of the World Medical Association.
[3]Reprinted with permission of the World Medical Association.

International Code of Medical Ethics declares that, "A physician shall act only in the patient's interest when providing medical care which might have the effect of weakening the physical and mental condition of the patient."

The purpose of biomedical research involving human subjects must be to improve diagnostic, therapeutic and prophylactic procedures and the understanding of the aetiology and pathogenesis of disease.

In current medical practice most diagnostic, therapeutic or prophylactic procedures involve hazards. This applies especially to biomedical research.

Medical progress is based on research which ultimately must rest in part on experimentation involving human subjects.

In the field of biomedical research a fundamental distinction must be recognized between medical research in which the aim is essentially diagnostic or therapeutic for a patient, and medical research, which is purely scientific and without implying direct diagnostic or therapeutic value to the person subjected to the research.

Special caution must be exercised in the conduct of research which may affect the environment, and the welfare of animals used for research must be respected.

Because it is essential that the results of laboratory experiments be applied to human beings to further scientific knowledge and to help suffering humanity, the World Medical Association has prepared the following recommendations as a guide to every physician in biomedical research involving human subjects. They should be kept under review in the future. It must be stressed that the standards as drafted are only a guide to physicians all over the world. Physicians are not relieved from criminal, civil and ethical responsibilities under the laws of their own countries.

## I. Basic Principles

1. Biomedical research involving human subjects must conform to generally accepted scientific principles and should be based on adequately performed laboratory and animal experimentation and on a thorough knowledge of the scientific literature.

2. The design and performance of each experimental procedure involving human subjects should be clearly formulated in an experimental protocol which should be transmitted for consideration, comment and guidance to a specially appointed committee independent of the investigator and the sponsor, provided that this independent committee is in conformity with the laws and regulations of the country in which the research experiment is performed.

3. Biomedical research involving human subjects should be conducted only by scientifically qualified persons and under the supervision of a clinically competent medical person. The responsibility for the human subject must always rest with a medically qualified person and never rest on the subject of the research, even though the subject has given his or her consent.

4. Biomedical research involving human subjects cannot legitimately be carried out unless the importance of the objective is in proportion to the inherent risk to the subject.

5. Every biomedical research project involving human subjects should be preceded by careful assessment of predictable risks in comparison with foreseeable benefits

to the subject or to others. Concern for the interests of the subject must always prevail over the interests of science and society.

6. The right of the research subject to safeguard his or her integrity must always be respected. Every precaution should be taken to respect the privacy of the subject and to minimize the impact of the study on the subject's physical and mental integrity and on the personality of the subject.

7. Physicians should abstain from engaging in research projects involving human subjects unless they are satisfied that the hazards involved are believed to be predictable. Physicians should cease any investigation if the hazards are found to outweigh the potential benefits.

8. In publication of the results of his or her research, the physician is obliged to preserve the accuracy of the results. Reports of experimentation not in accordance with the principles laid down in this Declaration should not be accepted for publication.

9. In any research on human beings, each potential subject must be adequately informed of the aims, methods, anticipated benefits and potential hazards of the study and the discomfort it may entail. He or she should be informed that he or she is at liberty to abstain from participation in the study and that he or she is free to withdraw his or her consent to participation at any time. The physician should then obtain the subject's freely-given informed consent, preferably in writing.

10. When obtaining informed consent for the research project the physician should be particularly cautious if the subject is in a dependent relationship to him or her or may consent under duress. In that case the informed consent should be obtained by a physician who is not engaged in the investigation and who is completely independent of this official relationship.

11. In case of legal incompetence, informed consent should be obtained from the legal guardian in accordance with national legislation. Where physical or mental incapacity makes it impossible to obtain informed consent, or when the subject is a minor, permission from the responsible relative replaces that of the subject in accordance with national legislation.

   Whenever the minor child is in fact able to give a consent, the minor's consent must be obtained in addition to the consent of the minor's legal guardian.

12. The research protocol should always contain a statement of the ethical considerations involved and should indicate that the principles enunciated in the present Declaration are complied with.

## II. Medical Research Combined with Professional Care (Clinical Research)

1. In the treatment of the sick person, the physician must be free to use a new diagnostic and therapeutic measure, if in his or her judgment it offers hope of saving life, reestablishing health or alleviating suffering.

2. The potential benefits, hazards and discomfort of a new method should be weighed against the advantages of the best current diagnostic and therapeutic methods.

3. In any medical study, every patient—including those of a control group, if any—should be assured of the best proven diagnostic and therapeutic method. This does not exclude the use of inert placebo in studies where no proven diagnostic or therapeutic method exists.

4. The refusal of the patient to participate in a study must never interfere with the physician–patient relationship.
5. If the physician considers it essential not to obtain informed consent, the specific reasons for this proposal should be stated in the experimental protocol for transmission to the independent committee.
6. The physician can combine medical research with professional care, the objective being the acquisition of new medical knowledge, only to the extent that medical research is justified by its potential diagnostic or therapeutic value for the patient.

### III. Non-Therapeutic Biomedical Research Involving Human Subjects (Non-Clinical Biomedical Research)

1. In the purely scientific application of medical research carried out on a human being, it is the duty of the physician to remain the protector of the life and health of that person on whom biomedical research is being carried out.
2. The subjects should be volunteers—either healthy persons or patients for whom the experimental design is not related to the patient's illness.
3. The investigator or the investigating team should discontinue the research if in his/her or their judgment it may, if continued, be harmful to the individual.
4. In research on man, the interest of science and society should never take precedence over considerations related to the well-being of the subject.

## THE NUREMBERG CODE[4]

1. The voluntary consent of the human subject is absolutely essential. This means that the person involved should have legal capacity to give consent; should be so situated as to be able to exercise free power of choice, without the intervention of any element of force, fraud, deceit, duress, overreaching or other form of constraint or coercion; and should have sufficient knowledge and comprehension of the elements of the subject matter involved as to enable him to make an understanding and enlightened decision. This latter element requires that before the acceptance of an affirmative decision by the experimental subject there should be made known to him the nature, duration and purpose of the experiment; the method and means by which it is to be conducted; all inconveniences and hazards reasonable to be expected; and the effects upon his health or person which may possibly come from his participation in the experiment.

    The duty and responsibility for ascertaining the quality of the consent rests upon each individual who initiates, directs, or engages in the experiment. It is a personal duty and responsibility which may not be delegated to another with impunity.
2. The experiment should be such as to yield fruitful results for the good of society, unprocurable by other methods or means of study, and not random and unnecessary in nature.
3. The experiment should be so designed and based on results of animal experimentation and a knowledge of the natural history of the disease or other

[4]Reprinted from *The Trials of War Criminals before the Nuremberg Military Tribunals,* (Washington, D.C.: U.S. Government Printing Office, 1948).

problem under study that the anticipated results will justify the performance of the experiment.

4. The experiment should be so conducted as to avoid all unnecessary physical and mental suffering and injury.

5. No experiment should be conducted where there is an *a priori* reason to believe that death or disabling injury will occur; except, perhaps, in those experiments where the experimental physicians also serve as subjects.

6. The degree of risk to be taken should never exceed that determined by the humanitarian importance of the problem to be solved by the experiment.

7. Proper preparations should be made and adequate facilities provided to protect the experimental subject against even remote possibilities of injury, disabilities, or death.

8. The experiment should be conducted only by scientifically qualified persons. The highest degree of skill and care should be required through all stages of the experiment of those who conduct or engage in the experiment.

9. During the course of the experiment the human subject should be at liberty to bring the experiment to an end if he has reached the physical or mental state where continuation of the experiment seems to him to be impossible.

10. During the course of the experiment the scientist in charge must be prepared to terminate the experiment at any stage, if he has probable cause to believe, in the exercise of the good faith, superior skill, and careful judgment required of him that a continuation of the experiment is likely to result in injury, disability, or death to the experimental subject.

## NURSES' CODE OF ETHICS (AMERICAN NURSES ASSOCIATION)[5]

The American Nurses Association (ANA) has developed a code for nurses that discusses the nurses' obligation to protect the patient's privacy, respect the patient's dignity, maintain competence in nursing, and assume responsibility and accountability for individual nursing judgments. This code states the nurses' ethical responsibilities and is summarized here:

1. The nurse provides services with respect for human dignity and the uniqueness of the client, unrestricted by considerations of social or economic status, personal attributes, or the nature of the health problems.

2. The nurse safeguards the client's privacy by judiciously protecting information of a confidential nature.

3. The nurse acts to safeguard the client and the public when health care and safety are affected by the incompetent, unethical, or illegal practices of any person.

4. The nurse assumes responsibility and accountability for individual nursing judgments and actions.

5. The nurse maintains competence in nursing.

[5]Reprinted with permission from *Code for Nurses with Interpretative Statements*, copyright 1985. (American Nurses Publishing: American Nurses Foundation/American Nurses Association, Washington, D.C.)

6. The nurse exercises informed judgment and uses individual competence and qualifications as criteria in seeking consultation, accepting responsibilities, and delegating nursing activities to others.
7. The nurse participates in activities that contribute to the ongoing development of the profession's body of knowledge.
8. The nurse participates in the profession's efforts to implement and improve standards of nursing.
9. The nurse participates in the profession's efforts to establish and maintain conditions of employment conducive to the high quality of nursing care.
10. The nurse participates in the profession's efforts to protect the public from misinformation and misrepresentation and to maintain the integrity of nursing.
11. The nurse collaborates with members of the health care profession and other citizens in promoting community and national efforts to meet the health needs of the public.

## CODE FOR NURSES: ETHICAL CONCEPTS APPLIED TO NURSING (INTERNATIONAL COUNCIL OF NURSES)[6]

The International Council of Nurses developed a code that discusses the role of nurses as they relate to people, their practice, society, their coworkers, and their profession.

The fundamental responsibility of the nurse is fourfold: to promote health, to prevent illness, to restore health and alleviate suffering. The need for nursing is universal. Inherent in nursing is respect for life, dignity and the rights of man. It is unrestricted by considerations of nationality, race, creed, color, age, sex, politics or social status.

Nurses render health services to the individual, the family and the community and coordinate their services with those of related groups.

### Nurses and People

The nurse's primary responsibility is to those people who require nursing care.

The nurse, in providing care, promotes an environment in which the values, customs and spiritual beliefs of the individual are respected.

The nurse holds in confidence personal information and uses judgment in sharing this information.

### Nurses and Practice

The nurse carries personal responsibility for nursing practice and for maintaining competence by continual learning.

The nurse maintains the highest standards of nursing care possible within the reality of a specific situation.

The nurse uses judgment in relation to individual competence when accepting and delegating responsibilities.

---

[6]Reprinted from *Bioethics Readings and Cases,* B. Brody, and H. Engelhardt. (Upper Saddle River, N.J.: Prentice Hall, 1987), pp. 393–394.

The nurse when acting in a professional capacity should at all times maintain standards of personal conduct which reflect credit upon the profession.

### Nurses and Society

The nurse shares with other citizens the responsibility for initiating and supporting action to meet the health and social needs of the public.

### Nurses and Co-Workers

The nurse sustains a cooperative relationship with co-workers in nursing and other fields.

The nurse takes appropriate action to safeguard the individual when his care is endangered by a co-worker or any other person.

### Nurses and the Profession

The nurse plays the major role in determining and implementing desirable standards of nursing practice and nursing education.

The nurse is active in developing a core of professional knowledge.

The nurse, acting through the professional organization, participates in establishing and maintaining equitable social and economic working conditions in nursing.

# Allied Health Codes of Ethics

## CODE OF ETHICS OF THE AMERICAN ASSOCIATION OF MEDICAL ASSISTANTS (AAMA)[7]

The AAMA has developed a Code of Ethics for Medical Assistants. The introduction says, "The Code of Ethics of AAMA shall set forth principles of ethical and moral conduct as they relate to the medical profession and the particular practice of medical assisting."

The Code then states:

Members of the AAMA dedicated to the conscientious pursuit of their profession, thus desiring to merit the regard of the entire medical profession and the respect of the general public which they serve, do hereby pledge themselves to strive for:

### Human Dignity

I.  Render service with full respect for the dignity of humanity;

*Confidentiality*
II.  Respect confidential information obtained through employment unless legally authorized or required by responsible performance of duty to divulge such information;

*Honor*
III.  Uphold the honor and high principles of the profession and accept its disciplines;

[7]Copyright by the American Association of Medical Assistants, Inc. Reprinted by permission.

*Continued Study*
  IV. Seek continually to improve the knowledge and skills of medical assistants for the benefit of patients and professional colleagues;

*Responsibility for Improved Community*
  V. Participate in additional service activities aimed toward improving the health and well-being of the community.

In addition to the Code of Ethics of the AAMA, a creed, or statement of intent, has been developed by this organization. The creed states:

> I believe in the principles and purposes of the profession of medical assisting.
> I endeavor to be more effective.
> I aspire to render greater service.
> I protect the confidence entrusted to me.
> I am dedicated to the care and well-being of all people.
> I am loyal to my employer.
> I am true to the ethics of my profession.
> I am strengthened by compassion, courage, and faith.

## CODE OF ETHICS FOR THE PROFESSION OF DIETETICS[8]

The American Dietetic Association and its Commission on Dietetic Registration are the vanguard of professional associations and credentialing bodies that have adopted a voluntary, enforceable code of ethics. They are summarized as follows:

The dietetic practitioner

  1. Provides professional services with objectivity and with respect for the unique needs and values of individuals.
  2. Avoids discrimination against other individuals on the basis of race, creed, religion, sex, age, and national origin.
  3. Fulfills professional commitments in good faith.
  4. Conducts him/herself with honesty, integrity and fairness.
  5. Remains free of conflict of interest while fulfilling the objectives and maintaining the integrity of the dietetic profession.
  6. Maintains confidentiality of information.
  7. Practices dietetics based on scientific principles and current information.
  8. Assumes responsibility and accountability for personal competence in practice.
  9. Recognizes and exercises professional judgment within the limits of his/her qualifications and seeks counsel or makes referrals as appropriate.
  10. Provides sufficient information to enable clients to make their own informed decisions.
  11. Who wishes to inform the public and colleagues of his/her services does so by using factual information. The dietetic practitioner does not advertise in a false or misleading manner.

[8]Reprinted with permission of the American Dietetic Association, copyright 1993. The American Dietetic Association. Reprinted by permission from *Journal of American Dietetic Association,* Vol. 99.

12. Promotes or endorses products in a manner that is neither false nor misleading.
13. Permits use of his/her name for the purpose of certifying that dietetic services have been rendered only if he/she has provided or supervised the provision of these services.
14. Accurately presents professional qualifications and credentials.
15. Presents substantiated information and interprets controversial information without personal bias, recognizing that legitimate differences of opinion exist.
16. Makes all reasonable effort to avoid bias in any kind of professional evaluation.
17. Voluntarily withdraws from professional practice under the following circumstances:
    a. If the practitioner has engaged in any substance abuse that could affect his/her practice.
    b. If the practitioner has been adjudged by a court to be mentally incompetent.
    c. If the practitioner has an emotional or mental disability that affects his/her practice in a manner that could harm the client.
18. Complies with all applicable laws and regulations concerning the profession.
19. Accepts the obligation to protect society and the profession by upholding the Code of Ethics for the Profession of Dietetics and by reporting alleged violations of the Code through the defined review process of the American Dietetic Association and its credentialing agency, the Commission on Dietetic Registration.

# CODE OF ETHICS OF THE AMERICAN HEALTH INFORMATION MANAGEMENT ASSOCIATION[9]

## Preamble

The health information management professional abides by a set of ethical principles developed to safeguard the public and to contribute within the scope of the profession to quality and efficiency in health care. This Code of Ethics, adopted by the members of the American Health Information Management Association, defines the standards of behavior which promote ethical conduct.

## Principles

The Health Information Management Professional

1. Demonstrates behavior that reflects integrity, supports objectivity, and fosters trust in professional activities.
2. Respects the dignity of each human being.
3. Strives to improve personal competence and quality of services.
4. Represents truthfully and accurately professional credentials, education, and experience.
5. Refuses to participate in illegal or unethical acts and also refuses to conceal the illegal, incompetent, or unethical acts of others.
6. Protects the confidentiality of primary and secondary health records as mandated by law, professional standards, and the employer's policies.
7. Promotes to others the tenants of confidentiality.

[9]Reprinted with permission of the American Health Information Management Association, (amended October 1991).

8. Adheres to pertinent laws and regulations while advocating changes which serve the best interest of the public.
9. Encourages appropriate use of health record information and advocates policies and systems that advance the management of health records and health information.
10. Recognizes and supports the Association's mission.

# CODE OF ETHICS OF THE AMERICAN SOCIETY FOR MEDICAL TECHNOLOGY[10]

## Preamble

The Code of Ethics of the American Society for Medical Technology (ASMT) sets forth the principles and standards by which clinical laboratory professionals practice their profession.

The professional conduct of clinical laboratory professionals is based on the following duties and principles:

## I. Duty to the Patient

Clinical laboratory professionals are accountable for the quality and integrity of the laboratory services they provide. This obligation includes continuing competence in both judgment and performance as individual practitioners, as well as in striving to safeguard the patient from incompetent or illegal practice by others.

Clinical laboratory professionals maintain high standards of practice and promote the acceptance of such standards at every opportunity. They exercise sound judgment in establishing, performing, and evaluating laboratory testing.

Clinical laboratory professionals perform their services with regard for the patient as an individual, respecting his or her right to confidentiality, the uniqueness of his or her needs and his or her right to timely access to needed services. Clinical laboratory professionals provide accurate information to others about the services they provide.

## II. Duty to Colleagues and the Profession

Clinical laboratory professionals accept responsibility to individually contribute to the advancement of the profession through a variety of activities. These activities include contributions to the body of knowledge of the profession; establishing and implementing high standards of practice and education; seeking fair socioeconomic working conditions for themselves and other members of the profession, and holding their colleagues and the profession in high regard and esteem.

Clinical laboratory professionals actively strive to establish cooperative and insightful working relationships with other health professionals; keeping in mind their primary objective to ensure a high standard of care for the patients they serve.

## III. Duty to Society

Clinical laboratory professionals share with other citizens the duties of responsible citizenship. As practitioners of an autonomous profession, they have the responsibility

---

[10]Reprinted with permission of the American Society for Clinical Laboratory Sciences, June 1995.

to contribute from their sphere of professional competence to the general well-being of the community, and specifically to the resolution of social issues affecting their practice and collective good.

Clinical laboratory professionals comply with relevant laws and regulations pertaining to the practice of clinical laboratory science and actively seek within the dictates of their consciences, to change those which do not meet the high standards of care and practice to which the professional is committed. As a clinical laboratory professional, I acknowledge my professional responsibility to:

> Maintain and promote standards of excellence in performing and advancing the art and science of my profession;
> Safeguard the dignity and privacy of my patient;
> Hold my colleagues and my profession in high esteem and regard;
> Contribute to the general well-being of the community; and
> Actively demonstrate my commitment to these responsibilities throughout my professional life.

## CODE OF ETHICS FOR RADIATION THERAPISTS[11]

The radiation therapist advances the principle objective of the profession to provide services to humanity with full respect for the dignity of mankind.

The radiation therapist delivers patient care and service unrestricted by concerns of personal attributes or the nature of the disease or illness, and non-discriminatory with respect to race, color, creed, sex, age, disability or national origin.

The radiation therapist assesses situations; exercises care, discretion and judgment; assumes responsibility for professional decisions; and acts in the best interest of the patient.

The radiation therapist adheres to the tenants and domains of the *Scope of Practice for Radiation Therapists.*

The radiation therapist actively engages in lifelong learning to maintain, improve and enhance professional competence and knowledge.

[11]Reprinted with permission of the American Society of Radiologic Technologists, August 10, 1997.

# Health Care Regulatory Credentialing Agencies

American Association of Medical Assistants
20 N. Wacker Dr., Suite 1575
Chicago, IL 60606-2903
(800) ACT-AAMA

American Association for Medical Transcription
P.O. Box 6187
Modesto, CA 95355
(800) 982-2182

American Association for Respiratory Therapy
1729 Regal Row
Dallas, TX 75235
(972) 243-2272

American Board for Occupational Health Nurses, Inc.
201 East Ogden Ave., Suite 114
Hinsdale, IL 60521-3652
(630) 789-5799

American Dietetic Association
430 N. Michigan Ave.
Chicago, IL 60611
(312) 899-0040

American Health Information Management Association (AHIMA)
233 N. Michigan Avenue
Chicago, IL 60601-5800
(312) 233-1100

American Health Management and Consulting, Inc.
140 Allens Creek Road
Rochester, NY 14618
(800) 638-0890

American Medical Association
515 N. State St.
Chicago, IL 60610
(312) 464-5000

American Medical Women's Association
801 N. Fairfax Street, Suite 400
Alexandria, VA 22314
(703) 838-0500

American Society for Clinical Laboratory Science
7910 Woodmont Avenue, Suite 530
Bethesda, MD 20814
(301) 657-2768

American Society of Clinical Pathologists
Board of Registry
2100 W. Harrison
Chicago, IL 60612
(312) 738-1336

American Society of Radiologic Technologists
15000 Central Ave., SE
Albuquerque, NM 87123
(505) 298-4500

Association of Physician Assistant Programs
950 N. Washington Street
Alexandria, VA 22314-1552
(703) 548-5538

Council on Social Work Education
1725 Duke Street, Suite 500
Alexandria, VA 22314-3457
(703) 683-8080

National League for Nursing
Career Information Services
61 W. Broadway
New York, NY 10009
(212) 363-5555

Registered Medical Assistant
710 Higgins Rd.
Park Ridge, IL 60068-5765
(847) 823-5169

Registered Medical Technologist
710 Higgins Rd.
Park Ridge, IL 60068-5765
(847) 823-5169

# Medical Web Sites

Please note that URLs may change over time.

AIDS Pathfinder
*www.nnlm.nlm.nih.gov/pnr/etc/aidspath.html*

American Association of Medical Assistants
*www.aama-ntl.org*

American Health Information Management Association
*www.ahima.org*

American Health Lawyers Association
*www.healthlawyers.org*

American Medical Association
*www.ama-assn.org*

American Nurses Association
*www.nursinworld.org/readroom*

American Telemedicine Association (ATA)
*www.atmeda.org*

AmericasDoctor.com
*www.americasdoctor.com*

Association for Responsible Medicine
*www.a-r-m.org*

CancerNet
*www.nci.nih.gov.hpage/cis.htm*

Centers for Disease Control (CDC)
*www.cdc.gov*

Certified Doctor
*www.certifieddoctor.org/verify.html*

Cleveland Clinic Foundation
*www.ccf.org*

Cybrary
*www.cybrary.info*

Findlaw
*www.findlaw.com*

HealthAnswers
*www.healthanswers.com*

Health Care Providers Service Organization (HPSO)
*www.hpso.com*

Healthfinder
*www.healthfinder.gov*

HealthIdeas
*www.healthideas.com*

Health Insurance Portability and Accountability Act (HIPAA)
*www.hhs.gov/ocr/hippa*

Hospice Foundation of America
*www.hospicefoundation.org*

Human Genome Project Information
*www.ornl.gov/hgmis/medicine/genetest.html*

IntelliHealth (from Johns Hopkins)
*www.intellihealth.com*

International Council on Infertility Information Dissemination
*www.inciid.org/ivf.htlm*

Joint Commission on Accreditation of Healthcare Organizations (JCAHO)
*www.jcaho.org*

Laboratory Values
*www.ghsl.nwu.edu*

Legal Information Institute: Tort Law
*www.law.cornell.edu/topics/tort.html*

Mayo Clinic Health Oasis
*www.mayohealth.org*

MedHelp International
*www.medhelp.netusa.net/index.htm*

Medical Journals
*www.medsite.com*

MedlinePlus
*www.nlm.nih.gov/medlineplus*

Medscape
*www.medscape.com*

National Association for Healthcare Quality
  *www.nahq.org*

National Cancer Policy Board of the Institute of Medicine
  *www.iom.edu*

National Center for Health Statistics
  *www.cdc.gov/nchswww/index.htm*

National Hospice and Palliative Care Organization
  *www.nhpco.org*

National Institutes of Health
  *www.nih.gov*

National Library of Medicine
  *www.nlm.gov*

Occupational Safety and Health Act
  *www.osha.org*

United Network for Organ Sharing (UNOS)
  *www.unos.org*

U.S. Department of Health and Human Services
  *www.hhs.gov*

U.S. House of Representatives
  *www.house.gov*

# Case Citations

*Agnew-Watson v. County of Almeda*, 36 Cal. Rptr. 2d 196 Ct. App. (Cal. 1994).
*Allen v. Mansour*, 681 F. Supp. 1232, E.D. (Mich. 1986).
*In re Axelrod*, 560 N.Y.S.2d 573, App. Div. (1990).

*In re Baby M*, 537 A.2d 1227 (N.J. 1988).
*Barnes Hospital v. Missouri Commission on Human Rights*, 661 S.W.2d 534 ( Mo.1983).
*Benduburg v. Dempsey*, 19 F.3d 557,11th Cir. (1994).
*Big Town Nursing Home v. Newman*, 461 S.W.2d 195 (Texas Civ.App.1970).
*Blank v. Palo Alto-Stanford Hosp. Ctr.*, 44 Cal. Rptr. 572 (Cal. Ct. App. 1965).
*Bondu v. Gurvich*, 473 So. 2d 1307 (Fla. Dist. Ct. App. 1984).
*Bouvia v. Superior Court*, 225 Cal. Rptr. 287 (Cal. App. 1986).
*Buchanan v. Kull*, 35 N.W.2d 351 (Mich.1949).
*Buckley v. Hospital Corp. of America, Inc.*, 758 F.2d 1525, 11th Cir. (1985).

*Child Protection Group v. Cline*, 350 S.E.2d 541 (W. Va. 1986).
*Cline v. Lund, 31 Cal. App.* 3d 755 (1973).
*Cruzan v. Director, Missouri Dep't of Health*, 497 U.S. 261 (1990).

*Darling v. Charleston Community Mem. Hosp.*, 211 N.E. 2d 253 (1965).
*Davis v. Davis*, 842 S.W.2d 588 (Tenn. 1992).
*DeMay v. Roberts*, 9 N.W.146 (Mich.1881).
*Doe v. Borough of Barrington*, 729 F.Supp. 376, (N.J. 1990).
*In re Doe*, 533 A2d 523 (R.I. 1987).
*Downs v. Sawtelle*, 574 F.2d 1, Cir. (1978).

*Fair v. St. Joseph's Hosp.*, 437 S.E.2d 875 (N.C. App. 1933).

*Garcia v. Elf Atochem*, N. Am., 28 F.3d 446, 5th Cir. (1994).
*Goff v. Doctors General Hospital*, 333 P.2d 29 (Cal.Ct.App. 1958).
*Goforth v. Porter Med. Assoc., Inc.*, 755 P.2d 678 (Okla. 1988).

*Grijalva v. Shalala,* 946 F. Supp. 747 (Ariz. 1996).
*Griswold v. Connecticut,* 381 U.S. 479 (1965).
*Grubbs v. Medical Facilities of America, Inc.,* 879 F. Supp. W.D. (Va. 1995).
*Guilmet v. Campbell,* 385 Mich. 57, 188 N.W.2d 601 (1971).

*Harris v. McRae,* U.S. 297 (1980).
*Harvet v. Unity Med. Ctr.,* 428 N.W.2d 574 (Minn. Ct. App. (1988).
*Hayes v. Shelby Memorial. Hosp.,* 726 F.2d 1543, 11th Cir. (1984).
*Heller v. Ambach,* 433 N.Y.S.2d 281 (1979).
*Hickman v. Sexton Dental Clinic, P.A.* 367 S.E.2d 453, (S.C. Ct. App. 1988).
*H.L. v. Matheson,* 450 U.S. 398 (1981).
*Hurlock v. Park Lane Med. Ctr. Inc.,* 709 S.W.2d 872 (Mo. Ct. App. 1985).

*James v. Jacobson,* 6 F.3d 233, 4th Cir. (1993).
*Jeczalik v. Valley Hosp.,* A.2d 90 (N.J. 1981).
*Jenkins v. Bogalusa Comm. Med. Ctr.,* 340 So.2d 1065, (La. Ct. App.1976).

*Kern v. Gulf Coast Nursing Home, Inc.,* 502 So.2d 1198 (Miss. 1987).

*Lambert v. Bessey,* 83 Eng. Rep. 220 (1681).
*Landeros v. Flood,* 551 P.2d 389 (Cal. 1976).
*Landau v. Medical Board of California,* 71 Cal. Rptr. (Cal. App. 1998).
*Love v. Heritage House Convalescent Ctr.,* 463 N.E.2d 478 (Ind. Ct. App. 1983).
*Lovelace Medical Ctr. v. Mendez,* 805 P.2d 603 (N.M. 1991).

*Maher v. Roe,* 432 U.S. 464 (1977).
*McLaughlin v. Cooke,* 774 P.2d 1171 (Wash. 1989).
*Mohr v. Williams,* 104 N.W.12 (Minn.1905).
*Moon Lake Convalescent Center v. Margolis,* 435 N.E.2d 956 (Ill. App. Ct. 1989).
*Morena v. South Hills Health System,* 462 A.2d 680 (Pa. 1983).
*Morrison v. MacNamara,* 407 A.2d 555 (D.C.1979).
*Murray v. Vandevander,* 522 P.2d 302 (Okla. Ct. App. 1974).

*Norton v. Argonaut Ins. Co.,* 144 So.2d 249 (La. App.1962).

*O'Neill v. Montefiore Hosp.,* 202 N.Y.S2d, 436, App.Div. (1960).

*Pardazi v. Cullman Med. Ctr.,* 838 F.2d 1155, 11th Cir. (1988).
*Parrish v. Clark,* 145 So. 848 (Fla. 1933).
*Patrick v. Burget,* 486 U.S. 94 (1988).
*People v. Gandotra,* 14 Cal. Rptr. 2d 896 (11th Cal. App. 1992).
*People v. Smithtown Gen. Hosp.,* 736, 402 N.Y.S.2d 318, Sup. Ct. (1978).
*Planned Parenthood of Central Missouri v. Danforth,* 428 U.S. 52 (1976).
*Planned Parenthood of Southeastern Pennsylvania v. Casey,* 50 U.S. 833 (1992).
*Polonsky v. Union Hospital,* 418 N.E.2d 620, (Mass. App. Ct. 1981).
*Poor Sister of St. Francis v. Catron,* 435 N.E.2d 305 (Ind. Ct. App. 1982).

*Quinby v. Morrow,* 340 F.2d 584, 2d Cir. (1965).
*In re Quinlan,* 355 A.2d 647 (N.J. 1976).

*Rodgers v. St. Mary's Hospital,* 556 N.E.2d 913 (Ill. App. Ct. 1990).
*Roe v. Wade,* 410 U.S.113 (1973).
*Rust v. Sullivan,* 500 U.S. 173 (1991).

*St. John's Reg. Health Ctr. v. American Cas. Co.,* 980 F.2d 1222, 8th Cir. (1992).
*Satler v. Larsen,* 520 N.Y.S.2d 378, App. Div. (1987).
*In re Schroeder,* 415 N.W.2d 436 (Minn. Ct. App. 1987).
*Skinner v. Oklahoma,* 316 U.S. 535 (1942).
*Smith v. Cote,* 513 A.2d 341 (N.H. 1986).
*Starks v. Director of Div. of Employment Section,* 462 N.E.2d 1360 (Mass. 1984).
*State v. Fierro,* 603 P.2d 74 (Ariz. 1979).
*State Dep't. of Human Services v. Northern,* 563 S.W.2d 197 (Tenn. Ct. App. 1978).
*Swanson v. St. John's Lutheran Hosp.,* 597 P.2d 702 (Mont. 1979).

*Teeters v. Currey,* 518 S.W.2d 512 (Tenn.1974).
*Thompson v. Brent,* 245 So.2d 751, (La. App.1971).
*Thompson v. Midwest Found. Indep. Physicians Ass'n.,* 124 F.R.D 154 (1988).
*Thor v. Boska,* 113 Cal. Rptr. 296, Ct. App. (1974).
*Tugg v. Towney,* 864 F. Supp. 1201, S.D. (Fla. 1994).

*United States v. Busse, Dey, Lupulescu, and Failla,* 833 F.2d 1014 (U.S. App. 1987).
*United States v. NME Psychiatric Hosps., Inc.,* No.94-0268.

*Watson v. Idaho Falls Consol. Hosp., Inc.,* 720 P.2d 632 (Idaho 1986).
*Weaver v. Ward,* 80 Eng. Rep. 284 (1616).
*Williams v. Summit Psychiatric Ctrs.,* 363 S.E.2d 794 (Ga.App.1987).
*Woolfolk v. Duncan,* 872 F. Supp. 1381, E.D. (Pa. 1995).

*Zatarain v. WDSU-Television, Inc.,* WI 16777 E.D. (La. 1995).
*Zucker v. Axelrod,* 527 N.Y.S.2d 937 (1988).

# Supplemental Cases for Discussion

## Tuskegee Syphilis Study

In 1929, the United States Health Service worked with state and local departments of health in six states to find a method to control venereal disease. The statistical reports that were conducted between 1930 and 1932 demonstrated a high rate of syphilis in Macon County, Alabama, where over 84 percent of the population was black and 40 percent of the men were infected with syphilis. The methods used for treating this disease consisted of the injection of mercury and other toxic compounds. Some men recovered with this treatment; others were made even more ill; and in some cases in which no treatment was given, the patient was able to live for several decades.

After funding ran out during the Depression to treat the disease, the researchers conducting the Tuskegee Study attempted to discover how severe this disease was if left untreated. For this study, the U.S. Public Health Service selected 600 men. Of these 600 research subjects, 400 of the men had syphilis and the other 200 non-syphilitic men became the control group. The infected patients were not told about the purpose or nature of the research. In fact, the researchers would refer to procedures such as spinal taps as "treatments" to induce patient participation. When some of the men in the control group developed syphilis over the course of the study, they were transferred into the research group without ever being told they had the disease. No treatment was ever given to any of the men to fight the disease.

In the early 1940s, penicillin was found to be effective against syphilis. The Tuskegee project could have been discontinued at this time, since there was no longer any need to study the course of this disease without treatment. However, the research project did continue. The researchers were able to track the men and make sure they did not receive antibiotics for any condition. In the 1960s, a researcher working for the U.S. Public Health Service tried to put an end to the project, which was now being conducted by the Center for Disease Control in Atlanta. When he was unsuccessful, he notified the press and ultimately the project was stopped. The public was outraged that poor black men had been subjected to a research project without their consent and denied treatment for a treatable disease in an attempt to gain what was seen as useless information. In 1973, the surviving patients received an out-of-court settlement of $37,500 for the infected men and $16,000 for the men in the control group. The families of men who had died also received compensation of $15,000 for the infected men and $5,000 for the uninfected men.

This was never a secret project. This project had been well publicized in medical journals. The people who read about the study did nothing to stop it.

(Summarized from G. Pence. *Classic Cases in Medical Ethics.* New York: McGraw Hill Publishing Company, 1990.)

## The Willowbrook State Hospital Case

Willowbrook State Hospital, an institution for mentally retarded children on Staten Island, experienced a large number of infectious diseases among its patients. Conditions at the hospital were not good, and most children suffered from hepatitis, measles, and parasitic and respiratory infections. Hepatitis, in particular, was a problem, since many of the children were not toilet-trained and the disease was spread through an oral-intestinal route. Researchers determined that nearly all susceptible children became infected with hepatitis during their first year at the hospital.

Between the years 1956 and 1970, 10,000 children were admitted to Willowbrook Hospital. Of those children, almost 800 were entered into a research project to gain information about the disease with the hopes of eventually developing an immunization against the disease. All the parents of the children in the research project granted written consent. The children were injected with the same strain of hepatitis that was already prevalent at the hospital.

The physician-researchers in charge of the project received intense criticism for subjecting the children to this research. The researchers defended their actions by stating that

a. the children that were used as subjects were unharmed or, at least, not made any more ill than they already were;
b. the children may have even benefited, since they were placed on an isolated unit and thus were not exposed to other infectious diseases;
c. the children in the study may have had a subclinical infection, which would render them immune to the hepatitis virus;
d. the children may have been better off as a result of the research, since the study added to the growth of information about the disease;
e. all the parents had given their informed consent.

The medical community was outraged about the experiment and raised the following objections:

a. mentally retarded persons, especially children, should not be used for research experimentation;

b. the children are unable to defend or speak for themselves;

c. there is a greater possibility of abuse with children than with adults;

d. the parents may have been coerced to grant consent, since the hospital was full and there was only space to admit children into the hepatitis unit;

e. the experiment did not appear to be therapeutic;

f. the benefits to the hospital and the community at large were minimal;

g. the experiments were designed to confirm *existing* studies about the effects of gamma globulin immunization for hepatitis;

h. researchers withheld from the nonresearch children (control group) an inoculation that may have been effective against hepatitis.

Since 800 children were isolated from other children, they did not acquire infectious diseases prevalent at the time. Ultimately, the claim that the children in the research study benefited from the project was upheld in court.

(Summarized from G. Pence. *Classic Cases in Medical Ethics.* New York: McGraw Hill Publishing Company, 1990.)

## Marguerite M. Case

Marguerite M., an 89-year-old widow, was admitted into the cardiac intensive care unit in Chicago's Memorial Hospital at 3:00 A.M. on a Sunday morning with a massive heart attack (myocardial infarction). Her internist, Dr. K., who is also a close family friend, has ordered an angiogram to determine the status of Marguerite's infarction (heart attack). Dr. K. has found that the angiogram and resulting treatment needs to be done within the first six hours after an infarction in order to be effective. The procedure is going to be done as soon as the on-call surgical team can set up the angiography room. The radiologist, who lives thirty minutes from the hospital, must also be in the hospital before the procedure can begin. At 4:30 A.M. the team is ready to have Marguerite, who is barely conscious, transferred from the intensive care unit to the surgical suite.

Coincidentally, at 4:30 A.M., Sarah W., an unconscious 45-year-old woman, is brought in by ambulance with a massive heart attack. The emergency room physicians, after conferring with her physician by phone, conclude that she will need a balloon angiography to save her life. When they call the surgical department to have the on-call angiography team brought in, they are told that the room is already set up for Dr. K.'s patient. They do not have another team or surgical room for Sarah W. A decision is made that Sarah, who needs the balloon angiography in order to survive, will receive the procedure.

Dr. K. is called at home and told that his patient, Marguerite, will not be able to have the angiogram. The hospital is going to use the angiography team for Sarah, since she is younger than Marguerite and has a greater chance for recovery. Unfortunately, it took longer than expected to stabilize Sarah before and after the procedure, and the six-hour "window" when the procedure could be performed on Marguerite passed. Sarah survived, made a full recovery, and returned to her family. Marguerite expired the following morning.

## The Robert W. Case

In September 1993, 50-year-old Robert W. was involved in a pickup truck accident that left him brain-damaged and unable to eat, drink, talk, or communicate his wishes. Two years later, his wife, Ruth, requested that her husband's doctors remove the feeding tubes that kept him alive. She stated that long before the accident, he had indicated that he would not wish to live in a helpless condition.

Robert's mother and sister objected to having his tubes removed and stated that he was minimally conscious and not comatose. The Supreme Court ruled in favor of the mother and sister in August 2001. The Court finding stated that families have no right to stop life support for conscious patients who are not terminally ill and who have left no explicit written instructions regarding this issue. Ironically, the patient died of pneumonia, with the feeding tubes still in place, one month before the court's ruling on the case. The Court, in a six to zero decision, stated that "absent clear and convincing evidence," that Ruth's decision was in accordance with her husband's own wishes or best interests, it would not have allowed the removal of life support.

Courts had previously allowed the removal of life support in cases in which the patient is terminally ill or in a comalike state. But the law is unclear on how families can proceed when patients are conscious but unable to express their wishes.

## Terri Schiavo: "The Face That Moved a Nation"

In October 2003, the face of Terri Schavino smiling at her mother caught the interest of the American public and the governor of Florida, Jeb Bush. Terri had been in a persistent vegetative state since 1990. Her husband, Michael, and her parents were friendly until a jury awarded $1 million to Terri, under Michael's control, in a medical malpractice lawsuit. The parents contend that Michael stopped his wife's therapy and used the money to pay lawyers' fees in an attempt to have his wife's feeding tube removed. Terri's husband states that he wanted to fulfill his wife's wishes that she not be kept living in a comatose or vegetative state. Her parents opposed having the tube removed, declaring that she is not comatose but rather appears to smile, blink, and is able to follow balloons and her parents as they move about her room.

Terri's feeding tube was removed as ordered by the court. There was a great amount of media attention over the case, including a photo of Terri Schiavo smiling up at her mother on the front page of many national newspapers. One week after the feeding tube was removed, Governor Jeb Bush and the Florida legislature ordered that the feeding tube be reinserted. It was.

(Kampert, P. "The Face That Moved a Nation," *Chicago Tribune*, October 23, 2003, 1, 25.)

## John F. and the HMO

John, a 34-year-old father of two children, is a member of an HMO in Texas. John has made several trips to his area HMO to seek medical attention since finding blood in his bowel movements. He had been taking large amounts of aspirin for persistent headaches but did not realize that this could cause internal bleeding. John was always seen by a physician's assistant, Robert M., at the HMO, but never by a physician. Robert didn't ask John about taking any nonprescribed medications. John didn't realize that he should mention the over-the-counter medication (aspirin) consumption. Robert tells John that he is unable to prescribe any tests for him, but tells him to return if he is not any better. Two days later, John is rushed to the area emergency room with a bowel hemorrhage.

## Marion and the Pacemaker

Marion is a 92-year-old patient who weighs 79 pounds. She has had poor eating habits for at least ten years and refused all attempts by her daughters to improve her nutrition. In addition, Marion had been a heavy smoker all her life and suffered frequent respiratory problems. During the past two years, she has become quite forgetful, has suffered a broken hip as a result of a fall out of bed, and has been treated for pneumonia. Her daughters, who have their own family responsibilities and cannot bring their mother to live with them, have found an excellent nursing home near them run by an order of Catholic nuns. In spite of Marion's protests, she enters the nursing home.

During her third week in the nursing home, Marion develops a cough, high temperature, and respiratory problems. She is hospitalized with a diagnosis of pneumonia. Marion immediately becomes disoriented and attempts to remove her intravenous and oxygen tubing. Since she tries to climb out of bed, her daughters must remain at her side. The attending physician tells the daughters that in addition to treatment for pneumonia, Marion will also need to have a pacemaker inserted to regulate her heartbeat. However, Marion would then be unable to return to the nursing home, since the facility is not equipped to care for someone recovering from surgery.

After thoughtful discussions with other family members, Marion's daughters tell the physician that they do not want to put their confused mother through the surgical procedure. They state that they want to spare her the pain of recovery from a surgical procedure, since she is quite confused and elderly. Further, they are concerned that their mother will not survive a surgical procedure in her frail condition. The physician seems to be understanding of this decision. However, the floor nurses take the daughters aside on several occasions to tell them that this is not a dangerous procedure and they need to sign a permit for the surgery. In fact, the daughters are made to feel that they are not acting in their mother's best interests by not signing the permit. Marion returns to the nursing home without the pacemaker. She lives another four years without any further cardiac problems.

## Emily A. and the Hernia Repair

Emily has been admitted for a two-day hospital stay for the repair of an umbilical hernia and a laparoscopic cholecystectomy (gall bladder removal) under a general anesthetic. Her recovery from the surgical repair is uneventful except that she develops a cough. The cough keeps Emily awake all night after surgery. She tells the nurses taking care of her about the cough, but they seem to think it is not serious and nothing is done other than taking Emily's temperature, which is normal. Emily is discharged, and her coughing becomes much more frequent once she is home. She develops pain around her hernia incision every time she coughs, and the surgical site has become inflamed. Emily still does not have a temperature. She calls her surgeon on the fourth day after surgery to explain her condition. He tells her that he doesn't treat internal medicine problems. He suggests that she call her internist. Emily calls her internist, who prescribes an antibiotic over the phone. Emily recovers after ten days.

## David Z. and Amyotropic Lateral Sclerosis (ALS)

David, who has suffered with ALS for twenty years, is now hospitalized in a private religious hospital on a respirator. He spoke with his physician before he became incapacitated and asked that he be allowed to die if the suffering became too much for him. The physician agreed that, while he would not give David any drugs to assist a suicide, he would discontinue David's respirator if asked to do so. David has now indicated through a prearranged code of blinking eye movements, that he wants the respirator discontinued.

The nursing staff has alerted the hospital administrator about the impending discontinuation of the respirator. The administrator tells the physician that this is against the hospital's policy. She states that once a patient is placed on a respirator, the family must seek a court order to have him or her removed from this type of life support. In addition, it is against their policy to have any staff members present during such a procedure. After consulting with the family, the physician orders an ambulance to transport the patient back to his home, where the physician discontinues the life support.

# Glossary

**Abandonment**   withdrawing medical care from a patient without providing sufficient notice to the patient.

**Acquired immune deficiency syndrome (AIDS)**   a disease resulting in infections that occur as a result of exposure to the human immunodeficiency virus (HIV), which causes the immune system to break down.

**Active euthanasia**   actively ending the life of or killing a patient who is terminally ill.

**Addiction**   an acquired physical or psychological dependence on a drug.

**Administrative law**   a branch of law that covers regulations set by government agencies.

**Advance directive**   the various methods by which a patient has the right to self-determination prior to a medical necessity; includes living wills, health care proxies, and durable power of attorney.

**Agent**   person authorized to act on behalf of a patient.

**Affirmative defenses**   allow the defendant (usually physician or hospital) to present evidence that the patient's condition was the result of factors other than the defendant's negligence.

**Allege**   to assert or declare without proof.

**Alternative dispute resolution (ADR)**   methods for resolving a civil dispute that do not involve going to court.

**Amniocentesis**   a test for the presence of genetic defects in which a needle is used to withdraw a small amount of amniotic fluid that surrounds the fetus in the uterus.

**Applied ethics**   the practical application of moral standards to the conduct of individuals involved in organizations.

**Arbitration**   submitting a dispute for resolution to a person other than a judge.

**Arbitrator**   a person chosen to decide a disagreement between two parties.

**Artificial insemination**   the injection of seminal fluid that contains male sperm into the female's vagina from her husband, partner, or donor by some means other than sexual intercourse.

**Artificial insemination donor (AID)**   a procedure in which a donor's sperm is used.

323

**Artificial insemination husband (AIH)** a procedure in which sperm from the woman's husband or partner is used.

**Associate practice** a legal agreement in which physicians agree to share a facility and staff but do not, as a rule, share responsibility for the legal actions of each other.

**Assumption of risk** a legal defense that prevents a plaintiff from recovering damages if the plaintiff voluntarily accepts a risk associated with the activity.

**Autopsy** a postmortem examination of organs and tissues to determine the cause of death.

**Beneficence** the action of helping others and performing actions that would benefit another person.

**Bioethics** also called biomedical ethics, the moral dilemmas and issues of advanced medicine and medical research.

**Bioethicists** persons who specialize in the field of bioethics.

**Bloodborne pathogens** disease-producing microorganisms transmitted by means of blood and body fluids containing blood.

**Borrowed servant doctrine** a special application of *respondeat superior* in which an employer lends an employee to someone else.

**Brain death** an irreversible coma from which a patient does not recover; results in the cessation of brain activity.

**Breach** neglect of an understanding between two parties; failing to perform a legal duty.

**Breach of contract** the failure, without legal excuse, to perform any promise or to carry out any of the terms of an agreement; failure to perform a contractual duty.

**Bureau of Narcotics and Dangerous Drugs (BNDD)** an agency of the federal government responsible for enforcing laws covering statutes of addictive drugs.

**Cap** limit.

**Capitation rate** a fixed monthly fee paid by an HMO to health care providers for providing medical services to patients who are members of that HMO.

**Cardiopulmonary** heart and lung function.

**Case law** also called common law, case law is based on decisions made by judges.

**Cease and desist order** a court order to immediately stop an activity and not attempt any further violation.

**Censure** to find fault with, criticize, or condemn.

**Checks and balances** designed by the framers of the Constitution so that no one branch of government would have more power than another and so that each branch of government is scrutinized by other branches of government.

**Civil law** concerns relationships between individuals or between individuals and the government, which are not criminal.

**Claims-made insurance** liability insurance that covers the insured party for only the claims made during the time period the policy is in effect (or policy year).

**Clearinghouse**   a private or public health care entity that facilitates the processing of nonstandard electronic transactions into HIPAA transactions (e.g., a billing service).

**Closing argument**   closing speech or summary made by the attorneys for both the plaintiff and the defendant.

**Comatose**   vegetative condition.

**Common law**   also called case law, common law is based on decisions made by judges.

**Comparable worth**   also known as pay equity, the theory that extends equal pay requirements to all persons doing equal work.

**Comparative negligence**   a defense, similar to contributory negligence, that the plaintiff's own negligence helped cause the injury; not a complete bar to recovery of damages but only damages based on the amount of the plaintiff's fault.

**Compensatory damages**   an amount of money awarded by the court to make up for loss of income or emotional pain and suffering.

**Competent**   capable of making a decision without mental confusion due to drugs, alcohol, or other reasons.

**Conscience clause**   legislation or regulation stating that hospitals and health care professionals are not required to assist with such procedures as abortion and sterilization.

**Consent**   the voluntary agreement that a patient gives to allow a medically trained person the permission to touch, examine, and perform a treatment.

**Consideration**   in contract law, consideration is something of value given as part of the agreement.

**Constitutional law**   the inviolable rights, privileges, or immunities secured and protected for each citizen by the Constitution of the United States or by the constitution of each state.

**Contraception**   birth control.

**Contract law**   that division of law that includes enforceable promises and agreements between two or more persons to do or not to do a particular thing.

**Contributory negligence**   conduct on the part of the plaintiff that is a contributing cause of injuries; a complete bar to recovery of damages.

**Controlled Substances Act of 1970**   a federal statute that regulates the manufacture and distribution of the drugs that are capable of causing dependency.

**Co-payment**   an agreed-upon fee paid by the insured for certain medical services; usually $10 to $20.

**Coroner**   a public health officer who holds an investigation (inquest) if a person's death is from an unknown or violent cause.

**Corporation**   a type of medical practice, as established by law, that is managed by a board of directors.

**Cost/benefit analysis**   also called utilitarianism, an ethical approach in which the benefit of the decision should outweigh the costs.

**Covered entities**    health care organizations covered under HIPAA regulations such as public health authorities, health care clearinghouses, and self-insured employers, life insurers, information systems vendors, and universities.

**Creditor**    person or institution to whom a debt is owed.

**Creed**    statement of intent.

**Criminal case**    one in which court action is brought by the government against a person or groups of people accused of committing a crime, resulting in a fine or imprisonment if found guilty.

**Criminal laws**    set up to protect the public from the harmful acts of others.

**Damages**    any injuries caused by the defendant; usually a monetary award is given as compensation.

**Data**    statistics, figures, or information.

**Debtor**    person who owes money to another person.

**Defamation of character**    making false and/or malicious statements about another person; includes libel and slander.

**Defendant**    person or group of people sued civilly or prosecuted criminally in a court of law.

**Deposition**    oral testimony that is made before a public officer of the court to be used in a lawsuit.

**Dereliction**    neglect, as in neglect of duty.

**Diagnostic Related Groups (DRGs)**    designations used to identify reimbursement per condition in a hospital; used for Medicare patients.

**Direct cause**    the continuous sequence of events, unbroken by any intervening cause, that produces an injury and without which the injury would not have occurred.

**Disclosed**    made known.

**Discovery**    the legal process by which facts are discovered before a trial.

**Discovery rule**    legal theory that provides that the statute of limitations begins to run at the time the injury is discovered or when the patient should have known of the injury.

**Discrimination**    unfair or unequal treatment.

**Doctrine of professional discretion**    means that a physician may determine, based on his or her best judgment, if a patient with mental or emotional problems should view the medical record.

**Double-blind test**    a research design in which neither the experimenter nor the patient knows who is getting the research treatment.

**Drug Enforcement Administration (DEA)**    a division of the Department of Justice that enforces the Controlled Substances Act of 1970.

**Due process**    the entitlement of all employees to have certain procedures followed when they believe their rights are in jeopardy.

**Durable power of attorney**    a legal agreement that allows an agent or representative of the patient to act on behalf of the patient.

**Duty**    obligation or responsibility.

**Electroencephalogram (EEG)**  test to measure brain activity.

**Embezzlement**  the illegal appropriation of property, usually money, by a person entrusted with its possession.

**Embryo**  unborn child between the second and twelfth week after conception.

**Empathy**  the ability to understand the feelings of another person without actually experiencing the pain or distress that a person is going through.

**Employee Assistance Program(EAP)**  a management-financed, confidential counseling referral service designed to help employees and/or their family members assess a problem such as alcoholism.

**Endorsement**  an approval or sanction.

**Employer Identification Number (EIN)**  a number assigned to an employer for purposes of identification.

**Employer Identifier Standard**  a standard number based on an employer's tax ID number or EIN that is used for all electronic transmissions.

**Ethics**  the branch of philosophy relating to morals and moral principles.

**Eugenic (involuntary) sterilization**  sterilization of certain categories of persons, such as the insane and feeble-minded, in order to prevent them from passing on defective genes to their children.

**Eugenics**  the science that studies methods for controlling certain characteristics in offspring.

**Euthanasia**  the administration of a lethal agent by another person to a patient for the purpose of relieving intolerable and incurable suffering.

**Exclusive Provider Organization (EPO)**  a type of managed care that combines the concepts of the HMO and PPO.

**Expert witness**  a medical practitioner or other expert who, through education, training, or experience, has special knowledge about a subject and gives testimony about that subject in court, usually for a fee.

**Expired**  died.

**Expressed contract**  an agreement that is entered into orally or in writing.

**Expulsion**  the act of forcing out.

**Feasance**  doing an act or performing a duty.

**Fee splitting**  an agreement to pay a fee to another physician or agency for the referral of patients; this is illegal in some states and is considered to be an unethical medical practice.

**Felony**  a serious crime that carries a punishment of death or imprisonment for more than one year. Examples are murder, rape, robbery, and practicing medicine without a license.

**Fetus**  unborn child from the third month after conception until birth.

**Fidelity**  loyalty and faithfulness to others.

**Fixed-payment plan**  a payment plan for medical bills that offers subscribers (members) complete medical care in return for a fixed monthly fee.

**Food and Drug Administration (FDA)**   an agency within the Department of Health and Human Services that ultimately enforces drug sales and distribution.

**Franchise**   a business run by an individual to whom a franchisor grants the exclusive right to market a product or service in a certain market area.

**Franchisees**   persons or companies who hold a franchise.

**Fraud**   the deliberate concealment of the facts from another person for unlawful or unfair gain.

**Fradulent**   deceitful.

**Garnishment**   court order that requires an employer to pay a portion of an employee's paycheck directly to one of the employee's creditors until the debt is resolved.

**Gatekeeper**   the person, such as a primary care physician, or entity, such as an insurance company, that approves patient referrals to other physicians or services.

**Gene therapy**   the replacement of a defective or malfunctioning gene.

**Genetics**   a science that describes the biological influence that parents have on their offspring.

**Gestational period**   time before birth during which the fetus is developing, usually nine months.

**Good Samaritan Laws**   state laws that help protect health care professionals from liability while giving emergency care to accident victims.

**Group practice**   three or more physicians who share the same facility and practice medicine together.

*Guardian ad litem*   court-appointed guardian to represent a minor or unborn child in litigation.

**Habituation**   the development of an emotional dependence on a drug due to repeated use.

**Health care plan**   an individual or group plan that provides or pays for medical care.

**Healthcare Integrity and Protection Data Bank (HIPDB)**   a national data bank that collects and reports disclosures of actions taken against health care practitioners, providers, and vendors for noncompliance and fraudulent activities.

**Health Insurance Portability and Accountability Act of 1996 (HIPAA)**   regulates the privacy of patient's health information.

**Health Maintenance Organization (HMO)**   a type of managed care plan that offers a range of health services to plan members for a predetermined fee per member by a limited group of providers.

**Human genome**   the complete set of genes within the 23 pairs of human chromosomes.

**Human Genome Project**   a research program funded by the federal government to "map" and sequence the total number of genes within the 23 pairs, or 46 chromosomes.

**Human immunodeficiency virus (HIV)**   the virus that causes the immune system to break down and can eventually result in the disease AIDS.

**Hypothermia**   state in which body temperature is below normal range.

**Implied consent**   an agreement that is made through inference by signs, inaction, or silence.

**Implied contract**   an agreement that is made through inference by signs, inaction, or silence.

**Indictment**   a written charge presented to the court by the grand jury against a defendant.

**Indigent**   a person who is without funds.

**Induced abortion**   an abortion caused by artificial means such as medications or surgical procedures.

**Informed (or expressed) consent**   consent granted by a person after the patient has received knowledge and understanding of potential risks and benefits.

*In loco parentis*   a person assigned by a court to stand in place of the parents and possess their legal rights and responsibilities toward the child.

**Inquest**   an investigation held by a public official, such as a coroner, to determine the cause of death.

**Institutional Review Board (IRB)**   a hospital or university board of members who oversee any human research in that facility.

**Integrity**   the unwavering adherence to one's principles; dedication to maintaining high standards.

**In-vitro fertilization**   the process of combining ovum and sperm outside of a woman's body.

**Joint Commission on Accreditation of Healthcare Organizations (JCAHO)**   an agency that oversees hospital accreditation standards.

**Laws**   rules or actions prescribed by a governmental authority that have a binding legal force.

**Liable**   legal responsibility for one's own actions.

**Libel**   any publication in print, writing, pictures or signs that injures the reputation of another person.

**Litigation**   a dispute that has resulted in one party suing another.

**Living will**   a legal document in which a person states that life-sustaining treatments and nutritional support should not be used to prolong life; a type of advance directive.

**Malfeasance**   performing an illegal act.

**Malpractice**   professional misconduct or demonstration of an unreasonable lack of skill with the result of injury, loss, or damage to the patient.

**Managed Care Organization(MCO)**   a type of medical plan that pays for and manages the medical care a patient receives.

**Mediation**   using the opinion of a third party to resolve a civil dispute in a nonbinding decision.

**Medicaid**   federal program, implemented by the individual states, to provide financial assistance for the indigent.

**Medical etiquette** standards of professional behavior.

**Medical ethics** moral conduct based on principles regulating the behavior of health care professionals.

**Medical informatics** the application of communication and information to medical practice, research and education.

**Medical practice acts** laws established in all 50 states that define the practice of medicine as well as requirements and methods for licensure in a particular state.

**Medicare** federal program that provides health care coverage for persons over 65 years of age as well as for disabled persons or those who suffer kidney disease or other debilitating ailments.

**Mercy killing** another term for voluntary euthanasia.

**Minimum necessary standard** means that the provider must make a reasonable effort to limit the disclosure of patient information to only the minimum amount that is necessary to accomplish the purpose of the request.

**Minor** a person who has not reached the age of maturity, which in most states is 18.

**Misdemeanors** less-serious offenses than felonies; punishable by fines or imprisonment of up to one year. These include traffic violations and disturbing the peace.

**Misfeasance** the improper performance of an otherwise proper or lawful act.

**National Organ Transplant Law of 1984** federal law that forbids the sale of organs in interstate commerce.

**Negligence** an unintentional action that occurs when a person either performs or fails to perform an action that a "reasonable person" would or would not have committed in a similar situation.

**Nominal damages** a slight or token payment awarded by the court.

**Nonfeasance** the failure to perform an action when it is necessary.

**Nontherapeutic research** research conducted that will not directly benefit the research subject.

**Office of Civil Rights (OCR)** the federal office that investigates violations of HIPAA.

**Occurrence insurance** also called claims-incurred insurance, liability insurance that covers the insured party for all injuries and incidents that occurred while the policy was in effect (policy year), regardless of when they are reported to the insurer or when the claim is made.

**Palliative care** care for terminally ill patients consisting of comfort measures and symptom control.

**Parenteral** medication route other than the alimentary canal (oral and rectal) including subcutaneous, intravenous, and intramuscular routes.

**Partnership** a legal agreement in which two or more physicians share the business operation of a medical practice and become responsible for the actions of the other partners.

**Passive euthanasia** allowing a patient to die by foregoing treatment.

**Plaintiff**   a person or group of people suing another person or group of people; the person who instigates the lawsuit.

**Posthumous**   after death.

**Postmortem**   after death.

**Precedent**   a ruling of an earlier case that is then applied to subsequent cases.

**Preempt**   overrule.

**Preferred Provider Organization (PPO)**   a managed care concept in which the patient must use a medical provider who is under contract with the insurer for an agreed-upon fee in order to receive copayment from the insurer.

**Privacy Rule**   a requirement that all covered entities under HIPAA must be in compliance with the privacy, security, and electronic-data provisions by April 14, 2003.

**Privileged communication**   confidential information that has been told to a physician (or attorney) by the patient.

**Problem-Oriented Medical Record (POMR)**   method of documentation that focuses on the patient's problems, and not just on the diagnosis.

**Prosecutor**   a person who brings a criminal lawsuit on behalf of the government.

**Protected Health Information (PHI)**   any individually identifiable information that relates to the physical or mental condition of the provision of health care to an individual.

**Proximate**   the injury was closely (proximately) related to the defendant's negligence.

**Proxy**   a person who acts on behalf of another person.

**Prudent person rule**   also called the responsible person standard, means the health care professional must provide the information that a prudent, reasonable person would want before making a decision about treatment or refusal of treatment.

**Public duties**   responsibilities the physician owes to the public.

**Punitive damages**   also called exemplary damages, monetary award by a court to a person who has been harmed in an especially malicious and willful way; meant to punish the offender.

**Quality of life**   the physiological status, emotional well-being, functional status, and life in general of the individual.

**Reciprocity**   the cooperation of one state in granting a license to practice medicine to a physician already licensed in another state. Reciprocity can be applied to other licensed professionals such as nurses and pharmacists.

**Regulations**   rules or laws made by agencies.

**Res ipsa loquitur**   Latin phrase meaning "the thing speaks for itself."

**Res judicata**   Latin phrase meaning "the thing has been decided."

**Respondeat superior**   Latin phrase meaning "Let the master answer" means the employer is responsible for the actions of the employee.

**Revocation**   the act of taking away or recalling, such as taking away a license to practice medicine.

**Revoked**   take away, as in revoke a license.

**Rider**   additional component to an insurance policy.

**Rigor mortis**   stiffness that occurs in a dead body.

**Risk management**   a practice to minimize the incidence of problem behavior that might result in injury to the patient and liability for the organization.

**Sanctions**   penalties or fines.

**Settle**   the act of determining the outcome of a case outside a courtroom; settling a case is not an indication of legal wrongdoing.

**Slander**   speaking false and malicious words concerning another person which brings injury to his or her reputation.

**SOAP**   medical charting that includes subjective (S), objective (O), assessment (A), and a plan (P) of treatment for the patient.

**Social utility method of allocation**   a method of determining the allocation of organs by giving them to people who will benefit the most.

**Sole proprietorship**   a type of medical practice in which one physician may employ other physicians.

**Solo practice**   a medical practice in which the physician works alone.

**Spontaneous abortion**   termination of pregnancy that occurs naturally before the fetus is viable.

**Standard of care**   the ordinary skill and care that medical practitioners use and that is commonly used by other medical practitioners in the same locality when caring for patients; what another medical professional would consider appropriate care in similar circumstances.

*Stare decisis*   Latin phrase meaning "let the decision stand."

**Statute of limitations**   the period of time that a patient has to file a lawsuit.

**Statutes**   laws enacted by state and federal legislatures.

**Sterilization**   the process of medically altering reproductive organs so as to terminate the ability to produce offspring.

**Subpoena**   court order for a person or documents to appear in court.

*Subpoena duces tecum*   Latin phrase meaning, "under penalty take with you"; a court order requiring a person to appear in court and to bring certain records or other material to a trial or a deposition.

**Subpoenaed**   ordered by the court.

**Surrogate**   representative of another person.

**Surrogate mother**   a woman who agrees to bear a child for another couple. The husband's sperm is implanted into the woman's uterus.

**Sympathy**   pity for someone else.

**Telemedicine**   the use of communications and information technologies to provide health care services to people at a distance.

**Terminally ill**   one whose death is determined to be inevitable.

**Therapeutic research**   a form of medical research that might directly benefit the research subject.

**Therapeutic sterilization**   sterilization undertaken to save the mother's life or protect her health.

**Third-party payers**   a party other than the patient who assumes responsibility for paying the patient's bills (for example, an insurance company).

**Tolerance**   a respect for those whose opinions, practices, race, religion, and nationality differ from our own.

**Tort**   a civil injury, or wrongful act, committed against another person or property that results in harm and is compensated in money damages.

**Tort law**   that division of law that covers acts that result in harm to another.

**Uniform Anatomical Gift Act**   a state statute allowing persons 18 years of age and of sound mind to make a gift of any or all body parts for purposes of organ transplantation or medical research.

**Unintentional torts**   such as negligence, occur when the patient is injured as a result of the health care professional not exercising the ordinary standard of care.

**United Network for Organ Sharing (UNOS)**   the legal entity in the United States responsible for allocating organs for transplantation.

**Utilitarianism**   an ethical theory based on the principle of the greatest good for the greatest number.

**Vesting**   a point in time, such as after ten years of employment, when an employee has the right to receive benefits from a retirement plan.

**Viable**   in the case of a fetus, ability to survive outside of the uterus.

**Viatical settlements**   allows people with terminal illnesses, such as AIDS, to obtain money from their life insurance policies by selling them.

**Vital statistics**   major events or facts from a person's life, such as live births, deaths, induced termination of pregnancy, and marriages.

**Waive**   give up a right.

**Wireless Local Area Networks (WLANs)**   a wireless system that is used by physicians and nurses to access patient information.

**Withdrawing life-sustaining treatment**   discontinuing a treatment or procedure, such as artificial ventilation, after it has started.

**Withholding life-sustaining treatment**   failing to start a treatment or procedure such as artificial ventilation.

# Index